Bon Appétit
Country cooking

Bon Appétit® Country cooking

Heather Maisner, General Editor

The Knapp Press
Los Angeles

Bon Appétit Country cooking

Editor   *Heather Maisner*

Art editor   *Sue Mann*

Assistant editor   *Hilary Davies*

Picture editor and stylist   *Antonia Gaunt*

Researchers   *Jonathan Walters Sue Seddon*

Art assistants   *Pam Carruthers Peter Saag Vicki Towers*

Assistant stylist   *Nadia Reif*

Project assistants   *Katy Franklin Mary Foster*

Meat consultant   *Frank Gerrard MBE*

Pastry consultant   *Arthur Perkins*

Recipes prepared for photography

Alex Dufort Dinah Morrison

Ruth Orme Rhondda Wraith

Production   *Clare Badham Mike Emery*

Consultant for American edition   *Norma MacMillan*

This edition of COUNTRY COOKING was produced by Marshall Cavendish Limited of London, with the kind assistance of the editors of *Bon Appétit* Magazine.

Published in England under the title
Country Cooking

Published in 1978 by The Knapp Press
5900 Wilshire Boulevard, Los Angeles, California 90036

Library of Congress Cataloging in Publication Data

Main entry under title: Bon appétit® country cooking.

1. Cookery, European. 2. Cookery, American.
I. Maisner, Heather. II. Bon Appétit.
III. Title: Country cooking.
TX723.5.A1B58   641.5'94   78-16857

ISBN 0-89535-006-8

Printed in England

Contents

Authors

Michael Bateman *Great Britain*
Editor of Lifespan, *Sunday Times Magazine*, and a leading authority on cooking, Michael Bateman has written and edited several books on food, including *Cooking People* and *Best British Meat Dishes*. He is currently preparing a *Man's Manual of Cookery* based on the expertise of top European chefs.

Wina Born *Holland and Belgium*
Wina Born is Dutch and lives in Amsterdam. She has written over forty books on food and wine, including *Famous Dishes of the World*, now translated into six languages. She writes on cooking and restaurants for the magazines *Avenue* and *Margriet*, and has a weekly program about food and wine on Dutch radio.

Caroline Conran *Italy*
Caroline Conran is the *Sunday Times Magazine* food correspondent. She is also the translator of Michel Guérard's revolutionary *Cuisine Minceur*, the author of many of Habitat's *Cook's Calendars*, co-author of *Poor Cook* and *Family Cook* and co-editor of *Best British Meat Dishes*. She has also just completed the translation of Michel Guérard's second book, *Cuisine Gourmande*.

Nina Froud *Russia and Poland*
Nina Froud has written thirty-eight books on international cooking, including *The Home of Russian Cookery* and the forthcoming *Food from the Soviet Union*. Part-Russian and part-Italian, she speaks nine languages and has written and translated several plays (including *Uncle Vanya* from the Russian). Food is her absorbing hobby, and she has traveled over most of the world collecting recipes.

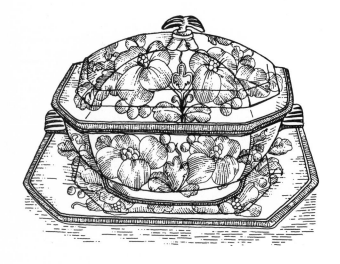

The Contributors

The Contributors

Robin Howe   *Greece and the Balkans, Austria-Hungary*
Robin Howe has written over twenty cook books, including *Balkan Cooking*, *Greek Cooking* and *Cooking from the Heart of Europe*. She and her husband now live in Italy, but before the war they lived in Budapest and Vienna, and traveled widely in central Europe and the Balkans.

Evan Jones   *North America*
Evan Jones is an American freelance writer and an authority on American cooking. He has written numerous articles on the subject and several books including *American Food: The Gastronomic Story* and *The Book of Cheese*. He also contributes to *Gourmet* magazine, the *International Review of Food and Wine*, *Travel and Leisure*, *Quest* and *Americana*.

Arne Krüger   *Germany and Switzerland*
Arne Krüger is an eminent chef and author of thirty books on both German and international cuisine, including *The Cook German Book* and *Cooking Round the World*. He edits a monthly magazine on food and wine called *Arne's Journal* and a magazine for chefs called *Chef International*. He writes articles on cooking and restaurants for several magazines including *Playboy* and *Feinschmecker* (*'Gourmet'*), Hamburg. He is now working on a history of German cooking.

Roger Lallemand   *France*
Roger Lallemand, *chef de cuisine* and a titular member of l'Académie Culinaire de France, is the author of the encyclopaedic *La Cuisine de Chez Nous*, a definitive work on French regional cooking in twenty-five volumes.

Anna Macmiadhacháin   *Spain and Portugal*
Anna Macmiadhacháin, whose great-grandmother was Spanish, has traveled extensively in Spain and Portugal with her husband, the painter and poet Padraig Macmiadhacháin. She is the author of *Spanish Regional Cookery*, the Iberian section in the *World Atlas of Food* and has contributed to, and illustrated, *Food for our Times*.

Inge Mitchell   *Scandinavia*
Inge Mitchell, born and educated in Aarhus, the capital of Jutland, Denmark, in 1960 became the first manager of the Danish Food Center in London, and now lectures extensively on Scandinavia and its cuisines. She has contributed to many British magazines, and has demonstrated the colorful preparation of Scandinavian cooking on television.

Photographers

Keith Collie   *Scandinavia*

Robert Golden   *Spain and Portugal, Greece and the Balkans*

Kenneth Griffiths   *Austria-Hungary, Russia and Poland*

Christine Hanscomb   *Italy*

Alan Randall   *Holland and Belgium*

Red Saunders   *North America*

Heini Schneebeli   *Germany and Switzerland*

Tessa Traeger   *France, Great Britain*

Illustrators

Vana Haggerty   *Black and white illustrations*

Anna Pugh   *Color illustrations*

Bon Appétit Country cooking

explores the European and North American culinary experience from Finland to Crete, from Ireland to Russia, and from Canada to Texas. It cuts across historical and political boundaries and looks back to a hypothetical moment in time, somewhere toward the end of the nineteenth century, before two world wars had politically divided and subdivided Europe, and before convenience foods had entered the home to jade the modern palate. At this time people looked to the immediate countryside for their food, and to their family repertoire of recipes for their cooking.

Central and Eastern Europe were then divided into four major areas of influence, dominated by the German, Austro-Hungarian, Turkish and Russian empires. These stamped the mark of their cuisines on the kingdoms they ruled, and vice versa, causing a cross-cultural culinary intermingling which is present today: for example, many dishes we consider typically Greek can be traced back to Turkey, some Viennese dishes are still called by their Yugoslavian names, and the Polish national soup, *borshch*, possibly began in the Ukraine.

Throughout history conquering and exploring nations have altered and developed eating habits everywhere: the cherry tree which is considered to be truly British was in fact

Introduction

The destiny of nations depends on the manner in which they are fed. *Brillat-Savarin (1775-1826)*

planted in Britain by the Romans; it was the Moors who first introduced into Spain those seemingly typical Spanish crops—melons, peaches, figs and apricots, almonds, oranges and lemons; and the potato and tomato, fundamental ingredients in the European diet, were brought to Europe from the New World as recently as the seventeenth century.

History imposes new contours on cooking, but it is landscape and climate that dictate basic ingredients. A French *bouillabaisse* is a subtle blend of native fish and local wine; the Central European predilection for imaginative cabbage and potato dishes evolved as a result of the harsh climate which was particularly favorable to these vegetables; and the Scandinavian versatility with fish grew out of their dependence on the sea to provide essential protein.

The invention and modification of cooking utensils added a further dimension to country cooking. In some cases the dish and its container have become virtually inseparable: in France the terrine is the name of both a pâté and the earthenware dish in which it is cooked, and the Russian *paskha* is sculpted by its paskha mold. Throughout Europe the baker's oven has defined certain dishes, which were left for slow cooking as the oven cooled after the baking of bread.

Some ingredients and dishes are as intrinsically linked to their places of origin as the landscape, but certain staples are found throughout Europe and North America. Meat, fish and vegetables provide basic nutrients, although meat cuts and cooking methods vary between countries, fish availability differs, and the type of vegetables to be found and a nation's attitude to them alter from place to place. Dried beans, peas and lentils are added to most stews and hotpots, and each country has its cereal staple, whether it be oats, wheat or rye. Pounding grain into flour and adding moisture is an ancient practice found all over Europe. This forms the basis for all pastry and pasta, pancakes and dumplings, which evolved as a means of making small amounts of protein stretch to feed a large family and developed into delicacies in their own right.

Regional specialties that traveled better than others have taken on the status of national dishes, and some have even gained international repute: French *coq au vin*, Austrian *Wiener Schnitzel*, British fish and chips, Russian chicken Kiev, Italian pizza, Greek hummus, the Scandinavian smörgåsbord. But there are many other lesser known yet delicious dishes that have been handed down through generations by word of mouth and are only just reaching the international printed page. Modern communication methods, transportation and packaging mean that today's cook is privileged as no other has been: it is possible to find ingredients from all over the world on sale in local shops.

Country Cooking brings into the home both familiar and lesser known traditional recipes, and reawakens the appetite to the dishes of our European and American heritage.

Meat-eating and meat-cooking habits everywhere are dictated primarily by geography and climate. In countries with a mild climate conducive to rearing cattle, beef and veal are usually the favorite meats; whereas in bleak mountainous areas goats and sheep provide the basic meat supply for the region.

In hot climates quick cooking and smaller pieces of meat are favored, whereas in cooler areas large cuts of meat are popular, roasted or simmered for several hours.

Religion plays an important part in determining meat-eating habits. Pork was forbidden in countries where the Turks were influential and the Moslem faith was adopted. The Jewish religion also denounced the eating of pork, and laid down rules for slaughtering animals which gave rise to a separate tradition of Jewish cuisine. The Christian Church dictated that no meat should be eaten for the forty days of Lent, and the Catholic Church also forbade the eating of meat on Fridays. But feast days were often meat-eating occasions, especially at Easter when roast lamb or kid was the traditional dish in many parts of Europe.

Economic factors dictate the amount and the kind of meat a nation consumes. Rich countries tend to eat more meat and leaner, more tender cuts. Americans traditionally eat more meat per head than any Europeans; and since high-quality meat has always been plentiful in our country we have tended to scorn the cheaper cuts, especially variety meats. Poorer nations have to make do with less meat and meat of poorer quality. As a result they have used their ingenuity to produce delicacies using every part of the animal including the brains, kidneys and liver.

Until relatively recently meat storage was a problem in all climates. Since it was difficult to keep animals alive during the winter, many were slaughtered in the autumn and the meat salted to be eaten during the cold months. Cooks learned to disguise the salty flavor of preserved meat with hot spicy sauces, for example *romesco* and *all-i-oli* sauces in Spain; or they simmered the meat with ingredients such as dried legumes, which would absorb the salty flavor. Although no longer necessary for storage purposes salt meat has remained popular: pickled pork and sauerkraut is a favorite German combination; the air-dried beef of Grisons is a famous Swiss delicacy, and the traditional New England boiled dinner is made with beef that has been 'corned' with salt, sugar, saltpeter and spices.

Different countries like their meat served in different ways. The French on the whole love tender cuts of meat which they eat *saignant* (rare). But they also know how to make the toughest meat tender: they may marinate mutton with wine and fresh herbs to improve the texture, or simmer shank of beef *en daube* for several hours, very gently, until it can be sliced with a spoon.

Veal, pork, beef and lamb form the basis of many country dishes; but their preparation and cooking are influenced by the religion and economy of each country

In Germany pork is traditionally the most popular meat: every part of the pig is used for roasting, steaming, broiling, boiling or preserving. Sausages are a German specialty: each region has its favorite methods of seasoning and combining the ingredients. There are *Bratwürste*, made of fresh, raw meat and *Bruhwürste*, made of smoked meat.

The Dutch eat less meat than many of their European neighbors: vegetables play a more important part in their diet, and local cheese is a valuable alternative source of protein. When they do eat meat it is usually pork. The Belgians, however, love meat: excellent beef is produced in the northern province of Flanders, and in the south, Ardennes ham is famous.

Lamb is more popular in Britain than anywhere else in Europe apart from the Balkans, and mutton has provided some of the best traditional British dishes. The hillsides of Wales and Scotland, and England's South Downs are ideal for grazing sheep. But British – particularly Scottish – beef is also of extremely high quality. Roast beef is the national Sunday dish, and roasting is probably the favorite British method of cooking meat.

The inhospitable climate and terrain of northern Scandinavia make cattle-rearing almost impossible – elk and reindeer are more common than beef. However sheep and goats do thrive in southern Norway and Sweden, where roast lamb is a traditional delicacy. In Denmark pork and bacon are the most popular meats – pigs outnumber people by two to one.

The pig is also the main source of meat in Spain and Portugal: roast suckling pig and pork tenderloin are great favorites for special occasions, and salt pork, bacon and hot, spicy pork sausages add flavor to everyday stews. Sheep, goats and wild boar provide meat, while beef is rarely eaten.

The Italians specialize in dishes made with variety meats, such as Tuscan broiled pork liver parcels, Venetian calf liver with onions and Florentine tripe. They are also famous for their Parma ham and many types of sausage.

Austrian butchers are known for their skill in slicing veal scallops on the bias, so that they stretch when pounded to make *Wiener Schnitzel*. They also offer forty different cuts of beef for making *Tafelspitz* (boiled beef), and beef is the basis for the traditional Hungarian goulash.

Charcoal grilled lamb and kid are the favorite Greek meats. Beef is quite rare in the Balkan countries generally, although some cattle are raised in Rumania, along with sheep and pigs.

In Russia beef and pork are equally popular. The Russians specialize in barbecuing meat, a tradition handed down from their nomadic ancestors; they also make neat little meat parcels wrapped in pasta or pastry which can be easily stored. In the hot southern provinces, where the cuisine is influenced by Turkey, lamb and mutton are the favorite meats. Polish hunter's *bigos*, a casserole made with a mixture of pork, beef, veal, lamb, venison, bacon and ham sausage, reflects the Poles' enthusiasm for meat. Roast pork flavored with caraway is a favorite here as it is in Germany.

America is the land of beef, and charcoal-grilled T-bone steak is perhaps the favorite national dish. For over two hundred years, ever since the West was taken over by settlers, fine cattle have been raised on the western plains, and these now provide two-thirds of our meat. Lamb is rarely eaten,

mutton almost never, although pork is quite popular, especially as spare ribs. Traditional American recipes reflect the time when meat was not so plentiful: chitterlings are made with pig's intestines and Brunswick stew with squirrel. Canadians eat a wider range of meat than their American neighbors and here pork is the favorite meat. But in the cold north of Canada only buffalo and reindeer can survive.

Butchers in every country have their own traditions and styles of meat cutting. Methods of cutting vary even within the same country: in Great Britain there are at least eight recognized ways of cutting beef, and twelve in North America. American methods reflect the European background of the American people: the method used by butchers in New York (originally New Amsterdam), for instance, is very similar to that used in Holland. French butchers have developed a particularly intricate way of cutting beef, based upon the separation of distinct muscles. This makes the portions of meat more uniform than those used in other countries.

With appropriate cooking any cut of meat can be made tender. Meat that comes from the most active parts of the animal, such as the muscles in the legs, shoulders and neck, is best cooked slowly in liquid for a long time. Meat from the less active muscles, such as the loin, is best cooked quickly in a dry heat. Fat is very important to the flavor and texture of meat, and fat from different parts of the same animal can vary considerably in taste and texture. If meat is overcooked it loses its natural fat and moisture, and eventually its flavor.

All meats can be transformed with imaginative and careful cooking, and cooks in every country have learned to make the most of the meats at their disposal.

Christmas display 1909

Fish and seafood

Fish have provided a wealth of free and nourishing food everywhere but, since they were best eaten fresh, fish-eating habits varied immensely from place to place. People living beside the warm waters of the Mediterranean could eat fresh tuna, red mullet, swordfish, rascasse, sea bass, sardines and anchovies practically all year round. But the changing seasons had more effect on the temperature of the deep waters of the Atlantic, and here they would eat flounder, halibut, herring, mackerel and whitebait through late spring and summer, and sprats, whiting, haddock and mackerel through winter and early spring. The contrast between a Scandinavian fish soup (see page 126) and a Provençale *bouillabaisse* (see page 47) demonstrates the world of difference between the sea fish of the north and south.

For those living inland but close to a river, the fish diet could be equally varied – pike, perch, shad, salmon, trout, carp, sturgeon, lampreys and eels abounded all over North America and Europe. It is only in recent times that several of these species have become scarce through over-fishing and pollution. Lampreys used to be so plentiful in Britain that people – including Henry I and Alexander Pope – are said to have died of a surfeit of them, but now they are very rarely found. Sturgeon were so plentiful in parts of Russia that in the days before refrigeration their roe, caviar, was sometimes used like tar to make roofs waterproof: but they are now so rare in Western Europe that if a sturgeon is caught in Britain, it is traditionally donated to the monarch. Even carp, which were originally brought to Europe from China and then bred in ponds, were so abundant in the eighteenth century that the French used to make a pâté from carps' tongues.

Smoking and pickling are the traditional ways of preserving the so-called 'oily' fish, which include herring, mackerel, sprats, eels and salmon. Fish with a lower fat content – the so-called 'white' fish, such as sole, flounder, cod, haddock, hake and turbot – can often be preserved by drying or salting.

Over time these methods of preserving accounted for some of the most characteristic country fish dishes – Scandinavian pickled herring, German rollmops, British kippers and smokies, Italian salted anchovies, Portuguese salt cod, Canadian and Scottish smoked salmon. Smoking over the sawdust from hard woods such as cedar, juniper or eucalyptus added a new dimension to the flavor of the fish; and pickling often provoked cooks to invent a whole repertoire of sauces to counteract the strong salty flavor. The modern cook can use frozen fish which provides a wider choice.

All fish are rich in protein, and oily fish provide essential vitamins too. In the past they have also been held to have a mystical significance: in ancient civilizations they often symbolized fertility – perhaps because of the vast numbers of eggs they produced, or perhaps because Venus was born from the waves. Certain shellfish, particularly crayfish, were considered to be aphrodisiacs. The fish became an early symbol

Fish and seafood

of Christianity, because the letters in the Greek word for fish, ΙΧΘΥΣ, are also the initials of the phrase 'Jesus Christ God's Son Savior'; and the Christian Church encouraged fish-eating by banning meat during Lent and on Fridays. The Jewish religion similarly determined fish-eating habits by banning any fish without scales and fins, that is all shellfish. In other circles, however, shellfish, particularly oysters, were considered good for the brain; and Louis XI of France is said to have invited the Sorbonne professors to oyster feasts 'lest their scholarship should become deficient'.

Several species of shellfish which used to be considered common are now great delicacies; the oyster is the obvious example. Farmed since at least the second century BC and still plentiful enough to be considered poor man's food in the nineteenth century, they are now an expensive luxury. Eels, although very popular in Germany, Holland and Belgium, have suffered the opposite fate in Britain. Until the eighteenth century they were usually served at the tables of the rich; now they are neglected, except when jellied.

Fish and shellfish, perhaps more than any other kind of food, have tended to foster national prejudices. The average Englishman probably regards frogs' leg soup and snails in garlic with the same suspicion that a Frenchman brings to jellied eels and fish and chips (do they really eat them straight out of the newspaper?). But fish have also inspired cooks to produce some of their proudest national recipes – such as Russia's sturgeon *à la Balakiriev*, America's oysters Rockefeller, France's pike *quenelles*, and Scandinavia's *gravad lax* – marinated salmon – and *fiskefars* – fish purée.

Today refrigeration and transportation make more varieties of fish available everywhere, and traditional fish recipes present a whole new range of culinary adventures.

Methods of preparing and cooking fish vary widely from country to country. In England, for example, cod is usually eaten fresh in steaks or fillets; whereas salt cod is popular all over the Mediterranean and in Scandinavia.

1 Pike 2 Ling 3 Tuna 4 Skate (ray) 5 Hake 6 Garfish 7 Freshwater bream 8 Conger 9 Grey mullet 10 Cod steak 11 Elver (small eel) 12 Carp 13 Haddock 14 Halibut 15 Eel 16 Mackerel 17 Pompano 18 Salt cod 19 Monkfish 20 Shad 21 Trout 22 Sea bass 23 Herring 24 Red mullet 25 Whitebait 26 Pilchard 27 Sprat 28 Salmon 29 Squid 30 Prawn 31 Crab 32 Scampi 33 Clam 34 Scallop 35 Spiny lobster (crawfish) 36 Shrimp 37 Oysters 38 Mussels 39 Dover sole 40 Lemon sole 41 Flounder 42 Brill

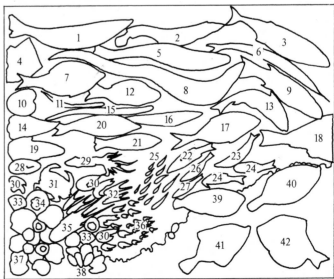

Vegetables

Vegetables, like other foods, have changed in popularity over the centuries; old favorites were discarded as new varieties arrived from other parts of the world. In the ancient civilizations of Europe, and until the Middle Ages, the staple vegetables were the root varieties: for example, turnips, radishes, carrots and leeks. Green vegetables, often used for flavoring soups and stews, included cabbage, spinach, turnip tops, cress, nettles and thistles. The Belgians ate Brussels sprouts as early as the thirteenth century, but it wasn't until the eighteenth century that sprouts became common elsewhere. Cauliflowers were introduced to Europe by Arab traders in the sixteenth century; peas and eggplant were brought from the Far East.

The biggest event in vegetable history was the discovery of the New World. European cooks were suddenly presented with a wealth of strange new ingredients: potatoes, yams, squashes, fava beans, string beans, avocados, peppers and tomatoes. They adopted them as their own, and today it is impossible to imagine Italian or southern French cuisine without tomatoes, and German or Irish cooking without the potato. On the other hand many cuisines have since tended to neglect root vegetables, such as beets, turnips, carrots and rutabaga. Country recipes, including Finnish rutabaga casserole (see page 140), German glazed turnips (see page 80), Russian *borshch* (see page 234) and Belgian *carrottes à*

Vegetable fashions change and different varieties of the same vegetable vary, altering the flavor and texture of a dish. The small cherry-red English tomato, for example, is far removed in flavor and texture from the fleshy Mediterranean variety.

1 Cabbage 2 Red cabbage 3 Spring greens 4 White cabbage 5 Brussels sprouts 6 Peppers 7 Jamaican hot peppers 8 Chili peppers 9 Pumpkin 10–12 Other varieties of squash 13 Zucchini 14 Romaine lettuce 15 Field lettuce 16 Escarole 17 Belgian endive 18 Bibb lettuce 19 Sweet potatoes 20–23 Red and white varieties of potato 24 Jerusalem artichoke 25–28 Different varieties of tomato 29–31 Green beans 32 Pearl onions 33 Leeks 34 Ordinary onions 35 Scallions 36 Garlic 37 Shallots 38 Spanish onion

l'ardennaise (see page 98) show just some of the delicious dishes they can provide.

Gardeners have had as much effect on the vegetables we eat as explorers, by developing new varieties and improving old ones. This process began as early as the fifteenth century, when the Frenchman Michaux first produced the fresh green peas that we know today, but which were quite unlike the pale dried variety that had been a staple throughout the Middle Ages. In the sixteenth century Italian gardeners discovered that the flavor of celery and fennel could be improved by covering the stems and bulbs with earth as they grew – a method which was later also used in France to produce the famous white asparagus of Argenteuil.

Modern technology has enabled some vegetables to be produced practically all the year round; but formerly country cooking depended heavily on the seasons. The first ripe tomato was a particularly sweet delight; and some dishes almost ritualistically marked the transition from winter to spring: Dutch *kruudmoes* with chopped green herbs (see page 88) and Finnish *kesäkeittdo* (see page 128) with crisp cauliflower flowerets, new potatoes, fresh green beans and spinach, baby carrots, radishes and shelled peas.

Different varieties of the same vegetable can vary enormously in flavor and texture, both between and within countries. An American cook may say there is no substitute for a mealy Idaho potato, which is ideal for baking, but to make a German salad you must use only waxy potatoes; for Czech potato dumplings your potatoes should be floury, but frying potatoes should be firm. To make an authentic Hungarian cabbage pancake you need a tightly packed white cabbage; but for a cabbage soup with walnut oil from Bourbonnais you should use the looser, greener, Savoy cabbage. A long firm crisp northern cucumber will make quite a different salad from a rotund seedy southern one. And a tiny cherry-red English tomato will alter the flavor and texture of a dish that really demands a fleshy Mediterranean or a pear-shaped Italian one. In fact Italian tomato sauces or soups taste more authentic if canned Italian tomatoes are used rather than fresh local ones.

Attitudes to vegetables vary greatly between nations: American, British and Russian cooks tend to think of them merely as accompaniments to meat, or as bases for soups; but the cooks of other countries accord them more importance. The French will often serve vegetables as a separate course in a meal; in Holland, when children ask what they are having for dinner, their mother replies by telling them what vegetable they will eat; national dishes such as French *ratatouille*, Swiss *rösti* and Polish stuffed cabbage are almost meals in themselves, and Balkan ingenuity with vegetables is unparalleled.

Whatever the vegetable and whatever the dish a European approach to vegetable cooking brings with it a world of rich new textures and flavors.

Beans, peas and lentils

Beans, peas and lentils satisfy the senses in taste, aroma and shape, while their color range is enormous. Nearly every Western country has a national dish based on the adaptable legume. Below are some of the many varieties.

Fava bean

Lima bean

Whole dried pea

Split green pea

Split yellow pea

Mung bean

Red kidney bean

Pinto bean

Flageolet (green)

Flageolet (white)

Black-eyed pea

Black or turtle bean

Soybean

Peanut

Chick-pea

French lentil

Egyptian lentil

Whole (Chinese) lentil

Whole brown lentil

Beans, peas and lentils in their dried form are essential ingredients of country cooking all over the world. They form the mainstay of many casseroles giving color, body and texture to the dish and enabling a small amount of meat to go a long way. Served alone they can form a fragrant purée, or they can be dressed (sometimes sprouted) to make a succulent salad.

Dried peas, beans and lentils, known collectively as legumes, are the edible seeds of leguminous plants. They grow in most areas of North America and Europe, as well as many other parts of the world. When dried, they are still rich in protein, minerals and vitamins, and they can be stored for up to nine months without losing any of their goodness. This meant that they were able to play an important part in the great journeys of the past. Sixteenth- and seventeenth-century explorers carried European varieties of peas and beans on their long sea voyages, and also brought back new, unknown varieties to Europe. The first families to journey into the American Midwest took legumes with them as a basic part of their food.

Today every Western country has a national dish based on dried peas, beans or lentils: there is French *cassoulet*, Italian *minestrone*, Mexican *chili con carne*, Dutch pea soup, Spanish *fabada asturiana*, American baked beans, and Greek *hummus*. Legumes satisfy the senses in taste, aroma and shape, while their color range is enormous: there are deep-red kidney beans, ebony-smooth black beans, delicate pale green flageolets, pretty speckled pinto beans and the red-gold, gray shades of lentils. They are simple to prepare and require little supervision during cooking. They are also deliciously adaptable, absorbing the flavors of the meat, herbs and spices with which they are cooked. The two legumes richest in protein – edible soybeans and peanuts – can also be used to make flour, seasoning, oil, curd and butter.

Dried beans, whole dried peas and whole lentils need to be soaked before cooking. A quarter of a cup of dried legumes provides enough for one portion, but it is best to cook more legumes than you need and save some for salads or soups.

The night before cooking wash the legumes in cold water, unless the package states otherwise, removing any that float. Drain. Add three to four times their volume of cold water and bring to a boil in a heavy saucepan. Cover tightly and remove from the heat. (If you forget to do this the night before, do it just a few hours before cooking, and it will still shorten the cooking time considerably.)

The water the dried beans have soaked in absorbs some of their vitamins, and can be used for cooking the beans; but it is very gassy so, to avoid flatulence, use fresh water for cooking.

Cover the legumes with ample water and simmer gently until they are tender. The cooking time will depend on the variety of legumes, how old they are, when they were harvested and how quickly they were dried; but as a general rule whole lentils take an hour, beans take 1½ hours or more, soybeans and

chick-peas 3–4 hours or longer. Some recipes suggest adding baking soda to the water to reduce cooking time; but this also destroys some of the vitamins in the legumes, so it is not to be recommended. Salt, on the other hand, slows down the cooking process, and it should not be added until the last half hour.

Always flavor legumes generously: the long cooking process tends to exhaust most herbs and spices, so add some more at the end. Legumes love olive oil and garlic, onions and tomatoes, parsley and thyme.

To make bean salads you can pour on the dressing while the beans are still hot; in this way the flavors are absorbed to the full. Legumes in general need lubrication: add a piece of salt pork or bacon while they are cooking, a big lump of butter, a splash of oil, or even a dollop of cream when they are done, to give them a rich, velvety texture.

To get the most food value out of legumes serve them with a cereal food such as rice, pasta or bread. Legumes have a particularly high level of certain amino acids, while grains have a much lower level. If you combine the two you get more complete, that is usable, protein than from either food alone.

Below is a guide to some of the principal beans, peas and lentils, and what you can do with them.

Fava beans

Fava beans are the beans the Romans used for casting votes; in fact archaeologists have found remains of them on Bronze Age sites. Called broad beans in Europe, favas resemble lima beans but are rounder. The young beans when fresh are a great delicacy and the dried ones too have a distinctive flavor. Use them to make a bean salad, or puréed and seasoned with lemon juice and salt for a Balkan hors d'oeuvre.

Lima beans

This flat, kidney-shaped bean, which is available in a variety of sizes, originated in Central America. It is now grown extensively in California, as well as in the South where it is called a calico or speckled butter bean. To make succotash: heat together in water to cover equal volumes of cooked corn kernels, cooked lima beans and cooked diced meat; thicken with 1–2 tablespoons sunflower seed meal (or flour), season with salt and pepper, and continue cooking until thick and soupy. To serve as a vegetable you can bathe lima beans in fresh tomato sauce flavored with celery. They go particularly well with roast pork.

Whole dried peas

Dried green peas are used to make the mushy peas that are traditionally served with British fish and chips. Cook the peas until tender, then leave to stand for 2–3 hours before re-heating. Stir vigorously with a wooden spoon, and season to taste. Delicious served with ham or corned beef too.

Split green peas

These are the ones for making pease pudding, which the old rhyme suggests would often cook over a medieval hearth till it was 'nine days old'. Soak 1 cup peas overnight, tie them in a muslin cloth and place in a saucepan of boiling salted water to cover. Add a ham bone or bacon scraps and simmer

for 2 hours or so until tender. Lift out the peas, purée them and add 2 tablespoons butter, a beaten egg, and salt and pepper to taste. Beat until thoroughly mixed, then tie up tightly in a floured cloth and boil for another 30 minutes. For extra flavor, add chopped onion or herbs. Serve with ham or bacon. You can also use split green peas for thick pea soup: the Dutch float chunks of smoked sausage or frank-furter in theirs. Or simply purée the peas to serve with pork.

Split yellow peas

Like the green ones, these are whole hulled peas that split naturally when dried. They can be eaten, as they are in India, as a spicy purée or as little cakes known as *tikki channeh dahl*: cook 1 cup yellow split peas in stock until very soft (3–4 hours). Purée them and add to the purée a handful of chopped fresh parsley, a 1 in piece ginger root, chopped, $\frac{1}{2}$ teaspoon salt, a crushed bay leaf and $1\frac{1}{2}$ teaspoons crushed cumin seed. Bind with egg; shape into croquettes and sauté in a skillet. Split yellow peas are also used to make a Swedish soup called *ärter med älask*, flavored with thyme, marjoram, ginger, bacon, onions and cloves (see page 128).

Mung beans

These are best known in the West as crunchy succulent bean sprouts (in fact you can also sprout edible soybeans, and any whole peas or lentils). Sprouting releases all the vitamins and minerals the beans contain into a form that is edible raw. To sprout them, soak 2 tablespoons mung beans overnight in water in a canning jar. Next day, drain them (you can fasten a piece of muslin over the top with the ring to do this), and put the jar in a dark place. Morning and evening rinse the beans with fresh water and drain again. Mung bean and lentil sprouts will be ready to eat in 3–5 days; peas and soy-beans take a little longer. Store the sprouts in a plastic bag in the refrigerator, and use in salads or sandwiches, or stir-fried with other vegetables.

Red kidney beans

These are the handsome shiny-red beans that make *chili con carne* even *look* hot. The Mexicans, who are big bean-eaters, love them seasoned with chili and topped with grated cheese; the Italians use them for a nourishing soup flavored with garlic and sage, and also cook them with tomato sauce, garlic and shredded lettuce, to serve as a separate vegetable.

The Russians cook them with damsons and garlic; the Spanish serve them in a tomato sauce, with rice, as a main course; the French use them for *potage à la Condé*, with red wine and bacon. Together with wax beans, chick-peas and chopped onion and celery, kidney beans make a colorful 'three bean salad', which is served in both Greece and America. While they are still warm, toss the beans in a gener-ous dressing of olive oil, vinegar or lemon juice, salt, pepper, mustard, a little chopped onion or garlic, and fresh chopped parsley, chives or tarragon.

Pinto beans

These pretty speckled brown or pink beans are popular in the southwest as their flavor blends well with chili powder and tomatoes. They are similar to the Italian borlotti bean, which is cooked with onions, ham bones and a pinch of cinnamon to make Venetian bean soup; add noodles to the soup and serve with lots of grated Parmesan. In Piedmont they bake borlotti beans with bacon and cinnamon slowly all through Saturday night to eat after church on Sunday.

Dried white beans

Four varieties of dried white beans are available in America: Great Northern, marrow, navy and pea. The French use white beans in *cassoulet* with pork, lamb, sausage and goose. The Italians add them to *minestrone*; the Spanish put them in the famous hot stew *fabada asturiana* with pork and *chorizo* sausage; we use them for sumptuous Boston baked beans, cooked all day in a slow oven with fat salt pork, molasses and seasonings; the Greeks cook them to a purée with olive oil, garlic, thyme, tomato purée and a bay leaf, and serve this cold with lemon juice, raw onion, salt and black pepper. By themselves they make a perfect accompaniment to roast lamb: cook them with garlic and rosemary, and crush a few spoonfuls of the beans at the end to make a creamy sauce; or add 2–3 tablespoons cream and 1 tablespoon chopped fresh parsley.

Flageolets

These pale green or white beans are related to the French white haricots, but have a more subtle flavor. They are grown in France and Italy and the majority are exported. Serve them as a vegetable with lamb, use them in bean salad, or cook them to a pretty pale green or white purée, garnished with fresh chopped parsley, to serve with lamb chops or kabobs.

Black-eyed peas

Also known as black-eyed beans or cow peas, these delicious, earthy beans were brought by the slaves to the Deep South where they are the mainstay of many 'soul food' dishes such as Hoppin' John, traditionally served on New Year's Eve: soak 1 cup beans overnight, then simmer with 1⅓ cups brown rice and 1 quart water for 30 minutes. Sauté a little chopped bacon, a chopped onion and a clove of garlic in oil, add to the beans and rice, and simmer for another hour or until tender. Finally add salt, pepper, and chopped fresh parsley and basil to taste.

Black or turtle beans

Good-looking shiny beans, these are popular in South American and Mexican cooking. Simmer them with cumin, oregano, onions, red peppers and cider vinegar and serve with fresh tomato sauce; or sauté a chopped onion, a clove of garlic and a tablespoon of fresh parsley in a little butter, mix with the black beans, and serve over rice.

Soybeans

This is the most nutritious bean of all: ½ cup soybeans is the protein equivalent of a 5 oz steak. They are used to make oil, flour, a pulp called okra, a fermented purée called miso, and a meat substitute, as well as the famous soy sauce which can be used in place of salt. Soybeans take longer to cook than others: allow about 4 hours after soaking. Add them to a tasty vegetable stew of parsnips, turnips, carrots and onions with plenty of garlic, marjoram and thyme; or stir-fry with chopped red and green peppers, onion and bean sprouts.

Peanuts

Not really nuts at all, peanuts are the second most nutritious legume. Their food value is often under-estimated: they can be used to make flour and bread, added to soups and stews and salads, or boiled and eaten whole. If you don't like peanut butter, maybe it's because you've never tasted the home-made variety: roast raw peanuts (still in their skins) on baking sheets in a 350°F oven for 15–20 minutes. Cool, then grind in a food mill or coffee grinder. Stir in a few spoonfuls of oil and salt to taste. Delicious!

Chick-peas

Cream-colored nut-like peas, chick-peas, or Spanish beans, garbanzo beans or ceci peas, originated in South America and are now used all over the world. They may take up to 6 hours to cook, even after soaking. Eat them whole as a cold snack, or in Greek hummus: purée 2½ cups cooked chick-peas, add 2–3 crushed cloves of garlic, ⅔ cup tahini (sesame seed paste), 2 tablespoons olive oil, a little lemon juice, salt and pepper to taste, and enough water to thin to the consistency of mayonnaise. Stir in 2 tablespoons chopped fresh mint and serve as an appetizer with piping hot Greek bread.

Lentils

The two varieties of lentils are the French, which is gray, and the red-orange Egyptian. Cook them as a vegetable (adding a little butter and parsley at the end) to serve with game, pork or rabbit; or make a lentil curry by boiling 1 cup lentils and a chopped onion in 1 pint water. Meanwhile fry the following in a skillet: 1 chopped clove garlic, 1 small onion, 1 red chili pepper, 2 cardamoms, 2 cloves, a 2 in cinnamon stick and 1 tablespoon curry powder. Add the cooked lentils, 1 tablespoon tomato purée, and a pinch of salt, and simmer for 10 minutes. For lentil soup: cook 1 cup lentils in water to cover with a crushed garlic clove, some chopped bacon slices, ½ lb skinned tomatoes, 2 chopped onions, salt, pepper and a clove. When the lentils and bacon are tender (in about 1 hour), add 1 lb diced potatoes and cook for 20 minutes more. Remove the clove, purée the soup, add 2 tablespoons lemon juice and serve hot, garnished with fresh chopped parsley.

Cereals are high in protein, vitamins and minerals. Ground into pastes with water they were man's first staple food, and the realization that cereal plants would produce food repeatedly, year after year, led to the first settlements and the beginning of agriculture. They were also natural emblems of the passing seasons, and as a result every ancient civilization worshipped a god of the harvest.

Certain kinds of cereal thrive in certain geographical areas, and have become almost national dishes in their own right: buckwheat in Eastern Europe and Russia, where it is cooked to a porridge called *kasha*; oats in the cool, wet areas of Scotland, Northern Ireland and the northern United States. Wheat is so adaptable that it grows anywhere. Corn and rice were taken to Europe from their original habitats – America and Asia respectively – and were adopted by the farmers and the cooks of Spain and Portugal, southern France, northern Italy and Rumania.

Cereals can be cooked whole, coarsely cracked into 'grits' and toasted, ground into coarse meal and cooked to a porridge, or ground to a fine flour to make breads and pastries. Grains can be eaten alone, or added to soups and stews, or sweetened to make puddings. They can also be used to make alcoholic drinks: beer and whiskey from barley, whiskey and vodka from rye, chicha from corn. Barley malt is used to make malted milk products. Sorghum, which grows in hot climates including the southern United States, is used to make a kind of wine and also a syrup.

Each individual cereal has its own specific uses that have been modified over the centuries.

Rice

Rice is believed to have originated wild in India, and it was being cultivated in China at least five thousand years ago. These two countries are still the major rice producers and consumers, although rice is now produced in many other countries. Over half of the world's population relies on rice as a staple food.

Rice grows best in flooded paddy fields in warm, wet climates. The grains are milled to remove the husk (making

Paddy fields in the Algarve: rice thrives best in warm wet climates. **far right** *Spiked ears of barley are used to make bread, whiskey and beer, and are delicious in country soups and stews*

Grains and grasses

brown rice) and then polished to remove the bran (making white rice). The grains can be short (slightly sticky when cooked and ideal for making rice puddings), medium as in Italian Arborio rice (used for risottos, sweet dishes, or for 'puffed' rice, which is similar to popcorn), or long, as in Patna or Basmati rice (dry and fluffy when cooked and perfect for savory dishes). Rice can be ground into rice flour, used for making cookies or thickening sauces.

There are several ways of cooking plain long-grain rice. One method involves covering the desired quantity of rice – usually about $\frac{1}{2}$ cup per person – with 1 inch of cold salted water. Bring to a boil, stir, and cook covered for $12\frac{1}{2}$ minutes. Allow to stand for a further $12\frac{1}{2}$ minutes before serving.

To cook brown rice, bring to a boil in twice its volume of cold salted water and simmer very gently for 30 minutes. Or, to give the rice a stronger, nutty flavor, sauté it first in a little butter, then add twice its volume of boiling stock and simmer until tender. Use about $\frac{1}{3}$ cup brown rice per person.

To make rice salad, cook $1\frac{1}{2}$ cups long-grain or brown rice until tender. Combine with chopped celery, chopped tomato and black olives and toss in $\frac{1}{4}$ cup vinaigrette dressing. Chill, and serve on a bed of lettuce.

Wheat
Wheat has been cultivated for at least nine thousand years and, together with barley, was the staple grain of all the ancient civilizations. The Egyptians were the first to add yeast to wheat dough to leaven it. It was partly the need for more wheat to feed the exploding population of Ancient Rome that inspired further expansion of the Empire: Britain, parts of Spain and northern Africa were Imperial 'granaries'.

There are three major types of wheat: the hard type, which grows well in North America and in Central Europe along the river Danube, yields 'strong' flour with a high level of gluten that makes a very light, protein-rich bread; soft wheat, which grows in Britain and northern Europe, contains less gluten and makes less airy bread; and durum wheat, which grows in hotter climates like southern Italy, is used to make macaroni products and semolina.

Whole grain wheat can be served just like rice, as an accompaniment to meat and vegetables. Simmer it in twice its volume of water and a little salt, tightly covered, for about 2 hours, until the grains are tender and all the liquid absorbed.

Frumenty is a wheat and milk pudding which the Romans introduced to all parts of Europe, and which still lives on today in the form of rice pudding. It was popular throughout the Middle Ages, either sweetened with honey or mixed with meat and vegetables to make a meal. To make a modern sweet *frumenty*, simmer $\frac{1}{2}$ lb whole grain wheat in 1 pint water until tender. Transfer the wheat to a buttered 1 quart baking dish with $1\frac{1}{2}$ pints milk, 2 beaten eggs, $\frac{2}{3}$ cup soaked raisins, 3 tablespoons honey, $\frac{1}{4}$ teaspoon each ground mace and ginger, and the grated rind of 1 lemon. Bake at 320°F for 1 hour, until set. Serve hot or cold.

Wheat, an emblem of the passing seasons and one of man's earliest foods

Oats
Oats are known to have been cultivated in the Near East as early as 2500 BC. They were distributed throughout Europe by the Romans, and proved hardy enough to survive in the cool, wet climates of Scotland, Northern Ireland and the northern United States. Oat groats were easily pounded into a coarse meal which could be combined with water and eaten raw, if necessary. But they were also cooked as puddings, cakes and gruel. Today oats can be bought as flour, oatmeal or rolled oats.

To make Scots porridge for 4, bring 1 pint water to a boil and sprinkle in $\frac{1}{3}$ cup oatmeal, stirring well with a wooden spoon (or a spurtle, if you're Scottish). Boil for 3 minutes. Add salt to taste halfway through cooking. Serve with a separate jug of milk, fresh cream or buttermilk. Add sugar or honey, if desired.

To make Swedish oatmeal wafers, melt $\frac{1}{3}$ cup butter in a saucepan, and stir in $\frac{2}{3}$ cup oatmeal, $\frac{1}{2}$ cup flour, $\frac{1}{3}$ cup sugar, $\frac{1}{4}$ teaspoon baking powder, 2 tablespoons light cream and 2 tablespoons light corn syrup. Drop teaspoons of the mixture onto buttered baking sheets and bake in the oven at 400°F for about 5 minutes. Cool for 1 minute before removing from the baking sheet.

Whole oat, wheat and rye grains can be sprouted like beans and used in salads, soups or bread doughs.

Millet
Millet, the staple of Eastern Europe, India and Africa, is a tiny, pale yellow grain. In the West it has been relegated to the ranks of bird-seed, but its high protein content makes it a valuable contribution to the diet. It is sold, ready-hulled, in health food stores and delicatessens. It should be cooked in four times its volume of water until all the liquid is absorbed. Its subtle, nutty flavor combines well with legumes, especially chick-peas as in North African *couscous*. It is also used for stuffing vegetables, adding to meatballs, and for desserts.

To make *couscous* for 6–8 people: soak $\frac{3}{4}$ lb cracked millet in water. Take a very large saucepan and sauté in plenty of olive oil: 2 lb cubed lamb, 1 chopped onion, 1 teaspoon ground coriander, 1 teaspoon crushed chili pepper, 1 teaspoon ground cumin, $\frac{1}{4}$ teaspoon saffron and 2 teaspoons salt. Add 2 quarts water or stock, cover and simmer for about 1 hour, until the meat is nearly tender. Add $\frac{1}{2}$ cup each of chopped onion, turnip, zucchini, eggplant, leeks, peppers, celery, raisins and chick-peas (these ingredients can vary according to taste and availability), and simmer for a further 30 minutes. Meanwhile line a metal colander with muslin, place the moistened millet inside it, cover it and put it to steam over the meat and vegetables for 30 minutes more. (This works just as well as a real *couscoussière*.) When all the ingredients are tender, arrange the millet in a large ring on a serving platter, drain the vegetables and place them in the center, and serve the meat with the gravy. Serve with the North African chili sauce – *harissa*.

To make a sweet pudding: cook $\frac{1}{2}$ lb millet in 1 quart milk in the top of a double boiler for 1 hour, stirring from time to time. Cool to lukewarm, add 2 beaten eggs and $\frac{1}{4}$ cup honey, beat well and cook for 10 minutes longer. Serve hot or cold with whipped cream.

Barley

Barley was cultivated by the Ancient Egyptians as early as 6000 BC, and was the chief bread grain of the Hebrews, Greeks and Romans. It was also the basic unit of the Sumerian measuring system, and was used as money in Ancient Babylon. In modern times, most of the barley crop of North America and Europe is used for making beer and whiskey. The barley sold for food is usually milled and polished or 'pearled', which unfortunately reduces the food value. But it is possible to buy 'pot' barley, which is de-husked but not polished, and therefore most nutritious. Barley is ideal for adding to soups and lamb stews.

To make Scotch broth for 4 people: cover $1\frac{1}{2}$ lb cubed boneless lamb with 1 quart water, add salt and pepper, bring slowly to a boil and simmer for $1\frac{1}{2}$ hours. Add 1 chopped carrot, 1 chopped turnip, 1 chopped onion, 2 sliced leeks and $\frac{1}{2}$ cup pot barley. Skim and garnish with parsley; or to serve the traditional way, strain and serve the broth first by itself. The Poles have a similar dish called *krupnik* (see page 237).

To make barley wine, said to cure all ills: wash and blanch $\frac{1}{4}$ cup pearl barley, add $1\frac{1}{2}$ quarts boiling water and simmer until reduced by half. Strain, reserving the barley to use in a soup, and add to the liquid $\frac{1}{3}$ cup raisins, $\frac{1}{3}$ cup sliced figs and another 1 pint boiling water. Simmer and reduce to 1 quart, adding $\frac{1}{2}$ oz licorice root halfway through. Strain. Dilute to taste.

Rye

Rye was first cultivated by the Ancient Romans; by the Middle Ages rye flour was commonly used throughout Europe to make bread. Rye became particularly popular in Central and Eastern Europe and Russia, where strong, dark rye bread accompanies many meals. The Scandinavians also use rye to make a lighter bread, sometimes flavored with honey, orange peel, fennel and anise.

To make Austrian *Pfeffernüsse*, little rye cakes traditionally served at Christmas: beat 3 eggs together and gradually add the juice and grated rind of 2 lemons and 1 cup confectioners' sugar. In another bowl stir together $1\frac{1}{4}$ cups rye flour, $\frac{1}{2}$ teaspoon each ground cinnamon, ground cloves, grated nutmeg and baking soda, and $\frac{1}{4}$ teaspoon each crushed cardamom seeds, crushed aniseed and salt. Add this to the egg mixture, and beat to form a smooth dough. Chill thoroughly. Drop spoonfuls of the mixture onto a greased baking sheet and bake in the center of a preheated oven for 10 minutes at 425°F. Sprinkle with confectioners' sugar to serve.

Corn

Corn probably grew wild in Mexico up to nine thousand years ago. It was the staple food of the American Indians when European explorers arrived in the sixteenth century. The early settlers adopted it as their own and took the new grain to Europe, where it is now grown in southern France, Italy, Spain and the Balkans. We remove the hull and germ to make hominy, which is then dried and cracked to make 'grits', a popular Southern breakfast dish. Cornmeal is popular all over America for muffins, breads and 'mushes'; in Italy it is made into *polenta* (see page 173) and in Rumania it is served as *mamaliga* (see page 216).

To make cornbread, combine $\frac{1}{2}$ cup sifted flour, $2\frac{1}{2}$ teaspoons baking powder, 1–2 tablespoons sugar, $\frac{3}{4}$ teaspoon salt and $1\frac{1}{2}$ cups yellow or white water-ground cornmeal. Beat together 1 egg, 2–3 tablespoons melted butter and $\frac{3}{4}$ cup milk and add to the dry ingredients. Pour the batter into a greased 9 in square pan and bake at 425°F for 25 minutes. Serve warm.

To cook corn on the cob, remove the husks and silk from ears of fresh corn and cook in boiling water, or half milk and half water, for 4–10 minutes, depending on the age of the corn. If you like, add 1 tablespoon sugar to the water. Drain and serve with plenty of butter, salt and pepper.

To make popcorn, heat 1 tablespoon oil in a popcorn popper or heavy saucepan with a tight-fitting lid and place on a moderate heat. Sprinkle in enough popcorn to cover the bottom of the pan and replace the lid tightly. Shake the pan frequently to prevent burning. When the popping sounds die down empty the popcorn into a large bowl and add salt and melted butter.

Buckwheat

The buckwheat plant has heart-shaped leaves and pretty white flowers, and the fruit looks rather like a beech nut. It is a very hardy plant, and like rye is grown mainly in Russia and Eastern Europe. The Austrians make buckwheat dumplings, flavored with bacon, chives and parsley. The Russians use whole or cracked buckwheat grains to make *kasha*, a porridge that can be used as the basis for many meat and vegetable casseroles (see page 234). They also use buckwheat flour to make *blini* – yeast pancakes (see page 233). We Americans and the French also have a version of buckwheat pancakes.

To make about 40 pancakes, sift together $\frac{1}{2}$ cup flour, $\frac{1}{2}$ teaspoon baking powder, $\frac{1}{2}$ teaspoon salt, 1 teaspoon baking soda and 2 teaspoons sugar. Stir in $1\frac{1}{2}$ cups buckwheat flour. Mix together $3\frac{1}{4}$ cups buttermilk and 2 tablespoons melted butter and beat into the dry ingredients. Cook on a lightly greased griddle or in a heavy skillet until golden on both sides. Serve hot with butter and maple syrup.

Each country has its grain; each grain has a specific use modified over the centuries.
Rice: 1 Short grain, polished 2 Short grain, brown 3 Arborio 4 Medium grain, brown 5 Patna 6 Long grain, brown 7 Basmati 8 Wild rice 9 Corn 10 Cornmeal 11 Pot barley 12 Pearl barley 13 Buckwheat 14 Buckwheat flour 15 Rye 16 Rye flour 17 Millet 18 Couscous 19 Wheat 20 Durum flour (semolina) 21 Oats 22 Rolled oats 23 Flaked oats 24 Oatmeal

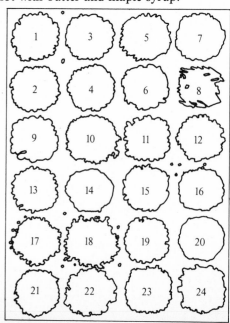

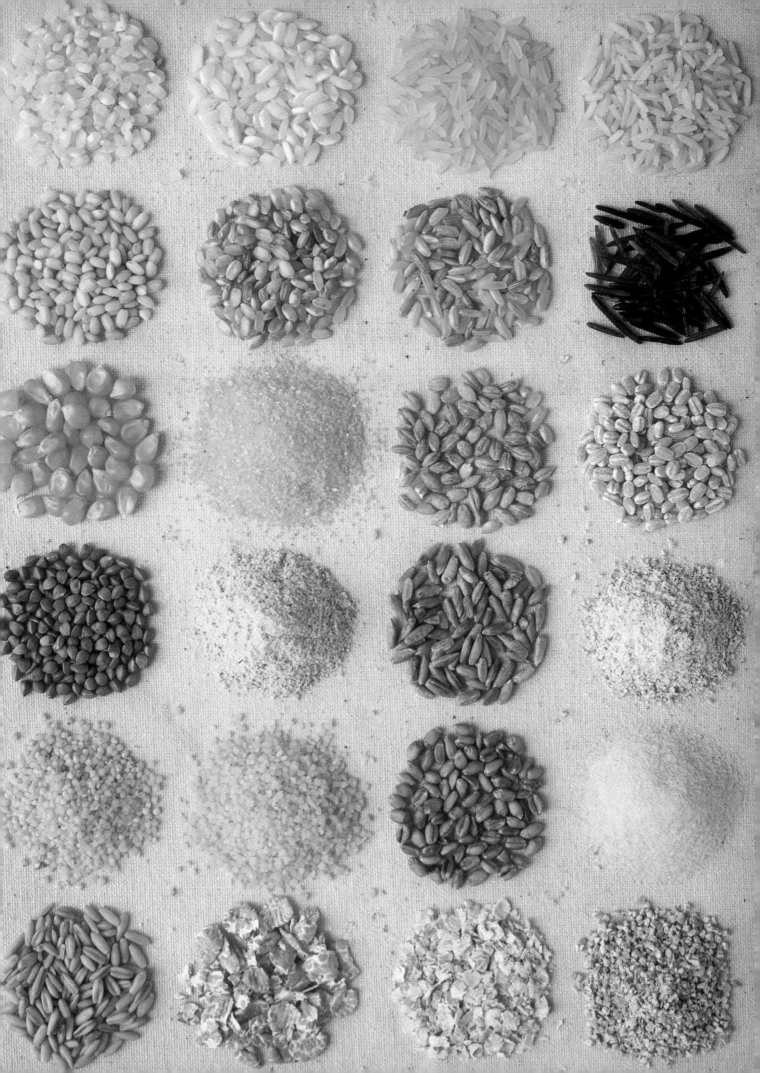

Pastry

astry – at first a plain, unleavened confection used to contain, cook or offset rich food – is thought to have evolved in Ancient Greece. The diet of a noble household included fritters made with buckwheat flour, oil and honey; griddle cakes dipped in wine and eaten hot; tarts filled with grapes and almonds; and wafers called *obolios*, which were baked between two flat irons and served with meats or dipped in sauces.

By the second century BC, in Rome, pastry was being eaten by rich and poor alike. Pastry-making became an industry, a respectable profession with its own guild. Roman bakers made cream and custard tarts, and savory 'dish pies' – pies baked in dishes. Pastry shells were used as plates, which were either eaten or discarded. Pastry scoops were used, rather like potato chips or crackers today, to dip in sauces that were served in communal bowls.

As pastry spread through Europe with the Roman Empire, its versatility increased, and it was used to complement foods, from meat and game to sweet custards and fruit. Raised pie crusts or 'coffins' shaped by hand became edible cooking containers, and pastry lids sealed in juices producing tender succulent meat. In times of scarcity pastry helped a small amount of meat to go further, and little turnovers, easily carried on journeys or to work in the fields, were also a convenient way of eating meat and other fillings in the days before forks were invented.

Pastry: from a simple filler to a culinary art – every country has a specialty:
1 Mazurek (Poland)
2 Karelian turnovers (Finland)
3 Curd tart (Great Britain)
4 Salt cod turnovers (Portugal)
5 Danish pastry
6 Caviar eclairs (Russia)
7 Pizza (Italy)

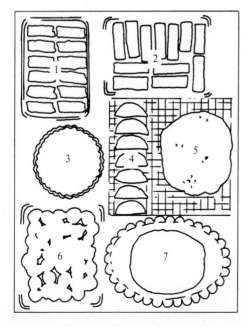

Apart from its practical functions, pastry was often used by the wealthy for decoration and even entertainment. At medieval banquets the table would be adorned with an impressive 'sotelte' – subtlety – made of sweetened paste and gelatin, which was not intended to be eaten. Depending on the occasion, it might represent a hunting scene, peopled with human and animal figures; a church, complete with altars and pews; a ship, fully armed; or a religious scene, such as the Trinity and the saints. In the Renaissance period table decorations became more animated: a Venetian cook book from the mid-sixteenth century describes 'Pies that the Birds may be alive in them, and fly out when it is cut up'; and an English nursery rhyme ('when the pie was opened, the birds began to sing') suggests that this kind of dish was not confined to Italy. At a royal wedding held in Munich in 1568 the guests saw a dwarf, dressed in a miniature suit of armor, emerge from a pie and perform somersaults along the table.

Pies intended for eating were often equally elaborate. One of the earliest English cook books, the *Forme of Cury*, which was compiled by Richard II's cook in 1390, gives recipes for 'grete pyes' containing beef, capons, chickens, mallards, rabbits, woodcocks, 'grete briddies' (large birds), dates, currants and prunes in a sauce thickened with bone marrow and egg yolks and flavored with spices. Another traditional medieval pie contained a pigeon inside a chicken inside a goose inside a turkey, with forcemeat in the spaces between. At the other extremity of the pastry scale were little sweet wafers or 'obleys' – descendants of the Ancient Greek *obolios* – served after meals with a spicy wine called '*hyppocras*'.

The simplest medieval wafer was made with flour and eggs sweetened with honey; but more elaborate versions contained wine, spices or olive oil. Throughout the Middle Ages there was a great rivalry between the wafer-makers, who later evolved into confectioners, and the pastry-cooks, who sold ready-made pie crusts and charged customers a small fee for the use of their large brick ovens.

The earliest pastries were made simply with flour and water, rather like a pasta dough. In the Middle Ages pastry was often seasoned with salt and sugar and colored with saffron or glazed with egg yolks to make it look attractive. Cooks of different nationalities developed their own characteristic methods of pastry making, using local ingredients. In northern Europe, particularly in Scandinavia, where rye grew more easily than wheat, rye flour was often used (see Finnish fish and pork pie, page 131, and Karelian turnovers, page 140). In wine-producing countries like France and Germany sweet pastry was sometimes flavored with wine.

Fat or oil was added to nearly all pastry doughs from the sixteenth century onwards, making pastry light and crumbly. Butter was used in dairy-farming areas; and in northern France 'butter paste' or puff pastry developed. The Austrians used their strong native flour to make miraculously light paper-thin leaves of dough brushed with melted butter (see strudel, page 206). A thrifty Danish cook found that he could make his pastry rise by adding yeast, thus saving on butter, while the British produced an ideal firm crust for hand-raised pies by adding suet melted in hot water. In warm southern climates so-called 'Spanish' puff paste was made using olive oil instead of butter.

By the nineteenth century pastry-making had developed into a diverse and delicate art form, encouraged by the great French chefs, in particular Carême, who invented choux pastry. He also created sweet specialties including *croquembouches* and *millefeuilles*, which have become classic items of pâtisserie.

One test of a good cook anywhere lies in the ability to make sound pastry, for it demands extreme care and attention to detail for complete success. The following general points are particularly important.

Shortcrust, tart and puff pastries need chilled fat, ice-cold water and cool hands; and the dough should be handled as little as possible. A marble slab makes an ideal rolling surface because it is cool, but a wooden pastry board will do just as well. Preheat the oven to 400°F. As different flours absorb different amounts of water, measure the water carefully and add it gradually; if you use too much the pastry will be hard and leathery, too little and it will be crumbly and difficult to handle.

When baking a pie or tart shell, butter the pie pan thoroughly to avoid sticking. Lift the dough gently onto the rolling pin and lay it over the pie pan. Press it gently into the corners (but do not stretch it or it will shrink again during cooking), and trim off the excess dough with a sharp knife. Prick it with a fork to allow air to escape.

If the shell is to be baked without the filling, line it with foil and fill it with dried beans or peas to act as a weight during cooking. About five minutes before it's ready, remove the foil and beans, and allow the surface to cook.

If making a pie, fill the pastry shell with the filling. Lay the 'lid' gently on top, press down firmly with a fork or spoon to make an attractive edging, and trim off any excess. Make a hole in the center of the lid with a fork or knife to allow steam to escape. The dough trimmings can be cut into shapes to decorate the top, which is then glazed with beaten egg into which a little salt has been stirred.

SHORTCRUST (PIE) PASTRY

This is the most commonly used pastry, suitable for all types of sweet or savory dishes.

To line 2 9-in pie pans or make a two-crust pie

2 cups flour
½ teaspoon salt
⅔ cup butter margarine, lard or shortening
4–5 tablespoons cold water

Sift the flour and salt into a mixing bowl. Work the fat into the flour for 2–3 minutes using the tips of your fingers or a pastry blender, until the mixture looks like breadcrumbs.

Add the water gradually and mix quickly with a knife. When the dough begins to stick together, knead it lightly in the bowl with one hand until it is firm and smooth.

It is possible to use the dough immediately; but it is better to let it rest for 15 minutes in a cool place. It will keep in a refrigerator for up to 2 days, wrapped in a plastic bag.

Preheat the oven to 400°F. Sprinkle some flour on a flat surface and on a rolling pin (but not on the dough), and roll out the dough evenly. After each roll turn the dough over and rotate it through 90°. Do not pull or stretch it, or it will shrink during cooking. Continue rolling until the pastry is about ⅛ in thick, then use as required.

TART PASTRY

This is a richer pastry, made in the same way as shortcrust, and ideal for sweet tarts. If the sugar is omitted it can be used for savory dishes as well.

To line 2 9-in tart pans

¾ cup butter
1 tablespoon sugar
1 egg
3–4 tablespoons cold water
2 cups flour
½ teaspoon salt

Mix the butter and sugar and cream lightly. Stir in the egg and a little water and make into a dough with the sifted flour and salt. Gather in one hand and knead lightly until it is firm and smooth. Add more water if necessary. Roll out as for shortcrust pastry, and bake in a preheated oven at 400°F.

PUFF AND FLAKY PASTRY

Puff pastry is the richest paste of all. It rises best when strong bread-making flour is used. Knead the butter in advance so that it is of the same consistency as the dough. Rest the dough between and after each rolling, and handle it as delicately as possible.

Flaky pastry is made with the same ingredients, but the butter is cut into small pieces and dotted over the dough in batches between folds and turns.

Makes an 8 in vol-au-vent, or 20–25 2½ in bouchées

2 cups flour
pinch of salt
¾ cup butter
8–10 tablespoons iced water
squeeze of lemon juice

Sift the flour and salt into a mixing bowl. Rub some butter (about 2 tablespoons) into the flour with your fingertips. Mix to a fairly firm dough with the water and lemon juice, and knead lightly on a floured surface until smooth.

Work the rest of the butter with a knife on a plate until it is as soft as the dough, then shape it into an oblong. Roll out the dough into a square, place the butter on one half of it, and fold the other half over it, pressing the edges together with the rolling pin.

Turn the dough so that the folded edge is to one side, and roll out into a rectangle 3 times as long as it is wide. Fold the bottom third up and the top third down and seal the edges as before by pressing them with the rolling pin. Wrap the dough in a plastic bag and leave to rest in a cool place or a refrigerator for 20 minutes.

Roll out the dough again, with the fold to one side as before. Fold, and leave to rest again. Repeat until the process has been completed 6 times altogether. After the dough has rested for the last time, roll it out to a thickness of about ⅛ in and cut as required. Glaze with beaten egg and bake in a preheated oven at 450°F.

HOT WATER PASTRY

This is sometimes called raised pastry, and is ideal for making raised meat pies.

Makes a case to fit a 9 × 5 × 3 in loaf pan or 4 individual pies

1½ cups lard
¾ cup water or milk
4 cups flour, sifted
1 teaspoon salt
beaten egg yolk to glaze

Bring the lard and water to a boil, and remove from the heat. Add the flour and salt and mix to a dough. Knead lightly, then leave in a warm place for 30 minutes. Roll out and use to line a buttered loaf pan or mold into shape around the base of an oiled and floured canning jar.

Fill with your chosen meat filling, glaze with beaten egg yolk, and bake for 30 minutes in a preheated oven (400°F), then reduce to 300°F and continue cooking for a further 1½ hours.

CHOUX PASTRY

This is a rich, light pastry which is quick and simple to prepare. It can be used for savory and sweet dishes.

Makes about 40 small éclairs, or 20 large ones

1 cup water
pinch salt
⅓ cup butter
1 cup flour, sifted
4 large eggs

Heat the water in a large saucepan with a thick bottom. Sprinkle in the salt. Add the butter, and bring to a boil. Remove from the heat and add all the flour. Mix well with a wooden spoon, return to the heat and cook, stirring all the time, until the mixture thickens and comes away from the sides of the pan.

Remove from the heat and add the eggs one by one, stirring constantly. Beat vigorously, either by hand or with an electric mixer, until very light.

Pipe the mixture onto a greased baking sheet through a pastry bag, and bake in a preheated oven at 400°F for 35 minutes until well risen and crisp. Leave until cold before filling.

A seventeenth-century bakery by Abraham de Bosse

Pasta was invented when Ceres, the goddess of the harvest, spurned Vulcan, the god of fire. He stripped all the wheat from her fields, ground it into flour, plunged it into the water of the Bay of Naples, cooked it over the flames of Vesuvius and dressed it with fragrant oil from the olive groves of Capri. Or so they say in southern Italy.

In fact pasta is older than the Roman gods: the Chinese were probably eating noodles or *mein*, made from a mixture of wheat and dried ground beans, more than three thousand years ago. By the eleventh century AD both the Indians and Arabs were making spaghetti-like noodles and the Arabs are thought to have introduced them to Europe: in the twelfth century the people of Sicily were making noodles which they still called by their Arab name, *itriyah* (literally, 'string').

A shortened form of this word, *trii*, is still a popular name for spaghetti in southern Italy.

The earliest ancestor of lasagne is a flat cake of dough called *laganon*, which the Greeks made. This was adopted by the Romans who called it *laganum*; Cicero and Horace both enthused about it in the first century BC and fifteen hundred years later lasagne was being enjoyed in places as far apart as Sumatra and London. Marco Polo mentions it when describing his travels in the East in the late thirteenth century, and it is referred to as 'loseyns' in the cook book compiled at the court of Richard II of England in 1390.

Macaroni and ravioli were popular in Italy by the Middle Ages: in *The Decameron* (1350) Boccaccio describes a distant country where 'on a mountain, all of grated Parmesan cheese, dwell folk that do nought else but make macaroni and ravioli . . .'. Macaroni is also found in the English *Forme of Cury*, where it is called 'macrows'. The English version of ravioli was 'tartlettes', and they were made by filling small cases of thin dough with a stuffing of ground pork, eggs, currants, spices and salt, and boiling them in salted water.

A Latin cook book compiled by the Vatican librarian in 1475 includes a recipe for 'a food called vermicelli: flour, well-sifted and white, well-kneaded with water, rolled into thin sheets and cut in pieces the length and width of a finger. If well drained in the sun, it will keep for 2 or 3 years. Cook them in a fatty broth and in a dish prepare them with fresh cheese and sweet spices. This pasta needs two hours of cooking.'

Throughout the fifteenth and sixteenth centuries pasta was a delicacy served at the great banquets given by Renaissance princes. *A New Book on How to Give Banquets*, compiled in the sixteenth century by the Duke of Ferrara's steward, includes macaroni cooked gently in milk and butter and served with a sweet sauce of honey and ricotta; lasagne baked with sole and shrimp; and spaghetti served with almonds, ricotta and sweet spices.

In 1641 the Pope was forced to decree that pasta stores should be at least twenty-five yards apart – an indication that by now pasta had become the food of the people. And not just the Italian people: in the German speaking world, *Nudeln* were an essential feature of the diet, served with meat or savory sauces or sweetened to make a dessert. The French transformed the German word into *nouilles* and served them *à l'italienne*. The Spanish devised many pasta recipes of their own such as *canalones* (see page 151). The Russians made meat-filled *pelmeni* (see page 235), which were probably descended directly from the Chinese *wun tun*, and *vareniki* with a cheese or sweet filling. And the Italians went on inventing more and more kinds of pasta: pasta *asciutta* – 'dry' pasta to serve with sauces and tiny shapes to garnish soups.

Cooks everywhere appreciated the versatility of pasta: served with butter and grated cheese (in the north of Europe) or olive oil and garlic (in the south), it made the simplest, yet most satisfying of meals. Stuffed pasta was an interesting way of using up leftovers, and making desserts; noodles made soups more substantial.

Pasta had many advantages: it could be stored for a long time; it could easily be carried on journeys, which made it popular among nomadic tribes; and it could be cooked in just a few minutes. Pasta could also form the basis for the most elaborate, exquisite dishes – such as the *pasticci* or *timballi*, combining meat and cheese and vegetable sauces, which were often served at the great formal dinners held in eighteenth-century Italy.

In addition to its practical advantages, pasta is also good for you. It is easily digested; it contains essential carbohydrates and vitamins. When served with a meat, cheese or fish sauce, it also provides a wide range of proteins.

The best, most nutritious pasta of all is made from durum wheat and eggs. Durum wheat is particularly hard, and when ground produces semolina, a yellowish granular substance, quite unlike the fine white flour of bread wheat. (Pasta *can* be made with bread flour, but it tends to go soggy when cooked, has less flavor, and less food value.) Sometimes

spinach is added to *pasta all'uovo* (egg pasta) to make *pasta verde*, which has an even smoother, creamier texture.

Southern Italy with its warm, dry climate was the original center of the pasta industry. Today a great deal of durum wheat – and pasta – is also produced and consumed in the United States.

In addition to the story of Vulcan and Ceres, many other myths have grown up around pasta over the centuries. Both Casanova and Lord Byron, for instance, claimed it was an aphrodisiac. One popular twentieth-century myth says that pasta is fattening: but in fact it is only as fattening as the butter you put on it. And another myth, equally untrue, says that fresh pasta is difficult to make at home. In fact it is easy – if time-consuming – to make yourself. Home-made pasta is quite delicious and very satisfying.

HOME-MADE EGG PASTA

Pasta is usually made on a wooden board, but if you are not used to doing it this way it is easier to make it in a large bowl.

Serves 4–6

2 cups flour
2 large eggs
2 teaspoons olive oil
a pinch of salt

Sift the flour, make a well in the center and crack the eggs into it. Add the olive oil and salt, and start stirring the flour from the sides of the well into the eggs with a fork.

When you have incorporated about half the flour, start working in the remaining flour with your hands. When you have a stiffish dough you can stop adding flour.

Knead the dough with the palms of your hands until it is fairly smooth and pliable.

Cut the dough into the same number of equal pieces as there are eggs. Roll out each piece into a thin strip, fold the strips into 3 and roll again. Repeat the performance 3 or 4 times to mix the dough thoroughly.

It is now ready for use. Roll it out into transparently thin sheets, cut into the required shapes, and cook in a large pan of boiling water for 2–5 minutes, or until *al dente* – tender but still firm.

Pasta – an aphrodisiac or the invention of a spurned god? There are as many myths as there are recipes for this nutritious food. The basic pasta dough (natural) can be cut into several widths and the flavor can be changed by adding more egg or spinach:

1 Fettuccine (with spinach)
2 Fettuccine (natural)
3 Vermicelli (with spinach)
4 Vermicelli (natural)
5 Tagliatelle (high in egg)
6 Tagliatelle (low in egg)
7 Ravioli made in a grid
8 Ravioli folded and cut
9 Canalones (Spain)
10 Vareniki with sour cream filling (Ukraine)
11 Pelmeni or noodle dumplings (Siberia)
12 Farfalle (Italy)
13 Ravioli with meat filling (Italy)

Regional and traditional recipes from Europe and North America

*Show me another pleasure like dinner
which comes every day
and lasts an hour.*

Talleyrand (1754–1838)

The enormous
diversity of the
French provinces:
Brittany and the
Massif Central

France is the gastronomic center of the world: no country has more diverse natural ingredients, or more human genius for transforming them into culinary delicacies. Each region of France has its own distinctive recipes, cooking methods and utensils based on local produce. The produce in the north of France differs considerably from that in the south, and there are differences between the plains, the mountains, the sea and the river banks.

In the cool far north of France, in Artois and Picardy, the soil is ideal for growing root vegetables such as turnips, beets, carrots and potatoes. The green pastures of Normandy feed the herds of cows whose rich milk makes *crème fraîche* and good butter. Here there are apple trees heavy with fruit for making apple tarts, cider and Calvados. The fertile la Beauce plain just below Paris provides the wheat that is used to make French bread; and across the Loire in Touraine, the so-called 'garden of France', green beans, cauliflower, celeriac, peas, leeks and other green vegetables grow in abundance. In the south, along the hot coastland, eggplants, green peppers and zucchini thrive as well as delicious peaches, melons, cherries, artichokes and asparagus; while toward the Alps fig and nut trees flourish and gnarled olive groves produce the rich oil that provides the basis for the region's many dishes.

Differences between east and west are less easily defined. The west coast however is rich in seafood – Breton lobster and tuna, pike from Nantes, mussels from Aunis and Saintonge – and the east boasts freshwater fish, splendid game and hops for making beer. In general the valleys of France – along the Loire, the Seine and the Rhône – are rich in fruit and vegetables.

French regional cooking depends on basic produce: the nature of the soil in any area determines the diet of the local people. Subtle differences in the soil of two regions which at first appear similar will lead to variations in produce. For example, the *sauvignon* (a variety of white grape) grown on the left bank of the Loire in Berry produces the wine of Sancerre; but from the same *sauvignon* on the right bank just opposite, in the Nevers district, comes the wine of Pouilly, known as 'Pouilly-fumé'. These same vines produce two different wines because of the soil, the way it is worked and the location of the hillsides.

Similarly, *la poularde de Bresse* has a world-wide reputation. Attempts have been made to raise the pullets in other parts of the country, apart from the sterile stretch of land in Burgundy between the small river Ain on the east, the Saône on the west, Dombes in the south and Franche-Comté in the north, but the results are never the same.

As soil and climate produce the distinctive raw materials of a region, so these two combine to dictate the cooking methods used by the local people. In the north of France an open fire used to be the traditional means of cooking: here meat was cooked, spit-roasted or simmered gently above the flames in a cast iron *chaudron*. Food could also be cooked overnight among the embers in closed earthenware pots. Dishes that needed long, slow cooking such as *gigot brayaude* from Auvergne, Languedoc *cassoulet* and *tripes à la mode de Caen* were often taken to the local baker to be cooked in his vast, wood-heated oven after the bread had been baked. These substantial dishes gained their unique flavor from the slow, gentle heat of the baker's oven.

In the hot south of France, however, where timber was less plentiful than in the temperate regions, enclosed charcoal ovens were used. Cooks could bake slowly or fry quickly without being exposed to a fierce heat for too long. In this southern climate the diet was naturally lighter and people ate salads, fresh fish and quick-fried chops.

Some traditional French recipes dispensed with ovens and pots entirely: *coquelet grillé aux sarments* from Brittany called for a chicken to be cooked over an open fire of vine shoots; in Saintonge an unplucked chicken was smothered with clay, buried in glowing embers and baked slowly overnight; while in Nevers an ancient recipe for *sanglier à la gauloise* demanded that you 'dig a deep hole in the ground and fill it with glowing embers. Wrap a well-seasoned leg of wild boar in a clean animal skin, place it in the hole, cover it with earth and leave overnight. The meat will be cooked by morning.'

The correct cooking vessel in general is as important to the end results of a dish as the ingredients it contains. Originally each region of France had its own particular utensils: Normandy had the *tripière*, a dish for cooking tripe; Périgord

From the vine to the bottle, and back to the field

the *pot à confit*, a preserving jar; Burgundy the *cocotte en fonte*, a deep cast-iron cooking pot with a tight-fitting lid; Brittany the *galetière* or *crêpe* pan; Bourbonne the *poêle à manche long*, a long-handled skillet, and Lorraine the *marmite à trois pieds*, a three-legged stewpot. The *daubière en terre*, a heavy braising pot with a tight-fitting lid, originated in Provence, but is now used everywhere for cooking meats and vegetables very slowly without letting the contents burn or losing any of the juices through evaporation; and the *diable*, an unglazed, porous clay container with a rounded top and bottom that fit firmly together, came originally from Limousin, but is now used in many parts of Europe for cooking potatoes without any liquid or fat.

Some dishes have even become synonymous with the pots they are cooked in: *terrine* is the name of both a pâté and the earthenware container in which it is cooked and served; and *kugelhopf* is the name of the fluted mold as well as the traditional Alsatian yeast cake cooked in it.

Just as the French have an appropriate pot for every dish, they also have an appropriate dish for every occasion. The French love festivals and celebrate them with traditional meals: *crêpes* for Candlemas, fritters for Shrove Tuesday and egg pâté for Easter. There are also special dishes in each region for the end of the harvest, the wine-gathering and the day the pig is killed. In early summer, hens that have stopped laying eggs are slaughtered, and cooks all over rural France use their ingenuity in turning the tough stewing chicken into a tender delicacy: in Berry the bird is boned and stuffed with pork, veal, nuts and brandy; in Normandy it is bathed in a cream and butter sauce; and in Béarn it is simmered slowly with assorted summer vegetables.

Each region of France is famed for its distinctive flavors based on local ingredients: *à la bourguignonne* means simmered in red Burgundy with salt pork, mushrooms and pearl onions; a dish cooked *à la provençale* will be flavored with garlic, olive oil, tomatoes and fresh herbs; and in Béarn, where every part of the goose is carefully preserved and used, the cooking is characterized by the goose fat used as a medium, instead of oil or butter.

It is above all in the invention of sauces that French cooks have shown their greatest genius, combining fresh local ingredients with good homemade stock to create exquisite tastes and textures. *Beurre blanc*, originally designed to complement the fish of the river Loire, uses Angevin shallots as a basis; the essential accompaniment to partridge or pork in the district near Perpignan is *sauce catalane*, made with tomatoes, oranges, garlic and olive oil; *béarnaise* sauce combines eggs, butter, wine and shallots with the distinctive flavor of tarragon to complement either meat or fish; and in Savoy a walnut and horseradish sauce, mixed with lemon juice and cream, accompanies magnificent freshwater fish from the mountain lakes.

French eating habits vary between the north and south. Most meals consist of several courses: soup or hors d'oeuvre, a meat dish and a vegetable dish, cheese and dessert. In the evening the meat course may be replaced by an egg or fish dish, a salad, or possibly a vegetable.

In the moderate climate of the north, where people are naturally industrious, lunch is taken between twelve and one o'clock. It is eaten quickly and work starts again at once. In the Midi, in southern France, lunch is taken later, at one-thirty to two o'clock. It is a more leisurely meal, often followed by a welcome siesta.

Since each French cook feels that his particular way of cooking is the correct one, there is an enormous number of French recipes for any given dish or ingredient. Techniques vary from one village to the next: no two Languedoc cooks will combine their cassoulet ingredients in quite the same way. The same is true of French *charcuterie*, wines and cheeses. Switzerland is generally known as 'the land of cheeses'; yet although there are many different varieties of Swiss cheese they are all of the Gruyère type. France on the other hand is the real land of cheeses: there is a world of difference in size, shape, ripeness, and, most of all, flavor

Goats' cheese and green peppers – nature's riches for the table

France

Dufy's Marché à Marseille – *where food is business as well as pleasure*

between Roquefort and Munster, Reblochon and Camembert, Crottin and Chavignol, the monumental Cantal and the minuscule Rocamadour.

French cuisine has been influenced a little by that of other countries: the Spanish occupation of Flanders and the north of France in the sixteenth century left a trace on the cuisine of the north; and the border provinces share some flavors and techniques with their neighbors: Basque and Languedoc cooks make spicy stews flavored with peppery sausages, reminiscent of Spain; the sausages, ham and *choucroute* of Alsace-Lorraine are almost as famous as those of Germany, and the cooking of the *Alpes* and the *pays niçois* are influenced by Italy. Certain man-made inventions have been introduced into France from other countries, such as mayonnaise from Spain, although this was, in fact, invented by a French chef. Also, the produce of the New World – potatoes, peppers, tomatoes, beans – was introduced to France in the seventeenth century as to every other European country, and was soon assimilated into most French dishes. The people of

Picardy practically claim to have invented their beloved potato; and it would be difficult to persuade a modern Provençal cook that tomatoes and peppers were once 'foreign' ingredients.

However, French cooking has affected other nations greatly: in the eighteenth century in particular, when the French language and manners were the height of fashion, French cooking was extremely influential. The Imperial court of Vienna, the nobility of pre-revolutionary Russia and the court of Frederick the Great of Prussia all abandoned their national way of life for that of France. French chefs were employed at every European court, and supervised the kitchens of every grand hotel.

While other countries have excellent cuisines, none is as diversified as the French. The people of France argue heatedly about the origin of certain dishes, the correct cooking methods and ingredients; yet for all their contradictory opinions on the subject, they are firmly united in their national reverence for food.

Hors d'oeuvre

TOURTE CHERBOURGEOISE (NORMANDY)
Scallop tart

In the port of Cherbourg on the Cotentin peninsula this tart is made using mild Normandy butter, or Cherbourg lard, which is a local delicacy. (Cherbourg is also famous for its small lobsters, the *demoiselles de Cherbourg*.)

Serves 6

Pastry
6 tablespoons softened butter
1 small egg
pinch of salt
1¼ cups flour, sifted

Filling
8 large scallops
2 eggs
1 egg yolk
⅓ cup milk
⅓ cup cream
salt
cayenne pepper
nutmeg
a few leaves of fresh tarragon and chervil, chopped
4 large mushrooms
2 tablespoons butter

Prepare the pastry by mixing the butter, egg and salt together, then adding the flour. Set aside in a cool place.

If using frozen scallops, allow them to thaw, then cut each into 3 or 4 pieces, slicing on a slant. Mix the 2 eggs and yolk, and pour in the milk and cream. Beat thoroughly, season with salt, cayenne and nutmeg, and finally add the chopped tarragon and chervil. Set aside in a cool place.

Peel and wash the mushrooms, chop them coarsely and put on one side. Sauté the scallop pieces gently in butter in a skillet, and season with salt and cayenne pepper. Before they are quite cooked, place on one side to cool.

Line a 7 in tart pan with the dough and garnish the bottom with the pieces of scallop and mushrooms. Pour the filling into the pastry shell, and place in the oven. Cook for about 30 minutes at 400°F.

Leave the cooked tart to cool for a while so that it can be removed from the pan easily. Slide it onto a flat, round ovenproof plate and return it to the oven for a few minutes. It must be served very hot.

left Tourte cherbourgeoise: *the delicate seafood subtlety of scallops*

QUICHE LORRAINE (LORRAINE)
Quiche Lorraine

In Lorraine *quiches* are sometimes made with puff pastry, which is said to have been invented here by Claude Gelée. (He later went on to become an artist better known as Claude le Lorrain.)

Serves 6

Pastry
6 tablespoons softened
  butter
1 small egg
a pinch of salt
1¼ cups flour, sifted

Filling
2 oz cheese
6 bacon slices
2 eggs
1 egg yolk
⅔ cup milk
⅔ cup cream
salt and pepper
grated nutmeg

To make the pastry, mix the butter with the egg and salt, and then add the flour. Put this on one side in a cool place.

Cut the cheese and the bacon into thin strips. Sauté the bacon quickly in a skillet but do not let it become brown or crisp.

Meanwhile mix together the eggs and egg yolk, milk, cream, salt and pepper, and a pinch of nutmeg.

Line a 7 in tart pan with the dough and arrange the strips of cheese and bacon on the bottom. Pour the filling into the pastry shell. Place in the oven and cook for 20–30 minutes at 400°F.

When the *quiche* is cooked, leave it to cool for a while so that it can be removed from the pan more easily and serve warm on a flat, round plate.

QUENELLES LYONNAISES (LYONS)
Pike quenelles

We should be particularly grateful to the unknown genius who invented pike *quenelles*, since he has enabled us to enjoy this tasty king of river fish without being inconvenienced by its numerous small bones.

Making *quenelles* is a delicate job and for this reason they are sold ready-made in many French grocery stores. In the Lyons region, *quenelles* are served not only with this Lyonnaise sauce but also with béchamel sauce and Nantua sauce, flavored with crayfish.

Serves 4

2 lb pike flesh
salt and pepper
grated nutmeg
3 egg whites
1 pint crème fraîche

Sauce
2 tablespoons butter
¼ cup flour
1 pint stock
1 teaspoon tomato
  purée
salt and pepper

Grind the fish and add salt, pepper and a little nutmeg. Place the ground fish in a large bowl and mix in the egg whites, stirring for a long time with a wooden spoon. Pass through a fine strainer and return to the bowl. Stand the bowl on crushed ice if possible, continue stirring the mixture, and add the *crème fraîche*. Correct the seasoning and chill.

To make the sauce, melt the butter in a heavy saucepan. As soon as it begins to foam add the flour and cook until the roux turns dark brown. Leave to cool.

Heat the stock and add it to the roux; beat until smooth and leave to simmer for a few minutes. Add the tomato purée, bring to a boil again, and correct the seasoning. Keep the sauce hot in a double boiler or over a very low heat.

To cook the *quenelles*, form the mixture into small fingers. Boil plenty of salted water in a large pan and plunge in 5 or 6 of the *quenelles* at a time. When they are firm and rise to the surface (after about 5 minutes), drain.

As the *quenelles* are cooked, place them in a buttered baking dish containing some of the sauce. Finally coat the *quenelles* with the rest of the sauce and place in the oven at 375°F for about 15 minutes. The *quenelles* should be served at once.

A simple Norman kitchen

OEUFS A LA NIVERNAISE (NEVERS)
Eggs cooked in wine

This popular Nevers dish has traveled well and is eaten in many parts of the world.

Serves 8

1 large onion, chopped
1 shallot, chopped
⅛ cup butter
1 quart red table wine
3 cloves of garlic,
  finely chopped
sprig of fresh thyme
1 bay leaf
salt and pepper
8 eggs
1 tablespoon flour
8 slices of bread
¼ cup cream
  (optional)

Fry the onion and shallot gently in ⅛ cup butter, but do not brown. Add the wine, garlic, thyme, bay leaf, salt and pepper. Simmer for 30 minutes.

Poach the eggs gently in the mixture, 2 at a time. The cooking liquid should be 'trembling' on the verge of boiling, but it must not boil. After a few minutes (not more than 4) drain the eggs; the whites should be firm, but the yolks still liquid.

When all the eggs are cooked, pour the wine into another pan, and reduce by boiling to 1 pint.

Meanwhile prepare a little *beurre manié* by working about 2 tablespoons butter into the flour with a fork until the mixture forms a smooth paste. When the wine is reduced, drop the *beurre manié* a little at a time onto the bubbling surface. Do not stir, but shake and rotate the pan for a few seconds until the sauce thickens. Leave the sauce on the lowest possible heat for a few minutes, and adjust the seasoning (it should be well spiced with pepper).

Brown the slices of bread lightly in the remaining butter, arrange them on the serving plate, and place a poached egg on each slice. Cover with the sauce. You can pour a little cream over the eggs just before serving if you wish.

Buying the good butter that so much French cooking demands

OEUFS A LA TRIPE (ORLÉANS)
Eggs with 'tripe'

This egg recipe was given its name to console the children, who traditionally were not allowed to eat tripe – a great deprivation in the Orléans region, especially at Jargeau, where it is the local specialty.

Serves 8

8 eggs
2 large onions,
  chopped
⅛ cup butter
3 tablespoons flour
1 pint milk
salt and pepper
freshly grated nutmeg

Cook the eggs for 10 minutes. Fry the onions gently in butter in a heavy saucepan without letting them brown. Sprinkle with flour to make a roux and leave to cook gently over a low heat for a few minutes. Take off the stove and leave to cool.

Boil the milk and pour it onto the cold roux; beat well, then cook gently, adding salt and pepper and finally a little freshly grated nutmeg. This onion sauce must be very smooth; if it is too thick you can add a little milk or cream.

Shell the hard-cooked eggs, cool them under a cold tap, and chop coarsely. Add them to the hot onion sauce, bring to a boil, correct the seasoning and serve.

Garlic – for a characteristic French flavour

ASPERGES A LA NORMANDE (NORMANDY)
Asparagus with cream sauce

Cooking in Normandy is characterized by rich cream and excellent butter – especially that of Isigny. Not far from Isigny, in Rouen, is 'The Butter Tower': some say that it was built with the dues paid to the Church by the village inhabitants, so that they could eat butter during Lent.

Serves 8

3 lb asparagus
salt and pepper
⅛ cup butter
1 cup cream
chopped fresh chervil

Scrape the ends of the asparagus spears, if necessary. Tie the asparagus in bundles and plunge them into boiling salted water. Cook gently for 10–15 minutes, until crunchy. Drain on a clean cloth and arrange on a long, ovenproof serving dish that has been liberally buttered.

Salt and pepper the cream; pour it over the asparagus and put the dish in a moderately hot oven (375°F) for 15 minutes. While cooking the cream will reduce and thicken. To serve, sprinkle with chopped chervil.

oups

SOUPE AU MOUTON (LORRAINE)
Mutton soup

Mutton soup has been made in Lorraine for hundreds of years. According to legend, it was Joan of Arc's favorite soup. She grew up in Lorraine, and her diet is said to have consisted almost entirely of different kinds of soup.

Serves 4

1 lb breast of lamb *¼ lb salt pork* *salt and pepper* *a handful of fresh* *lima beans (or* *dried ones soaked* *overnight)* *3 carrots* *2 turnips* *1 white of leek* *a piece of cabbage* *1 clove of garlic* *slices of toasted bread* *½ cup crème fraiche*	Place the lamb and salt pork in a large saucepan, cover with 1½ quarts of cold water and bring to a boil. Skim, add salt and pepper, the beans and chopped vegetables, and simmer gently for 1 hour or until tender. After cooking, take out the meat and vegetables, place them in a deep dish and keep them hot, to be served after the soup. (A Lorraine cook would broil the lamb for a few minutes to bring out the flavor.) To serve the soup, rub a tureen with the garlic, then line with the slices of toasted bread, sprinkle with *crème fraiche*, and pour in the broth. Serve at once.

The pastures of the Landes – once so marshy that shepherds wore stilts

POTAGE AUX GRENOUILLES (ALSACE)
Frogs' leg soup

Frogs are becoming increasingly scarce in Alsace. Since the marshes have been drained, frogs are gradually disappearing, to the despair of gourmets . . . and storks which are also very fond of eating frogs.

Serves 8

3 shallots *¼ cup butter* *24 frogs (48 frogs' legs)* *1 cup white wine* *1 quart stock* *salt and pepper* *2 egg yolks* *½ cup cream* *croûtons to serve*	Peel and finely chop the shallots, and brown them in butter in a large saucepan. Add the frogs' legs, cover and leave to sweat on a very low heat for about 10 minutes. Then add the white wine, stock, pepper and salt and cook for about 30 minutes. When the frogs' legs are tender, drain them and discard the small bones. Keep the meat hot in a little stock. Thicken the rest of the stock with the egg yolks and cream. Heat without boiling and stir gently. Correct the seasoning and add the frogs' legs. Serve very hot in a soup tureen, with croûtons on a separate dish.

SOUPE AU CANTAL (AUVERGNE)
Cantal cheese soup

Cantal is one of the oldest French cheeses: it was mentioned in the writings of Pliny the elder nearly two thousand years ago. Although it looks very much like Cheddar, it is smoother in texture and has a stronger flavor.

Serves 6–8

2 large onions *¼ cup butter* *1½ quarts stock or water* *salt and pepper* *¼ lb rye bread in* *slices, slightly* *dried in the oven* *½ lb Cantal cheese* *(or sharp Cheddar)* *2–3 tablespoons crème* *fraiche (optional)*	Peel and finely chop the onions, and fry them gently in butter in a heavy saucepan. Do not let them brown. Add the stock or water, salt and pepper, and bring to a boil. Simmer gently for 30–40 minutes. In a serving bowl arrange alternate layers of rye bread and sliced cheese. When the broth is cooked, correct the seasoning and pour it over the bread and cheese. Serve very hot, sprinkled with freshly ground pepper. If you wish to leave out the onions, strain the broth before adding it to the bread and cheese. To improve the flavor of the soup add 2 or 3 tablespoons of *crème fraiche* at the last moment.

SOUPE AUX CHOUX A L'HUILE DE NOIX (BOURBONNAIS)
Cabbage soup with walnut oil

Bourbon walnut oil is a famous delicacy, especially the kind that comes from the small town of Gannat, a few miles from Vichy. Until very recently this walnut oil was still pressed in the traditional way on an old stone mill.

Serves 6

2 small heads of Savoy cabbage, chopped
1 large onion, chopped
¼ cup walnut oil
1½ quarts stock or water
salt and pepper
3 potatoes, thinly sliced
5 thick slices stale white bread, toasted

Sauté the cabbage and onion rapidly in half the walnut oil. Meanwhile, heat the stock or water, adding salt and pepper. Add the cabbage and onion to the stock, then add the potatoes. Cover and cook for 1 hour.

After cooking beat the soup to mash the potatoes. Pour the soup into a tureen lined with the toasted slices of bread. Sprinkle the rest of the walnut oil over the soup and serve.

SOUPE SAVOYARDE (SAVOY)
Vegetable and cheese soup

Soups are an essential part of the Savoy diet. But there was a time when, in order to defend themselves from their attackers, Savoy householders tipped pots of boiling soup over their enemies.

Serves 4

3–4 turnips
1 large onion
1 lb potatoes
3 celeriac (celery root)
2 whites of leeks
6 tablespoons butter
1 quart stock
salt and pepper
5 large stale bread slices
1 pint milk
¼ lb Beaufort cheese (or substitute Gruyère)

Peel the vegetables and chop them finely. Fry them gently in ¼ cup butter in a saucepan, but do not let them color. Cover and leave to sweat for 30 minutes on the lowest possible heat. Then add 1 quart of stock, salt and pepper, cover and cook gently for 45 minutes.

Meanwhile, cut the bread into cubes and fry quickly in the remaining butter until crisp and golden.

Just before serving heat the milk to boiling and add this to the soup; correct the seasoning with salt and pepper.

Line a soup tureen with the croûtons and strips of Beaufort cheese. Pour the soup over the top and serve very hot.

A harvest near Calais – clothes change but the work still goes on.

GARBURE (GASCONY)
Cabbage and ham soup

Like all French country soups, *Garbure* can be mixed with wine to make a *goudale* or 'guzzle': when only a few spoonfuls of soup are left in your dish, pour in a glass of wine.

Prepare dried beans 24 hours in advance.
Serves 6

1 lb piece of ham
¾ lb fresh lima beans (or 1 cup dried ones, soaked overnight)
1 large onion stuck with a clove
2 cloves of garlic
sprig of fresh thyme
bay leaf
salt and peppercorns
6 carrots
3–4 turnips
2 leeks
1 lb potatoes
1 small head of white cabbage
¼ lb confit d'oie (preserved goose)
parsley

Place the ham, beans, onion, garlic, thyme and bay leaf in a stockpot containing 1½ quarts of cold water and bring to a boil. Season with salt and a few peppercorns. Cook for 50–60 minutes. Peel and wash the carrots, turnips, leeks, potatoes and cabbage, and cut them into medium-sized pieces. Add them to the soup and cook for another 45 minutes.

About 15–20 minutes before serving, add the drained *confit d'oie* cut into 4 and the coarsely chopped parsley. Leave the soup to simmer gently. Serve the meat and soup separately with slices of crusty bread and pickles.

SOUPE TOURANGELLE (TOURAINE)
Touraine vegetable soup

Touraine has been called 'the garden of France', and this vegetable soup exhibits the perfect richness and gentle mildness of the Loire Valley, where Touraine lies.

Serves 6

3–4 turnips
1 large onion
2 celeriac (celery root)
3 whites of leeks
¼ small cauliflower
¼ cup butter
1½ quarts stock or water
salt and pepper
¼ cup peas
¼ cup green beans
fresh chervil to garnish
1 tablespoon crème fraiche

Peel and chop the vegetables and wash them thoroughly. Gently fry all except the green beans and the peas in butter, without letting them brown. Cover with the stock or water and add salt and pepper. (It is better to use good homemade stock if you can, but take care not to add too much salt.) Simmer for 45 minutes.

Add the peas and the thinly sliced green beans and simmer for a further 20–30 minutes. Serve in a tureen garnished with several leaves of chervil, a pat of butter and a tablespoon of *crème fraiche*.

To make this into a creamed soup, blend it or purée in a food mill, add more cream and reheat it gently, skimming frequently.

right Soupe tourangelle: *many vegetables blended make one creamy soup.*

France

Fish

COQUILLES SAINT-JACQUES AU CIDRE (NORMANDY)
Scallops cooked in cider

Lucie Delarue-Mardrus, the Norman poet, wrote: 'The perfume of my country lies in an apple.' It also lies in a bowl of cider. The people of Normandy have great respect for this drink and have established a museum in its honor at Valogne – a must for any visitor interested in good eating.

Serves 4

20 scallops
salt and pepper
1 lemon
1 quart hard cider
6 tablespoons butter
¼ cup flour
1 cup crème fraîche
1¼ cups mushrooms
a drop of Calvados
  or applejack
  (optional)

If using frozen scallops, allow them to thaw. Add salt, pepper and the juice of 1 lemon to the cider, and poach the scallops gently in this mixture, without boiling. When they are tender, after about 10 minutes, drain and keep hot in a little butter in a covered pan.

Boil the cider cooking liquid to reduce it by one half. Meanwhile make a little *beurre manié* by mixing the flour with 2 tablespoons softened butter. Add this to the reduced cooking liquid and beat in well. Bring to a boil, add the *crème fraîche* and leave to simmer for 10 minutes or until the sauce becomes thick and smooth.

Correct the seasoning and strain the sauce over the scallops. Heat the scallops gently in the sauce for 2–3 minutes. Clean the mushrooms and saute them in the remaining butter. Season and add to the sauce.

A drop of Calvados may be added before serving.

FILETS D'ALOSE A L'OSEILLE (ORLÉANS)
Shad fillets with sorrel

When sorrel is cooked with fish it has the effect of softening the bones and even making them disappear. This aids digestion and also adds to the succulence of certain fish, particularly shad, which is akin to herring and found in plenty in the great river Loire that flows through the beautiful province of Orléans.

Serves 4

1 shad weighing
  2–3 lb, filleted
2 lb sorrel
6 tablespoons butter
salt and pepper
1¼ cups dry white wine
1 cup crème fraîche

Cut each shad fillet to make 8 pieces altogether.

Meanwhile select and wash the sorrel, and chop coarsely into long, thin shreds. Place in a heavy saucepan with 2 tablespoons butter, salt and pepper, and leave to sweat on a very low heat for 5–10 minutes.

Spread a layer of cooked sorrel in a deep, well-buttered baking dish. Pile the pieces of shad on top, with a spoonful of sorrel between each one, pour the white wine over them, add salt and pepper and cook in the oven (350°F) for about 15 minutes.

When the fish is tender, pour the liquid into a small saucepan and boil to reduce by half; add the *crème fraîche* and reduce again to a thick, smooth sauce. Test the seasoning. Pour the sauce over the shad pieces, put back in the oven for 2–3 minutes and serve immediately.

CARPE A L'ALSACIENNE (ALSACE)
Marinated carp

There was a time when 'officers of taste' hailed not only the flesh of the carp, but also its tongue and roe. The tongue, together with anglerfish liver and crayfish tails, was added to a renowned pâté, frequently served at the sumptuous table of Cardinal de Rohan, Bishop of Strasbourg in 1779.

Prepare 2 days in advance.
Serves 4

1 carp weighing 2 lb,
  cut in thick steaks
salt and pepper
2 cloves of garlic
sprig of fresh thyme
bay leaf
⅓ cup oil
1 large onion, chopped
3 shallots, chopped
3 tablespoons flour
1 pint dry white wine
parsley

Place the carp steaks in a deep dish; season with salt and pepper, add the crushed cloves of garlic, the thyme and bay leaf, and sprinkle with half the oil. Leave in a cool place for 24 hours.

Next day, brown the onion and shallots gently in the rest of the oil in a deep earthenware casserole, sprinkle with the flour, stir and leave to cook for 5 minutes. Stir in the dry white wine and 1 pint water. Bring to a boil, add the garlic, thyme and bay leaf from the marinade, and a bunch of fresh parsley. Test the seasoning, which should be strong. Add the carp steaks and cook for 45 minutes.

When tender, drain the steaks and reassemble the carp in a deep serving dish. Boil to reduce the cooking liquid by one quarter and pour over the carp. Serve cold the following day.

BROCHET BEURRE BLANC (BRITTANY)
Pike with white butter sauce

There are many stories about the origin of *beurre blanc*. The Bretons of Nantes offer this explanation: at the turn of the century, the Marquis of Goulaine had in his service an excellent cook called Clémence. One day when the Marquis was expecting guests Clémence asked her kitchen maid to make a béarnaise sauce. The maid began to carry out the cook's orders, but she forgot the tarragon and did not make an emulsion of the egg yolks. The butter simply beaten with the shallots made a new sauce which, to Clémence's great shame, had to be served to the guests. But the Marquis and his guests found the novelty delicious and this 'spoiled sauce' soon became known as *beurre blanc*.

Serves 4

1 onion, finely chopped
1 carrot, finely chopped
1 pint white wine
sprig of fresh thyme
parsley
bay leaf
2 cloves
salt and pepper
1 pike weighing 2 lb

White butter sauce
2 shallots, chopped
⅓ cup Muscadet wine
  vinegar
¾ cup butter
salt and pepper
juice of 1 lemon (optional)
cayenne pepper (optional)

First make a *court-bouillon*: add the onion and carrot to 2 quarts of water and the white wine with some thyme, parsley, bay leaf, 2 cloves and salt and pepper. Simmer for 45 minutes, then leave to cool.

Place the cleaned pike in a fish kettle with the cold *court-bouillon* and poach gently without boiling until tender (about 25 minutes).

Meanwhile, prepare the white butter sauce: place the shallots in a heavy saucepan with the Muscadet vinegar, and reduce until almost dry. Away from the heat, add pats of softened butter and beat continuously until you have a thick foam. Season with salt and pepper. At this point you can add the lemon juice and a trace of cayenne pepper.

Serve the drained pike as soon as it is cooked and the *beurre blanc* separately in a sauceboat.

Selling every fish in the world – the old Paris fish market

BOUILLABAISSE (PROVENCE)
Bouillabaisse

All along the Mediterranean coast from Menton to the Spanish frontier, every cook has his own recipe for bouillabaisse, each using slightly different ingredients. But connoisseurs will tell you that the authentic bouillabaisse can only be found between Marseilles and Toulon; and that it is of divine origin. It is said that Venus made bouillabaisse for her husband, Vulcan, so that he would fall into a deep sleep, leaving her free to visit her numerous lovers. For its unique flavor, bouillabaisse depends on fish which are native to the Mediterranean alone; this version uses American fish.

Serves 10

2 large leeks
2 onions
½ lb bulb Florence fennel
1 cup olive oil
13 lb fresh fish and
* shellfish (e.g. pompano,*
* sea perch, red snapper,*
* halibut, eel, scallops,*
* lobster, shrimp, clams,*
* mussels)*

5 cloves of garlic
¾ lb tomatoes,
* skinned and chopped*
2 tablespoons tomato
* purée*
sprig of fresh thyme
bay leaf
sprig of fresh rosemary
large pinch of ground
* saffron*
salt and pepper
1 stale baguette
* (French bread loaf)*
¼ cup Ricard or Pastis
parsley
1¼ cups grated
* Gruyère cheese*

Rouille sauce
1 clove of garlic
1 red chili pepper
salt and pepper
2 egg yolks
1 cup olive oil

Cut the leeks, onions and fennel into fine strips or *julienne*, and braise them in 2 tablespoons of olive oil in a large stock pot. Wash the fish, pat dry and cut into medium-sized pieces. Braise the fish trimmings – heads, bones and skin – with the vegetables. Stir from time to time.

Add 2½ quarts of water, the garlic, the tomatoes, tomato purée, thyme, bay leaf, rosemary and saffron. Season and bring to a boil. Simmer for 45 minutes, then strain.

Meanwhile, to prepare the croûtons, cut the *baguette* into thick slices, rub with garlic if liked, and bake in the oven (300°F) until pale golden brown and crisp.

Put the pieces of fish into a large saucepan. Sprinkle with the remaining olive oil and a little Ricard or Pastis. Stir. Pour the strained stock over the fish and cook very fast for 10 minutes. Add the shellfish and cook for another 5 minutes. Correct the seasoning.

Make the rust-colored rouille sauce by crushing the garlic and chili pepper to a paste in a mortar. Add salt, pepper and the egg yolks, then add the olive oil, drop by drop, stirring continuously. Test the seasoning, and serve in a sauceboat with 2 or 3 tablespoons of fish soup added.

Drain the fish carefully and place in a large, deep dish. Sprinkle with some of the fish soup. Serve the rest of the soup in a tureen garnished with chopped parsley. Serve the croûtons, grated Gruyère cheese and rouille sauce separately.

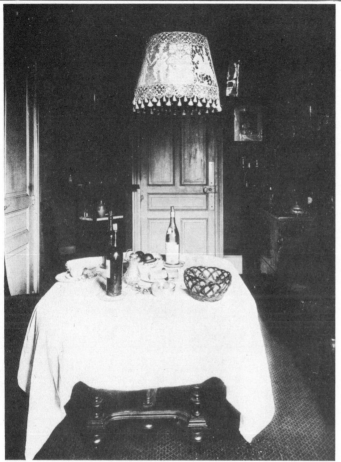

The careful formality of the French home

THON A LA BRETONNE (BRITTANY)
Tuna fish with cauliflower

This specialty is greatly prized by the Breton fishermen, who traditionally had to sell all the fine delicate fish such as sole, turbot and anglerfish, keeping only the more common fish for themselves. Sometimes they could not resist a good piece of tuna, which they called '*faire dimanche*' (making believe it's Sunday).

In Brittany this dish is served with navy beans, which are cooked separately and added to the cauliflower and potatoes when drained.

Serves 6

⅔ cup butter	In a large saucepan, melt the butter and add the onions; leave to brown. Add the tuna fish, season and turn occasionally.
2 large onions, chopped	
a piece of fresh tuna fish, about 3 lb	
salt and pepper	Add the garlic, cauliflower and the tomatoes. Add the white wine, bring to a boil and test the season-
2 cloves of garlic, crushed	ing. Add the thyme, bay leaf and parsley. Cover
1 medium cauliflower in flowerets	and cook very gently for 1 hour.
3 tomatoes, skinned and quartered	When the tuna fish is tender, remove and keep hot. Add peeled potatoes to the sauce and cook them gently for 30 minutes. The starch of the potatoes will thicken the sauce.
1 pint dry white wine	
a sprig of fresh thyme	Cut the tuna fish into serving pieces and arrange
bay leaf	on a plate. Take the thyme and bay leaf out of the
a bunch of parsley	sauce and pour over the fish. Serve, sprinkled with
1 lb small potatoes	tarragon and finely chopped chives.
chopped fresh tarragon	
chopped chives	

HOMARD A L'ARMORICAINE (BRITTANY)
Lobster à l'armoricaine

There will always be doubts as to the origin of this world-famous specialty which has two names: *homard à l'armoricaine* and *à l'américaine*. However, it is possible that they are in fact two separate recipes.

L'homard à l'armoricaine was inspired by a dish prepared by Breton fishermen and enhanced in the seventeenth and eighteenth centuries by the use of spices imported into Nantes by slave ship captains.

L'homard à l'américaine was created by Pierre Fraisse, a native of Bercy or Sète: inspired by *l'homard à la provençale* or *à la Bonnefoy*, he named his dish to please his friends across the Atlantic.

Serves 8

7 lb lobster (4 or 5 lobsters of 1½–2 lb each)	Shell the lobsters and cut into sections. Cut the bodies in half lengthwise and take out the creamy parts: set aside to be used later. Season the lobster pieces well and add them to very hot oil, in a large pan. Remove and add the onions and shallots. Leave them to sweat under a lid for several minutes.
salt and pepper	
⅓ cup oil	
2 large onions, chopped	
4 shallots, chopped	Stir once, then sprinkle with brandy and flambé.
⅓ cup old brandy (known in Brittany as gouttechique)	Add the well crushed garlic, the cider and the tomato purée, which is not obligatory but gives the sauce a much prettier color. Finish off with a
2 cloves of garlic, crushed	bouquet of parsley, thyme and bay leaf, and a pinch of cayenne pepper. Bring to a boil and
1 quart very dry hard cider	adjust the seasoning; the dish should be quite spicy. Return lobster and leave to simmer for 15–20
1 tablespoon tomato purée (optional)	minutes.
parsley	Meanwhile, mix the butter with the creamy parts of the lobsters and about 1 tablespoon of flour.
sprig of fresh thyme	When the lobster pieces are tender, remove from
bay leaf	the pan and keep warm. Reduce the cooking liquid
cayenne pepper	for 1 minute and then thicken with the butter
⅓ cup butter	mixture. The sauce should not be too thick. Pour
flour	it over the lobster pieces, bring back to a boil, and adjust the seasoning. Serve with rice in a separate dish.

ECREVISSES A LA CRÈME (NEVERS)
Crayfish with cream sauce

Enthusiasts in the Nevers region sometimes overdo the use of pepper and cayenne pepper, adding a peculiar 'lift' to this dish. Often referred to as 'amorous crayfish', this specialty seems to be quite an aphrodisiac.

Serves 4

3 shallots, finely chopped	Fry the shallots gently in butter in a heavy pan without letting them brown. Clean and wash the crayfish and sauté with the shallots. Stir in the
⅓ cup butter	white wine, salt and pepper, cover and cook for
24–30 crayfish	about 3–5 minutes. When the crayfish are tender,
1 pint dry white wine	take them out and keep warm in a covered casserole.
salt and pepper	Pour the white wine into a heavy saucepan and
1¼ cups crème fraiche	reduce by half. Add the *crème fraiche* and reduce
cayenne pepper	again to form a thick sauce. Adjust seasoning and
a few fresh tarragon leaves, chopped	add a pinch of cayenne pepper. Pour the sauce over the crayfish and bring to a boil.
	Serve in a deep dish, garnished with tarragon.

GRENOUILLES A LA CRÈME (LYONS)
Frogs' legs with cream sauce

Grenouilles à la crème is typical of the sort of dish created by the women of Lyons and Bresse. These cooks, commonly known as *cordons bleus*, have made this region famous for its simple and delicious cooking. Among the great *cordons bleus* are 'Mère Niogret', 'Mère Blanc' and 'Mère Brazier' to mention only a few.

Serves 4

*32 frogs
(64 frogs' legs)
salt and pepper
a little milk
⅓ cup flour
⅓ cup butter
1 cup cream
parsley
garlic (optional)
vinegar (optional)*

Season the frogs' legs with salt and pepper. Place them in a deep bowl with the milk, and leave for 30 minutes. Drain and coat with flour.

Melt some butter in a large skillet until sizzling, almost brown. Drop in the frogs' legs a few at a time and brown well. Place the cooked frogs' legs on a large plate in the oven preheated to 325°F to keep hot. When they are all done pour over the cream and return to the oven for several minutes.

Serve sprinkled with chopped parsley. It is a local custom to garnish this dish with a little chopped garlic or a dash of vinegar – or both.

LAMPROIE A LA BORDELAISE (GUIENNE)
Lampreys cooked in wine

Lampreys, which resemble eels but have finer flesh, have been a specialty in the Bordeaux region for a long time. In fact the poet Ausonius, who was born in Bordeaux in 309, was the first person to divulge this recipe using Bordeaux wine as a base. Lampreys were in great demand even with the Ancient Romans, who always included them in their magnificent banquets and feasts.

Serves 6

*2 or 3 lampreys weighing
about 3 lb (or
substitute eel)
salt and pepper
¼ cup oil
5–6 whites of leeks,
sliced
3 shallots, finely
chopped
2 cloves of garlic,
crushed
¼ cup brandy
1 pint red Bordeaux
wine
¼ cup diced cooked ham
(optional)
sprig of fresh thyme
bay leaf
parsley
croûtons to serve*

Buy live lampreys, plunge them into boiling water, then wash thoroughly in cold water. Bleed them and collect the blood, keeping it for later. Cut off the end of each lamprey's tail, make an incision around the neck and pull out the central nerve. Cut the lampreys into 4 or 5 pieces. Season with salt and pepper.

Heat the oil in a large pot and put in the pieces of lamprey. Add the whites of leeks and the shallots; braise gently, then add the crushed garlic.

Sprinkle with brandy and flambé. Add the red wine and bring to a boil, then add the chopped ham if used, thyme, bay leaf and a small bunch of parsley. Correct the seasoning. Cover and cook gently for 30 minutes.

When the pieces of lamprey are tender, remove them and the leeks, place in a deep serving bowl and keep warm. Reduce the cooking liquid, thicken it with the lamprey blood and test the seasoning. Strain the sauce over the lampreys and the leeks. Serve with a separate dish of croûtons.

MOUCLADE A LA CRÈME (AUNIS-SAINTONGE)
Mussels in cream sauce

It is odd to find a French regional recipe containing curry. But in times gone by slave-trading captains would disembark at the Atlantic ports, with African slaves and spices in the holds of their ships. The negro slaves were sometimes employed as servants in the huge, wealthy residences along the coast at Aunis, Saintonge, La Vendée and Nantes. Some were promoted to cooks, and made abundant use of the produce from their own countries, especially curry.

Serves 4

*2 quarts mussels
1 cup dry white wine
sprig of fresh thyme
bay leaf
parsley
pepper
a pinch of curry
powder
¼ cup cream
2 tablespoons butter
(optional)
flour (optional)
salt*

Scrape and wash the mussels thoroughly, using several changes of water. Drain thoroughly, making sure no sand remains on the shells.

Put the mussels in a large pan, add the white wine, thyme, bay leaf, parsley and a pinch of pepper. Bring to a boil, shake the pan and remove the mussels with a slotted spoon as they open; discard any empty shells. Arrange the mussels in a single layer, very close together, in a large ovenproof serving bowl.

Reduce the cooking liquid and add the curry powder. Add the cream and leave to simmer for a while, until the sauce is smooth, but not too thick. If necessary, thicken the sauce with the butter mixed with a little flour. Adjust the seasoning. Strain the sauce over the mussels, place the dish in a moderate oven (350°F) for 4–5 minutes, and serve immediately.

This recipe can be made without the curry powder.

Mouclade à la crème: *the spices of the east bring their exotic flavor to this dish.*

Choosing the best – while it's on the hoof

CASSOULET TOULOUSAIN (LANGUEDOC)
Cassoulet

Every town in the Languedoc has its own recipe for cassoulet – Toulouse, Castelnaudary, Castelsarrasin, Carcassonne, Montauban, Bergerac – and each claims that its own cassoulet is best.

Soak the dried beans overnight
Serves 6

1 lb fresh or
1⅓ cups dried navy beans
¼ lb fresh pork sides,
  chopped
1 bouquet garni
4 cloves of garlic
3 large onions
1 clove
1¼ lb each breast and
  shoulder of lamb
salt and pepper
¼ cup goose fat
3 tablespoons flour
1 tablespoon
  tomato purée
2½ quarts chicken stock
thyme (optional)
bay leaf (optional)
1¼ lb confit d'oie
  (preserved goose)
1 cervelas (cooked
  pork sausage)
¾ cup dry breadcrumbs

Put the fresh or soaked beans into a large pan with the pork, cover with cold water and bring to a boil. Skim the surface, then add the bouquet garni, a clove of garlic and a large onion stuck with a clove. Leave to cook gently.

Season the lamb pieces with salt and pepper and brown them in the goose fat in a 6–8 quart pot. When the meat is well browned, add 2 large finely-chopped onions. Leave to braise for a few minutes, then sprinkle in the flour, stir and cook for a moment.

Add lamb, onions, tomato purée and remaining garlic to the beans. Cover with stock. Bring to a boil and adjust the seasoning. (You can also add a sprig of thyme and a bay leaf if you wish.) Simmer for 1 hour.

When the beans and meat are tender, remove them with a slotted spoon and strain the sauce. Place the drained beans and meat on a large earthenware plate, with the *confit d'oie* cut into 6, 6 slices of pork, and 6 thick slices of *cervelas*. Pour the sauce over and sprinkle with breadcrumbs. Put the plate into the oven preheated to moderate (350°F), cook for a good 15 minutes, and then serve. The top should be lightly browned.

M*eat*

STUFATU (CORSICA)
Stufatu

We don't know whether the most famous Corsican of all, Napoleon Bonaparte, liked *stufatu*. The emperor was not much of a gastronome. His favorite dishes were a simple roast chicken or a broiled side of lamb with beans or lentils, although he did play a part in the creation of the celebrated *poulet Marengo* which his accomplished cook, Dunand, prepared on the eve of the Battle of Marengo.

Stufatu can be made with beef or lamb.

Serves 4

1¼ lb beef chuck
¼ lb boneless pork
¼ cup olive oil
1 large onion, sliced
3 cloves garlic, crushed
finely chopped parsley
⅓ cup diced smoked ham
¼ lb bacon, in thin strips
3 small tomatoes,
  skinned and chopped
¼ cup white wine
salt and pepper
1 quart beef stock
¾ lb macaroni
1¼ cups grated cheese,
  preferably Parmesan

Cut the beef and pork into small pieces. Brown them in the oil in a large pan. Add the onion, garlic, parsley, ham, bacon and tomatoes. Pour in the white wine, season with the salt and pepper and leave to sweat for a few minutes. Then add about 1 quart of stock and cook for 2–3 hours.

Meanwhile boil plenty of salted water and cook the macaroni. When it is *al dente*, drain thoroughly.

In a large casserole, put a ladleful of the beef-pork mixture in its sauce, which is called *stufatu*, spread over it a layer of macaroni and sprinkle with cheese. Repeat this process – *stufatu*, macaroni, cheese and so on until all the ingredients are used up.

Cook in a slow oven (300°F) for 30 minutes before serving.

France

STEAK AU POIVRE (PARIS – ILE DE FRANCE)
Peppered steak

This very Parisian specialty is of fairly recent origin. Some say that it was being served at the Hôtel de Paris in Monte Carlo in 1910, some that it was on Maxim's menu in 1920. Others claim that it wasn't created until as late as 1930 and then by a Monsieur Lerch, chef at the Restaurant Albert on the Champs-Élysées. At that time he was buying his meat frozen from South America. It was of excellent quality and remarkably tender but lacking in flavor. One day, when some clients who had drunk a number of aperitifs sat down to their meal, the head waiter Albert told the chef to season their steaks liberally with pepper, thinking that this was the only way these somewhat tipsy clients would taste the meat. Monsieur Lerch duly coated the steaks with a layer of crushed peppercorns.

This specialty now appears on the menu of almost every Parisian restaurant.

Serves 4

4 thick slices of boneless
  sirloin steak
  weighing 6 oz each
salt
2 tablespoons peppercorns,
  crushed
¼ cup oil
4 tablespoons butter
¼ cup brandy or
  Armagnac or
  good Burgundy
⅓ cup veal stock
⅓ cup cream
freshly ground pepper

Season the steaks with the salt and crushed peppercorns. In a sauté pan heat the oil and butter. Brown the steaks and cook as preferred.

When the steaks are cooked on both sides, remove from the pan and place on a shallow serving platter. Keep hot.

Pour off excess fat from the pan. Add the brandy to the remaining juices, heat to deglaze and then flambé. Add the veal stock and boil to reduce. Add the cream and allow to simmer gently until the sauce is thick and smooth. Check the seasoning and add more pepper if necessary.

Pour the sauce over the steaks. Serve immediately with French fried or sauté potatoes on a separate dish.

CHAROLLAIS A L'ECHALOTE (BURGUNDY)
Steak with shallots

The small city of Charolles has been famous for producing the best beef in France ever since the ninth century. It is noted for many culinary specialties such as rabbit stew, jugged goose, vegetable and bacon soup, chicken in wine – and this succulent steak with shallots.

Serves 4

3 shallots, finely minced
¼ cup white wine
1 thick piece of boneless
  sirloin steak
  weighing 1½ lb
salt and pepper
¼ cup oil
⅓ cup butter
chopped parsley

Put the shallots into a skillet and leave them to sweat without browning. When they are soft, add the white wine and reduce to form a thickish sauce.

Meanwhile, season the steak with salt and freshly ground black pepper. (Cut into 4 pieces before cooking if you wish.) Heat the oil and 2 tablespoons butter in another skillet. When the mixture is sizzling, add the steak. Turn and cook according to preference. Take off the heat, but keep warm.

Take the sauce off the heat, season and add the remaining softened butter and a little chopped parsley.

Cut the steak into 4 if you have not already done so, and place on a serving platter. Pour the sauce over the steak and serve with small new potatoes, browned in butter.

CERVELLES EN MEURETTE (BURGUNDY)
Brains cooked in red wine

Meurette is a Burgundy specialty – a stew made with local red wine. It is most commonly made with fish; but it can also be prepared with eggs (*oeufs en meurette*) and, of course, with brains. This recipe uses calf brains; if you use beef brain, one will be enough for four people but if you use lamb brains, you will need one for each person.

Prepare the brains 1 hour in advance.
Serves 4

2 calf brains
salt
lemon juice
1 carrot, finely chopped
1 large onion,
  finely chopped
¼ cup butter
1 clove of garlic
parsley
sprig of fresh thyme
bay leaf
sugar
1 pint red Burgundy
  wine
pepper
several slices of bread
  dried in the oven
1 egg yolk
chopped parsley

Soak the brains in cold water for 1 hour, then skin them carefully, removing the veins and the membrane. Poach the brains in water with salt and lemon juice for 15–20 minutes. Do not allow to boil. Drain the brains and keep warm.

In a saucepan, gently fry the carrot and onion in half the butter, but do not let them brown. When the vegetables are soft, add the brains, the garlic, the bouquet garni (parsley, thyme and bay leaf tied together) and a little sugar. Add the wine, season and leave to simmer for 15–20 minutes.

When the brains are tender, drain them and arrange on slices of bread on a serving platter. Keep warm.

Reduce the cooking liquid by boiling and strain into a small saucepan. Add small pats of the remaining butter, beating continuously. Finally, remove from the heat and beat in the egg yolk. Correct the seasoning. Pour over the brains and sprinkle with parsley.

Charollais à l'échalote: *the best steak treated with all due reverence*

FOIE DE VEAU A LA BAUGEOISE (ANJOU)
Stuffed calf liver

The cooking of Anjou is full of character and originality. Rabelais, who was born in the Loire Valley, was instrumental in spreading its fame and is also said to have helped originate one of the region's specialties: he once stopped at an inn in Anjou to order a good meal for some distinguished guests who would be arriving the next day. The inn-keeper, whose means were limited, simply chopped up some goose flesh and fresh pork, which he cooked in a cauldron with herbs and seasonings. The mixture, served cold in earthenware bowls, proved a great success with Rabelais and his guests. The dish was later called *rillettes*.

Stuffed calf liver is another Anjou specialty.

Prepare cauls 1 hour in advance.
Serves 4

4 bacon slices
6 chicken livers
salt and pepper
¼ lb sausagemeat
4 cauls 8 × 8 in, soaked
  in lukewarm water
  for at least 1 hour
8 slices of calf liver,
  each weighing
  about 3 oz
2 large onions, sliced
a sprig of fresh thyme
bay leaf
a sprig of parsley
¼ cup Cognac
1¼ cups white wine
chopped parsley
⅔ cup crème fraiche
  (optional)

First, make the stuffing: cut the bacon into small pieces and heat in a skillet until the fat runs. Add the chicken livers, sauté them, season, and pass through a food mill. Mix the purée with the sausagemeat and check seasoning.

Dry the cauls and spread them out flat. On each lay a slice of calf liver. Season and spread a thin layer of stuffing on each slice. Cover with a second slice of liver. Wrap in the caul.

Place the cauls in a flameproof casserole. Add the onions, thyme, bay leaf, parsley, Cognac and white wine. Bring to a boil. Season again. Cover and cook gently for 45 minutes. The cooking can be done in the oven but if so frequent basting is necessary.

When cooked, remove the cauls; place them on a serving platter and keep hot. Reduce the cooking liquid, strain and check the seasoning. Pour the sauce over the cauls and serve sprinkled with chopped parsley. *Crème fraiche* may be added to the sauce just before serving.

above *Crushing apples to make Normandy's superb cider and calvados*

TRIPES A LA MODE DE CAEN (NORMANDY)
Caen tripe

Everything is to be found in a dish of tripe and this dish even improves with reheating. We recommend that you use a *tripière* (special saucepan for tripe) as they do in Normandy; and we join the chef-poet Jean Le Hir in saying:

> *That finally what provokes*
> *Is the juice in which it soaks,*
> *That earthy, fragrant, unctuous sauce*
> *Golden, rich with fragrant force.*
> *Served as is right*
> *In a plate that almost burns,*
> *It joyfully earns*
> *Applause for such delight.*
> *Thus spake my old father puffing his*
> * pipe,*
> *Talking that day of Caen tripe.*

Prepare at least 36 hours in advance.
Serves 12

10 lb mixed tripe
1 calf foot
3 carrots, sliced
4 large onions, sliced
4 leeks, sliced
1 celery stalk
  (optional)
3 cloves of garlic
parsley
a sprig of fresh thyme
bay leaf
¼ cup Calvados or
  applejack
2 quarts dry hard cider
salt and pepper
a few peppercorns
2 or 3 cloves

Soak the tripe and the calf foot in cold water for 24 hours. Wash well, blanch, rinse and drain. Cut the tripe into wide strips and the foot in half lengthwise.

Place in a large saucepan with a tightly fitting lid. Add the carrots, onions, leeks, a small stalk of celery if you wish, garlic and bouquet garni made up of the parsley, thyme and bay leaf. Pour in the Calvados and the cider. Add enough water for the liquid to reach the rim of the saucepan.

Bring to a boil, add salt and pepper, and finally a few peppercorns and 2 or 3 cloves tied in a piece of muslin so that they can be removed easily later. Simmer gently for 7–9 hours, or even longer.

At the end of the cooking time discard the bouquet garni and the peppercorns and cloves. Take out the calf foot, remove the bone and cut the meat into pieces. Return the meat to the tripe. Check the seasoning and serve very hot.

The unspoiled countryside of the Loire

right Tripes à la mode de Caen: *Calvados and cider combine in this 'earthy, fragrant, unctuous sauce'.*

GIGOT BRAYAUDE (AUVERGNE)
Peasant leg of lamb

The word *brayaud* means 'a peasant who loves his food'. At Riom in the Auvergne at the beginning of June there is a 'brayauds' parade' which brings together all the farmers of the region. After the parade they gather to consume local delicacies such as the *omelette brayaude* (potatoes, bacon, ham, cream, cheese and eggs) which precedes the *gigot*.

Gigot brayaude is usually served either with Brussels sprouts mixed with whole cooked chestnuts, or with the tiny grey-green Puy lentils of the Haute-Loire. After four hours of cooking, the leg of lamb may be covered with thickly sliced potatoes, which soak up all the flavors of the meat juice as the lamb finishes cooking.

The Auvergne in spring

Serves 4

1 leg of lamb weighing 3 lb, skin and fat removed *salt and pepper* *3 or 4 cloves of garlic* *3–4 large slices of fatty bacon* *¼ cup butter or margarine* *2 carrots, thickly sliced* *2 large onions, thickly sliced* *1 quart stock* *a sprig of fresh thyme* *bay leaf* *chopped parsley*	Season the lamb with salt and pepper. Insert garlic cloves into the meat, and wrap the slices of bacon around it. Heat the fat in a flameproof casserole. Add the carrots and onions. Sweat for about 10 minutes. Add the stock, thyme, bay leaf and parsley. Put in the lamb. Bring to a boil and check seasoning. Cover and cook very gently on the top of the stove for 5 to 6 hours. The meat should be so tender that it can be sliced with a spoon, with no need for a knife.

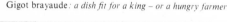
Gigot brayaude: a dish fit for a king – or a hungry farmer

MOUTON A LA CHAMPENOISE (CHAMPAGNE)
Champagne lamb

Champagne, that effervescent nectar which has traveled the world, is rather better known than La Champagne, the somewhat 'poor' province of France where it is made. The drink owes everything to La Champagne – to its soil, its climate, and to the monk from Champagne, Dom Perignon, who is said to have invented it.

This recipe for shoulder of lamb can be accompanied by a purée of split peas, much favored in the district.

Prepare 2 days in advance.
Serves 4

1 shoulder of lamb weighing 2 lb, boned, with skin and fat removed *1 large onion, sliced* *1 carrot, sliced* *2 cloves of garlic, crushed* *a sprig of fresh thyme* *bay leaf* *¼ cup vinegar* *1 pint Ay champagne or dry white wine* *¼ cup oil* *5 or 6 juniper berries* *¼ cup butter* *salt and pepper* *a little stock or water* *1 calf foot, blanched* *2 tomatoes, quartered*	Tie the shoulder of lamb with string and leave to marinate for about 48 hours with the onion, carrot, garlic, thyme, bay leaf, vinegar, wine, oil and juniper berries. Just before cooking drain the shoulder and wipe with a clean cloth. Drain the vegetables thoroughly. Heat the butter in a large flameproof casserole and turn the meat in it. When it is well browned add the vegetables from the marinade. Allow to sweat for about 10 minutes, then season with salt and pepper. Add the marinade and a little stock or water to cover the shoulder. Cut the calf foot in half lengthwise, add this and finally the tomatoes. Cook 1–2 hours, depending on the quality of the meat. When the meat is tender, remove it, carve into slices and arrange on a serving platter. Keep hot. Reduce the cooking liquid, strain it and check the seasoning. Pour over the meat and serve immediately.

Poultry and game

ESTOUFFADE DE PERDRIX AUX LENTILLES (AUVERGNE)
Braised partridge with lentils

Le Puy, the capital of Velay, offers many mouth-watering delicacies: asparagus, *godiveau* forcemeat, chestnuts, *andouille* sausages, hare with mulberries, blue cheese and the delicious *Verveine du Velay* liqueur. But most famous of all are the tiny green *lentilles du Puy*, which go perfectly with this succulent stuffed partridge.

Serves 4

2 or 4 thin slices
  of fatty bacon
2 large partridges
  or 4 young ones
salt and pepper
¼ cup lard
2 carrots, sliced
2 cloves of garlic
2 large onions
  (1 sliced)
1¼ cups white wine
2 cups small green
  Puy lentils
1 clove
a sprig of fresh thyme
parsley
bay leaf

Wrap a slice of bacon around each cleaned partridge and season inside with salt and pepper.

Heat the lard in a saucepan and brown the partridges. Add the carrots, garlic and the sliced onion, and leave to sweat for a few minutes. Pour in the white wine and about ⅔ cup water, and bring to a boil. Check seasoning, cover and simmer for about 2 hours, or 45–50 minutes for small birds.

Meanwhile put the lentils in a pan of cold salted water and bring to a boil. Add the other onion, with the clove stuck into it, and the thyme, parsley and bay leaf tied into a bouquet garni. Simmer for 45 to 50 minutes.

When the lentils are tender, remove the bouquet garni and the onion and clove. Add the drained lentils to the partridges and simmer for 15–20 minutes more. Remove partridges and lentils.

Reduce the liquid, check the seasoning and strain.

To serve: cut the partridges in half and arrange the pieces on top of the lentils on a serving dish. Pour over some of the sauce and serve the remainder in a sauceboat.

What vintage champagne will come from these grapes?

FAISAN EN BARBOUILLE (BERRY)
Casseroled pheasant

Today Berry is noted for the excellence of its game, particularly the pheasant from Sologne. At one time it was famous as the birthplace of King Louis XI. He was one of the first campaigners against fraudulent food practices and decreed that 'whoever sold rotten eggs would be pilloried, the aforementioned eggs to be left for small children to throw in the faces of the deceivers to make them a laughing-stock to everybody. . . .'

Serves 4

1 pheasant cut
  into 8 pieces
salt and pepper
6 tablespoons butter
1 carrot, diced
1 onion, diced
2 tablespoons flour
¼ cup Cognac
1 cup red wine of the
  region (Reuilly or
  Quincy)
1 cup stock
a sprig of fresh thyme
bay leaf
parsley
1 small celery stalk
  (optional)
1 clove of garlic, crushed
¼ lb fresh pork sides,
  diced
¼ lb button
  mushrooms, whole
12 pearl onions

Season the pheasant pieces and brown in half the butter in a heavy pot. Add the carrot and diced onion; stir, and allow to sweat for a minute. Then sprinkle with flour, stir and cook gently for 5 minutes.

Shower with Cognac and flambé. Add the red wine, the stock and a bouquet garni of thyme, bay leaf, parsley and celery if liked. Finally add the garlic. Bring to a boil, check the seasoning, cover and cook gently for 50–60 minutes.

Meanwhile sauté the pork in the rest of the butter. When the pheasant is tender, transfer it to another pan. Add the mushrooms, the whole pearl onions and the pork, and pour the sauce over the top. Cover and simmer for about 30 minutes.

RABLE DE LIÈVRE A LA JURASSIENNE (FRANCHE-COMTÉ)
Marinated saddle of hare

This saddle of hare is traditionally served with morels, which grow abundantly in the Jura. The ones from Morteau are particularly famous.

If you want to make the saddle for four people, leave on the two thighs.

Prepare this dish 24 hours in advance.
Serves 2

1 saddle of hare
several strips of
  bacon for larding
1 onion, sliced
1 carrot, sliced
sprig of fresh thyme
bay leaf
parsley
1 pint white wine of
  the region (Arbois)
salt and pepper
6 tablespoons butter

Sauce
the hare's liver,
  chopped
1 onion, chopped
  with some parsley
a pinch of flour

'Lard' the saddle by inserting lardoons in small incisions in the flesh. Place the saddle in a deep dish with the onion and carrot. Add the thyme, bay leaf, parsley and the white wine. Season with pepper. Allow to marinate for 24 hours.

The next day drain the saddle (reserving the liquid), pat it dry and put in a roasting pan with the butter. Season with salt. Cook in the oven (400°F) until tender (25 minutes). Throughout the cooking time baste and turn the meat frequently. Do not overcook; the flesh should remain pink in the middle.

Meanwhile fry the liver, onion and parsley in a saucepan without letting it brown. Stir in a pinch of flour and cook for 2–3 minutes. Add the strained liquid from the marinade. Simmer for 30–40 minutes. Check the seasoning.

When the hare is tender, place on a serving dish and pour the sauce over it.

France

LAPIN AUX PRUNEAUX (FLANDERS-ARTOIS)

Rabbit with prunes

This dish, which can be served with chicory, braised red cabbage, Brussels sprouts and many other vegetables, is always served with potatoes in Flanders. According to local legend the potato was 'invented' by the eighteenth-century chemist Parmentier. Of course this isn't true, but Parmentier certainly encouraged potato farming in the region, especially after the famine of 1785.

Prepare prunes 12 hours in advance.
Serves 4

1 rabbit cut in pieces
$\frac{1}{4}$ cup oil
$\frac{1}{4}$ cup butter
salt and pepper
1 carrot, sliced
1 large onion, sliced
1 clove garlic
$2\frac{2}{3}$ cups red wine
$\frac{1}{4}$ cup vinegar
a sprig of fresh thyme
bay leaf
parsley
fresh sage
fresh savory
36 prunes, soaked overnight

Brown the rabbit pieces in a mixture of half oil and half butter. Season with salt and pepper. When the pieces are well colored, add the carrot and the onion. Stir, cover and allow to sweat.

Add the clove of garlic, 1 pint red wine and the vinegar. Bring to a boil and check the seasoning. Finally add the thyme, bay leaf, parsley, sage and savory tied into a bouquet garni. Cook for 45–60 minutes, depending on the age of the rabbit.

Meanwhile cook the prunes: put them into a pan with the remaining red wine and $\frac{2}{3}$ cup water. Simmer gently for 5–20 minutes.

When the rabbit is almost cooked, drain and reserve the liquid. Place the rabbit pieces in a flameproof casserole, add the prunes and pour over the liquid. Cover and simmer for about 20 minutes.

If the sauce is very thin, thicken it just before serving with a little butter mixed with a little flour.

CANARD A LA DUCHAMBAIS (BOURBONNAIS)

Duck with wine and cream sauce

There are many stories about the inventor of this rich, velvety Duchambais sauce; some say a certain French nobleman, M Du Chambet, took the recipe in 1815 from some Austrian soldiers who camped in his chateau at La Palisse, not far from Vichy.

Serves 4

1 duck weighing 4 lb
salt and pepper
$\frac{1}{4}$ lb bacon, in thin strips
3 shallots, finely chopped
$\frac{1}{4}$ cup vinegar
$\frac{1}{2}$ cup red wine
1 cup stock
2 oz pork liver, in thin strips
1 clove of garlic
3 tablespoons Cognac
1 cup cream

Cut the duck into 8 pieces and season with salt and pepper. Lightly brown the bacon. Remove and set aside.

Sauté the duck pieces in the bacon fat until golden brown all over. Add the shallots and cook gently until tender but not brown. Pour off the fat from the casserole and keep it to sauté the liver and potatoes later.

Add the bacon strips to the duck. Add the vinegar, red wine and stock. Bring to a boil, cover and cook gently for 40–50 minutes.

When the duck is tender pour the liquid into a saucepan, and boil to reduce by half, thus creating the sauce base.

Sauté the pork liver pieces in a little of the fat, then chop them with the clove of garlic. Stir in the Cognac and add this to the sauce base, boil for several minutes, then add the cream and reduce until the sauce is thick. Check the seasoning.

Simmer the duck in the sauce for 5–10 minutes and serve with sauté potatoes or peas.

left *French cooks use their ingenuity to turn the humble chicken into a tender delicacy for example, bathed in cream and butter sauces or stuffed with veal, nuts and brandy*

POULE FARCIE BÉARNAISE (BÉARN)

Béarnaise stuffed chicken

This dish is a descendant of the seventeenth-century 'boiled fowl' which the rough and greedy King Henri IV wanted his subjects to cook every Sunday. The original recipe included far more garlic: the king himself ate several cloves daily, which did not prevent him from having considerable success with the ladies.

Serves 6

$\frac{2}{3}$ cup chopped cooked ham
1 clove of garlic, chopped
2 cups fresh breadcrumbs
chopped parsley
chopped chives
$\frac{1}{2}$ lb sausagemeat
salt and pepper
1 stewing chicken (4 lb)
1 lb carrots, sliced
3 whites of leeks, chopped
1 onion, chopped
1 piece celeriac (celery root), chopped
1 small head of green cabbage, blanched and chopped
a sprig of fresh thyme
bay leaf
parsley
$\frac{1}{2}$ lb fresh lima beans, or dried ones soaked overnight
croûtons, dill pickles and coarse salt to serve

Mix the ham, garlic, breadcrumbs and a little parsley and chives with the sausagemeat. Season with salt and pepper, and stuff the chicken with this mixture. Sew up the opening and truss the chicken.

Place the chicken in a large pan. Cover with cold water, bring to a boil, skim and salt. Add the carrots, leeks, onion, celeriac and green cabbage, and a bouquet garni of thyme, bay leaf and parsley.

After cooking for 45 minutes, add the lima beans. Cook for another hour at least, depending on the age of the chicken. If the chicken requires further cooking, the vegetables can be removed and drained and the chicken left to cook alone in the broth.

To serve, cut the chicken into pieces, and the stuffing into slices. Arrange on a serving platter with the vegetables around them. Remove the bouquet garni from the broth, and pour it, unstrained, into a tureen.

Serve croûtons to accompany the broth, and pickles and coarse salt for the chicken.

Lapin aux pruneaux: *the sweet taste of prunes enriches a simple dish*

The golden light of Provence

COQ AU VIN DE CHANTURGUE (AUVERGNE)
Chanturgue coq au vin

Coq au vin is one French dish which appeals to cooks far and wide. Wine has the effect of making tender the toughest chicken, and combines to produce a delicious aroma.

Legend has it that this dish was first presented to the Gauls by Caesar. He transformed an old scrawny chicken into a delicious dish by long, slow cooking in a regional wine, well seasoned with a variety of fresh herbs. Invited to share this dish, the Gauls had to admit that the knowledge and experience of the Romans could only benefit them, and they were obliged to surrender and accept the civilization and rule of Rome.

The chicken is served straight from the casserole, so that when the lid is lifted the guests can inhale the rich aroma of the sauce. In the Auvergne fresh button mushrooms or small broiled sausages are often added. Also, the chicken's blood is reserved and added at the end to give a stronger flavor.

Serves 6

1 chicken (about 4 lb)
  cut in 12 pieces
1 tablespoon vinegar
salt and pepper
¼ cup lard
15 pearl onions
¼ lb bacon cut into
  large strips
¼ cup flour
¼ cup Cognac
1¼ pints red
  Chanturgue wine
sprig of fresh thyme
bay leaf
parsley

If possible, when the bird is killed and bled, carefully reserve the blood and add the vinegar to prevent it from coagulating. Season the chicken pieces with salt and pepper.

Melt the lard in a flameproof casserole and lightly brown the onions and bacon. Remove and set aside. Add the chicken pieces to the fat and brown well. Return onions and bacon to the pan, add the flour, stir, and put into the oven (425°F) for 5 minutes.

Remove from the oven, sprinkle with the Cognac and flambé if desired. Pour on the wine, bring to a boil and check the seasoning. Add thyme, bay leaf and parsley in a bouquet garni. Cover and cook gently at 350°F for 2–3 hours, depending on the tenderness of the chicken.

Immediately before serving add the chicken's blood. Stir but do not let it boil. Serve in the casserole.

FRICASSÉE DE VOLAILLE A LA NORMANDE (NORMANDY)
Chicken with cider and cream

Normandy is famous for its excellent apples, particularly the Calville variety, which have given rise to wonderful desserts like apple tart and *bourdelot*, a whole apple cooked in puff or pie pastry. But apples are also used in savory dishes, like this creamy chicken fricassée. Small chickens may be used instead.

Serves 6

6 firm apples,
  peeled and cored
¼ cup butter
a pinch of confectioners'
  sugar
1 chicken weighing 5 lb
salt and pepper
flour
18 pearl onions
¼ cup Calvados or
  applejack
2¼ cups dry hard cider
½ lb mushrooms
1¼ cups crème fraiche

Place whole apples in a baking dish with 2 tablespoons butter and the confectioners' sugar, and bake in a slow oven (300°F) for 50–60 minutes.

Cut the chicken into 12 pieces, season with salt and pepper and coat with flour. Brown them lightly in ¼ cup butter in a flameproof casserole; add the onions and allow to cook for 10 minutes.

Sprinkle with Calvados and flambé. Add the cider and bring to a boil. Check seasoning, cover and cook gently for 30–40 minutes.

Sauté the mushrooms (whole if small enough) in the remaining butter, and season with salt and pepper.

When the chicken pieces are tender, arrange them on a large platter. Cover with mushrooms and surround with baked apples. Keep hot.

Reduce the cooking liquid by boiling. Add *crème fraiche* and cook until the sauce is smooth and creamy. Check the seasoning and pour over the chicken, mushrooms and apples. Serve immediately.

Vegetables

left Fricassée de volaille*: the russet apples of Normandy lend their rough flavor to a succulent chicken.*

right *A centuries-old mill in Provence which still produces olive oil today*

RATATOUILLE NIÇOISE (PROVENCE)
Ratatouille

This rich vegetable dish has become almost an emblem of Provence. It should be cooked slowly and tenderly and served either hot with roast pork or cold as an hors d'oeuvre.

Serves 4

1 cup olive oil
2 large onions, sliced
4 ripe tomatoes,
  skinned, seeded
  and chopped
3 cloves garlic, crushed
fresh or dried herbs of
  Provence – basil, parsley
salt and pepper
3 medium-sized
  zucchini, sliced
3 eggplants, diced
3 peppers (red or
  green or both),
  seeded and sliced

Heat half the oil in a saucepan. Add the onions and brown them slowly. Add the tomatoes, garlic and herbs, season with salt and pepper. Cover and cook very gently over a low heat.

Heat the rest of the oil in a skillet and sauté the zucchini a few at a time. Then sauté the eggplants and finally the peppers. As they are ready add them to the onions and tomatoes in the saucepan.

When all the vegetables are combined in the casserole, check the seasoning, cover and simmer gently until very soft, about 40–60 minutes.

Baking country bread a hundred years ago

GRATIN DAUPHINOIS (DAUPHINÉ)
Dauphiné potatoes

The Dauphiné region is well known gastronomically for its *gratins*, dishes cooked with grated cheese and sometimes breadcrumbs. Be sure that the potatoes you use for *gratin dauphinois* will remain firm during the cooking.

Serves 4

1¼ pints milk
6 tablespoons butter
salt and pepper
2 lb potatoes
1 clove garlic, crushed
1 cup cream
nutmeg (optional)
¼ cup grated
 Gruyère cheese

Boil the milk in a large heavy pan. Add the butter and season with salt and pepper.

Meanwhile peel and wipe the potatoes with a clean cloth (do not wash them). Then cut them into wafer-thin slices. Put them in the boiling milk and add the crushed garlic. Simmer very gently until tender.

Add the cream, simmer for a moment, check the seasoning and grate in a little nutmeg if desired.

Transfer to a buttered earthenware *gratin* dish and sprinkle with the grated cheese. Cook in a moderate oven (350°F) for 15 minutes, until the top is well browned. Serve hot.

SALSIFIS A LA NORMANDE (NORMANDY)
Salsify or oyster plant with cream sauce

This cream-colored root vegetable is very popular in winter in France. Its delicate, sweet flavor is complemented in this traditional dish by cream sauce and tarragon.

Serves 4

juice of 1 lemon
2 lb salsify or
 oyster plant
¼ cup butter
¼ cup flour
1¼ cups milk
¼ cup cream
salt
pepper (optional)
chopped fresh tarragon

Put half the lemon juice in a bowl of cold water and place the salsify in the water as you peel them. Then cut into 1½ in pieces. Put into a saucepan of cold water with the rest of the lemon juice. Add a pinch of flour to the water to preserve the color of the salsify. Bring to a boil and cook gently until tender.

Meanwhile prepare a roux with the melted butter and flour. Allow to cool, then add the boiling milk. Cook this white sauce for 2–3 minutes, stirring all the time. Add the cream and season to taste.

When the salsify are tender, drain and add to the cream sauce. Bring back to a boil. Serve sprinkled with tarragon.

The salsify can be gratinéed; put them in a baking dish with the cream sauce, sprinkle with grated cheese and put in the oven (350°F) for about 10 minutes. Omit the tarragon.

CÈPES A LA LIMOUSINE (LIMOUSIN)
Cèpes in cream sauce

Limousin cooking is said to be rather undistinguished, but this is very shortsighted since these people, who manufacture the most beautiful china, have also created exquisite delicacies to serve upon it.

Serves 4

1½ lb fresh cèpes or
 good, firm mushrooms
salt and pepper
¼ cup butter
¼ cup oil
1 medium onion,
 chopped
1 shallot, chopped
1 cup cream
chopped parsley

Wash the cèpes or mushrooms and pat dry. Slice diagonally. Season with salt and pepper.

Heat the butter and oil in a skillet until very hot. Sauté the cèpes a few at a time until lightly browned. The fat must be very hot so that the cèpes fry quickly.

Meanwhile, in a separate pan, sauté the onion and shallot. When lightly browned, add the drained cooked cèpes. Stir the mixture and add the cream. Simmer gently for 10 to 15 minutes.

Some people also add a pinch of chopped garlic.

Sprinkle with chopped parsley and serve straight from the pan.

Desserts

TERRINÉE NORMANDE (NORMANDY)
Normandy rice pudding

In Normandy, it is traditional to cook this *terrinée* overnight in a baker's oven.

Serves 6

1 cup rice
½ cup sugar
a pinch of salt
grated nutmeg or ground cinnamon
1½ pints milk, boiled and cooled

In a casserole combine the rice and sugar. Add a pinch of salt and nutmeg or cinnamon. Stir in the cooled milk. Cook in a slow oven (275°F) for about 1¾ hours.

CLAFOUTIS LIMOUSIN (LIMOUSIN)
Black cherry pudding

When the eminent members of the Académie Française were compiling their dictionary, they defined the word *clafoutis* as 'a kind of fruit tart'. The people of Limousin protested, declaring that the *clafoutis* was nothing like a tart and that it could only be made with black cherries. Academicians finally admitted that the local inhabitants were right and immortalized their description of 'black cherry pudding'.

In fact other cherries can be used with equal success, but they must never be pitted.

Serves 6

2 cups flour
3 eggs, beaten
¾ cup sugar
a pinch of salt
1¼ cups boiled milk, cooled
1½ lb small black cherries, stalked but not pitted
3 tablespoons butter

In a large mixing bowl combine the flour, eggs and ⅔ cup of the sugar, then add the pinch of salt. Beat thoroughly, add the cooled boiled milk, and continue beating until the mixture is smooth.

Wash cherries, drain and leave to dry on a clean cloth for a few minutes. When quite dry, add them to the mixture.

Liberally butter an 8 in deep pie plate and pour in the cherry mixture. Bake in a moderately hot oven (400°F) for 30–40 minutes, until the *clafoutis* is risen and golden brown.

Remove from the oven and allow to cool before serving sprinkled with the remaining sugar.

KUGELHOPF (ALSACE)
Kugelhopf

While the Polish king Stanislas Lescincsky (Louis XV's father-in-law) was in exile in Lorraine, he is supposed to have had the idea of sprinkling a rum-flavored syrup over a kugelhopf. As he was reading *The Thousand and One Nights* at the time he called the new dessert 'Ali-baba'. Later the name was shortened to 'baba'. So it is that Alsace has the kugelhopf and Lorraine the rum baba, two delicious cakes linking two food-loving provinces.

Prepare 2 hours in advance.
Serves 12

1 cup milk
1 cake compressed yeast
⅔ cup butter
4 cups flour
½ cup sugar
pinch of salt
2 large eggs, beaten
⅔ cup raisins, soaked in water or kirsch
⅓ cup almonds

Heat the milk over a very low heat and mix ¼ cup of it with the yeast. Make sure the milk is not too hot. Melt ½ cup butter in the remaining milk.

Sift the flour into a large mixing bowl. Make a well in the center and add the sugar, salt and eggs. Combine them together well, and then add the milk, butter and yeast.

Knead for 20–25 minutes, until this very elastic dough no longer sticks to the bowl or to the fingers. Add the raisins and the almonds.

Butter a *kugelhopf* mold with the remaining butter, and place the dough in it. Leave in a warm place, covered with a clean cloth, until the dough has risen to the top of the mold (about 2 hours).

Bake in a moderate oven (350°F) for 40–45 minutes. On no account open the oven door during the first 20 minutes.

A garden . . . a meal: Le Repas *by Monet*

BEIGNETS AU FROMAGE BLANC (CHAMPAGNE)
Cottage cheese fritters

In this region cottage cheese fritters are often accompanied by a glass of champagne. They may also be flavored with a local liqueur such as marc champagne or ratafia.

Prepare 1–2 hours in advance.
Serves 6

½ lb well drained cottage cheese 2 egg yolks a little liqueur (optional) ¾ cup flour, sifted 2 tablespoons sugar a pinch of salt oil for deep frying vanilla-flavored sugar	In a large mixing bowl combine the cheese, egg yolks, liqueur if used, flour, sugar and salt. Beat thoroughly with a wooden spoon until the mixture is smooth and rather thick. Set aside for 1–2 hours. Form the mixture into small balls and drop them with a spoon into very hot oil in a deep fat fryer. When the balls are light and fluffy and golden brown, drain them and serve hot, sprinkled with the vanilla-flavored sugar.

CRUCHADES AUX CONFITURES (AUNIS-SAINTONGE)
Cornmeal fritters with apricot jam

Cognac is the 'oral treasure' of the Aunis-Saintonge region on the west coast of France, and is used to enhance many simple dishes.

Serves 6

1 pint water
a pinch of salt
2 tablespoons sugar
1¾ cups cornmeal
¼ cup Cognac
oil for deep frying
¼ cup apricot jam
	Boil the water in a saucepan with the salt and sugar. As soon as it comes to a boil, sprinkle in the cornmeal gradually, stirring all the time with a wooden spoon.
	    Continue cooking gently until the mixture is very thick and smooth; remove from the heat and stir in the brandy. Spread over a greased baking sheet or a large flat plate.
	    When cold, cut the mixture into triangles with a pointed knife and deep fry these in very hot oil until golden brown. Drain, and sandwich them together with a spoonful of apricot jam.

Cruchades aux confitures: Cognac is the secret ingredient that makes cornmeal an extravagance.

*Eating and drinking
keep body and soul together.*

German proverb

Painted shutters keep out the North Sea gales.

Germany is a rich agricultural country with many cuisines. The powerful German Empire, unified in 1871, consisted of what had been several loosely integrated kingdoms dominated to the west by Prussia, Saxony and Bavaria. Each kingdom had its own specialties, which it shared during the brief four decades of unity, and some of these such as *Königsberger Klopse* from East Prussia have now achieved the status of a German national dish. Underlying the instability of political boundaries are the immutable boundaries of climate and geology. In the main, regional specialties are dictated by what has always been traditionally grown, raised or caught in an area; and Germany can be gastronomically divided into three regions which stretch across the country horizontally: the coastal area of the north and the mountainous south sandwich between them the rich, flat plains of the midlands.

The northern region is noticeably influenced by its neighbors, Holland, Scandinavia and Russia, but its most important element is the sea. This is Germany's only coast, and it supplies all her sea fish. Germans love fish: they marinate and pickle the prolific herring to produce world-famous rollmops, and they make particularly delicious smoked eel, buckling and sprats. The cuisine of this region is designed primarily to keep out the cold and damp. Hearty soups made from cabbage, bacon, lentils or peas thickened with sour cream are ubiquitous. This strong agricultural area, which produces sugar beet, potatoes, hops and barley, also boasts two of the most sophisticated cities in Germany, Hamburg and Berlin. Hamburg gave birth to the hamburger, perversely known in Germany as *Deutsches Beefsteak*; but the culinary specialties of Berlin are manifold and the appetites of its inhabitants legendary. Berlin pickled cucumbers, hot plum doughnuts, and Christmas *Baumkuchen*, an immense tubular cake of concentric rings, are irresistible. This area also houses the delightful Vierlande on the banks of the river Elbe, which is famous for its ducks and chickens.

The central area, more conservative in its cuisine as in its life style, formerly contained Saxony and Westphalia. Westphalian ham, served in rosy diaphanous slices, is as delicious as *prosciutto*, especially served with slices of nutty pumpernickel. Westphalian casseroles of pork and lima beans, and heavily peppered dishes of beef ribs seem ideally designed to produce a thirst, which is best quenched by Dortmunder beer. Frankfurt, to the east, is synonymous with the world-famous sausage, and also remarkable for its light 'green sauce' made from chopped herbs mixed with oil, vinegar and a little sugar. To the east, Thuringia is the home of the potato dumpling and a mouth-watering fruit tart, topped with egg and rum custard. Saxony offers buckwheat pancakes drenched in sugar-beet syrup and dark fragrant cakes of honey dough while Silesia, strongly influenced by its Polish neighbors, has sour cream and poppy seeds, beer soup and delicious carp recipes.

Germany and Switzerland

The fertile basin where the Danube flows

From cabbage to sauerkraut

A chapel in Upper Bavaria

In the south of Germany, there is a perceptible lightening of culinary mood. Dumplings give way to tiny, featherlight *Spätzle*, made from wheat flour, and potatoes cooked with apples take on a new dimension in the famous country dish *Himmel und Erde* (Heaven and Earth). Cheese from the dairy herds of Bavaria comes into its own, and vines planted by the Romans grow along the banks of the Rhine and Moselle rivers. Fresh salmon is a local specialty, and the favorite meats are pork, veal and venison, often served with mushrooms fresh from the Black Forest. The strudel of Bavaria are filled with a savory fish and cabbage mixture, as well as the conventional fruit.

German cooking is the product of both a healthy, well-run agriculture and native good housekeeping. Meat is the mainstay of their cooking and, like the English and to a certain extent us Americans, Germans have an uneasy suspicion that a meal without a substantial meat content is a snack in disguise. The supreme meat has always been pork, and German cooks can do magical things with it: the most famous dish is, perhaps, pickled pork with sauerkraut, but it is also used in pot roasts, as tenderloin, as spare ribs and fresh pork sides. Turned into bacon (*Speck*), smoked or otherwise, pork becomes the *sine qua non* of the German housewife, and is used in soups and stews, cooked on its own or with potatoes to make a savory pancake.

Veal is also widely eaten, especially in the south where it is served as *Schnitzel* in dozens of different ways. However, one of the surest gastronomic indications that you are in Germany is the goose. The best geese are raised in what was formerly Pomerania in the north, and the best of them go to make the divine *Spickgans*, breast of goose smoked over a beechwood and juniper fire.

The sausage has been raised almost to an art form, and there are said to be as many sausages or *Würste* as there are major towns. They range from the gourmet delights of goose liver and truffle to frugal pork fat, blood and onions.

Cabbage is the national vegetable, served shredded and salted as sauerkraut, or red and pickled. Asparagus is the delight of the midlands and the south, and mushrooms are found everywhere.

Germany and Switzerland

witzerland is not linked historically to Germany, but geographically; and like Germany it is a classical tourist country. With three languages and cultures it inevitably has a greater selection of recipes. In the west the cooking is influenced by France, in the south by Italy, and in the north by Germany. French influence can be seen in the sauces and cooking methods; Italian in the imaginative use of veal, spaghetti and *polenta*; and German in the bean and bacon hotpots and meat cooked with apples and onion.

However, Switzerland does have its own dishes – most of them using cheese. Apart from the well-known *fondue*, there is *raclette* from the Valais district. This consists of a creamy cheese – preferably Conches or Bagnes – which is allowed to melt in front of the fire, and is then scraped up and served with baked potatoes and scallions. Gruyère cheese forms a basis for many cheese stews, soups, pies, fritters, soufflés and tarts. And, of course there is cheesecake.

Among the lesser known Swiss specialties are preserves and jams, such as the delicious black cherry jam. Fruit is used in soups, sometimes even with chocolate and wine, and a very special Swiss dessert is the cherry soufflé from Basle.

Certain foods are obviously associated with certain landscapes. In Germany poppy seeds in bread, cakes and puddings belong automatically to the Silesian kitchen, and seafish and meatballs to the East Prussian; Mecklenburg conjures up thick jams made from many different fruits and served with the Sunday roast; Pomerania means flounder and smoked eels. Switzerland, on the other hand, suggests huge rounds of cheese, beef dried in the clean cold air of Graubünden, and Westphalian raw ham.

One thing is certain: whatever the changes in politics and boundaries, the diet remains constant.

left *Alpine herdsmen sixty years ago and* **below** *the splendor of the Swiss Alps today*

Winter along the Rhine

Hors d'oeuvre

SAHNEHERINGE (SILESIA)
Herring salad

It is difficult to associate this dish with one particular area as it is so popular throughout northern Germany. One thing is certain, it did not originate on the coast, for it requires salted herrings, which were transported inland in large barrels. Housewives added sour cream and apples to modify the salt taste of the herrings.

Prepare this dish 1 day in advance
Serves 6–8

8 large salted herring fillets	Soak the salted herring fillets in cold water for at least 4 hours, changing the water several times. Prepare a marinade with the vinegar, water and sugar and place the fillets in the mixture for a few hours.
1 pint sour cream	
1 large dill pickle, chopped	
2 firm tart apples, chopped	Drain the fillets, arrange them on a serving plate, and pour the sour cream over them. Sprinkle the pickle, apples, onions and chives over the top. Serve with baked potatoes, lager and *schnaps*.
2 onions, chopped	
4 teaspoons chopped chives	

Marinade
3 tablespoons vinegar
3 tablespoons water
3 tablespoons sugar

Soups

MARKKLÖSSCHENSUPPE (BERLIN)
Marrow dumpling soup

Beef marrow is a Berlin specialty: it can be served on toast with finely chopped celery heart, or sprinkled with grated cheese and broiled; or made into strongly flavored marrow dumplings – the essence of this soup. In preparing the dumplings be sure to allow enough time for them to stand.

Serves 4

5 oz fresh marrow	Crush the marrow and mix it with the egg yolk, breadcrumbs, parsley, nutmeg and salt. Beat the egg white until stiff and add to the mixture. Leave to stand for about 10 minutes.
1 egg, separated	
1 cup fresh breadcrumbs	
¾ cup chopped parsley	
a pinch of grated nutmeg	Bring the beef stock to a boil. Form small dumplings with a teaspoon (dipping it each time in hot water) and drop them into the stock. Cook the dumplings until tender.
1 teaspoon salt	
1 quart beef stock	

RÜBCHENSUPPE MIT ENTE (MECKLENBURG)
Turnip soup with duck

This is a popular 'leftovers' meal after a Sunday roast. It is a hearty soup, almost like a stew. A goose carcass or the bones and crackling from roast pork may be used instead of a duck. If there isn't enough meat you can add some pork spareribs. The soup is flavored with traditional 'pot herbs' – finely chopped vegetables – and with beef extract, which has been a favorite ingredient in German soups and stews since the mid-nineteenth century when it was first produced commercially.

Serves 4

carcass and giblets of a roast duck	Brown the giblets quickly in 2 tablespoons lard. Cut up the carcass, and put with the giblets, pot herbs and spareribs, if used, into a pan with 2 quarts of water. Simmer for 45 minutes. Strain the soup, discard bones, chop the meat finely and set aside.
6 tablespoons lard	
1 cup chopped 'pot herbs' – leeks, onions, carrots, celery heart, parsley	
¼ lb pork spareribs, chopped (optional)	In another pan cook the remaining lard and sugar together to a caramel and brown the turnips. Pour in enough duck stock to cover them and simmer for 30 minutes.
2 teaspoons sugar	
1 lb turnips	
2 tablespoons butter	Beat the butter and flour together and beat this gradually into the rest of the stock over a gentle heat. Finally combine all the ingredients, add the meat extract and season with salt and pepper.
¼ cup flour	
2 teaspoons beef extract	
salt and pepper	

Marrow dumpling soup: guaranteed to keep out the cold

Germany and Switzerland

BUTTERMILCHSUPPE (EAST PRUSSIA)
Buttermilk soup

This is a soup to eat in summer; served chilled on sultry evenings it is a real delicacy. Depending on the season, strawberries, raspberries, gooseberries or grapes can be served with it. You must not neglect this soup for a moment while you are making it, as it can easily spoil.

Serves 4

1 quart buttermilk
a strip of lemon rind
2 tablespoons sugar
1 tablespoon potato flour
1 cup sour cream

Heat the buttermilk with the lemon rind and sugar in a deep pan or double boiler. Beat constantly to prevent curdling. (The hotter it gets, the more likely it is to curdle.)

Dissolve the potato flour in a little water, and when the buttermilk begins to rise quickly add this to it. Bring back to a boil, remove from heat and beat again. Remove the lemon rind and add the sour cream. Serve hot or cold.

BÜNDNER GERSTENSUPPE (GRISONS)
Grisons barley soup

This is an ancient recipe from the eastern Swiss canton of Graubünden or Grisons. It is important to make it with a good rich stock, and add a generous quantity of cream.

Serves 4

1½ lb crushed ham bones
½ lb fresh pork sides or bacon
½ cup pearl barley
1 cup sour cream
1½ cups chopped chives

Simmer the ham bones and pork sides or bacon in 1½ quarts unsalted water for 1½ hours. Skim the surface. Strain the stock and cook the barley in it for about 30 minutes until the grains are tender, but not soft. Stir in the cream, add the chives and bring to a boil once more.

In Switzerland this soup is served with ham pastries or spinach-flavored cakes.

GELBE ERBSENSUPPE (BERLIN)
Yellow pea soup

In the past fifty years this recipe has fallen into ill repute as it has been adopted as a standard army dish. The soup can't help that: it is doomed to taste good and cost little.

Prepare the peas 12 hours in advance.
Serves 4–6

1 lb (2 cups) dried yellow peas, soaked
1 small piece of ham
6 bacon slices, chopped
¼ cup drippings
1 leek
2 onions
2 carrots
¼ celeriac (celery root)
1 lb potatoes, peeled and diced
salt and pepper
4 cooked German sausages, sliced
fresh celery leaves

Boil the peas for 1 hour and drain. In 4–6 cups fresh water, simmer the peas and ham for a further hour.

Heat the bacon with the drippings in a separate pan, fry the finely chopped leek, onions, carrots and celeriac, then add to the soup. Add the potatoes, salt and pepper to taste, and simmer for 30 minutes. Finally add the sausages and celery leaves, and simmer for a further 5 minutes.

SCHNIPPELBOHNENSUPPE MIT ÄPFELN (WEST PRUSSIA)
Bean soup with apples

A fruity summer meal: the combination of fruit with meat and vegetables is characteristic of German cooking. If you like a stronger taste you can add sausages or slices of cooked beef brisket to this soup. The beans should be cooked until they are just tender, not soft.

Serves 6–8

1 lb green beans
¾ lb potatoes, diced
2 quarts beef stock
a bunch of summer savory
1 lb cooking apples, peeled, cored and sliced
¼ lb bacon, chopped
1 onion, finely chopped
4 teaspoons flour
2 teaspoons vinegar
salt
a little sugar

Remove the strings from the beans and cut them diagonally into small pieces. If the beans are over-ripe use only the white seeds inside. Simmer the beans, potatoes and stock for about 1 hour. Add the summer savory for the last 15 minutes, and the apples for the last 10 minutes.

In a separate large pan brown the bacon with the onion. Sprinkle with flour and cook for a few minutes; then gradually add a little bean stock. Add this to the soup and finally season to taste with vinegar, salt and sugar.

BIERSUPPE MIT SCHNEEBERGEN (SILESIA)
Beer soup with floating islands

Beer accompanies most German meals and is also an important ingredient in many dishes. This soup is traditionally made with German brown beer; if this is not available, use dark beer.

Serves 4

1½ pints brown beer
¼ cup sugar
a pinch of salt
grated rind of 1 lemon
2 cloves
a good pinch of ground cinnamon
4 teaspoons cornstarch
2 eggs, separated
2 teaspoons confectioners' sugar

Bring the beer, sugar, salt, lemon rind and spices slowly to a boil. Mix the cornstarch with a little beer and add to the soup. Boil for a few minutes. Mix the egg yolks with 2 teaspoons of water, remove soup from the heat, and add yolks. (Take care that the yolks do not curdle.)

Beat the egg whites until stiff, add the confectioners' sugar and beat again, then place spoonfuls on top of the soup. Put in a hot oven (425°F) for a few minutes to brown the surface.

BRAUNE KÄSESUPPE NACH BASLER ART (BASLE)
Basle brown cheese soup

This simple soup has a surprisingly delicate flavor. It suits almost every occasion and is especially good as a light snack served with cheese and the wonderful air-dried meat prepared in the countryside near Basle.

Serves 4

¼ cup butter
8 teaspoons flour
beef stock
salt and pepper
2 teaspoons beef extract
3 tablespoons sour cream
1 cup grated Gruyère cheese

Cook the butter and flour in a heavy pan until lightly browned, then gradually add 1 quart beef stock and beat until smooth and creamy. Stir in salt, pepper, beef extract and sour cream.

Divide the soup between 4 deep bowls and sprinkle with a thick layer of grated cheese. Serve with crusty white bread.

HAGEBUTTENSUPPE (MECKLENBURG)
Rosehip soup

For this traditional Mecklenburg recipe you need fresh, ripe rosehips and a lot of patience to clean the fruit and remove the hairy seeds.

Serves 4

½ lb rosehips, seeded
¼ cup butter
2 teaspoons flour
juice of ½ lemon
¼ cup sugar
⅔ cup Madeira wine
⅔ cup red wine
a pinch of ground cinnamon
1 cup whipped cream

Put the rosehips in a pan with a little water and cook gently. When they are tender, press them through a strainer, reserving the cooking liquid.

Meanwhile melt the butter in a separate pan and add the flour to make a roux. Gradually add the rosehip liquid, lemon juice, sugar and Madeira wine. Bring to a boil, then add the rosehips, red wine and cinnamon.

Serve with ladyfingers and decorate with whipped cream.

Grains and savories

RISOTTO CON FUNGHI (TICINO)
Mushroom risotto

In Ticino, the Italian-speaking part of Switzerland, risotto is often served as an accompaniment to roast meat; prepared with ham and mushrooms, as in this recipe, and served with a fresh green salad, it becomes a satisfying main course.

Serves 8

1 cup diced onions
¼ cup butter
2 cups rice
1 cup chopped mushrooms
½ cup diced cooked ham
5 cups stock
salt and pepper
1 parsley root, chopped
Parmesan cheese, grated

Cook the onions in butter until transparent, then add the rice. Stir well, and do not let the onion brown. Add the mushrooms, ham, stock, salt, pepper and parsley root.

In 20 minutes the rice should have absorbed all the liquid and the risotto will be ready. Sprinkle with Parmesan cheese to serve.

GRAUPEN UND ZWETSCHGEN (RHINELAND)
Pearl barley and plums

This dish can be served on its own as a main course or as an accompaniment to ham or cold roast beef. It is an autumnal delicacy, eaten when plums are ripening in the lanes and gardens of the Rhineland.

Prepare the plums 24 hours in advance.
Serves 4

1¼ cups pearl barley
¼ cup butter
1 teaspoon salt
4 teaspoons sugar
1 lb plums, halved, pitted, sprinkled with sugar and left for 24 hours

Place the barley in a pan with the butter and 1 quart of water, cover and simmer gently for 45 minutes. Add the salt, sugar and the prepared plums and cook uncovered for a further 20 minutes to allow some of the liquid to evaporate. The mixture should be thick enough to eat with a fork.

RAMEQUINS (SWITZERLAND)
Ramekins

Hot cheese dishes are very popular in Switzerland; and no wonder, in a country where so many varieties of cheese are produced. These small cheese tartlets with delicate creamy centers are best eaten with the fingers, hot from the oven. If necessary the pastry shells can be made the day before; then the filling is quickly poured into them and the tartlets are cooked for a few minutes until golden brown.

Makes about 40 tartlets

pie or puff pastry made with 3½ cups flour (p. 30)
1 lb full fat cheese, such as Brie, sliced thinly
1 cup light cream
2 eggs
salt and pepper
a little grated nutmeg

Line shallow muffin tins with paper-thin pastry and prick with a fork. Mix the sliced cheese, cream, eggs, salt, pepper and nutmeg into a smooth batter. Fill the tart shells three-quarters full and bake in the oven (350°F) for 20 minutes. (If you are pre-cooking the shells in advance, they need only 10 minutes in the oven, and 10 minutes more when filled.)

Summer: nineteenth-century needlework from Switzerland

NEUENBURGER FONDUE (NEUCHÂTEL)
Neuchâtel fondue

Swiss cheese dishes like fondue and *raclette* (cheese melted over a fire and served with baked potatoes) were invented by mountain herdsmen living in remote huts on the high-lying pastures. They were simple to prepare, and made nourishing, substantial evening meals.

Fondue is traditionally made in a flat-bottomed earthenware pot, called a *caquelot*, which will rest easily on a small alcohol lamp, keeping the dish hot without letting the cheese burn. The same wine that is used for making the fondue – a sparkling white wine – should be drunk with the meal.

Serves 4

1 clove of garlic, cut in half
1¾ cups sparkling white Neuchâtel wine
¼ cup butter
1¼ lb grated or finely sliced full fat cheese (half Emmenthal and half Gruyère)
1 teaspoon potato flour
¼ cup kirsch
pepper
plenty of white bread, cubed

Rub the fondue pot with the cut clove of garlic. Gently warm the wine in the pot. Little by little add the butter and the grated cheese, stirring constantly until it melts. Take care not to use too high a heat otherwise the cheese will become stringy and the fondue will be spoiled. Mix the potato flour with the kirsch and stir into the fondue, which will thicken immediately. Add a little pepper, but no salt. Place the fondue in the middle of the table on an alcohol lamp.

To eat the fondue all the guests spear cubes of white bread on long two-pronged forks, dip them into the cheese and pop them, dripping, into their mouths. According to an old custom a man who loses his cube of bread in the fondue must pay for a round of wine or kirsch; and a woman must give every man in the party a kiss.

Fish

GEFÜLLTER MAIFISCH (BERLIN)
Stuffed May fish

The traditional May fish is in fact a garfish, which is most plentiful in the month of May. It is caught in the Baltic and transported fresh to Berlin. Garfish has bright, leaf-green bones, which have the advantage of being easy to see and thus avoid, when you are eating the fish. If garfish is not available, mackerel may be used instead.

Serves 4

4 garfish
2 tablespoons flour
¼ cup butter

Stuffing
¼ cup chopped cooked ham
4 tomatoes
4 slices of white bread without crusts
a sprig of parsley
salt
¼ cup milk

Clean and salt the insides of the fish. Make the stuffing by grinding the ham, tomatoes, bread, parsley and salt together, and adding the milk. Loosely stuff the fish with this mixture and sew up the open sides. Coat the fish in flour and brown in plenty of butter, then cook in a moderate oven (325°F) for 30 minutes.

Serve with potato salad.

Fishing – a constant pleasure

SCHELLFISCH MIT MILCHREIS (POMERANIA)
Haddock with creamed rice

For many years this dish has been served at weddings and in traditional restaurants in Pomerania. Use very fresh fish.

Serves 4

1 cup rice
salt
1 cup heavy cream, partly whipped
2 lb haddock
1 onion, stuck with 2 cloves
¼ bay leaf
a dash of vinegar (optional)
1 lemon, cut into wedges
parsley

Simmer the rice with a pinch of salt and the cream mixed with a little water. Add more water if it dries out.

Salt the inside of the fish and poach gently in salted water with the onion and bay leaf. Do not allow the water to boil fiercely, otherwise the fish will break up. If you prefer the fish to be really firm, add a dash of vinegar to the water.

Arrange the fish and rice on a long serving platter and garnish with lemon wedges and parsley.

FORELLENFILETS 'BEAU RIVAGE' (LAKE GENEVA)
'Beau rivage' fillets of trout

This dish was as popular in Swiss farmhouse kitchens as in rich town households, for trout was no luxury to those living close to the lakes. The sea trout found in Lake Geneva and Lake Constance are much larger than delicate brook trout.

Serves 4

¼ cup butter
1 cup diced shallots
salt and pepper
2 large trout, filleted but not skinned
juice of 1 lemon
¼ cup chopped mushrooms
2 tomatoes, chopped
4 teaspoons chopped parsley
¼ cup white wine
⅔ cup sour cream

Butter a shallow baking dish and line with a thick layer of shallots. Sprinkle with salt. Season the fillets of trout with salt, pepper and lemon juice, lay them in the dish and cover with mushrooms, tomatoes and parsley.

Pour over the white wine, cover with foil and cook in the oven (350°F) for 15–20 minutes. Take out of the oven and pour the liquid into a pan. Add the sour cream and cook the sauce for a few minutes to reduce slightly, then pour it back over the trout.

Serve in the same dish, and pass buttered potatoes, endive salad and chilled white wine.

Meat and poultry

KÜMMELFILET VOM SCHWEIN (BERLIN)
Pork tenderloin with kümmel

At one time Berlin was particularly famous for the *schnaps* and liqueurs distilled in the city. Later many distillers from East Prussia moved to Berlin, including all the makers of *kümmel*, a liqueur flavored with caraway seeds; and consequently many Berlin recipes include *kümmel*. This dish is traditionally served on a bed of mashed potatoes.

Serves 4

2 pork tenderloin
salt and pepper
4 teaspoons flour
¼ cup butter
¼ cup brandy
¼ cup kümmelschnaps or
  kümmel liqueur
1 cup beef stock
2 teaspoons finely
  ground caraway seeds
2 tablespoons finely
  chopped parsley

Sprinkle the pork with salt and pepper and coat in the flour. Brown in half the butter until just tender but still pink inside. Set the meat aside and keep hot.

Scrape the juices from the skillet into a small pan and add the brandy, *kümmelschnaps*, stock and remaining butter. Bring to a boil. (This can be done in a chafing dish at the table if you prefer.) Remove pan from the heat and stir in the caraway seeds.

Slice the pork; arrange the slices on a bed of mashed potatoes and pour the sauce over the top. Finally garnish with fresh parsley.

SÜLZKOTLETT (BERLIN)
Ham slices in aspic

Aspic jelly is very popular in the cuisine of nothern Germany: jellied pork and goose in aspic are particular favorites. Traditionally the jelly was made out of boiled bones and skin from pork or veal.

Prepare this dish half a day in advance.
Serves 4

¼ celeriac (celery root),
  peeled and sliced
¼ leek, sliced
1 carrot, sliced
1 bunch parsley roots,
  chopped
salt
1 quart stock
4 thick smoked ham
  slices (bone in)
¼ cup white wine
2 tablespoons vinegar
1 tablespoon sugar
2 envelopes unflavored
  gelatin
1 tomato, sliced
¼ green pepper, cut in
  strips and blanched in
  boiling water

Simmer the celeriac, leek, carrot, parsley roots and salt in the stock for about 20 minutes, until tender. Add the ham slices and simmer for about 1 hour, until they are cooked. Strain off the broth and add to it the wine, vinegar, sugar and dissolved gelatin. This cools to form the aspic.

Arrange the cooked vegetables in a deep dish, or in 4 individual dishes. Pour over a little aspic, then place the ham on top and cover with tomato and green pepper. Finally cover completely with aspic and allow to set for several hours.

Invert onto a plate for serving and serve sauté potatoes and rémoulade sauce separately. (This sauce is made by adding chopped dill pickles, capers, parsley, chervil, tarragon and an anchovy fillet or anchovy paste to mayonnaise.)

EISBEIN AUF SAUERKRAUT (BERLIN)
Pickled pork with sauerkraut

This most celebrated dish, which originated in Berlin in the heyday of the Prussian Empire, later became popular all over Germany. For good results, the seasoning and correct cooking time are most important.

Serves 4

1 onion
4 lb smoked pork picnic
  roast
1 bay leaf
5 coriander seeds
5 coarsely ground
  black peppercorns
4 teaspoons salt

Sauerkraut
2 lb sauerkraut
¼ cup pork drippings
2 onions, finely chopped
5 juniper berries
1¼ cups white wine
1 potato, peeled and
  grated
2 teaspoons sugar

Cut the unpeeled onion in half and brown the cut surfaces in a skillet. (This gives the gravy a better color.)

Cover the meat with water, add the onion, bay leaf, spices and salt and simmer for 1½ hours.

When the pork is nearly cooked, roughly chop the sauerkraut and bring it to a boil with 1 pint liquid from the pork. Melt the drippings in a separate pan and fry the onions until golden brown. Add to the sauerkraut together with the juniper berries and wine.

After 40 minutes add the potatoes and mix well. Cook for a further 10 minutes. Finally, add the sugar to take the edge off the sourness. Arrange the sauerkraut and pork on the same platter, and serve with mashed potatoes.

Pickled pork with sauerkraut: a generous measure of white wine sweetens this Berlin speciality.

Grape harvesting in the past

GEFÜLLTE SCHWEINSBRUST MIT KRÄUTERN (RHINELAND-PFALZ)
Stuffed pork with herbs

In Lower Saxony, this dish is prepared with plain tart apples, but in the Rhineland herbs, raisins and exotic spices are added as well.

Serves 4

2 lb fresh pork sides, boned
salt and pepper
3 tablespoons pork drippings

Stuffing
2 apples, peeled and finely chopped
¼ cup oil
2 teaspoons chopped fresh marjoram
2 teaspoons chopped fresh sage
2 parsley roots, chopped
4 teaspoons chopped parsley
1 teaspoon chopped fresh spinach leaf
1 teaspoon crushed coriander seeds
1 teaspoon ground cardamom
¼ teaspoon ground cinnamon
¼ teaspoon dried lemon balm
¼ teaspoon salt
2 teaspoons finely ground black pepper
¼ cup raisins, finely chopped
¼ cup chopped almonds

Stew the apples in oil until soft. Add the herbs, spices and salt and pepper. After a few minutes, add the raisins and almonds and mix thoroughly.

Rub the pork with salt and pepper, score the skin at ½ in intervals and stuff with the fruit mixture. Stitch the open edges together. Melt the drippings in a pan, add the meat and place in the oven (425°F) for 30 minutes, basting frequently. Pour 1 cup of water over the meat, reduce oven temperature to 350°F and cook for a further hour.

Serve with a mixed salad of potatoes, pickles and radishes, dressed with oil and vinegar. Beer and *schnaps* are good accompaniments.

SÄUERLICHE HAMMELKEULE (WESTPHALIA)
Marinated leg of lamb

In the close season when there was no fresh game, the more well-to-do German families used to eat this 'mock venison' – a marinated leg of lamb, mutton or pork prepared in the same way as real venison. The larding is most important.

Prepare this dish several days in advance.
Serves 6

1 leg of lamb, boned
½ lb bacon, cut in strips
lard
1 cup fresh breadcrumbs
1 pint sour cream
a sprig of parsley
chives
salt and pepper

Marinade
2 carrots, chopped
2 onions, chopped
2 quarts buttermilk
1 cup vinegar
1 bay leaf
1 teaspoon sugar
12 peppercorns, crushed
1 teaspoon salt

Combine the ingredients for the marinade in a large earthenware casserole, place the meat in it and leave for a few days.

Dry the meat and insert the bacon in small incisions in the meat. Melt the lard and brown the meat all over. Add a few spoonfuls of the marinade, cover and cook in a moderate oven (350°F) for about 1½ hours or until just tender.

Remove the meat and thicken the gravy by adding the breadcrumbs and then the sour cream. Finally season with the herbs and salt and pepper. Cut the meat into slices, pour the sauce over it and serve with roast potatoes or potato salad.

GROSSE BUTTERBOHNENKERNE MIT SCHWEINEBAUCH (WESTPHALIA)
Broad beans with belly of pork

Lima bean fans can be found everywhere. Once you have eaten fresh lima beans you wonder how you ever lived without them. They are best picked very young, before their outer shell becomes hard. Then they can be cooked just like other spring vegetables – simmered until tender and tossed in butter – or cooked with fresh pork sides the Westphalian way.

Serves 4

2 lb lima beans, shelled
½ lb fresh pork sides
salt
1 parsley root
¼ cup diced onion
4 bacon slices
¼ cup butter
¼ cup flour
summer savory
pepper

Place the beans in a saucepan with the piece of pork, cover with water and bring gently to a boil. Add salt and parsley root, and simmer until tender (about 15 minutes). Strain, reserving the liquid.

In a separate pan brown the onion and bacon in the bacon fat, then remove the onion and bacon. Melt butter and add the flour to make a roux. Stir in the onion and bacon and thin with some of the bean cooking liquid. Add the beans and a little summer savory. Cut the pork into thick slices, add to the beans and season to taste.

Germany and Switzerland

HIMMEL UND ERDE (RHINELAND)
Heaven and earth

This winter dish, the German relative of Dutch 'hot lightning', has always been popular in the fruit-growing district around Cologne. It is served as a dish by itself or with fried liver. The apples should be very tart.

Serves 6–8

2 lb potatoes, peeled and thickly sliced
2 lb apples, peeled, cored and quartered
a strip of lemon rind
4 teaspoons sugar
¼ lb bacon, diced
2 large onions, sliced
salt and pepper
1 lb blood sausage, sliced

Boil the potatoes in salted water until tender. Drain and mash. In another pan cook the apples with the lemon rind and sugar until soft. Mix the potatoes with the apples and beat until smooth.

Fry the bacon separately, remove from the pan and brown the onions in the same fat. Add both to the apple and potato mixture. Season with salt and pepper, and serve in a dish with slices of blood sausage on top.

BERNER PLATTE (BERNE)
Bernese platter

This Bernese platter closely resembles the 'garnished sauerkraut' of eastern France. But the people of Berne do not like this comparison: theirs is a local dish, steeped in tradition.

Serves 6

2 onions, sliced
¼ cup butter or lard
2 lb green beans, trimmed
1 cup stock
½ lb pork spareribs
½ lb bacon
4 smoked ham slices (bone in)
4 Vienna or Frankfurter sausages
4 ham sausages

Brown the onion slices in butter or lard, then add the green beans. Cook them for a few minutes over a fierce heat, stirring constantly. Pour in the meat stock, add the pork spareribs and the bacon, which gives the dish its savory aroma, and leave to cook, covered, for about 1 hour.

In the last 20 minutes add the ham slices and sausages. Strain off the liquid and arrange the vegetables on a china serving platter with the meat and sausages.

Serve with French mustard, boiled potatoes tossed in butter and herbs, and beer.

HOPPELPOPPEL (BERLIN)
Hodgepodge

Hoppelpoppel is a popular, colorful expression like 'mishmash' or 'hodgepodge'; and that's exactly what it is: pieces of meat and vegetables mixed together in the same pan. *Hoppelpoppel* can be eaten at any time of day or year, but it is generally regarded as a snack to accompany a glass of beer.

Serves 4

¼ cup lard or butter
1 cup diced leftover roast beef or pork
1 cup diced cooked ham
1 cup diced sausages
1 lb potatoes boiled in their skins, cooled and chopped
2 onions, finely chopped
4 eggs, beaten
salt and white pepper
3 tablespoons chopped parsley

Heat the fat in a large skillet and fry the meat and potatoes. Add the onions, eggs, salt and pepper, stirring all the time. Sprinkle with chopped parsley and serve immediately on hot plates.

SCHLODDERKAPPES (RHINELAND)
Schlodderkappes

This is one of those renowned stews that can be made at any time of the year. It is prepared rather like Irish stew, with alternate layers of meat and vegetables; and it also improves on reheating. Caraway seeds give it a characteristic flavor.

Serves 4

2 lb head of white cabbage
2 lb potatoes, diced
1½ lb pork spareribs, diced
1 teaspoon salt
¼ teaspoon pepper
1¼ pints stock
¼ teaspoon caraway seeds
4 teaspoons chopped celery leaves

Separate the cabbage leaves, cut out the thick central veins and blanch in boiling water. Arrange the potatoes, cabbage and meat in layers in a flameproof casserole and sprinkle with salt and pepper. Pour in the stock, cover and simmer for 1 hour. Towards the end of the hour add the caraway seeds and celery leaves.

Serve with lager and *schnaps*.

FALSCHER HASE (BERLIN)
Mock hare

This meat loaf – the traditional Sunday lunch – is sometimes made in the shape of a cowering hare; but otherwise the recipe has nothing to do with game.

Serves 4

½ lb beef chuck steak
1 lb shoulder of pork
2 fresh juniper berries
1 teaspoon dried marjoram
2 bread rolls, soaked in milk
1 leek, chopped
2 onions, chopped
5 small link pork sausages
4 eggs, beaten
salt

Cut the meat into cubes and mix with the juniper berries and herbs. Then pass through the grinder twice with the rolls, leek and onions. Add the sausage meat, eggs and salt and mix thoroughly.

With dampened hands, either shape the mixture into a long roll and place on a greased baking sheet, or press it firmly into a greased loaf pan and place in a roasting pan containing water. Cook in a moderate oven (350°F) for 1–1½ hours, until the meat is golden brown and, when skewered, no longer runs red.

Arrange the 'mock hare' on a serving platter and serve with sauté potatoes.

Working in the kitchen: *a German jigsaw puzzle of a hundred years ago*

KÖNIGSBERGER KLOPSE (EAST PRUSSIA)
Königsberg meatballs

Königsberg was once the capital of East Prussia, and these meatballs are among the few specialties from its fine cuisine which have remained with us to this day. Königsberg meatballs are now regarded as almost the national dish of Germany.

Serves 4

¼ *lb boneless pork*
¼ *lb boneless beef*
¼ *lb bacon*
2 onions
2 slices white bread,
  soaked
1 teaspoon chopped
  anchovies
4 eggs
salt and pepper
1 teaspoon dried
  marjoram

Sauce
¼ *cup butter*
4 teaspoons flour
¼ *cup cream*
2 egg yolks
2 teaspoons vinegar
1 teaspoon sugar
2 teaspoons capers
1 teaspoon dried
  marjoram
salt and pepper

Grind together the meat, onions and bread. Add the anchovies, eggs, salt, pepper and marjoram. Mix thoroughly. With dampened hands, form medium-sized balls and simmer in boiling salted water for 20 minutes or until just tender. Remove the meatballs carefully with a slotted spoon.

Make a roux with the butter and flour and gradually stir in the cooking liquid. Beat the cream with the egg yolks and add this to the sauce with the vinegar, sugar, capers, marjoram, salt and a little pepper. Add the meatballs to the sauce, heat gently and serve hot.

Boiled potatoes and beer go well with this dish.

KOHLROULADEN (BERLIN)
Stuffed cabbage

Traditional Berlin restaurants compete to produce the tastiest stuffed cabbage. The dishes are judged on the success of the creamy sauce as well as the meat stuffing.

Serves 4

1 large head of white
  cabbage
2 slices of stale brown
  bread

Stuffing
¼ *lb lean ground beef*
¼ *lb ground pork*
4 teaspoons diced bacon
2 slices of white bread,
  soaked in milk
2 teaspoons beef extract
2 teaspoons salt
2 teaspoons pepper

Sauce
10 bacon slices
¼ *lb tomatoes, skinned*
  and chopped
1 cup sour cream
2 teaspoons flour
salt and pepper
4 teaspoons paprika
¼ *cup chopped parsley*

Combine all the ingredients for the stuffing and mix thoroughly. Make a deep cut in the base of the cabbage and simmer in salted water with the bread for 30 minutes. Then carefully remove the leaves from the stalk. Make a bed with 3–4 leaves, place a little meat mixture in the center of each, roll up and secure with string. Repeat until all the leaves and stuffing are used up.

Fry the slices of bacon in a large pan. Place the stuffed cabbage on top and allow to brown on a low heat. Add about 1 cup water, cover and cook for 20–30 minutes. Add the tomatoes, sour cream and the flour mixed with a little water. Cook for another 10 minutes. Season with salt, pepper and paprika and garnish with parsley.

Baked potatoes and beer go well with this dish.

Königsberg meatballs: a national dish from a town that's no longer German

Traditions, like cobble-stones, live on in the small towns of Germany.

GEDÄMPFTE KALBSBRUST (RHINELAND)
Stuffed breast of veal

This is a particularly delicious Sunday dish, handed down through the generations of a Düsseldorf family. One stuffing is given below, but another version combines meat, bread, herbs, kidney fat and raisins, and yet another uses vegetables, finely chopped cabbage, caraway seeds, bread cubes and sour cream. Whichever recipe is used, the stuffing is always generously seasoned with pepper or paprika.

Serves 4

1 kg breast of veal
2 potatoes
2 onions
1 carrot
¼ *head celery*
150 g butter
4 tablespoons sour cream
2 teaspoons flour
4 teaspoons parsley
½ *bay leaf*
2 teaspoons capers
salt and pepper

Stuffing
250 g lean veal
100 g streaky bacon
100 g gammon
5 anchovy fillets
3 eggs
3 onions
a sprig of parsley
rind of ¼ lemon
¼ *teaspoon*
  ground cloves
1 teaspoon paprika
¼ *teaspoon cinnamon*
salt

First prepare the stuffing. Mince the meat, onions, bacon, gammon, parsley, lemon rind and anchovies together, then add the eggs, salt, cinnamon, cloves and paprika. Spread this on the veal and roll up.

Melt 125 g butter in a frying pan and brown the meat all over. Add 250 ml water, the vegetables and bay leaf. Cook, covered, on a gentle heat for about 1½ hours. Add more water if necessary and make sure that the vegetables do not burn.

Transfer the meat to a serving dish and keep hot. Thicken the cooking liquid with 25 g butter mixed with flour, and add the sour cream, capers, salt, pepper and parsley. Bring gently to the boil, stirring all the time, and pour over the meat.

Serve with cauliflower and creamed potatoes.

SCHWEINSKEULE MIT KRUSTE (POMERANIA)
Smoked pork in breadcrumbs

Ham and pork preserves are prepared and eaten all over Germany, but Westphalian ham is the most famous. There are two main varieties of ham: smoked, which is eaten raw, and cured (sometimes also smoked), which is boiled and baked for eating. In this recipe a smoked pork roast is first boiled and then baked; and it is best to leave the natural fat on the pork, as it improves the crust.

Prepare 24 hours in advance.
Serves 12

4 lb boneless smoked
  pork roast
12 cloves
salt
2 cups dry breadcrumbs
⅓ cup brown sugar
¼ cup butter

Cover the pork with cold water, bring to a boil and skim. Simmer for about 50 minutes; then take out the pork, cool slightly and remove the skin. Spike the pork with cloves, sprinkle with salt and place in a roasting pan with a little water. Bake in a moderate oven (350°F) for a further 50 minutes. Keep the water constantly topped up.

Take out the pork and cover with breadcrumbs, sugar and butter until a crust is built up. Return to the oven at a higher temperature (400°F) for about 30 minutes or until golden brown.

Cool the pork, slice and serve with potato salad, and white wine from the Palatinate.

Cook with rabbit and pheasant: *from a porcelain plate of 1811*

SCHINKENAUFLAUF (GRISONS)
Ham soufflé

When the Swiss talk about 'ham', they are usually referring to the air-dried, lightly salted raw ham or beef of Grisons.

Serves 4

½ lb smoked ham
1 cup cream
1 cup fresh breadcrumbs
4 eggs, beaten
pepper
4 teaspoons chopped
  parsley
4 teaspoons chopped
  chives
puff pastry made with
  2 cups flour, rolled
  out thinly (p. 30)
⅓ cup chopped pistachio
  nuts

Grind the ham to a paste, add this to the cream, breadcrumbs and eggs and season with pepper, parsley and chives. (Salt should not be necessary in this recipe as the ham adds sufficient flavor.)

Butter a 9×5×3 in loaf pan, coat it with flour and line with pastry. Press the pastry firmly against the sides of the pan and prick with a fork. Pour in half the ham mixture, cover with pistachio nuts and then add the rest of the ham mixture.

Cook in the oven at 350°F for about 45–60 minutes until risen and brown on top. If necessary cover the surface with foil to prevent burning. Cut the warm soufflé into thick slices and serve with brown bread and butter.

ZÜRCHER LEBERSPIESSLI (ZURICH)
Liver kabobs

Zurich has been a cultural center of Switzerland ever since the Reformation; and visitors come to enjoy its worldly delights as well as its intellectual ones. However, all the traditional dishes are very simply prepared – no doubt reflecting the influence of Calvin and his followers.

Serves 4

1¼ lb calf liver
salt and pepper
2 sage leaves
12 thin bacon slices

Cut the liver into 12 slices 1 in wide and 2½ in long and season with salt, pepper and crushed sage leaves.

Wrap each piece of liver in a slice of bacon and spear 3 of them on each of 4 metal skewers. Fry the kabobs and serve with apple sauce, fried onion rings and fried potatoes.

ZÜRCHER KALBSGESCHNETZELTES (ZURICH)
Veal cutlets

This lightning dish from Switzerland has achieved world renown; but, like many well known specialties, it is often prepared incorrectly. The Swiss cook always makes it at the last minute and serves it piping hot straight from the pan, which is the way it should always be done.

Serves 4

1 lb veal round steak
  or cutlets, cut into thin
  strips
4 teaspoons flour
¼ cup butter or 4
  teaspoons oil
¼ cup diced onion
½ cup wine
1 teaspoon meat extract
⅔ cup cream
salt and white pepper

Pound the veal thoroughly, then coat in flour. Melt the butter in a skillet and sweat the onion until it is translucent. Add the meat and fry it very quickly over a high heat. Stir all the time.

When the meat is lightly browned, remove from the pan and keep warm. Add the wine to the skillet and allow it to bubble for several minutes, then add the meat extract and finally the cream.

Remove the sauce from the heat. Season the meat with salt and pepper, return to the pan, toss in the sauce and serve immediately. The best accompaniments are *Rösti* and white or rosé wine.

*Houses coated with
snow like bread cubes
in a fondue*

Vegetables

GUTES GÄNSEKLEIN-RAGOUT (POMERANIA)
Goose ragout

This dish was traditionally eaten the day before an autumn or winter festival. While the geese were being prepared for roasting, the goose trimmings, which were regarded as a particular delicacy, were carefully preserved. This ragout served to whet the appetite for the crispy roast to follow.

Serves 4

*1 kg goose trimmings
(wings, gizzard, heart,
neck)*
2 onions, chopped
1 carrot, finely chopped
*¼ root of celeriac,
finely chopped*
1 leek, chopped
*250 g dried fruit, soaked
in water*
80 g dripping
2 cloves
vinegar
5 peppercorns
4 teaspoons sugar
2 teaspoons salt

Brown the trimmings and onion in the dripping. Add a little water, the carrot, celeriac, cloves, salt and peppercorns, and simmer for 10 minutes. Then add another 250 ml water, the leek, and the dried fruit, and cook for another 30–40 minutes, until the meat is tender.

Stir frequently to avoid burning, and make sure that the meat remains covered in liquid. Finally season to a sweet-sour taste with a dash of vinegar and sugar. (Some cooks like to thicken the ragout with a basic white sauce.)

Serve with jacket potatoes.

ARTISCHOCKEN MIT MARK (ZURICH)
Artichokes with ox marrow

This dish belongs to the fine cooking tradition of Switzerland's city restaurants. It has long been served in the guild houses of Zurich, which still today offer excellent hospitality.

Serves 4

8 globe artichoke hearts
125 g raw ham, diced
30 g onion, diced
*50 g grated Appenzell
or Emmenthal cheese*
150 ml Madeira wine
125 g ox marrow, soaked
10 g parsley, chopped
juice of 1 lemon
salt

Cook the artichoke hearts in water with salt and lemon juice for about 1 hour. (Use an enamelled pan as artichokes become discoloured when cooked in metal pans.)

Drain the artichokes and place in a buttered, shallow, fireproof dish. Sprinkle with ham, onion, parsley, and the ox marrow. Finally add the wine and cover with grated cheese. Cook in a hot oven (220°C, 425°F, Gas 7) until the top is golden brown.

Serve with steak, and white wine from Zurich.

Rösti: *potatoes and cheese – a simple, satisfying dish*

RÖSTI (URI)
Fried potatoes

This Swiss national dish is usually made with potatoes that have been boiled in their skins the previous day. They are peeled and diced, fried gently in butter, then formed into a pancake and inverted onto a plate with the golden brown crust uppermost. This particular version from Uri, however, is made with raw potatoes and cheese – and sometimes cream is added as well.

Serves 6

1 cup grated Emmenthal or Gruyère cheese *1 cup cream (optional)* *⅓ cup butter* *1¼ lb potatoes, peeled and grated* *salt*	Stir the cheese into the cream (if used). Melt the butter in a large heavy skillet. Sprinkle the grated potato with salt, pile into the pan and fry for about 20 minutes. turning occasionally. Halfway through cooking, add the cheese (or cream and cheese). When the potatoes are tender, turn the *Rösti* onto a warm plate and serve with a fresh salad or crusty bread and coffee.

GLASIERTE RÜBCHEN (SILESIA)
Glazed turnips

During the past hundred years certain vegetables have been sadly neglected in Germany, particularly the rutabaga and the turnip. But here is a delicious old recipe from Silesia for sweetly glazed turnips, eaten with boiled or roast pork.

Serves 6

5 tablespoons butter *1 tablespoon sugar* *1¼ lb turnips, washed and cut in half* *1 quart stock* *4 teaspoons flour* *salt and pepper* *pork spareribs (optional)*	In a large pan melt the butter, add the sugar and stir continuously with a wooden spoon until the mixture becomes a light brown caramel. Add the turnips and brown gently for about 5 minutes. Add enough stock to half cover the vegetables and simmer gently for 15 minutes. Mix the flour to a paste with a little of the remaining stock and add to the sauce to thicken it slightly. Cook for a few minutes more, stirring constantly, and season to taste with salt and pepper. You can make this dish into a complete meal by simmering some pork spareribs to make stock, and adding the meat to the turnips. Serve with parsley, buttered potatoes and a glass of Frankfurt wine.

KARTOFFELSALAT (GERMANY)
Potato salad

Potato salad is prepared differently in every part of Germany. In the south, in Baden-Württemberg and Bavaria, the cooked potatoes are steeped in a dressing of oil, vinegar, sugar, mustard and chopped onion. In the north mayonnaise is added; and in the east the potato salad is mixed with diced dill pickles and quartered hard-cooked eggs. The basic preparation tends to be the same everywhere.

Prepare 1 hour in advance.
Serves 6–8

2 lb firm potatoes *1 cup vinegar* *2 teaspoons sugar* *⅓ cup water* *⅓ cup finely chopped onion* *2 teaspoons mild mustard* *⅓ cup oil* *2 tablespoons mayonnaise (optional)* *1 cup diced dill pickles (optional)* *4 hard-cooked eggs, quartered (optional)*	Boil the potatoes in their skins for 25 minutes, drain and peel off the skins. Meanwhile combine the other ingredients, mixing thoroughly. Cut the potatoes into thin slices, and while they are still warm toss them in the dressing. Leave to stand for at least 1 hour.

The contrasting landscapes of Switzerland

Desserts

KLÖSSE UND BIRNEN (MECKLENBURG)
Dumplings and pears

The former province of Mecklenburg, the region between Berlin and the Baltic, was well known for its fresh fruit and delicious fruit recipes. In fact fruit tarts are often served here as part of the main course with stewed or roast meat. The following recipe, whether served hot or cold, makes an excellent dessert or a light evening meal.

Serves 6–8

The dumplings
½ cup butter
4 eggs
½ teaspoon salt
a pinch of grated nutmeg
3 tablespoons fresh breadcrumbs

Pears
2 lb ripe pears, peeled, cored and halved
2 tablespoons sugar
juice of 1 lemon
2 teaspoons cornstarch

Beat the butter with the eggs until foamy, and season with salt and nutmeg. Add the breadcrumbs, stirring constantly. If the mixture becomes too stiff, add a little water.

Drop tablespoonsful of the mixture into boiling water and cook for about 7 minutes. Remove with a slotted spoon and place in a serving dish.

Simmer the pears in 1½ quarts water with the sugar and lemon juice for 10–15 minutes or until tender. Remove the pears and add them to the dumplings. Thicken the cooking liquid with cornstarch and pour this over the pears and dumplings.

ZITRONENPUDDING (MECKLENBURG)
Lemon pudding

Lemons do not grow in Mecklenburg; but together with raisins and rum they have long been shipped from the Mediterranean into the busy ports of the region – Wismar and Rostock – and now form part of the local diet.

Serves 4

½ cup butter
1 cup flour
1 cup milk
1 vanilla bean
½ cup sugar
5 eggs, separated
juice and grated rind of 2 lemons
a pinch of salt
custard or cherry sauce
chopped almonds

Make a basic white sauce with the butter, flour and milk. Stir with a wooden spoon until the mixture begins to leave the sides of the pan.

Split the vanilla bean lengthwise and scrape the soft black center into the sugar. Add the egg yolks, lemon rind and juice, sugar and salt to the sauce and mix. Beat the egg whites stiffly and fold in.

Butter a baking dish and pour in the mixture. Place the dish in a pan containing water and cook in the oven at 350°F for 1 hour.

Serve the pudding warm with custard or cherry sauce, sprinkled with chopped almonds.

Make cherry sauce by simmering 1 lb pitted cherries very gently until soft and then adding about 1 tablespoon of sugar and 2 teaspoons of cornstarch mixed with water. Cook for a few minutes more, stirring all the time, then leave to cool.

SCHWARZBROTPUDDING (WESTPHALIA)
Black bread pudding

The Westphalians are so enthralled with this dessert that they call it 'the food of the gods'. Perhaps they are exaggerating; but the recipe is very adaptable and can be made with more fruit or sweetener according to taste.

Serves 8

3 eggs, separated
1 cup sugar
1 vanilla bean
½ teaspoon ground cinnamon
4 cups fresh Westphalian black breadcrumbs
butter
½ lb cranberries, stewed with lemon juice
3 squares semisweet chocolate, grated
whipped cream

Cream the egg yolks, sugar, vanilla from the bean and cinnamon together. Beat the egg whites until very stiff and fold into the mixture, then add the breadcrumbs, stirring gently.

Butter a 1½ quart soufflé dish; place a layer of berries on the bottom, about 1 in deep. Then add half the bread mixture, the chocolate, the rest of the berries and finally the rest of the bread mixture. Cover with foil and bake in the oven (350°F) for 50 minutes.

Allow the pudding to cool completely and then decorate with whipped cream

BENTHEIMER MOPPEN (RHINELAND)
Bentheim honey cakes

Bentheim is the birthplace of these sweet, spicy little cakes which are traditionally served at Christmas.

Prepare at least 5 days in advance.

Makes about 50 small cakes

⅔ cup honey
3 tablespoons butter
1 egg
⅓ cup sugar
1 teaspoon ground cinnamon
1 teaspoon ground cloves
3 cups flour, sifted
2 teaspoons baking powder
½ cup chopped almonds

Frosting
1 tablespoon lemon juice
2 cups confectioners' sugar

Melt the honey and butter gently in a pan and allow to cool. Meanwhile beat the egg with the sugar until creamy and add this to the cooled honey mixture together with the spices, flour, baking powder and chopped almonds. Mix well. Leave for 4 days in the refrigerator.

On the fifth day, shape the mixture into small balls the size of hazelnuts. Place on a greased baking sheet well apart and bake in a moderate oven (350°F) for 7–10 minutes. Allow to cool.

Beat the lemon juice gradually into the confectioners' sugar, and add about 1 tablespoon of water to make frosting that will coat a spoon. Frost the cakes and keep for at least 1 day before serving.

SAHNEPLINSEN (SILESIA)
Creamy crêpes

Plinsen is the Silesian word for those thin egg pancakes which the French call *crêpes.* They can be served with either sweet or savory fillings. These sweet ones make a delicious dessert; but as they are very filling they can alternatively constitute an entire evening meal.

Serves 4

¾ cup cornstarch
4 eggs, separated
1 cup sour cream
½ teaspoon salt
sugar
butter
¼ teaspoon ground cinnamon
cranberry, strawberry or black cherry jam
whipped cream (optional)

Mix the cornstarch with 4 teaspoons water. Add the egg yolks, sour cream, salt and 2 teaspoons sugar. Beat the mixture until smooth. Beat the egg whites stiffly and fold into the batter.

Cook 4 crêpes, one at a time, in a heavy buttered skillet until golden brown on both sides. Sprinkle with cinnamon and sugar, spread with jam and, if you wish, decorate with a dollop of whipped cream.

Gathering cherries

BERLINER PFANNKUCHEN (BERLIN)
Plum doughnuts

These deep-fried doughnuts are very popular during the winter months, particularly around New Year. At holiday time they are cooked and sold piping hot at street stalls all over Germany.

Makes about 16 doughnuts

1¼ cakes compressed yeast
1¼ cups lukewarm milk
6 cups flour
¼ cup sugar
2 eggs
1 egg yolk
grated rind of 1 lemon
a pinch of salt
a few drops of vanilla
¼ cup butter, melted
⅔ cup plum jam
oil for deep frying

Dissolve the yeast in half of the lukewarm milk (not too hot or the yeast will be killed). Sift the flour into a mixing bowl, make a well in the center and pour in the yeast mixture. Sprinkle a little of the sugar over the top, place a dish towel over the bowl and leave to rise in a warm place for 15 minutes.

Now add the eggs, the yolk, the rest of the sugar, lemon rind, salt, vanilla and finally the melted butter and the remaining milk. Beat until the mixture forms a manageable dough. Place this on a floured board and roll out to the thickness of a finger. Cut into 3 in circles. Put a spoonful of plum jam in the center of half the circles and place another circle on top. Press the edges down firmly with dampened fingers.

Put the doughnuts in a warm place to rise for 10 minutes. In the meantime, heat the oil in a deep fat fryer. Deep fry the doughnuts until golden brown all over. Sprinkle with sugar while they are still warm.

SEMMELPUDDING (POMERANIA)
Bread pudding

The Pomeranians are considered particularly cautious people. However, through the large port of Stettin the region has gained worldwide contacts, which have had an effect on local cooking and eating habits. The rum, lemon juice and almonds used in this recipe are typically 'foreign' ingredients.

Prepare the dried fruit 24 hours in advance.

Serves 4

4 teaspoons sugar
¾ cup butter
6 eggs, separated
4 cups fresh breadcrumbs
1 cup milk
⅓ cup raisins
⅔ cup currants, both soaked overnight and chopped
1 cup chopped almonds
1 cup rum

Sauce
4 eggs
1 cup white wine
juice of ¼ lemon
1 cup sugar
2 teaspoons cornstarch

Beat the sugar with ⅔ cup butter until creamy, add the egg yolks and continue to beat. Little by little add the breadcrumbs and milk and beat until the breadcrumbs have absorbed the liquid.

Beat the egg whites until stiff, then add them to the mixture with the dried fruit, almonds and finally ¾ cup of rum. Pour the mixture quickly into a buttered soufflé dish, place in a pan containing water and bake in the oven for 1 hour at 350°F.

While the pudding is warm, invert it onto a plate and sprinkle with the remaining rum.

Beat the sauce ingredients vigorously in a double boiler over a low heat. As soon as the foam begins to rise, remove from the heat to prevent the sauce curdling, and continue beating for 1 minute. Pour over the pudding and serve immediately.

BASLER KIRSCHPFANNKUCHEN (BASLE)
Basle cherry soufflé

The city of Basle lies on the border of Switzerland near to Germany and France. Nevertheless its eating habits have remained unchanged and barely affected by outside influences for hundreds of years. Desserts such as this, made with stale bread rolls called *weggli*, are also popular in southern Germany, where the rolls are known as *Wecken*.

Serves 6

¾ cup butter
1 cup sugar
8 eggs, separated
1 cup grated unpeeled almonds or hazelnuts
¼ cup flour, sifted
1¼ tablespoons ground cinnamon
¼ teaspoon baking powder
1 lb bread rolls, soaked in 1¼ cups hot milk and drained
3 tablespoons cookie crumbs
2 lb cherries, pitted
confectioners' sugar

Beat the butter and sugar together in a large bowl until creamy, then gradually add the egg yolks, beating all the time. Stir in the nuts, flour, cinnamon and baking powder, then the softened bread. Fold in the stiffly beaten egg whites, and finally add half the cookie crumbs and the cherries.

Butter a soufflé dish, sprinkle with the remaining cookie crumbs and fill with the cherry mixture. Cook the soufflé in a moderate oven (350°F) for 1 hour. When it is cooked sprinkle the surface with confectioners' sugar, and serve hot or cold.

Plum doughnuts: a sweet winter treat

It is the part of a wise man to feed himself with moderate pleasant food and drink.

Baruch Spinoza (1632–1677)

Windmills, canals and flat green polder land – the essential Dutch landscape

The vast wet forests of the Ardennes camouflage a wealth of game.

The quiet reflection of trees in a canal: here may be found the prized eels of Flanders.

Holland and Belgium are often referred to in a single breath, as if they were really one country which happened to be divided in two. It's true that in the past they have often shared a common fate – they were both dominated by Spain for three hundred years – but they always clung tenaciously to their national characteristics. The contrasts between the two countries become increasingly apparent the more you get to know them; and they are constantly pointed out in the insulting and witty jokes that the Dutch and Belgians tell at one another's expense, in which the Belgians are inevitably shown to be stupid and the Dutch incredibly mean.

The two races certainly have vastly different attitudes to food. The paintings of Pieter Breughel celebrate a positively orgiastic delight in the pleasures of eating and drinking, and this shameless enthusiasm still survives unchanged in Belgium. In the paintings of the Dutch masters of the seventeenth and eighteenth centuries, we see tables heavy with beautiful food and rich drinks, but no people indulging themselves; the overall impression is one of opulence and plenty, but not of sensuality. They say that the Belgians eat for pleasure, while the Dutch eat for necessity. Certainly they both eat very well.

By nature the Dutchman is cautious, thrifty and home-loving. He does not like to behave extravagantly, nor does he want to be considered ostentatious and therefore a snob. He disapproves of spending his hard-earned money on such transitory things as food and drink. The Belgian on the other hand is not the slightest bit bothered by such considerations; he believes that those who have a lot of butter should spread it on thick. When he goes out to dine he won't worry about the cost of a bottle of wine, as long as it is good. His wife will dress up in her best clothes, with all her jewels on show, often looking as if she is posing for one of Rubens' voluptuous portraits. It is no coincidence that the Belgians are the biggest consumers of French champagne, and that they drink about ten times as much as the Dutch, although the price is the same in both countries.

Brussels has more restaurants, per head of population, than Paris; and when the Belgians are not eating out, they like to have an equally luxurious meal at home. Perhaps a plump and respectable lady cook will be employed for the evening, or they may go out to buy food from the *traiteurs* – shops where you can buy the most exquisite ready-prepared food: plates of salmon, dressed crab, stuffed duckling, sauces and cakes and pies. On Saturdays, when people have been out shopping all day and are too tired to cook, these shops are always overflowing with eager customers.

Allowing for the different mentality of these two races it is not surprising that very different cooking traditions have developed in Holland and Belgium, even though they make use of many of the same raw materials.

The Dutch cuisine tends to be quite simple; it is said that the Dutch are more concerned with quantity than with quality,

Holland and Belgium

The exposed landscape of Holland – only the underwear has changed since the nineteenth century.

and certainly their most popular traditional recipes are all very substantial. This is understandable: the country has an extremely exposed landscape and the people have always used a lot of their energy fighting against the elements. As children they learn to bicycle along open roads on the polder land reclaimed from the sea by dikes, and not surprisingly they take with them thick slices of bread filled with huge pieces of local cheese – cycling into the wind is hungry work!

Traditional Dutch cooking is packed with calories, and comes into its own with heart-warming winter dishes. The most typical recipe is the *stamppot*, a hotchpotch of vegetables: kale, sliced green beans, or endive are mashed with potatoes to make a stiff solid mixture, served with fat smoked sausages on the top. (The Dutch have an expression for tough guys which means literally 'men brought up on *stamppot*'.)

The Dutch soil is ideal for growing vegetables, and the people eat quantities of them in both winter and summer. Not long ago every well-to-do family would serve two vegetables with the meat course; and when Dutch children ask their mother, 'what are we having to eat today?' she will often just tell them what vegetables she is going to cook.

The Dutchman has a sweet tooth. He drinks medium sweet sherry. He will eat his fried eel, game, chicken and many meat dishes accompanied by a sweet fruit sauce, and will often want to add sweet sauces to such fashionable dishes as

fondue bourguignonne, curry and pâté. Even the little savory snacks which are served along with an aperitif are often garnished with a square of pineapple or candied ginger. Every city in Holland has its traditional pastries: Amsterdam *korstjes* (honey crusties), *Arnhemse meisjes* ('Arnhem girls'), Weesp *moppen* (cookies), Gouda *stroopwafels* (syrup waffles), and Utrecht *sprits* (shortcake), to name but a few.

The Dutch have a slightly prudish attitude towards food. They are cautious in their use of herbs, consider garlic somewhat anti-social, and shy away from all unusual fish and meat. Variety meats such as brains, liver, kidneys and heart have never been popular, and even today only sweetbreads appear regularly on restaurant menus, while liver and tongue might be eaten occasionally at home. The same is true of fish. The Dutch are fond of haddock, sole, cod and herring, but more adventurous they are not. Eels are bought ready-smoked and live ones on sale in fish markets are considered rather awful. As for shellfish, they have never been popular with the Dutch, except in the province of Zeeland; most of the delicious mussels and oysters which are caught there are exported directly to Belgium and France. More unusual sea creatures like ray, sea eels, red mullet, and even crabs are despised, although the humble shrimp has always found grace.

Although Dutch cooking is traditionally plain, simple and homely, the exotic influence of the colonies is becoming increasingly evident even in the most conventional house-

Pickled herrings and chopped onions are the street food of Holland

and linguistic divisions of the country. The north is Flemish-speaking and the south French-speaking, with Brussels (where everyone is bi-lingual) marking the dividing line. The Flemish language is much older than Dutch; it is more melodious, and filled with many archaic and literary words which to a Dutchman sound very odd. In the south, in the Ardennes region, the people speak a French dialect, and the whole area is very strongly influenced by France, especially in all culinary matters.

The southern Ardennes region has vast sombre woods and a climate which tends towards fog and rain; but its superb cuisine, which has made the Ardennes world-famous, fully compensates for the bleakness of the landscape. Here small wild trout, found practically nowhere else in Europe, abound in the rivers; and in the hunting season wild boar, deer, and even the increasingly rare partridge can be found. The local cooks are noted for their exquisite sauces flavored with herbs, cream and wine in which they dress these succulent fish and meats. The inhabitants of the Ardennes come from old Celtic stock and have been famous since Roman times for their delicious home-cured ham, which they smoke over fires of juniper wood. The meat is so tender and so delicately flavored that it can be eaten in thick slices. Even the smallest butcher's in the Ardennes will have these hams hanging up, wrapped in the traditional red and white checked cotton cloths and prepared by the butcher himself.

The Belgians are known as some of the best beer brewers in the world. There are breweries in small villages, in old abbeys, and even in the center of Brussels. Many of them still use the traditional methods of brewing with live yeast, so each beer has its own distinctive taste and character. Just like wine it is matured in wooden barrels, and then in carefully corked bottles. There is nothing as delicious as Flemish Burgundy, accompanied by brown peasant bread and slices of Ardennes ham. It is not surprising that the Belgians have always used this beer in their cooking, and it serves the same inspiring role as wine in so many French recipes.

The green and fruitful province of Flanders, in the north of Belgium, shares with Holland the windy grey North Sea coast and the vast expanses of flat polder land. Flanders was a prosperous seafaring and merchant power in the thirteenth and fourteenth centuries, and it is still dotted with picturesque medieval towns with steep-gabled roofs and little market squares. This is dairy farming country, rich in high quality meat and delicious butter. Fat eels abound in the ditches and canals, and the northern cooks prepare them in all sorts of ways. They know how to make the most of everything that comes from the sea, and even the smallest shellfish, little snails and tiny fishes are incorporated in their recipes. Mussels are a national dish; and so too are shrimp, which are still sometimes caught in the medieval way by men who ride out into the breakers on the backs of Belgian horses.

The following recipes illustrate the rich sensual flavors of Belgian dishes and show how Dutch cooking combines relatively plain recipes with the occasional somewhat startling use of an unlikely spice. No longer can the Belgians really insult the Dutch so confidently about the plainness of their cuisine, nor can the Dutch mock the Belgians for their love of strange, rich flavors.

holds. In the seventeenth century the riches of the Indonesian archipelago poured into Holland, and Amsterdam became the wealthiest and most lively city in Europe. Then a forest of masts bobbed up and down in the harbor, and the tall stately warehouses were filled with the rich aroma of pepper, nutmeg, cinnamon and cloves. At first the kitchen maids of the rich merchants and then the ordinary Dutch people experimented with these exotic spices, and learned to use them to enliven their dishes. Cinnamon, nutmeg and cloves went into pastries, cakes and stewed fruits; nutmeg was added to nearly all vegetables from lima beans to endive; and cloves gave a pungency to stewed meat and such vegetables as red cabbage; while lots of coarsely ground pepper went into the *stamppot* and other heavy dishes.

When respectable Dutch families went to settle in the Dutch colony of Indonesia throughout the seventeenth century, Indonesian methods of cooking came into fashion. Later the repatriated families stayed true to their *rijsttafel* (mixed rice dish), and now since the war, when people no longer have cooks to prepare such complex dishes for them, there is a new vogue of eating out in Indonesian restaurants. At home people make their own simple versions of the Indonesian *nasi goreng*, or the Chinese-Indonesian *bami*, and this has become so popular that many families who have no contact at all with Indonesia still have a weekly *nasi goreng* day. Indeed many modern Dutch housewives are more at home with Indonesian spices than the traditional European herbs.

In contrast to the plain, homely cooking of old Holland, Belgian cuisine is far more varied, reflecting the geographical

Soups and eggs

OSSESTAARTSOEP (DRENTHE)
Oxtail soup

This winter soup is considered a complete meal in itself. It comes from the province of Drenthe in the east of Holland and is traditionally flavored with the root of Hamburg parsley; a bunch of parsley may be used as a substitute.

Serves 6

2 oxtails, chopped
1 piece of bacon rind
1 carrot, sliced
bay leaf
1 parsley root
1 onion, chopped
1 leek, chopped
1 celery stalk, chopped
2 large potatoes, peeled and chopped
1 cup barley
a drop of vinegar
salt and pepper
parsley to garnish
2 slices of bread without crusts
butter

Trim excess fat from the oxtail pieces, place them with the bacon rind, carrot, bay leaf and parsley root in a roasting pan and bake in a moderate oven (350°F) for 15 minutes. Transfer to a large saucepan, add at least 2 quarts of water and simmer for 4–5 hours.

Strain. Remove the meat from the bone and return to the strained stock. Add the onion, leek, celery, potatoes and the barley, and simmer for another 30 minutes or until the vegetables are tender. Add a drop of vinegar for flavoring, season to taste and sprinkle with parsley. Serve with strips of bread fried in butter.

ERWTENSOEP (HOLLAND)
Pea soup

This is Holland's favorite national dish. In winter you can get a cup of pea soup absolutely anywhere in a Dutch town – in restaurants, cafés, railroad stations, factory canteens. And in the country, when the canals are frozen over and people make long trips from village to village on skates, they will often stop on the way for a cup of steaming hot soup served at open-air stalls. Pea soup was a mainstay of army and navy rations; in fact the Dutch navy used to have a pea soup day once a week, even when it was serving in the tropics. The navy-style soup was so thick you could stand a spoon up in it.

Pea soup should be served in an old-fashioned soup tureen.

Prepare peas several hours in advance.
Serves 6

2 cups split peas, soaked
1 pig's foot
¼ lb salt pork
salt
4 potatoes
4 leeks
1 celeriac or celery root
1 head of celery
1 smoked sausage
black rye bread
parsley
pepper

Put the soaked split peas in a pan with 3 quarts of water and add the pig's foot, the pork and some salt. Simmer for 2 hours, until the peas are tender.

Add the thinly sliced vegetables and the sausage and cook for a further 30 minutes. Use a wooden spoon to mash the peas. Do be careful at this stage not to burn the bottom of the pan!

Remove the pig's foot, sausage and pork, and pour the soup into a tureen. Slice the sausage and meat from the foot and serve separately. Cut the pork into slices and serve on the rye bread.

Garnish the soup with chopped parsley and a generous amount of coarsely ground black pepper.

SOUPE AU LARD (ARDENNES)
Bacon soup

This soup–stew is very popular in the autumn and winter in the cold, bleak Ardennes region of Belgium. The local bacon and ham are smoked over juniper wood, which gives them a wonderful flavor.

Serves 8

1 lb Canadian bacon, in one piece
2 bay leaves
a sprig of thyme
2 teaspoons peppercorns
4 potatoes, chopped
2 or 3 celery stalks, chopped
2 leeks, chopped
3 small turnips, chopped
¼ head of green cabbage, chopped
1 large carrot, chopped

Place the bacon in a saucepan with the herbs and peppercorns and simmer gently in 2 quarts of water for at least 1 hour.

Remove the bacon and strain the stock. Return the bacon and stock to the saucepan with the vegetables, and simmer together for another 30–35 minutes.

Remove the bacon. Cut off and discard the fat, and cut the lean meat into cubes. Return these to the soup and serve immediately.

KERVELSOEP (FLANDERS)
Chervil soup

This soup, which came originally from Flanders, is now almost the national soup of Belgium, and with good reason, for it brings out the delicate flavor of chervil.

Serves 6

1 small onion, sliced
1 leek, sliced
1 potato, diced
1 tablespoon butter
1½ quarts stock
¼ cup potato flour
2 tablespoons milk
¾ cup finely chopped chervil
salt and pepper

Fry the onion, leek and potato gently in the butter for 15 minutes, then add the stock and simmer for about 1 hour until soft.

Blend to a purée and return to the pan over a low heat. Mix the potato flour with a little milk, and use this to thicken the soup.

Just before serving add the finely chopped chervil, and salt and pepper to taste.

An example of the Dutch fondness for elaborately decorated homes

Kruudmoes: *a spring dish of fresh herbs that combines sweet and savory tastes to play upon the senses*

OSTENDSE VISSOEP (BELGIUM)
Ostend fish soup

Ostend has a marvelous fishmarket, and the town is famous for its shrimp and its fish dishes. Traditionally the stock for this soup was made from shrimp shells.

Serves 6

Fish stock
fish trimmings
salt and pepper
parsley
1 celery stalk, chopped
1 carrot
1 slice of lemon

6 tablespoons butter
1 celery stalk, chopped
3 carrots, chopped
1 leek, chopped
1 clove of garlic
thyme
bay leaf
2 tablespoons tomato purée
1 whiting, filleted
1 sole, filleted
¼ cup rice flour
¼ cup cream
½ lb shelled shrimp
¼ cup brandy
1 sprig of parsley

Make stock out of the fish heads and bones, salt and pepper, a little parsley, 1 stalk of celery, 1 carrot and the slice of lemon, all simmered in 1½ quarts of water for 1 hour. Strain the stock.

Melt the butter and sauté the rest of the vegetables, together with the garlic, thyme and bay leaf. Add this to the fish stock with the tomato purée and the pieces of fish. Cook until the fish is tender, about 30 minutes.

To thicken the soup, mix the rice flour with the cream, and stir this in. Just before serving add the shrimp and the brandy, and garnish with parsley.

KRUUDMOES (GELDERLAND)
Herb mash

This is a very old peasant recipe from the east of Holland. It was traditionally eaten in early spring when the first green shoots of vegetables and herbs appeared in the gardens. After a long winter with nothing but salted vegetables and dried beans and peas the people longed for the taste of fresh vegetables and herbs.

Serves 6

1 cup barley
¼ lb salt pork
¼ lb Gelder or Frankfurter sausage
4–5 tablespoons finely chopped green herbs (chervil, chives, celery, sorrel)
1 cup raisins
1 quart buttermilk
apple syrup or molasses

Simmer the barley in 1 quart of water for 1½ hours.

Place the piece of pork and the sausage in a large pan with 1 quart of water. Bring to a boil and simmer for 30 minutes. Add the barley and simmer for 15 minutes. Add the herbs and raisins and simmer for another 15 minutes. All the water should be absorbed or evaporated.

Remove the pan from the heat and stir in the buttermilk. This dish can be eaten either cold or lukewarm and is traditionally served with a spoonful of thick, dark apple syrup added to each bowl.

A dried-fish stall in Ostend c. 1900

GROENTESOEP (HOLLAND)
Vegetable soup

In Holland this soup was traditionally served for Sunday lunch. The broth would be left to simmer gently while the family went to church, and when they got back everybody drank a cup of coffee while the vegetables were cooked. This is a summer version of the soup; in winter you can use a carrot, a leek, a slice of celeriac or celery root and sprouts.

Serves 4

¼ lb stewing beef, cut in pieces
salt and pepper
peppercorns
bay leaf
a few celery stalks
parsley sprigs
5 small carrots
1 young leek
1 piece of cauliflower
1 tablespoon dried breadcrumbs, soaked in 2 tablespoons milk
¼ lb ground beef
nutmeg
8 green beans
a few tablespoons of fresh peas
¼ cup vermicelli
1 tablespoon chopped parsley
1 tablespoon chopped chervil

Make a stock by simmering the stewing beef, salt, peppercorns, bay leaf, celery and parsley in at least 1½ quarts of water for 2 hours. Strain the stock and replace the meat.

Clean and chop the vegetables. Mix together the breadcrumbs, ground beef, pepper, salt, and nutmeg, and make into small balls. Add these meat balls, all of the vegetables and the vermicelli to the stock, and simmer for 20–35 minutes. Garnish with chopped parsley and chervil, and serve.

KAMPER STEUR (OVERIJSSEL)
Sturgeon from Kampen

The beautiful old Hansa town of Kampen at the mouth of the river IJssel is famous for its funny stories. And here is how this fishless dish got its name: up until the seventeenth century sturgeon could be caught in the river IJssel, and the people of Kampen feasted on sturgeon and fresh caviar. But the fish began to die out, until there was only one left. The people of Kampen were so fond of their sturgeon that they hung a little silver bell around his neck, to warn the fishermen not to catch him. And when he finally died of old age the people named this egg dish after the lost sturgeon of Kampen.

Serves 4

4 eggs
2 tablespoons butter
¼ cup flour
1¼ cups stock
2 teaspoons prepared mustard
parsley

Hard cook the eggs, shell and cut them in half lengthwise. Place in a warm dish.

Make a roux with the butter and flour, and stir in the stock to make a thick, creamy sauce. Add the mustard. Pour the sauce over the eggs and garnish with parsley.

This simplest of egg dishes, kamper steur, *is named after the most highly prized of fish, the sturgeon.*

WATERZOOI (GHENT)
Waterzooi

This dish originated in the proud and rebellious town of Ghent, where it is still a specialty served in the best restaurants. The Emperor Charles V (1500–1558), who was born in Ghent, loved this dish; he spent the last years of his life in a Spanish monastery where, it is said, he often wept with longing for his *waterzooi*.

The dish falls somewhere between a soup and a stew, and is flavored with traditional 'pot herbs' – a handful or two of finely chopped carrot, onion, leek, celery and parsley.

Serves 8

2 lb beef shin bones
finely chopped pot herbs (carrots, onion, leek, celery and parsley)
thyme
bay leaf
salt and pepper
1 good-sized chicken
7 tablespoons butter
6 tablespoons flour
6 leeks, chopped
2 large onions, chopped
2 large carrots, sliced
1 celery stalk, chopped
4 egg yolks
1 cup cream
chopped parsley
chopped chervil

Make a stock by simmering the bones in 3 quarts of water with the pot herbs, thyme, bay leaf, salt and pepper. Strain the stock and cook the chicken in it until tender.

Make a roux with 3 tablespoons butter and the flour, and stir in 2 quarts stock. Cook the vegetables gently in the remaining butter. Beat the egg yolks with cream, add a little of the thickened stock, and then gradually add this to the rest of the stock.

Divide the cooked chicken into pieces, place them in a deep dish, arrange the vegetables around them and pour the sauce over the top. Sprinkle with parsley and chervil, and serve with bread and butter.

Paling in't groen: *eel prepared in the grand manner – laid on glass and coated with a delicate green sauce*

ish

VLAAMSE KABELJAUW (FLANDERS)
Flemish cod

This deliciously simple recipe from the Flemish coast must be prepared with very fresh fish. Belgian connoisseurs buy their cod from the little town of Nieuwpoort.

Serves 4

4 cod fillets
salt and pepper
lemon juice
2 onions, cut into fine rings
¼ cup butter
¾ cup white wine
parsley

Sprinkle the cod with salt and pepper and some lemon juice.

Fry the onion rings in the butter until they are golden brown. Place the fillets of fish in a liberally buttered ovenproof dish and the onions on top of them. Pour on the wine, cover and bake in a moderate oven (350°F) for 30 minutes. (If the dish has no lid then cover it with foil to prevent the fish drying out.)

Serve with a garnish of parsley.

PALING IN'T GROEN (FLANDERS)
Eel in the green

A dish from the Flemish countryside, this used to be a specialty of the garden restaurants along the river Schelde, just outside Antwerp. On fine summer evenings people would eat *paling in't groen* under the old chestnut trees and watch the ships pass by.

Serves 6

2 lb eel, cut in pieces
salt and pepper
thyme
2 tablespoons butter
¼ cup finely chopped spinach
¼ cup finely chopped sorrel
2 tablespoons chopped parsley
1 tablespoon chopped burnet
1 sprig of tarragon, chopped
1 tablespoon chopped chervil
1 pint white wine
4 egg yolks
lemon juice

Rub the eel pieces with salt, pepper and thyme. Melt the butter in a large heavy pan and add the spinach, sorrel, parsley, burnet, tarragon and chervil, with the pieces of eel on top. Add the wine and bring to a boil. Simmer for 10 minutes on a very low flame.

Beat the egg yolks, add a little of the wine liquid and return this to the rest. Stir until it thickens. (Be careful not to let it boil, or it will curdle.)

Arrange the pieces of eel on a glass serving dish. Add a little lemon juice to the sauce and pour this over the eel. Serve chilled, with brown bread and butter.

PALING IN BIERSAUS (FLANDERS)
Eels in beer sauce

This extremely rich dish is often served on the popular feast days which are still part of the Flemish way of life. It makes use of the wonderful eels – as thick as a child's arm, as they say – which abound in the ditches of the polder land.

Ideally, the beer for this recipe should be the famous *Gueuzelambiek*, a dark heavy beer with a rich and creamy flavor.

Serves 4–6

¼ lb fat bacon, cubed
¼ cup butter
12 small onions, whole
¼ lb small mushrooms, whole (or large ones, sliced)
1 clove of garlic, crushed
2 lb eel, cut in pieces
salt and pepper
1 cup brown beer
2 bay leaves
¼ cup cream
¼ cup flour

Melt down the bacon cubes in half the butter and fry the small onions, the mushrooms and the garlic until tender.

Remove the onions, garlic and mushrooms. Dip the pieces of eel in flour, season with salt and pepper and fry them in the same butter. As soon as they brown, pour the beer over them, together with about ½ cup water and the bay leaves. Simmer gently for about 20 minutes or until the eel is tender. Add the onions, mushrooms and cream.

Mix the rest of the butter to a paste with the flour, and add it little by little to the cooking liquid until it makes a thick sauce.

Serve immediately with creamed potatoes or

Flemish fishermen returning home across the sand dunes

NASI GORENG (DUTCH INDONESIA)
Indonesian rice dish

This dish comes from Indonesia where it was a popular break-fast dish, using up leftover rice and meat. It was also called 'the pyjama dish', because it was so informal. People returning from the colonies introduced it to Holland where it has become so popular that many families now have a *nasi goreng* day at least once a week, and Indonesian restaurants and stores sell it cold and ready-prepared in plastic bags.

Sambal, a hot paste made with red chili pepper, garlic and fried onions, is served with it and can be bought in all Dutch grocery stores. *Nasi goreng* is often also served with *kroepoek*, large crispy wafers made out of dried shrimp fried in hot fat.

Serves 4

2 cups long-grain rice
salt
¼ cup oil
1 large onion, or
 1 medium onion and
 1 shallot, finely chopped
2 cloves of garlic, chopped
1–2 teaspoons sambal
1 teaspoon powdered
 cumin
1 teaspoon ground
 coriander
¼ lb lean meat, finely
 chopped
¼ lb shelled shrimp
4 eggs

Simmer the rice with salt until the grains are dry and separate. Heat the oil and fry the onion and garlic together with the *sambal*, cumin and coriander until the onion is a light golden color.

Remove from the pan and fry the meat very quickly in the same oil. Add the rice and fry until it is golden. Add the onion and then the shrimp, and mix well together. Meanwhile, fry the eggs in a separate pan.

Transfer the *nasi goreng* to a large warm dish and serve with the fried eggs on top. In Holland the *sambal* jar is put on the table and each person helps himself to as much as he can stand.

TRUITE A L'ARDENNAISE (ARDENNES)
Trout Ardennes style

Small wild trout, still plentiful in the rivers of the Ardennes, are delicious served with this wine and herb sauce that reveals the French influence on the cooking of this region.

Serves 4

4 trout
salt
1¼ cups water
1¼ cups white wine
1 carrot, chopped
1 shallot, chopped
thyme
bay leaf
2 cloves
crushed peppercorns
3 tablespoons butter
3 tablespoons flour
1 tablespoon chopped
 parsley
a few sprigs of parsley

Rub the trout with salt. Bring the water and wine, carrot, shallot, herbs and spices to a boil in a large heavy pan. Put in the trout, bring back to a boil, cover and simmer on a very low heat for 10 minutes (rainbow trout need longer).

Remove the fish and keep warm. Strain the liquid and reduce by boiling to half the amount. Combine butter, flour and chopped parsley, and thicken the liquid by stirring in this mixture a little at a time.

Serve with new potatoes, butter and parsley sprigs, and Luxembourg Moselle wine.

MARINE STOKVIS (OVERIJSSEL)
Dried salt cod with mustard sauce

Salt cod was the traditional diet of the Dutch navy, served every Friday on plain white china.

Prepare the cod 24 hours in advance
Serves 4

1 lb dried salt cod
1 cup rice
2 lb potatoes
4 onions, sliced
butter
4 egg yolks
dill pickles

Mustard sauce
3 tablespoons butter
5 tablespoons flour
1 pint fish stock
1–2 teaspoons prepared
 mustard

Soak the cod in cold water for 24 hours, changing the water 3 times. Remove the skin and bones. Cut the fish into strips, roll these up and tie them with string. Boil in a large pan with plenty of water for 45–90 minutes, depending on the quality of the fish.

Meanwhile, cook the rice and the potatoes. Cook the onions in butter until they are transparent.

To make the mustard sauce melt the butter, stir in the flour, add the stock gradually, then the mustard.

Serve each part of the meal on a separate dish: the salt cod rolls, the onions, potatoes, rice and mustard sauce: and place a glass with an egg yolk in it next to each person's plate.

The traditional way of eating this dish is as follows: tip the egg yolk on to your plate. Add the potatoes and mash them together. Add the fish, onions, rice, and dilute with a little cod water. Finally add the mustard sauce and a few dill pickles.

Maid with a Milk Jug *c. 1660: Vermeer loved to portray the simple daily activities of his people.*

M*eat, game and vegetables*

GENTSE HUTSPOT (GHENT)
Ghent hotpot

This is a traditional autumn or winter dish straight out of Breughel's time. It probably derives from the Spanish *olla podrida*, introduced to Belgium by Spanish soldiers in the sixteenth century. It is usually cooked in large quantities and the ingredients can vary according to taste and the availability of produce.

Serves 10–12

1 lb breast of lamb, boned
1 lb ribs of beef
salt and pepper
2 pig's feet
¼ lb Canadian bacon
1 bouquet garni of parsley, thyme and bay
1 shallot (optional)
2 lb large carrots, cut into chunks
2 lb leeks, cut into large pieces
8 white turnips
8 small onions, whole
½ head of white cabbage
2 lb potatoes, quartered
8 small pork sausages
chopped parsley

Rub the meats with salt and pepper. Place the lamb, beef, feet and bacon in a saucepan. Cover with water, bring gently to a boil, skim, and simmer for about 1–1½ hours, until tender.

Add the bouquet garni and shallot, if used, then the vegetables, cut up in large pieces, and the sausages. Simmer for about 1 hour or until the vegetables are tender. Skim again if necessary.

Strain off the stock. Place the meats in the center of a large dish and surround with the vegetables. Sprinkle with parsley and pour over some of the stock. To be authentic make sure you have Belgian or German mustard on the table.

Gentse hutspot: *basic ingredients for a feast worthy of Breughel's* Peasant Wedding *(c. 1567)*

FILET DE PORC A L'ESCABÈCHE (HAINAUT)
Pork tenderloin à l'escabèche

This recipe became popular in Belgium during the Spanish occupation in the sixteenth century. Over the years it has become somewhat more sophisticated than the Spanish *escabeche*.

Prepare this dish 24 hours in advance.
Serves 4

Marinade
¼ cup white wine
¼ cup vinegar
1 clove of garlic, whole
a few juniper berries
a sprig of thyme
a sprig of tarragon,
 finely chopped
bay leaf

2 lb pork tenderloin
salt and pepper
1 lb tomatoes, skinned,
 seeded and chopped
1 carrot, chopped
1 large onion, chopped
1 celery stalk, chopped
1 red pepper, chopped
¼ cup oil
a few sprigs of tarragon
2 cloves of garlic
6 tablespoons butter
parsley
1 lemon, sliced

Rub the meat with salt and pepper and leave in a bowl with the marinade ingredients for 24 hours. Drain.

Cook the vegetables gently in the oil with a little chopped tarragon and 2 crushed cloves of garlic. Add the marinade and simmer gently for about 30 minutes.

Fry the meat quickly on all sides in hot butter. Add the cooked vegetables with their liquid (if you wish you can remove the bay leaf, the juniper berries and the whole clove of garlic).

Cook the meat slowly until it is tender, about 1 hour. Then place the meat in a deep dish, skim the fat off the liquid and pour this over the meat.

Allow to cool. Cut the meat into slices and serve cold with the sauce, garnished with chopped parsley and slices of lemon.

In Friesland, where water forms natural boundaries, even pigs must travel by boat.

LEIDSE HUTSPOT (HOLLAND)
Leyden hotpot

In 1584 the city of Leyden was besieged by the Spaniards for many months and by the autumn the people were starving. At last the Prince of Orange ordered that the dikes around the city should be broken. During the night of October 3 the Spaniards fled from the rising waters and by dawn their camp was empty. One courageous boy went out of the city gate to look at the camp, and on a dying fire he found an enormous pot of delicious orange-colored stew. He took the pot back to his starving family. From that day onwards the people of Leyden have eaten hotpot on October 3 to celebrate their salvation. However, the potatoes included in this recipe are certainly not authentic, since potatoes were still unknown in Holland in the sixteenth century. The original dish was probably prepared with white beans.

Serves 4

1 lb flank steak
2 onions, chopped
1¼ lb carrots, sliced
2 lb potatoes, diced
salt and pepper

Bring 1 quart of water to a boil. Put in the meat and simmer for 1½ hours, until nearly tender. Add the onions, carrots, potatoes and salt, and cook for another 30–45 minutes until all the ingredients are tender and most of the liquid has evaporated. Add more salt if necessary, and a generous amount of pepper. Serve with the meat sliced on top of the vegetables.

HETE BLIKSEM (DRENTHE)
Hot lightning

Variations of this traditional winter dish can be found as far away as Silesia, in modern Poland. The Germans in Westphalia also cook a similar dish called 'Heaven and Earth', and here the local dialect is close to Dutch.

Serves 8

2 lb cooking apples
2 lb eating apples
4 lb potatoes, chopped
salt
ground cloves
¾ lb blood sausage, cut
 in thick slices
butter

Peel and core the apples and cut them into pieces. Simmer the cooking apples in a little water in a heavy pan for about 20 minutes. Add the potatoes and eating apples, and cook them all together for about 30 minutes or until they are soft. Mash them with salt and ground cloves.

Fry the slices of blood sausage in butter (very fat sausage needs no butter). Stir the fat into the mashed potatoes and apples, and arrange the slices of sausage on top to serve.

VLAAMSE KARBONADEN (FLANDERS)
Flemish chops

This famous Belgian recipe probably dates from the early Middles Ages, when bread was still used to thicken sauces. Flour was not used for thickening until the sixteenth century.

The name of the dish is a little confusing because it doesn't use chops, but brisket of beef.

Serves 4

¼ cup beef drippings	Heat the drippings in a large pan with a lid and fry the brisket until it browns all over. Remove the meat and fry the onions in the same fat until they change color. Sprinkle with flour and cook for a few minutes. Add the beer, stirring all the time, and when it forms a froth add the meat, herbs, sugar, vinegar, salt and pepper. Cover the pan and simmer for about 1½ hours. Spread mustard on both sides of the bread and add this to the pan. If necessary add a little more water, and leave to simmer for another hour, during which time the bread will thicken the sauce. Serve with boiled potatoes and a simple boiled vegetable, such as cabbage or carrots.

1 lb brisket of beef, cut into pieces
3 onions, sliced
1 tablespoon flour
1 pint dark beer
bay leaf
thyme
parsley root or leaves
1 tablespoon sugar
2 tablespoons vinegar
salt and pepper
mustard
1 thick slice of brown bread without crusts

RAGOUT DE MOUTON A L'ARDENNAISE (ARDENNES)
Ardennes lamb stew

This is a lot of meat to cook for just four people, but whatever is left over is delicious to eat on the following day, especially when served cold with Ardennes brown bread and mustard, and, of course, the good brown ale brewed in the local abbeys.

Serves 4

2 lb boned shoulder of lamb
2 cloves of garlic
2 tablespoons butter
2 large carrots, cut into strips
2 turnips, cut in half
1 large onion, cut into rings
¼ head of green cabbage, finely chopped
1 pint white wine
1 pint stock
2 lb potatoes, quartered
salt and pepper

Tie the meat into shape with string. Stick 4 half cloves of garlic into it. Melt the butter and lightly brown the meat on all sides.

Lower the heat and add the carrots, turnips, onion and cabbage. Heat the wine and stock together and pour over the meat and vegetables. Bring to a boil and leave to simmer for 30 minutes. Add the potatoes and simmer for another 30 minutes.

Remove the meat from the pan and cut it into thick slices. Arrange these on a large serving dish with the vegetables around them, and keep hot.

Boil the broth until it is reduced to a thick sauce, and if necessary thicken with a little butter mixed to a paste with flour. Season to taste. Pour some sauce over the lamb and serve the rest separately.

ROGNONS A LA LIÉGEOISE (ARDENNES)
Liège kidneys

This classic dish comes from the town of Liège in the east of Belgium. Juniper berries grow wild in the moorland region of the Ardennes near Liège, and they give this recipe its distinctive flavor.

Traditionally the kidneys are prepared and served in a flameproof earthenware dish.

Serves 4

2 slices of fat bacon
butter for frying
2 calf kidneys with some of the fat
salt and pepper
2 lb small new potatoes
12 juniper berries, crushed
1 tablespoon brandy

Melt down the bacon in the butter. Remove the bacon and fry the kidneys quickly on both sides. Season with salt and pepper, cover and cook slowly on a low heat for 20 minutes.

Meanwhile parboil the potatoes, then fry in butter until crisp and golden.

Add the juniper berries to the kidneys and continue cooking until the meat is tender. Then add the brandy and the potatoes.

Enter any one of the
herbalist stores in
Amsterdam and your
senses are assailed by the
pungent aromas of the
east.

VLAAMS KONIJN MET PRUIMEN (FLANDERS)
Flemish rabbit with prunes

In Flanders this is a very popular holiday dish. The recipe
must be very old, since this combination of sweet and sour
flavors was most popular during the Middle Ages.

Prepare the rabbit and the prunes 24 hours in advance.
Serves 4

Marinade
¼ cup wine vinegar
¼ cup water
bay leaf
a sprig of thyme
2 cloves of garlic,
  crushed
6 peppercorns
parsley

1 young rabbit
1 leek, chopped
1 carrot, chopped
flour
6 tablespoons butter
1 pint red wine
a sprig of thyme
bay leaf
1 lb prunes, soaked
  overnight
2 tablespoons redcurrant
  jelly

Cut up the rabbit and place it with the leek and
carrot and marinade ingredients in a bowl. Leave
for 24 hours, turning the meat occasionally.

Remove the meat from the marinade and dry thoroughly. Coat lightly with flour and fry quickly in
hot butter. Strain the marinade and warm it slightly.
Add a dash of this to the rabbit with the red wine.
Bring gently to a boil, then add another sprig of
thyme and another bay leaf, cover and simmer for
1 hour.

Add the soaked prunes and simmer for another
30 minutes or until the meat is tender.

Remove the rabbit pieces and keep hot in a serving
dish. Boil the sauce to reduce it slightly, then add the
redcurrant jelly. Pour over the rabbit to serve.

HAZEPEPER (DRENTHE)
Hare pepper pot

This was often referred to as 'the men's dish' because it was
prepared by the men who hunted hares. The big hares that
live on the Dutch heathland eat a lot of heather, which gives
their flesh a particularly spicy flavor.

Prepare 24 hours in advance.
Serves 6

1 hare
1 pint red wine
1 tablespoon vinegar
peppercorns
thyme
bay leaf
1 tablespoon diced lean
  bacon
6 tablespoons butter
1 onion, chopped
1 carrot, sliced
¼ cup flour
10 cocktail onions
the hare's liver, chopped
salt
chopped parsley

Cut the hare into pieces (keeping the liver separate)
and put into a marinade of the wine, vinegar, plenty
of crushed peppercorns and all the herbs. Leave for
24 hours, then remove the hare pieces, dry them and
coat them in flour.

Fry the bacon cubes in ¼ cup butter, add the pieces
of hare and fry quickly all over. Add the strained
marinade, chopped onions and carrot, and simmer
for about 1½ hours. Remove the meat and keep
warm in a deep dish.

To make the sauce, melt the remaining butter
over a low heat, stir in the flour and cook until light
brown. Stir in the liquid that the hare was cooked
in, together with the bacon and the cocktail onions,
and allow to thicken. Finally add the liver and a few
more crushed peppercorns. Season to taste with
salt. Pour the sauce over the hare and garnish with
parsley. Serve with mashed potatoes, red cabbage
and apple sauce.

left A Street in Delft, *Vermeer c. 1660*

Holland and Belgium

A plentiful harvest of wheat gives evidence of the natural richness of Dutch soil.

KONIJN MET STROOP (LIMBURG)
Rabbit with apple syrup

This Sunday dish was traditionally left simmering in the pot while the family went to church. Apple syrup is a favorite ingredient in Dutch cooking, but if you cannot buy it you could substitute maple syrup, simmered for fifteen minutes with half a cooking apple.

Prepare this dish 3 days in advance.
Serves 4–6

1 large rabbit
3 bay leaves
3 cloves
1 onion, chopped
3 tablespoons vinegar
⅓ bottle white wine
⅓ cup butter
salt and pepper
⅓ cup apple syrup
10 cocktail onions

Cut the rabbit into pieces and place in a bowl with a marinade made of bay leaves, cloves, chopped onion, vinegar and just enough white wine to cover. Leave for 3 days.

Remove the meat, reserving the marinade. Drain, pat dry and brown in hot butter. Season with salt and pepper. Add a little warm water, the strained marinade liquid, the apple syrup and the cocktail onions. Cover and simmer gently for about 2 hours.

Serve with boiled potatoes and a green vegetable.

VIJFSCHAFT (UTRECHT)
Five-meal

This Utrecht dish from the heart of the country gets its name because it is composed of five main ingredients. It is traditionally served with fried bacon or sausages.

Prepare the beans 24 hours in advance.
Serves 8

¾ cup dried red
* kidney beans, soaked*
* overnight*
3 lb potatoes, cut into
* pieces*
1¼ lb carrots, chopped
2 onions, sliced
2 cooking apples, peeled,
* cored and sliced*
salt and pepper
1–2 tablespoons corn-
* starch or potato flour*
6 tablespoons butter

Cook the beans in the water they have soaked in for at least 30 minutes. Add the vegetables and apples with a little salt, and cook until tender (about 45 minutes). Strain off the liquid. Use 1–2 tablespoons of it to make a paste with the cornstarch or potato flour. Stir over a low heat, add the butter and dilute the paste with more of the cooking liquid until you have a thick sauce. Season with pepper and pour over the vegetables to serve.

Carrottes à l'ardennaise: *winter carrots Ardennes-style, steeped in the strong smoky flavor of locally cured bacon*

CAROTTES A L'ARDENNAISE (ARDENNES)
Ardennes carrots

This simple and tasty Belgian peasant dish is popular in the villages in the Ardennes. It is best served with roast pork or with *boeuf bouilli* (boiled beef).

Serves 8

¾ lb Ardennes bacon
  (strong flavored, lean
  smoked bacon), diced
2 large onions, sliced
¼ cup flour
2 lb carrots, cut into
  strips
salt
1 teaspoon sugar
chopped parsley

Fry the bacon slowly together with the sliced onions. Sprinkle with flour, stirring continuously, and when the flour begins to color stir in 1¼–1½ cups warm water, stirring all the time.

Add the carrots and cook slowly, uncovered, with some salt and the sugar for about 45–60 minutes, allowing as much water as possible to evaporate. Serve garnished with parsley.

BRUINE BONEN MET APPELTJES (BETUWE)
Beans with sweet apples

This dish comes from the fertile part of Holland that lies between the Rhine and Waal rivers. Here there are huge apple orchards, and the local women traditionally dry apples to cook in the winter.

Prepare the beans and apples 24 hours in advance.
Serves 8

2 cups dried red kidney
  beans, soaked overnight
⅓ lb dried apples, soaked
  overnight
1 lb fat bacon, in one
  piece
1–2 tablespoons
  cornstarch or potato flour

Cover the soaked beans and apples with 1 quart of fresh water, add the piece of bacon, and simmer until they are tender (about 1½ hours).

Drain off the liquid and thicken with the potato flour or cornstarch to make a sauce. Slice the bacon; arrange it on top of the apples and beans, and pour the sauce over the top. Serve with boiled potatoes.

Desserts

KRAMIEK (FLANDERS)
Raisin bread

On fine Sunday afternoons at the turn of the century when Belgian parents took their children to the park or the country, they would often go to open-air restaurants to eat *kramiek* and cottage cheese. Nowadays this raisin bread is still popular with afternoon coffee.

Serves 6

4 cups flour
1 cake compressed yeast dissolved in ¼ cup lukewarm milk
3 tablespoons butter, melted
2 teaspoons salt
¼ cup sugar
1½ cups raisins

Sift the flour into a mixing bowl. Make a well in the center and pour in the yeast mixture and the melted butter. Sprinkle the salt around the edge of the flour and scatter the sugar over it. Make a strong flexible dough by kneading from the center outwards, adding more lukewarm milk if necessary.

Place the dough in a large bowl, cover with a damp cloth, and leave to rise in a warm place for about 1 hour. Mix in the raisins and let the dough rise again for about 1 hour.

Knead once more quickly, form the dough into a round loaf, and leave to rise on a greased baking sheet until double in size. Bake in a hot oven (400°F) for about 30–45 minutes.

JAN-IN-DE-ZAK (NORD HOLLAND)
John in the sack

This traditional dessert was used to 'fill you up' when a meal was somewhat scanty, or on a 'leftovers day.' Also the farmers' wives would give it to their husbands when they went to work in the fields.

Serves 6

1 cake compressed yeast
1 cup warm milk
2¼ cups flour
salt
1 egg
1 cup mixed dried fruit: currants, raisins, candied peel
2 tablespoons butter, melted
1¼ tablespoons brown sugar
cinnamon

Dissolve the yeast in a little of the warm milk. Sift the flour into a large mixing bowl, make a well in the center and pour in the yeast mixture. Sprinkle salt around the edge, break the egg into the center and knead to a firm dough, adding the rest of the milk. Finally add the dried fruit.

Cover the dough with a damp cloth and leave to rise for about 30 minutes. Wet a clean cloth with warm water, sprinkle some flour on it and tie the dough up in it loosely. Hang the bundle in a pan with plenty of boiling water and cook for 2½ hours.

Remove the cake, drain and cut it into slices.

Make a sauce from the melted butter and brown sugar with a little cinnamon and pour this over the hot cake. Or you can spread butter and sugar on the slices and on top of that pour some hot milk.

REP-JE-DEN-BRIJ (BETUWE)
Hurry-the-porridge

This rich sweet dish that used to be eaten as a main course is now served as a dessert. It originates from the fruit-growing area of Holland, between the Waal and Rhine rivers.

Prepare currants a few hours in advance.
Serves 8

1⅓ cups currants, soaked
2⅓ cups rice
3 lb cooking apples, peeled and sliced
1 bottle medium sweet white wine
butter
sugar
cinnamon

Drain the currants, and simmer with the rice and apples in the wine for about 30 minutes, until a rather thin purée is formed (if necessary add some water). Stir occasionally.

Serve hot in individual bowls with a pat of butter and a sprinkling of sugar and cinnamon.

EIERS EN BEIERS (ZEELAND)
Eggs and gooseberries

A summer dish from the southern Dutch province of Zeeland, where the rich soil is ideal for growing soft fruits like gooseberries and raspberries.

Serves 4

1 lb gooseberries
½ cup sugar
a pinch of cinnamon
4 eggs

Simmer the gooseberries until they turn into a pulp and then push them through a strainer. Add the sugar and cinnamon.

Beat the eggs and stir them into the gooseberries. Leave to cool, then sprinkle with more cinnamon.

BEGIJNERIJST (FLANDERS)
Saffron rice

This old Flemish dish can be seen in the paintings of peasant life by Pieter Breughel the Elder. The *begijnen* are members of a Dutch religious sisterhood not bound by vows. The order was founded in the twelfth century, and the enclosed courtyard buildings erected for it in the Middle Ages are still found today in the beautiful towns of Bruges and Lier. They say that when children went to visit their old 'aunt beguine' she would cook this dish for them, and tell them that all the little children in heaven are *begijnerijst* with a silver spoon.

Serves 6

¾ cup short-grain rice
1 quart milk
½ stick of cinnamon
¼ cup sugar
a few threads of saffron
dark brown sugar

Cook the rice quickly in plenty of water for 10 minutes. Drain it and return to the pan with all but 3 tablespoons of the milk and the cinnamon. Simmer for about 1 hour on top of the stove or in the oven.

Heat the remaining milk until it is lukewarm, and mix it with the sugar and saffron. Add this mixture to the rice so that it becomes a bright yellow color. Pour the thick rice porridge into individual bowls, and allow to cool before serving, sprinkled with brown sugar.

These big dray-horses were once a common sight on all Belgian farmland.

SPECULAAS (HOLLAND)

These decorative cookies are traditionally eaten at the feast of St Nicholas on December 6, although they are popular all year round to serve with coffee.

The name *speculaas* comes from the Latin word for mirror: the wooden mold in which the cookie is made is the mirror image of the cookie. Antique molds are very attractive, and are much sought-after by collectors. The most traditional design shows a pair of lovers; and it was customary for sweethearts to give one another *speculaas* on St Nicholas' Eve.

Prepare 24 hours in advance.
Makes 8–10 speculaas or 20–30 small cookies.

⅔ cup butter
1¾ cups flour
1 teaspoon baking powder
⅔ cup brown sugar
¼ teaspoon salt
1 teaspoon milk
2 teaspoons speculaas spices (a mixture of ground cloves, ginger, cinnamon, cardamom and coriander)
1 cup chopped almonds

Cut the butter into small pieces and rub into the sifted flour and baking powder. Add the sugar, salt, milk and spices and knead quickly until you have a smooth dough. Finally add the almonds, and leave to rest overnight.

Lightly flour a pastry board, roll out the dough and cut out the figures or fancy shapes with a *speculaas* mold or cookie cutter. Place the figures on a greased baking sheet and bake in a moderate oven (350°F) for 15–20 minutes until the *speculaas* are crisp and brown.

POIRES CUITES (LIÈGE)
Pears cooked in wine

As autumn days become shorter and colder, ladies appear in the main streets of Liège selling delicious hot pears from handcarts and calling out in the local dialect 'cutès peûres'. The soft hot pears are best eaten crushed on buttered brown bread.

Serves 4

1¼ cups brown sugar
1 teaspoon cinnamon
1 cup red wine
4 large, ripe, firm pears, peeled

Add the sugar and cinnamon to the wine. Bring to a boil and allow to cook to a syrup. Place the pears whole in an ovenproof dish with their stems uppermost, pour the liquid over them and bake for at least 30 minutes in a moderate oven (350°F). Baste once or twice while they are cooking. Serve hot.

Poires cuites: *cook pears in wine and brown sugar until tender, and eat them crushed onto brown bread and butter.*

Speculaas: *the lover and his lass are the traditional shapes for these spicy sweet cookies*

PLATTEKAASTAART (BRABANT)
Cottage cheese tart

This delicious tart is a specialty of the area just south of Brussels. The villagers who live here on the edge of the Zonien Forest form an island of Flemish speaking peoples surrounded by the Walloons, or French speakers, and their cooking is very different from that of their neighbors.

Serves 8

1¾ cups flour
¼ cup sugar
2 teaspoons salt
1 cake compressed yeast, dissolved in ¼ cup warm milk
¼ cup butter, melted
1 egg, lightly beaten
5 tablespoons apple sauce
1 cup cottage cheese
2 egg yolks
2 teaspoons vanilla sugar
¼ cup crumbled macaroons
¼ cup ground almonds
2–3 tablespoons milk
a dash of rum
2 egg whites, stiffly beaten

Sift the flour into a mixing bowl. Scatter 2 tablespoons sugar over it and the salt around the edge. Make a well in the center and pour in the yeast mixture, the melted butter and the lightly beaten egg.

Start kneading from the center outwards, and make a flexible dough. Leave to rise in a warm place for about 1 hour, until it doubles in size. Roll the dough out flat and line a buttered pie pan with it. Spread a thin layer of apple sauce over the dough.

In a mixing bowl mix together the cottage cheese, remaining sugar, egg yolks, vanilla sugar, macaroons, almonds, cold milk and rum, then fold in the egg whites. Pile this mixture on top of the apple sauce.

Bake in a moderate oven (350°F) for about 45 minutes, until golden brown.

Holland and Belgium

LA TRULEYE (LIÈGE)

Beer and gingerbread

A hearty sweet dish from the old workmen's quarters of the industrial town of Liège.

Serves 4

1½ cups spiced gingerbread crumbs
1 quart beer
⅔ cup brown sugar
a pinch of cinnamon
a pinch of nutmeg
1 egg, beaten
a pat of butter

Simmer the gingerbread crumbs in the beer with the sugar, cinnamon and nutmeg until it turns into a thick porridge (about 1 hour). Remove from the heat, cool slightly, and add the beaten egg and some butter. Serve while still lukewarm, in individual deep bowls.

PRUIMENKREUZE (FRIESLAND)

Prune pudding

This old peasant recipe is said to be good for the digestion; but it also makes a delicious dessert.

Prepare the dried fruit 24 hours in advance.
Serves 6

1⅓ cups prunes
1 cup raisins
a piece of lemon peel
2 tablespoons apple syrup or molasses
2 tablespoons butter
a drop of vinegar
1–2 tablespoons cornstarch or potato flour

Soak the prunes, raisins and lemon peel overnight in 2 quarts of water.

Cook slowly in the same water until tender, about 30 minutes. Remove the lemon peel. Add the syrup, butter and vinegar and thicken with cornstarch or potato flour.

Serve either warm or cold.

BOERENJONGENS EN MEISJES (HOLLAND)

Farm boys and girls

These traditional Dutch drinks are served in large cut glass bowls with decorative ladles at weddings and on other festive occasions. They should be prepared six weeks in advance, and each recipe will serve approximately fifteen people.

Farm boys (Boerenjongens)

1 cup water
1 cup sugar
a stick of cinnamon
2½ cups white raisins
1½ pints brandy (Dutch white grain-brandy if possible)

Bring the water, sugar and cinnamon to a boil, add the raisins and simmer until they swell. Transfer to a bottle, pour the brandy in, and seal the top. Leave for 6 weeks.

Farm girls (Boerenmeisjes)

1⅓ cups dried apricots
1¾ cups water
1½ cups sugar
a piece of lemon peel
1½ pints brandy

Soak the apricots in the water with the sugar and lemon peel for 48 hours. Transfer to a bottle, pour in the brandy and seal the top. Leave for 6 weeks.

FRIESE BOEREN-KOFFIE (FRIESLAND)

Friesian farmers' coffee

This heart-warming Dutch drink originated in the cold northern province of Friesland. In winter, when the lakes and canals are frozen over, everybody, from the little children to the old people, goes out skating, and there are skating races in every village. After the races a dance is often held, and it is then that this wonderful 'coffee' is drunk.

Serves 8

3 egg yolks
¼ cup flour
a pinch of cinnamon
a pinch of nutmeg
1 cup sugar
1 teaspoon melted butter
1 quart beer (light or dark)
⅔ cup hot strong black coffee
⅔ cup brandy

Beat the egg yolks with the flour, cinnamon, nutmeg, sugar, melted butter and ½ cup beer.

Bring the rest of the beer to a boil. Skim off the froth. Pour slowly into the egg mixture, beating vigorously with a fork. Set on a low heat and bring almost to boiling point, stirring continuously. But do not boil or the eggs will curdle.

Remove from heat, add the hot coffee and brandy, and serve very hot.

*There is no love sincerer
than the love of food.*

Bernard Shaw (1856–1950)

*Three aspects of the
British countryside:
lush Oxfordshire
meadows,*

*the hills where Welsh
sheep graze,*

*and burns where the
Scottish salmon leap*

British food may seem distinctive, but it is a compound of many foreign influences. Britain's early invaders included Celts who came from Europe in 700 BC, the Romans who arrived in 55 BC, the Angles, Jutes, Saxons and Danes, and finally in the eleventh century, the Normans.

The Celts, whose strain still survives in Wales and Cornwall today, organized farms around a central main building which was the hall. This was for strategic and military purposes, but it also shaped eating habits, raising mealtimes to social occasions. The Celts taught the Britons how to bake in ovens; until then only the baking stone or griddle was used. They grew wheat, ground the grain in querns, made dough and baked it in earth ovens. They made solid puddings called frumenty (see page 25) by softening grain with milk and sweetening it with honey, a formula which still lives on in the form of rice pudding. They kept cattle, pigs and sheep, and made butter and cheese. They brewed their own ale from barley, an art which had been developed in Egypt. In fact they established the pattern of British traditional eating.

Britain was part of the Roman Empire for almost four hundred years from 43 AD to 410 AD. The distinctive Mediterranean flavor of Roman cooking had little permanent effect on British food, although the Romans introduced some salty sauces and cooking pots, as well as the cherry tree which is now thought to be characteristically British.

After the Romans came the North Europeans. Loosely called Danes, but including seamen-adventurers from the coasts of Holland, Germany, Norway and Sweden, as well as Denmark, they exploited the east of England for centuries, sometimes settling down. They introduced their skills of drying, salting and smoking fish and meat, an art of preserving which was essential to their life style for it sustained them through the long sea voyages and the harsh northern winters, when there was no forage for animals. The Briton still enjoys his early heritage of smoked and salted foods in ham, bacon and fish.

The Normans, who invaded Britain in the eleventh century, provided the most long-lasting influence on British food. They improved the vines the Romans had planted, built carp ponds for 'meatless days' and developed a cider industry. They brought their sophisticated Norman cooks with them and introduced new ideas about spicing and flavoring foods.

British kings annexed large parts of France in the early part of the Middle Ages which affected British eating habits at the very highest level. Later, Elizabethan merchant-adventurers roamed the world, and brought back new foods that changed eating patterns. In the nineteenth century colonization led to the importing of many foods including wheat from Canada, beef and lamb from Australia and New Zealand, sugar from the West Indies, cocoa from West Africa, citrus and dried fruit from South Africa and spices and exotic fruits from the Far East.

Great Britain

Gathering the harvest of the sea: Dyce's Pegwell Bay

Britain's diet owes much to the peoples it has conquered; it also owes a great deal to its geography. The damp climate makes for rich green pastures that are ideal grazing for cattle. English beef is highly prized but even it cannot compare with the excellent Scottish beef from the great herds of Angus. The hilly Welsh countryside and the South Downs of Sussex county provide grazing for sheep which are among the best in the world. The windy wet lands of Wales and Ireland are fine for growing large potato crops; and the flat landscape of East Anglia county, with its longer hotter summers, is perfect for producing high yields of wheat. The lovely vales of Hereford and Evesham, and rural Kent (known as the Garden of England) produce apples, cherries and strawberries; and the area around Aberdeen in Scotland yields most of Britain's raspberry crop.

The Scottish climate suits hardier foods. Oatmeal is the staple diet of the north, for 'oats will grow where wheat will not, and deer will graze where sheep cannot' and it is used in cereal, in cookies and in cakes. There is an abundance of game: partridge, woodcock and pheasant; and salmon and trout are fished from the lochs.

Inevitably, an island nation will derive much from its shores and offshore fishing. British fishermen catch large North Atlantic cod and haddock, and also fine fish such as turbot and sole. Dover sole is second to none. There has always been an abundance of lobster, oysters, mussels, scallops, prawns and shrimp.

Throughout the centuries, the British have survived on a good, if somewhat rough, basic diet of adequate meat and plentiful carbohydrate (wheat in the south, and oats in the less arable parts of Scotland). Most country households of the past had a pig and some chickens, which also meant eggs. In the tradition of all good country cooking, the British utilize every last part of the animal; in fact it is said of the pig that everything is used except its squeak. Surplus milk is used to make Britain's excellent cheeses.

The British take a modest view of their traditional dishes. They are not presented in the glamorous way of other nations, but they are good for all that. There's oxtail stew, and brawn or 'pig's cheese', made from the meat of a pig's head; and beef cheek and Bath chap (the cheek of the pig); there are soups and stews made gelatinous with slow-boiled calf foot, and pig's foot and cow-heel. And there are the many country pork sausages, ground with dry bread or zwieback and flavored with herbs such as thyme and sage.

In the north of England there's the prized tripe: the washed, scrubbed, bleached inner stomach of oxen, soft and honeycombed in texture. On the coast, the fishermen have their own long-tested recipes: Cornwall's stargazey pie, a bizarre dish of humble pilchards cooked with the heads sticking out of the pastry; and Cornish pasty, a pastry turnover with potatoes, vegetables and perhaps a little meat.

The Scots treasure the head of the cod, and cook it stuffed with oatmeal and the fish's liver. The Scottish islands have dozens of traditional dishes which use vitamin-rich cod liver and have names that sound, perhaps, more romantic than the dishes: Haggamuggi (fish stomach filled with chopped fish liver and steamed); Krampus (fish livers cooked with oats and barley), as well as Krus and Flakki and Mugilden and Sangster which are all very nourishing, but an acquired taste. And then there's haggis – the national sausage, a mixture of chopped variety meat, spiced, mixed with oatmeal, sewn up in a sheep's stomach, and steamed.

In spite of their reputation for cooking plain and fresh ingredients simply, the British don't actually like bland flavors. Throughout their history they have invented sauces which are fruity and salty, hot, strong and spicy. Fiery mustard which brings tears to your eyes is Britain's only native spice but it is an important one since it combines with fat to aid the digestion and is ideal for spreading on fatty meats.

The British are great picklers; they pickle meat with peppercorns (corned beef), and mace and chili peppers and allspice; they pickle vegetables, especially onions and cucumbers, and they pickle hard-cooked eggs; they make piccalilli – a mustard pickle of raw vegetables; they pickle walnuts, which are delicious added to stews. The British have grown to love the strong hot flavors brought back by the eighteenth-century settlers in India. They've teamed them up with salt, soy sauce from China, and combined them with vinegar to produce those most famous of all English table sauces, Worcestershire Sauce and Yorkshire Relish. With the

addition of tamarind (a sticky, lemon-sour dried fruit from India) the sauces have become thick and fruity and survive as HP and A1 and Daddy's Sauce. They are hot, sweet and sour, and no modern truckers' café would be without them.

The pattern of the working day has had much to do with the style of British eating. Before the Industrial Revolution brought millions of people to the towns, the British were very much a nation with country customs – early to rise and early to bed. Breakfast at eight in the morning was a substantial meal; even in the eighteenth century there was a good plate of cold meats and ale to drink, but by the nineteenth century it assumed massive importance, as found in the writings of Dickens and Thackeray. This was the beginning of the three or four course breakfast: oatmeal to start with, then fish (usually smoked haddock or kipper); then bacon and eggs, finishing with toast and marmalade – that wonderful conserve made from bitter Seville oranges, which the British have made their own. There were many other filling breakfast dishes: hams and potted brawn, sausages, kidneys, pork pies, hot and cold, and deviled bones, all eaten with plentiful cups of coffee or Indian tea.

As countryfolk moved to the towns in the nineteenth century, the old practice of an early dinner at five or six o'clock began to change. The meal was eaten later, and as a result a midday break became necessary. Lunch was born: first of all modestly, crackers and wine; then growing into the substantial meal we know today. At the same time the famous British institution, afternoon tea, came into being. Tea became a ritual in which the hostess would entertain her friends, while her husband was still at work; it was an excuse to produce the finest bone china and prettiest lace tablecloths. It was also a chance to show off: make delicately thin sandwiches (cucumber sandwiches for summer); bake special breads and buns and loaves (like the Welsh specialty bara brith); produce homemade strawberry and raspberry jams and preserves and jellies and, especially in the counties of Devon and Cornwall, clotted cream as stiff as butter; or make special local cakes, like Maids of Honor, Eccles cakes, lardy cakes, Banbury cakes, Sally Lunns; or larger set pieces, like seed cakes and fruit cakes – the magnificent Dundee cake, with its decoration of sliced almonds; and, of course, traditional scones and muffins and dropcakes made of oats.

The main meal itself marks a sharp social division in Britain, and until recently it was the rich who dined in the evening, and the poor who had their main meal in the middle of the day. (The working man's 'high tea' also differed from the genteel afternoon tea in that it included savory dishes.) But the nation joins as one for the traditional meal, which forms a family union in millions of homes – the Sunday roast: leg of lamb or shoulder of lamb with mint sauce; pork with crispy crackling, sour apple sauce and sage and onion stuffing; and, most traditional of all, beef rolled and tied and roasted to a turn, served with Yorkshire batter pudding which has cooked with the meat juices – soft and tender in the middle, ballooning and crisp around the edges – a magnificent combination, served with roast potatoes and fresh vegetables.

Whether it's the British lunch, tea or dinner that inspires you, the following selection of recipes will bring just some of Britain's heritage into your home.

Yorkshire's green and pleasant dales

Soups and a savory

Cock-a-leekie: *the most famous of British soups*

COCK-A-LEEKIE SOUP (SCOTLAND)

Next to Scotch broth, cock-a-leekie is the most famous of British soups. In one form or another it's been known since the fourteenth century – as a thick soup of stewing chicken cooked to shreds. The Scots first added leeks, and later still prunes.

Serves 6–8

1 stewing chicken, trussed
the giblets, heart, liver
and neck
1¼ lb leeks, white part
only, sliced lengthwise
1 onion, chopped
2 tablespoons rice
salt
12 prunes (optional)

Cover the chicken and giblets with cold water in a saucepan large enough just to contain the bird. Bring to a boil. As scum rises, keep skimming until no more appears. Now add the leeks, onion, rice and salt to taste. Lower the heat until the liquid is simmering so slowly that the surface just trembles with gently breaking bubbles. Cook for 2–2½ hours.

Remove the bird and giblets, and serve the soup with the leeks in it. The bird is served as the main course with potatoes and green vegetables.

To make a really thick soup which is a meal in itself, shred the chicken meat after cooking and return it to the pan. For a rich flavor, much liked by the Scots, wash a dozen prunes and add them to the soup when you put the chicken in to simmer.

WELSH RAREBIT (WALES)

The Welsh were traditionally the dairy farmers of Britain, and during the growth of London they became the first city dairymen, walking their cows through the streets and selling milk by the jugful. The Welsh used to be famous for their cheeses, but now not even Caerphilly is made in Wales any more. However, Welsh rarebit is still served everywhere – the perfect foil to a long evening of beer, and beer is best to drink with it.

Serves 4

1 tablespoon butter
3 tablespoons strong ale
(or beer)
salt and abundant freshly
ground pepper
1 cup grated Cheddar
cheese
4 pieces of toast,
buttered
English mustard
(optional)

Melt the butter in a saucepan, and add the beer and seasoning. Just before it boils add the cheese and beat until creamy. Pour onto the toast. Place under the broiler for half a minute until it browns, and serve.

Freshly made English mustard can be added. It can also be served on bread fried in bacon fat.

THICK PEA SOUP (LANCASHIRE)

This Lancashire version of one of the most traditional British soups is tasty and nourishing. It is also inexpensive, and a great comfort on winter evenings. Although made with lentils rather than dried peas, it's still called pea soup.

Serves 4

2 small carrots, diced
1 onion, sliced
about 1 lb ham bone
3¼ cups water
1¼ cups lentils
a pinch of salt and
pepper

Put the carrots and onion in a pan with the bone and water, and simmer with the lid on for 1 hour.

Remove the bone, add the lentils, and check the seasoning. Cook on a very low heat until the lentils are soft – 30–40 minutes.

Fish

An island people, the British have always relied on the sea for food.

FISH AND CHIPS (GREAT BRITAIN)

Fried fish was sold in pubs by street-sellers centuries ago but not with chips; separate street-sellers did, however, sell baked potatoes. The chip, or French fry, imported from Europe, met up with the fried fish less than a hundred and twenty years ago, and fused to form an instant British tradition. Hygiene laws now prevent it, but ideally fish and chips should be eaten with the fingers from the torn pages of a daily newspaper, preferably scandalous.

Serves 4

2 lb potatoes, peeled
vegetable oil for deep
*   frying*
4 pieces of fresh cod or
*   haddock, filleted (with*
*   skin left on)*
lemon slices for garnish

Batter
2 cups self-rising flour
¼ teaspoon baking powder
1 teaspoon salt
water

To make the batter sift the flour, baking powder and salt into a bowl. Beat in water little by little until the mixture is about the consistency of light cream. Leave to stand about 30–45 minutes to develop elasticity. If left any longer the batter begins to lose strength.

Cut the potatoes lengthwise into French fries at least ½ in wide. Pat them dry with paper towels. (Washing removes the starch, which is fine for potato chips but not French fries.)

Pour the vegetable oil into a deep fat fryer (if the pan is 6 in deep, put in about 3 in vegetable oil). Heat the oil until it gives off a faint, almost invisible, blue smoke (about 350°F). Fry the chips in small batches, and when they start to brown remove them with a slotted spoon. Drain on paper towels (or in a wire frying basket, which is more effective). If you like chips brown and crispy, raise the temperature of the oil to about 375°F and put the chips back in the pan for a minute or two. Put the chips in a warm oven, in a dish lined with paper towels, while you cook the fish.

Keep the oil at about 350°F. Dip each piece of fish into the batter, drawing it backwards and forwards 2 or 3 times to coat it fully. Then lower it gently into the hot oil, with the skin side down to prevent it curling.

Fry 2 pieces at a time depending on the size of your pan. After 4–5 minutes turn the fish over. Cook until gently browned (8–10 minutes). The heat of the oil seals the batter, and this acts as a kind of pressure cooker around the fish so that it cooks in its own steam and stays moist and juicy.

Serve the fish with the chips and slices of lemon.

right *Honest to goodness British fish and chips*

Great Britain

KEDGEREE (ENGLAND)

The British tend to take their many kinds of excellent smoked fish for granted: from smoked salmon to fat kippered herrings and bloaters (herrings smoked whole for days), from moist, succulent Arbroath smokies to ordinary smoked haddock, split lengthwise before being smoked. Kedgeree is one of the few dishes in which the smoked fish isn't eaten whole and plain. Although its name comes from the British Raj, this British breakfast dish owes little to its Indian grandparent *Khichri*, which combined rice and lentils.

Serves 4

1¼–1½ cups long-grain rice
salt and pepper
½ lb smoked haddock
butter or oil for frying
1 teaspoon curry powder
2 eggs, beaten
scallion to garnish

Cook the rice in boiling salted water until it is tender. Drain, if necessary.

Put the haddock in a shallow pan and cover with boiling water. Simmer for 10 minutes, then drain, cool and remove the bones and skin. Flake the fish.

Heat the butter or oil in a large skillet, stir in the curry powder, cook for a minute, then add the rice, turning it well. Add seasoning and stir in the fish. When hot, add the eggs and stir gently until they start to set. Garnish and serve at once.

Any cooked white fish can be used instead of smoked haddock. Curry paste or a generous pinch of cayenne pepper are alternatives to curry powder. Hard-cooked eggs are sometimes crumbled into kedgeree instead of beaten egg, in which case a little cream can be stirred into the finished dish.

BROILED DOVER SOLE (SOUTH-EAST)

It is a happy accident for England that Dover sole is found off her shores. This large oval flat fish is finer than any other kind of sole in the world. The flesh is firm, and the flavor more delicate than its close relatives the Torbay and lemon sole. Dover sole can be steamed or poached but it's really best when plain broiled.

Serves 4

4 whole Dover sole
melted butter
lemon slices and watercress for garnish
salt and pepper

Wash the sole well, and pat dry with paper towels. Brush both sides with melted butter and place under the preheated broiler, skin side uppermost. Cooking time varies with size, but allow about 15 minutes altogether for a large fish. Halfway through, turn the fish and finish cooking, basting all the time with melted butter. Season.

Serve the sole complete with skin and head, garnished with lemon wedges, more melted butter and watercress. You eat the white flesh on top first, then lift the bones off, revealing the second layer of white flesh, which is easily separated from the black skin.

Some recipes suggest removing the skin before cooking, and sometimes the head too; but you lose some of the flavor this way.

The French have created hundreds of sole dishes with fine sauces; but the British boast they have the perfect fish and it needs no disguise. The lesser varieties of sole may be served with béarnaise sauce, sauce tartare or sauce diable.

Meat

ROAST BEEF AND YORKSHIRE PUDDING (YORKSHIRE)

Roast beef is one of the most famous of all British dishes and rightly so, since the British climate lends itself perfectly to the rearing of beef cattle. Strictly speaking the roasting should be done on a spit over an open fire; but this method of roasting in the oven uses the dripping juices from the meat to wonderful effect, producing a pudding which is moist in the middle and crispy around the edges.

Serves 8–12

4 lb rib or sirloin roast of beef
flour
salt and pepper

Yorkshire pudding
1¾ cups flour
4 eggs
1 cup milk
1 cup water
salt and pepper

Preheat the oven to very hot (450°F). Meanwhile, prepare the batter. Sift the flour into a large bowl. Make a well in the center, add eggs and beat well. Add milk and water, gradually beating out any lumps until you have a thick creamy batter. Season and leave to stand for 1 hour.

Coat the meat lightly with seasoned flour, and place on a broiler pan with a rack. The pan will catch the juices as the meat cooks. Baste with these juices every 20 minutes.

Reduce the heat to 350°F and roast for about 1½ hours (or 18 to 20 minutes to the pound) for medium rare meat.

Half an hour before the meat is ready, remove the broiler pan and pour off the fat. Put another pan under the meat to catch the last juices. Pour the batter in the original roasting pan to a depth of ½ in, and return to the oven with the meat. The juices will now drip down onto the batter, flavoring it. The center will remain soft but the outside will start to swell up. For a really fluffy Yorkshire pudding, place the batter on the top shelf for the last 10 minutes and dribble any pan juices from the meat over the pudding.

Serve the beef with any of the de-fatted pan juices, English mustard, grated fresh horseradish or horseradish sauce.

STEAK AND KIDNEY PUDDING (GREAT BRITAIN)

This dish is one of the glories of the British kitchen, combining a steamed beef suet dough with beef and kidneys. It's a heady delight to the foreigner: simple, yet surprising in its rich, fragrant flavors.

Serves 6

1½ lb chuck steak, cut
   into cubes
½ lb beef kidney, cleaned
   and chopped
flour
salt and pepper
1¼–1¾ cups beef stock

Suet crust
4 cups self-rising flour,
   sifted
½ lb fresh beef suet,
   grated
1 teaspoon salt
about 1 cup water

Grease a 1½-quart steaming mold. Mix the flour, suet and salt lightly. Add as little water as possible, stirring with a wooden spoon until the dough leaves the sides of the bowl. Divide into 1 large and 1 small piece and roll each out on a floured board to ½ in thick. Use the larger piece to line the mold. The smaller piece will be the lid.

Coat the pieces of meat in seasoned flour and put in the lined mold. Cover with some of the stock, reserving the rest for later. Dampen the top edge of the suet crust, and paste down the lid, trimming away any excess dough with a sharp knife. Tie a floured cloth and a piece of foil over the top of the mold to seal it.

Place the mold in a large saucepan filled with enough boiling water to come halfway up the sides of the mold. Cover with a lid and simmer for 3 hours, checking that the water doesn't boil dry. Just before serving uncover the pudding, make a hole in the top and add more boiling stock.

Serve with boiled potatoes and green vegetables.

Under a plain exterior lies the savory richness of steak and kidney.

Pork pies: *the ideal meal for a journey or a picnic*

PORK PIES (LEICESTERSHIRE)

Pork pies belong to a fine tradition, and many counties have their own version. The most famous are Melton Mowbray pork pies, which are pinker than most because a little anchovy paste is added to the pork mixture.

Makes 4 individual pies

raised pastry (see
   page 111)
1¼ lb boneless pork,
   finely chopped
salt and pepper
anchovy paste
beaten egg to glaze

Gravy
1 cup stock
unflavored gelatin

Oil and flour the outside of a small canning jar. Divide the dough into 8 pieces – 4 large pieces for the bases, and 4 smaller ones for the tops. Roll out and mold the larger pieces of dough in turn around the bottom of the jar, loosening them as you work, so that they don't stick. It's rather like making clay pottery, and it's a skill which comes gradually: too hot and the dough is too soft, too cold and it's too hard to work. Make 4 pie cases in this way. Fill each with the chopped pork mixed with salt, pepper and anchovy paste to taste. Put on the lids, crimp and decorate with pastry shapes. Make holes for the steam to escape.

Wrap the pies in collars of greased foil tied with string, and cook on baking sheets in the middle of a hot oven (400°F) for 20 minutes. Reduce the heat to 300°F and cook for another 1 hour 40 minutes. Don't open the oven during cooking.

Meanwhile make a gravy with the stock and enough gelatin (see package instructions) so that it will set when cool. Traditionally the stock should be made from boiling pork trimmings with a pig's foot, sage and marjoram. Other accepted flavorings are nutmeg, mace, raisins or currants.

About 10 minutes before the pies are ready remove the foil collars and brush them with beaten egg to glaze. When done, remove them from the oven and switch it off. Pour the hot gravy into the holes through a funnel. Return to the cooling oven and leave to set overnight. Outside they should be firm and crisp; inside meaty, juicy and jellied.

As a variation, add chopped cooked ham and proportionately less pork. This produces a pie with more flavor and color.

IRISH STEW (IRELAND)

This traditional Irish dish has always been made with mutton; lamb would be considered too good. A cheaper version uses shanks; a richer one the best chops or cutlets. During the long slow cooking the potatoes dissolve to make the gravy thick and creamy.

Serves 6

3 lb boneless lamb, trimmed of fat
2 lb potatoes, peeled and sliced
a pinch of dried thyme
1 tablespoon chopped parsley
salt and pepper
1 lb onions, sliced

Slice the meat. Fill a casserole with a layer of potatoes, sprinkle with thyme and parsley then meat, salt and pepper and onion. Continue until all the ingredients are used up, finishing with a thick layer of potatoes.

Add about 2½ cups water and cover with a tight lid, sealed with foil if necessary. Bake in an oven preheated to 300°F for 2 hours, or cook over a gentle heat on top of the stove for the same time. Check from time to time that the dish isn't boiling dry. The potatoes should cook to a pulp.

LANCASHIRE HOTPOT (LANCASHIRE)

This nourishing, simple dish from Lancashire makes the most of one of the most economical cuts of meat.

Serves 6

3 lb potatoes, peeled and sliced
salt and pepper
3 lb lamb arm chops, trimmed
2 lb onions, peeled and sliced

Put a layer of potatoes in a casserole. Season and cover with meat, then onion. Continue layer by layer, ending with potatoes. Do not add water (as you do for Irish stew).

Put on a closely fitting lid, add sealing foil if necessary, and bake in the middle of an oven preheated to 300°F for 2 hours. Half an hour before the end take off the lid and raise the heat to 400°F to brown the top layer of potatoes.

BOILED CORNED BEEF (ENGLAND)

Corned beef dates back to the days before 'Turnip' Townshend devised a method of keeping animals alive through the winter by feeding them on turnips. Until then all meat was salted and preserved through the winter. Salted beef, a staple of the British merchant navy for several centuries, became known as corned beef because of the peppercorns used to flavor it.

Prepare at least 7 days in advance.

Serves 6

3 lb boneless brisket of beef
3 carrots, sliced
3 onions, chopped

Spices
1 lb (2 cups) salt
2 teaspoons saltpeter
2 cloves garlic, sliced
3 bay leaves
10 cloves
¼ teaspoon mace
20 peppercorns

Pound the spices together and rub or brush onto the meat. Place in an earthenware dish, cover and leave for 7 days. Twice a day turn the meat over, rubbing in the spices. The salt and saltpeter have a preservative effect, and also give the meat its attractive reddish color.

After 7 days rinse off the spices and tie the meat into a good shape for boiling. Place it in a large saucepan, cover with cold water, and add the carrots and onions. Bring to a boil and simmer, covered, until tender (2 hours).

Serve hot with dumplings and vegetables. Corned beef can also be served cold and pressed: remove the cooked beef from the pan and put it between 2 plates with a heavy weight on top. Leave it in a cold place overnight. Serve thinly sliced, with mustard and pickles.

BOILED BEEF AND CARROTS, WITH DUMPLINGS (ENGLAND)

Boiled beef and carrots is one of Britain's great warming winter dishes, glorified in a Victorian music hall song called just that. It's actually boiled corned beef, which you can buy already corned, or prepare at home using the previous recipe.

Soak the corned beef 12 hours in advance.

Serves 6

3 lb corned beef, soaked in cold water overnight
12 peppercorns
2 bay leaves
a bunch of parsley
6 whole peeled pearl onions
1¼ lb carrots, peeled

Dumplings
1¾ cups self-rising flour, sifted
¼ cup finely chopped beef suet
2 sprigs of parsley, finely chopped, or some dried thyme
about ¼ cup water

Drain the meat and place it in a large saucepan. Cover it with fresh cold water, adding peppercorns, bay leaves, parsley and onions. Bring to a boil, cover, then lower heat to a gentle simmer and cook for 2½ hours. Add the carrots after 1½ hours.

Meanwhile, mix the dumpling ingredients together with as little water as possible. Roll into pieces the size of golf balls. A quarter of an hour before the meat is ready, add the dumplings, keeping the lid on firmly while they cook.

ROAST PORK (ENGLAND)

The best cut of the pig for roasting is the loin. British cooks score the skin of this cut with a sharp knife to produce a characteristic crunchy crackling around the meat. Roast pork is traditionally served with sage and onion stuffing and a tart apple sauce.

Serves 8

5 lb loin of pork
vegetable oil or salt

Stuffing
1 lb sausagemeat
1 onion, finely chopped
1 cup fresh white breadcrumbs
1 beaten egg
2 tablespoons chopped fresh sage

Apple sauce
1 lb cooking apples, peeled, cored and chopped
water

Preheat the oven to 400°F. Combine the stuffing ingredients, mixing thoroughly, and spread on the bottom of a roasting pan.

Score the skin of the pork deeply with a sharp knife. Rub vegetable oil into the cuts – this will become the crackling – or rub it with salt, but not salt *and* oil – this doesn't work. Place the pork on top of the stuffing and roast it for 2–2½ hours. It's important not to undercook pork, but nor should it be allowed to dry out. As a general rule allow 25 minutes to start, then 28 minutes per pound.

To make the apple sauce, simmer the apples gently with 2 tablespoons of water – no sugar – until they become a purée.

Great Britain

BAKED HAM (ENGLAND)

The British are rightly proud of their hams, which are sweeter and moister than European hams. Before sugar was imported they were cured with honey. More recently honey was often replaced with molasses. Most counties have their own special styles, though the most famous is the York ham, lightly smoked over oak chippings. It is sweet and delicate compared with the rich, dark Bradenham hams from Suffolk.

A whole ham may weigh up to twelve pounds. Traditionally served at Christmas, it will keep you going for some time, even if you have to provide for several people.

Prepare 2 days in advance.

1 dry-cured 'old' ham (10–12 lb)
brown sugar and cloves for glaze, or white breadcrumbs for crust

Flavoring
2 onions, chopped
2 carrots, chopped
3 celery stalks, chopped
3 cooking apples, chopped
2¼ cups dry hard cider
1¾ cups molasses or ⅓ cup brown sugar
a small bunch of parsley
12 peppercorns

Immerse the ham in cold water and leave it for 24 hours, changing the water several times. (Some very salty hams need longer, so ask your butcher.)

Remove the ham and scrub it well. Put it in a large pan with the flavoring and bring to a boil. Simmer very gently for 5 hours, adding more liquid if necessary as it evaporates. Remove the pan from the heat and leave the meat to cool in the cooking liquid overnight.

The next day skin the ham. Score the fat with criss-cross knife cuts and stud it with cloves. Sprinkle with brown sugar and put in the top of a very hot oven (450°F) for 5–15 minutes.

For a different finish: after removing the skin, put the ham in a moderate oven (350°F) until the fat starts to melt. Remove and press plenty of fine white breadcrumbs into the fat. Return to a hot oven (425°F) to brown (about 10 minutes).

The oak tree – a symbol of the English countryside

BRAWN (ENGLAND)

Brawn, a molded jelly of pig's head trimmings, cooked with herbs and vegetables, is served cold as a main course or an appetizer. It's usually a grayish color but a prettier pink brawn can be produced by using salted pork. Ask your butcher to salt a pig's head for you a few days in advance.

Prepare 24 hours in advance.
Serves 4 (or 8 as an appetizer)

½ salted pig's head
1 lb beef cheek, shank or knuckle
1 pig's foot
12 peppercorns
4 cloves garlic, crushed
a bunch of parsley
1 large onion
6 carrots
2 celery stalks
juice of 1 lemon, strained
salt and pepper

If salted, first soak the head for 2 hours.

Put the head, the meat, peppercorns, garlic, parsley and all the vegetables together in a large saucepan. Cover with water, and simmer for 4 hours on a gentle heat. Skim, remove the meat and reserve the liquid.

When the meat is cool enough to handle, strip it away from the bones. Pull the skin away from the tongue, remove the hairy bits and tough gristle around the snout.

Chop all the selected meat and slice the tongue. Add the lemon juice and extra salt and pepper to taste. Place the meat in a suitably sized mold or round pan and cover with 1¼–1¾ cups cooking liquid. This becomes jelly when cooled.

Cover the brawn with wax paper. Place a plate on top with a heavy weight on it, and leave overnight to set. It can be kept in the refrigerator for several days if necessary. When ready to serve loosen the brawn by standing the mold in a pan of boiling water for up to 10 seconds, then unmold.

Serve cold with mustard and salad.

VEAL AND HAM PIE (ENGLAND)

Meat pies made with raised pastry are a peculiarly British tradition; they were once called coffins, or coffers, because of their square, long shape. They are usually prettily decorated with pastry pieces, then glazed. To make this pie you need either an 8–9 in straight-sided loaf pan, or springform cake pan, or a waisted metal pie mold sold in special kitchen stores. These have clips which unfasten when the pie is cooked.

Serves 6

lard or butter, softened
2 lb veal stew meat, cut in small cubes
1¼ lb ham, uncooked cut into small cubes
seasoned flour
4 hard-cooked eggs
stock made from veal trimmings, jellied

Raised pastry
1 cup lard
¾ cup water or milk
4½ cups flour
1 teaspoon salt
beaten egg yolk for glaze

Bring the lard and water or milk to a boil, and remove from the heat. Sift in the flour and salt and mix to a dough. Knead lightly and leave in a warm place for 30 minutes. Divide into 2 pieces, 1 to line the pan and the other for the lid, and roll them out on a floured board. Re-roll any scraps to make decorative leaves and flowers.

Rub the inside of the mold with softened lard or butter. Line the pan with the large piece of dough, pressing into place. Roll the veal and ham in seasoned flour and use to fill the pastry case, placing the hard-cooked eggs at equal intervals. It is important to fill the case right up to the top.

Moisten the edges, fix the dough lid on top and cut away any surplus with a knife. Decorate with leaves or flowers and brush with beaten egg yolk.

Make holes for steam to escape. Bake in the middle of a hot oven (400°F) for 30 minutes to set the pastry, then lower the heat to 300°F for another 1½ hours. Top up with the warmed stock and leave to set.

Serve cold with English mustard and a green salad.

Grouse, the richest of game birds, needs only simple accompaniments to offset its heady and sensuous flavour.

Poultry and game

GROUSE (SCOTLAND)

Grouse is eaten within a strict season in Scotland and hung for some days to develop a 'gamey' flavor. It is traditionally served with bread sauce, gravy and game chips (potato chips).

Serves 4

4 whole young grouse
flour
a pinch of cayenne pepper
8 bacon slices
4 thick slices of bread,
  crusts removed

Bread sauce
1¼ cups milk
1 onion, studded with
  12 cloves
salt and pepper
2 cups fresh white
  breadcrumbs
1 tablespoon butter, or 2
  tablespoons cream

Game chips
1 lb potatoes, peeled
  and thinly sliced
vegetable oil for deep
  frying

Preheat the oven to 400°F. Clean the birds, if necessary (some cooks believe in leaving the insides in, but it makes for an excessively strong flavor).

Coat the birds lightly with flour and cayenne pepper. Tie 2 slices of bacon over the breast of each one and place each bird on a slice of bread in a roasting pan. Roast for 25 minutes. Remove the bacon and roast for 5 more minutes.

Heat the milk gently in a double boiler and add the onion. Cook without boiling for 30 minutes, then discard the onion. Season with salt and pepper, and stir in breadcrumbs until the sauce is smooth but not solid. Check the seasoning, then add butter or cream and beat until smooth.

Soak the potatoes in cold water to remove surplus starch, then pat each slice dry with paper towels. Heat a pan of cooking oil to 350°F, and deep fry the potatoes, a few at a time, until they begin to brown. Drain each batch on paper towels. Reheat the fat to 350°F – it will have lost heat – and quickly re-brown the game chips.

PIGEON PIE (ENGLAND)

The British are great pigeon-fanciers. Today's modern dove-cotes tend to contain racing pigeons, but originally their ancestors bred and fed doves for eating. There are few countrymen, however, who haven't enjoyed pigeon pie at one time or another.

Serves 4

2 young pigeons, cleaned
2 bacon slices, or
  2 slices of smoked ham,
  cut into small pieces
¼ lb beef chuck, cut into
  thin pieces
flour
salt and pepper
the yolks of 4 hard-cooked
  eggs
1¼–1¾ cups stock

Pastry
¼ cup butter and lard,
  in equal parts
2 cups flour, sifted
¼ cup cold water

Gently work the fat into the flour with the tips of the fingers until it becomes crumbs. Moisten with water, mold into one piece, and leave in a cold place until ready to roll out.

Cut the pigeons in half, through the breastbone. Roll them and the bacon and beef in seasoned flour. Line a casserole with half the beef and bacon, then all the pieces of pigeon. Over the top crumble the hard-cooked yolks. Finally add the rest of the meat and enough stock to cover.

Roll out the dough fairly thickly and cover the casserole with it, crimping the edges with a fork. Make a hole for steam to escape. Put the pie in the middle of an oven preheated to 400°F. Bake for about 30 minutes until the pastry begins to brown. Then cover with foil and put in the lower part of the oven, reducing heat to 300°F and cook for another 1½ hours.

If you prefer you can leave the pigeons whole and stuff them with ground ham and hard-cooked eggs or use only pigeon breasts, allowing 1 pigeon per person.

ROAST GOOSE (ENGLAND)

This is traditional fare for Christmas ('Christmas is coming and the goose is getting fat') and Michaelmas (September 29), when they are not so fat. The cooked goose yields a great deal of fat, which many cooks prize for making tender pastries, and for light frying. It should be stored in the refrigerator.

Serves 6

1 goose weighing about
  10 lb

Sage and onion stuffing
1 large onion
the liver of the goose,
  chopped
8 cups fresh white
  breadcrumbs
¼ cup finely chopped
  beef suet
1 egg, beaten
grated rind of 1 lemon
1 tablespoon dried sage
2 teaspoons salt
1 teaspoon freshly ground
  pepper

Apple sauce
1 lb cooking apples,
  peeled, cored and
  thinly sliced
1 tablespoon butter

To make the stuffing cook the onion in boiling water in a covered pan for 10 minutes to soften. Drain, chop finely and mix with the other ingredients. Put the stuffing inside the bird.

An average goose weighs 10lb and, using the slow method, takes 5¼ hours to cook. (Allow 15 minutes for every 1 lb difference in weight.) Preheat the oven to 400°F then reduce to 275°F when you put in the bird.

For the quick method, allow a total of about 2 hours for an 8–10 lb bird and 1½ hours for a 7 lb bird. Preheat the oven to 400°F. Place the goose in a roasting pan and cook for 30 minutes. Then remove and prick lightly with a fork so that the surplus fat can run out. Lower the heat to 350°F and continue to cook. To prevent burning, cover the breast and wings with foil.

Serve with mashed potatoes, Brussels sprouts and apple sauce.

Melt the butter in a pan, add the apple slices and cook very gently, without water, until the apples turn to a mush. Don't add sugar; the sauce should be sharp to counteract the richness of the goose.

SADDLE OF HARE (GREAT BRITAIN)

Before the Industrial Revolution stepped up the population and lowered British standards of eating, every countryman supplemented his diet with food from the wild. The rich (thanks to his gamekeeper) and the poor (by courtesy of the poacher) had ample access to all sorts of game, especially rabbit and hare. The most famous hare dish is jugged hare, a rich stew which is thickened at the last moment with the blood. But to many the most delicious hare dish is the saddle – that is, the shoulders and back – simply roasted.

Serves 4

the saddle of a large hare
2–4 bacon slices
melted butter, milk or
  beer for basting

Forcemeat
meat from the legs of the
  hare, finely chopped
the hare's liver
2 bacon slices, chopped
1 cup fresh white
  breadcrumbs
¼ cup finely chopped beef
  suet
1 egg, beaten
grated rind of 1 lemon
stock made from
  trimmings, to moisten
chopped parsley
salt and pepper

Sauce
cornstarch
1 cup hot stock
1 tablespoon redcurrant
  jelly

Mix all the forcemeat ingredients together and stuff the saddle, holding it in place with foil.

Preheat the oven to 400°F. Put the stuffed saddle in a roasting pan and cover with the bacon. Put in the oven, and after 10 minutes reduce heat to 350°F. Roast for 1½ hours, but check after 1 hour, because hares vary in age and toughness. The youngest hare, a leveret, will cook in 45 minutes. Baste at intervals with the melted butter or milk or beer to keep it moist. Remove the foil for the last 15 minutes.

When the hare is ready, remove it from the oven. Make a sauce with the remaining juices, stirring in a little cornstarch dissolved in cold water, the hot stock, and some redcurrant jelly.

Salads

Plowing the fields a century ago

SALADS (ENGLAND)

The ancient art of salad making has its roots in medicine and owes much to the skills of the herbalist. The lettuce, for example, was known to promote relaxation, even sleep. Chicory was a cure for gout. Other salad plants were thought to have an exhilarating effect on the nervous system. These two British salads are each from a different century. The ingredients should be arranged decoratively and with great care.

SIXTEENTH CENTURY SALAD

Serves 6

12 spinach leaves,
  washed and dried
6 cabbage leaves, finely
  shredded
2 hearts of lettuce,
  sliced
2 oranges and 2 lemons,
  sliced and sugared
6 dill pickles, sliced
¼ cup raisins or currants
24 blanched almonds,
  sliced in half and
  browned in butter
4 dried figs, chopped
12 green olives
2 tablespoons capers

Dressing
3 parts olive oil to 1 of
  wine vinegar
sugar
a little freshly made
  English mustard
salt and pepper

Until the sixteenth century British salads tended to be mixtures of greenery including leeks, fennel, watercress, purslane, borage, mint, parsley and sage. The Elizabethans began to add hard-cooked eggs and later all kinds of cold meats, especially chicken. The famous salmagundi, an Elizabethan supper dish, consisted of a meat salad garnished with hard-cooked eggs, anchovy, pickles and beet, served on a bed of green salad plants. Elizabethan salads were prettily decorated with violets, primroses, borage leaves, marsh marigolds, rosemary, elder, and yellow flowers from broom to nasturtium.

Arrange the ingredients attractively and decorate with flowers. Just before serving pour over the dressing.

SEVENTEENTH CENTURY SALAD

Serves 6

6 hard-cooked eggs, cold
4 leeks, white part only,
  cooked and cooled
12 asparagus spears,
  cooked and cooled
¼ head of cauliflower (in
  flowerets), lightly cooked
3 French or Belgian
  endives, cooked and
  halved
¼ cup currants
6 fresh sorrel leaves,
  chopped
6 spinach leaves,
  chopped
1 bunch of watercress,
  shredded

Dressing
3 parts oil to 1 of vinegar
a pinch of cinnamon and
  ginger

The Elizabethan merchant seamen brought back many new vegetables: the Virginia potato, the Jerusalem artichoke (known as the Canadian potato), globe artichokes, asparagus, cauliflower, chard and beet. In the seventeenth century raw vegetables were included in 'boiled' salads, from which many modern ideas about salads derive – the inclusion of cooked beet, most of all.

Arrange the ingredients prettily on a plate with the sorrel, spinach and watercress sprinkled over. Pour over the dressing at the last moment before serving.

British tea

SCONES (SCOTLAND)

Before the invention of the kitchen range in the nineteenth century few homes had ovens: so the nearest to baking was to cook on a griddle pan, a flat metal tray placed over the embers of the fire. The finest product of griddle cooking is the scone, which Scotland may claim as its own.

Makes about 12 scones

2 cups flour
2¼ teaspoons baking powder
¼ cup butter or margarine, cut into small pieces
¼ cup sugar
about ¼ cup sour milk

Sift the flour with the baking powder and work in the fat. Add the sugar and milk until you have a dough which is stiff enough to roll out. Roll out on a floured board to ½ in thick. Using a cookie cutter, cut into 2½–3 in circles.

If you have a griddle or a large heavy skillet, heat it on top of the stove. Or you can use an electric hotplate, set to low. Grease the 'griddle' with a paper towel dipped in oil. Cook the scones for 5 minutes and, when risen, flip over and cook 5 minutes more. If the scones begin to burn, lower the heat; if they are not rising properly, raise it.

These days it's more common to bake scones on a greased baking sheet at 450°F for 15–20 minutes.

Scones are best eaten freshly made, split open and buttered, with jam and whipped cream.

SHORTBREAD (SCOTLAND)

The pride of Scottish cooking, and one of Scotland's gastronomic exports. The mixture has to be kept as cold as possible before cooking, so that the shortbread will be crisp. If you are unable to obtain rice flour, use 2 cups all-purpose flour with ½ cup cornstarch instead.

1 cup butter, cold from refrigerator
¼ cup sugar
1¼ cups all-purpose flour, sifted
1 cup rice flour
¼ teaspoon salt

Cut the butter into tiny pieces, and work into the sugar until well combined. Mix the flour, rice flour and salt, and work into the butter and sugar mixture. To do this use a knife, fork, or pastry blender rather than the fingers, in order to keep it as cool as possible. Mold into a ball, and cool in the refrigerator for 30 minutes. Flatten out the pastry to ½ in thick and pat into shallow, greased and floured baking pans.

Prick with a fork, and using a knife mark out the shapes into which you will cut the shortbread later – strips or triangles. Preheat the oven to very hot (450°F) and cook the shortbread for 5 minutes. Turn down to moderate (350°F) and cook for up to 30 minutes more, checking every 10 minutes. When the shortbreads start to turn a pale golden color they are ready.

Sprinkle with sugar, and leave to cool before removing from their containers. Store in airtight tins.

A British tea of lardy cake, Dundee cake, Madeira cake, bara brith, muffins, crumpets, scones and shortbread.

Great Britain

MADEIRA CAKE (GREAT BRITAIN)

British cakes began as yeasted breads, enriched with dried fruit. In the seventeenth and eighteenth centuries, cooks found out how to use beaten eggs to make light cake mixes. This one became popular in Victorian times, eaten, as its name implies, with a glass of rich, sweet Madeira wine.

Makes a 6 in cake

½ cup butter (at room temperature)
½ cup sugar
4 large eggs, beaten
grated rind of 1 lemon
1½ cups self-rising flour
1–3 tablespoons milk
1–2 slices of candied peel, washed and dried

Line a deep 6 in cake pan with buttered brown paper. Sprinkle with flour. Preheat the oven to 350°F.

In a bowl cream together the butter and sugar with a wooden spoon until light and fluffy. Beat the eggs in gradually, add the grated lemon rind, then sift in the flour, stirring well. The mixture should be soft enough to drop from the spoon; if not, add a little milk. Pour the mixture into the greased cake pan. Level off the top by spreading it with a wet knife.

Bake the cake in the middle of the oven. After about 20 minutes decorate the top with candied peel. Cook for 30–60 minutes altogether, until the cake is browning nicely. Ovens vary enormously, but you can test for readiness by pressing the top of the cake with your fingers. If the top is springy, it is done. If it is still moist, it needs longer.

When the cake is ready, leave it in the pan to cool for 10 minutes, then unmold it onto a cake rack.

CRUMPETS (MIDLANDS)

Crumpets were an Anglo-Saxon invention. In early times they were hard pancakes cooked on a griddle rather than the soft and spongy crumpets of Victorian times, made with yeast. Northern crumpets were flatter. The crumpet-makers of the Midlands and London developed the characteristic holes, by adding extra baking powder to the yeast dough.

Prepare 2 hours in advance.
Makes 12 crumpets

1 teaspoon sugar
2¼ cups warm water
½ cake compressed yeast (or active dry yeast according to the instructions on the package)
4 cups flour
1 teaspoon salt
1 teaspoon baking powder

Dissolve the sugar in a little warm water; mix with the yeast and leave until it starts to ferment – about 10 minutes. Sift the flour into a mixing bowl with the salt and baking powder, and beat in the yeast and warm water gradually, until creamier than a dough but not as runny as a batter; halfway in between. Leave to stand for 1½–2 hours in a warm place (not hotter than 80°F).

Cook the crumpets on a greased hotplate (set to low) or in a large heavy greased skillet. The batter should be poured into crumpet rings, which are like circular cookie cutters, or you can make 1 large crumpet the size of a dinner plate, and cut it into squares after cooking, as they do in the north. The crumpets are ready after 8–10 minutes. Don't turn them over. The top is left uncooked, because it is later to be toasted.

To serve: toast the crumpets on the flat side first, then on the side with the holes. Butter thickly and eat very hot.

MUFFINS (GREAT BRITAIN)

In Victorian times muffins and crumpets were sold by street-sellers who carried them in trays on their heads, but the muffin is almost extinct now – except in home cooking.

Prepare at least 1 hour in advance.
Makes 16 muffins

½ cake compressed yeast
1½ cups warm milk
1 teaspoon sugar
4 cups flour, sifted
1 egg
2 tablespoons melted butter
1 teaspoon salt

Dissolve the yeast in the warm milk and stir in the sugar to help activate the yeast. In 10 minutes it should start to froth and be ready to use.

Mix the flour and the yeast and milk mixture. Stir in the beaten egg and the butter, and add the salt.

Knead this dough on a floured surface for about 10 minutes, until it is light and elastic. Make it into a rounded lump, place it on a greased baking sheet, and cover with a plastic bag. Leave until it doubles in size (less than 30 minutes in a warm kitchen).

Cut the dough into pieces and roll them into rounds 3 in across and ½ in thick. Return them to the greased sheet, and leave to rise a second time, for about 20 minutes.

Cook the muffins over a low heat on a lightly oiled griddle or in a buttered skillet for 8 minutes on each side, or bake in a low oven (325°F) for 20 minutes. They double in size, and are ready when lightly browned.

Serve at once, split in half and buttered, or with jam and cream like scones for tea. Muffins are also delicious the following day, toasted.

Tea cakes on sale at the village fête

Great Britain

An Irish tea-house at the end of the nineteenth century

BARA BRITH (WALES)

Sweet Welsh breads are descendants of the earliest cakes and they are still as popular as ever in Wales today. Bara brith is a yeasty dough enriched with dried fruit and its name means 'speckled bread'.

Prepare 3 hours in advance.
Makes 1 fruit loaf

1⅓ cups raisins and
  currants, mixed
⅓ cup candied peel
1⅓ cups warm water (or
  milk)
⅓ teaspoon apple pie spice
1 cake compressed yeast
⅓ cup brown sugar
4 cups flour
1 teaspoon salt
⅓ cup lard (or butter)
1 egg, beaten

Leave the fruit and peel to soak in the warm water, adding the spice. Cream the yeast with sugar, adding some of the warm, spicy water.

Sift the flour and salt, and rub in the lard. Add the egg little by little, beating all the time. Add enough of the water in which the fruit has been soaking to make a loose but not too sticky dough. Knead for 10 minutes, then cover with a plastic bag and leave to rise in a warm place for about 1 hour.

Drain the dried fruit and candied peel and mix into the dough. Knead again, and put in a greased 4½ × 2½ × 1½ in loaf pan. Leave to rise a second time.

Bake in a preheated oven (450°F) for 15 minutes, then turn down heat to 375°F to cook for another 45 minutes. Remove from the oven and leave for 10 minutes to set. Then unmold onto a cake rack to cool.

DUNDEE CAKE (SCOTLAND)

The top of this classic Scottish tea cake is distinctively studded with almonds, its center thick with fruit and scarlet halved cherries.

Makes a 7–8 in cake

1 cup butter, softened
1 cup sugar
5 eggs, beaten
2⅓ cups self-rising flour
⅓ cup raisins
⅓ cup currants
⅓ cup chopped candied
  peel
1 cup ground almonds
⅓ cup candied cherries,
  halved
1½ tablespoons grated
  lemon rind
¾ cup blanched almonds,
  halved

Line a deep 7–8 in cake pan with buttered brown paper. Preheat the oven to 300°F.

Cream the butter and sugar until smooth and fluffy. Stir the eggs into the mixture gradually, sifting in the flour little by little. Then stir in all the other ingredients except the halved almonds.

Put the mixture in the cake pan and level off with a dampened knife. Decorate with the almonds. Bake in the middle of the oven for 1½ hours. Check by piercing the center of the cake with a skewer to see if it is done; the skewer should come out dry. If it is sticky, the cake needs more cooking.

When it is done, turn off the oven but leave the cake in for 5 minutes before unmolding it onto a cake rack to cool.

For a darker, richer cake use brown sugar and a tablespoon of molasses instead of the sugar.

LARDY CAKE (ENGLAND)

Lardy cakes are very rich and very sweet and eaten traditionally only for special occasions – high days and holidays and harvest festivals in particular.

Dough
¾ cake compressed yeast
warm water to mix
2½ cups flour
½ teaspoon salt

Filling
⅔ cup raisins
⅓ cup sugar
⅓ cup lard
1 teaspoon apple pie spice

Syrup
¼ cup sugar
3 tablespoons water

Mix the dough and leave it to rise in a warm place. When it has doubled in size, punch it down and roll into a rectangle ½ in thick. Spread one-third of the filling onto two-thirds of the dough. Fold into 3, putting the uncovered dough into the center first. Give the dough a half turn and repeat the rolling and spreading twice more.

Put the square cake on a baking sheet and leave to rise for 30 minutes. Bake in a hot oven (425°F) for 20–25 minutes. Meanwhile boil the sugar with the water to make a syrup. As soon as the cake is removed from the oven place it on a rack to cool and paint with the hot syrup to give it a nice shiny top.

If a round cake is required, select an 8 in pan and tuck the dough in, rounding the corners with your hand.

SEED CAKE (GREAT BRITAIN)

Caraway seeds have long been used in British cooking, and at one time caraway seed cookies were prepared to mark the end of the sowing of the spring wheat. These cookies later evolved into this distinctive caraway-flavored tea cake.

Makes an 8 in cake

½ cup butter, softened
½ cup sugar
2 eggs, beaten
2 cups self-rising flour
3 tablespoons caraway seeds
a pinch each of ground cloves and cinnamon
2–3 tablespoons milk

Line a deep 8 in cake pan with buttered brown paper and sprinkle with flour. Preheat the oven to 350°F.

Cream the butter with the sugar. Place the mixing bowl over a saucepan of hot water, and beat the eggs into the butter and sugar mixture. When combined, sift in the flour with the caraway seeds and spices, adding milk as necessary to make a soft mixture.

Fill the cake pan with the mixture, leveling the top with a dampened knife. Put in the middle of the oven and bake for 45 minutes.

Test with a skewer. If the skewer comes out dry the cake is done; if sticky it needs longer. Leave the cake to cool in the turned-off oven for 5 minutes, then unmold it onto a cake rack.

OATCAKES (SCOTLAND)

In the damp climate of Scotland where wheat is sometimes difficult to grow, oats have grown easily for centuries. These griddle cakes are among the simplest of all oat recipes.

Makes about 20 oatcakes

1½ teaspoons salt
2⅔ cups medium-ground oatmeal
2 tablespoons bacon fat or lard
up to 1¼ cups boiling water
some fine oatmeal for rolling out

Mix the salt into the oatmeal. Melt the bacon fat in a little of the boiling water and stir into the medium oatmeal, gradually adding just enough water to make a soft dough. On a board sprinkled with fine oatmeal roll out as thinly as possible.

Cut into triangles. Cook on a fairly hot greased griddle or electric hotplate (turned to low) until the edges start to curl – about 5 minutes.

Oatcakes can also be baked on a greased baking sheet on the top shelf of a hot oven (425°F). Leave them in the oven to dry out, with the door open.

Desserts

TRIFLE (GREAT BRITAIN)

Trifle is an ideal dessert for children's parties. It goes down well with adults too in its alcoholic form known as 'tipsy cake', with the cake base soaked in sherry or brandy.

Serves 6

6 ladyfingers, split in half lengthwise
homemade jam
up to ⅔ cup sherry or brandy
1¼ cups whipped cream
12 blanched almonds
⅓ cup candied fruit (cherries, angelica etc)

Custard
2½ cups milk
4 egg yolks
2 tablespoons vanilla sugar or sugar and vanilla extract

To make the custard heat the milk, egg yolks and vanilla sugar in a double boiler, stirring all the time until the mixture thickens, and taking care it doesn't burn or stick. When ready, the custard will coat a spoon.

Spread the ladyfingers with jam. Arrange them on the bottom of a pretty glass bowl and pour the brandy or sherry over them. Cover with the warm custard, and place in a cold place to set. Decorate the trifle with whipped cream, arranging almonds and candied fruit on top.

You can also make the trifle without custard: soak the ladyfingers in the brandy or sherry. Cover them with lemon or orange-flavored gelatin, which you pour on just at the point of setting, so that the ladyfingers don't absorb the gelatin. For children's parties trifle can be made with gelatin *and* custard *and* whipped cream.

GOOSEBERRY FOOL (ENGLAND)

Like trifle, the word fool was used to indicate a dish of little importance, a little nothing, a folly. The English fool is a dish of great simplicity – a mixture of cream and fresh fruit purée. It can be made with any fresh, seasonal fruit – raspberries, strawberries, redcurrants, blackcurrants or gooseberries.

Prepare at least 1 hour in advance.
Serves 4

¾ lb gooseberries, washed and topped and tailed
½ cup sugar
1¼ cups whipping cream
1–2 tablespoons half-and-half (optional)
lemon or orange rind, finely grated

Put the gooseberries in a heavy saucepan with the sugar and 1 tablespoon of water. Cook on a very gentle heat. As the gooseberries cook, crush them with a wooden spoon.

After 20–30 minutes remove from the heat, and pass the fruit purée through a strainer, pressing it down with a wooden spoon. (You could use a liquidizer, and then strain it.) Let the mixture cool.

Pour the cream into a bowl and beat to form stiff peaks. If it is particularly solid, add a little half-and-half to make it smoother and softer.

Fold the fruit purée into the cream. Put in a pretty glass bowl or into individual glasses, and chill for at least 1 hour. Decorate with grated lemon or orange rind before serving.

The airy elegance of a well made trifle

SYLLABUB (ENGLAND)

A delicious cream dish which is thoroughly British, syllabub was originally made by the dairyman milking his cow into a pail, in which he had put a measure of sherry. The foaming froth was then skimmed off to serve at breakfast. An eighteenth century refinement was to color the syllabub prettily – green, yellow or red, using spinach juice, saffron or cochineal.

Serves 4–6

1¼ cups heavy cream
⅓ cup dry white wine (or dry sack or sherry)
¼ cup sugar
grated rind and juice of ½ lemon

Beat all the ingredients together to a stiff froth. Spoon into individual glasses and when chilled decorate them with a little grated lemon rind.

You can also make syllabub with sweet white wine, or hard cider, and orange instead of lemon.

BREAD AND BUTTER PUDDING (GREAT BRITAIN)

One of the most historic of all British dishes, bread and butter pudding originated as a simple Tudor dish combining old bread and dried fruit. It has never lost its popularity, partly because of its economical use of stale bread. A solid bread pudding, without the added custard, has been served in British boarding schools and other institutions for centuries.

Serves 4–6

¼ cup butter, softened
8–10 slices of white bread, crusts removed
a pinch of ground cinnamon
⅓ cup currants
⅓ cup raisins

Custard
2½ cups milk
4 egg yolks
½ teaspoon apple pie spice

Butter a baking dish or pan. Butter the slices of bread on both sides and line the bottom of the dish with a single layer of bread, cut to fit. Sprinkle with spice and dried fruit. Cover with more layers of fruit and bread, until all the ingredients are used up.

Beat the milk, eggs and spice and pour over the bread. Leave for 30 minutes to soak up the liquid. Bake in a preheated moderate oven (350°F) for 20–30 minutes, until the top is crisp.

SUET PUDDINGS (GREAT BRITAIN)

Sweet suet puddings are characteristically British and steamed treacle pudding, spotted dicks, jam roly-polies and college pudding are an unforgettable part of British school days. Suet puddings emerged in the seventeenth century with the introduction of the pudding cloth – until then animals' stomachs had been used, and puddings were mostly savory, like haggis and black sausage.

COLLEGE PUDDING (GREAT BRITAIN)

One of the most famous British suet puddings.

Serves 6

4 cups self-rising flour, sifted
1 teaspoon baking powder
a pinch of ground ginger
1 cup finely chopped beef suet
1¼–2½ cups warm milk
2 eggs
½ cup sugar
1⅓ cups mixed dates and currants, chopped
¼ cup butter, softened

Mix all the ingredients together except the butter. Divide the mixture into 2 pieces, and roll each into an oblong ½ in thick. Spread 1 oblong with softened butter and cover it with the other piece. Roll them up together into a cylinder.

Wrap in a floured cloth, leaving room for the pudding to expand, and tie the bundle securely. Put it in a deep pan of boiling water, cover and cook for 1½ hours. Cut into slices and serve hot with custard sauce.

JAM ROLL AND SPOTTED DICK (GREAT BRITAIN)

By the nineteenth century the suet pudding served with jam was the mainstay of the English laborer and working man. Children love it.

Serves 4–6

1¾ cups self-rising flour, sifted
½ cup finely chopped beef suet
⅔ cup water
⅔ cup currants (optional)
hot jam or syrup to serve

Mix the dough, and on a floured board roll it out into a long sausage 3 in in diameter. Tie it in a floured cloth and cook over steam for 45 minutes, or plunged in boiling water for 30 minutes. Serve with heated jam or syrup.

To make spotted dick, add the currants to the mixture.

SUSSEX POND PUDDING (SUSSEX)

This is one of the most sophisticated versions of 'suet pud'. When cut open the richly scented lemon liquid inside runs thickly onto the plate and surrounds the pudding like a pond.

Serves 4–6

1¾ cups self-rising flour, sifted
½ cup finely chopped beef suet
1 teaspoon baking powder
⅔ cup milk
⅔ cup water
⅔ cup brown sugar
½ cup butter, cut in small pieces
1 thin-skinned lemon, washed and pricked with a fork

Mix together the flour, suet, baking powder, milk and water to make a dough. Cut into 2 parts, 1 to line the mold, the other as a lid. Roll out.

Grease a 1½ quart steaming mold, and line with the dough. Mix the sugar and butter together and put half into the mold. Put the lemon on top. Cover with the rest of the sugar and butter. Dampen the rim, and press down the lid, trimming off excess dough with a sharp knife. Cover with foil, then a cloth tied with string, leaving room for the pudding to expand.

Place in a large saucepan with boiling water that reaches halfway up the sides of the mold and cook for 3 hours. Check to see that the water does not boil dry. (Longer cooking can only improve a suet pudding.)

To serve: gently ease the pudding from the sides of the mold with a knife and turn upside-down onto a serving plate. Serve with cream.

Great Britain

SUMMER PUDDING (GREAT BRITAIN)

Every traditional cuisine has ways of using up yesterday's bread, but none is more beguiling than this summer pudding – a chilled, scarlet treat of raspberries and redcurrants.

Serves 4–6

1 lb raspberries
1 lb redcurrants
sugar to taste
about 12 thin slices of yesterday's bread

Wash and drain the fruit. Remove stalks from the raspberries. With a fork, pull redcurrants from their stalks. Put in a saucepan with the sugar, cover and heat gently until the juices run. Strain off a few tablespoons of juice and reserve.

Cut the crusts off the bread. Butter a 1-quart mold or soufflé dish and line the bottom and sides with the bread slices, trimming each piece to make a neat fit. Keep some pieces to make a lid.

Pile the fruit into the mold and cover with bread. Cover the pudding with a plate and put a heavy weight on top, then chill for 8 hours or so, long enough for the juice to penetrate and soak the bread with its rich flavor.

To serve, put a large plate over the mold, turn upside-down and ease the pudding out gently. There may be some bald patches where the juice hasn't soaked in, so pretty it up with the juices you have reserved. Serve alone or with cream.

The fruit may vary according to availability.

MINCE PIES (GREAT BRITAIN)

Mincemeat is Christmas fare; but it derives from a very old practice of preserving meat by mixing it with minced and chopped dried fruits, to which suet and later brandy are added to improve the keeping qualities. Even now, without the meat, a good mincemeat is made months before it's needed to give it time to mature. It will keep for years.

Prepare long in advance.
Makes about 3 lb mincemeat

2 cups raisins
1 cup currants
1½ lb cooking apples, peeled, cored and chopped small
⅔ cup finely chopped beef suet
a pinch each of grated nutmeg, ground cinnamon and mace
½ cup chopped blanched almonds
⅔ cup sugar
¼ cup brandy
grated rind and juice of 1 lemon

Wash and drain the dried fruit, and wipe dry. Mix together with the apples, suet, spices, almonds and sugar, stirring well. Stir in the brandy and lemon rind and juice. Put the mincemeat into jars, cover with wax paper, and store. Do not fill the jars to the top as the mixture will expand.

The pies
Makes 20 pies

pie pastry made with 2¾ cups flour (see p. 30)
mincemeat
beaten egg yolk
sugar

Roll out the dough and cut out 20 3-in circles and 20 2½-in circles. Use the larger ones to line shallow muffin tins and put a spoonful of mincemeat in each. Cover with dough lids and press down firmly. Brush with egg yolk. Bake for 20 minutes in a fairly hot oven (400°F). Sprinkle with sugar before serving.

CHRISTMAS PUDDING (ENGLAND)

Every family has its own recipe for this most celebrated of all English puddings. It began in the Middle Ages as frumenty: a pudding of grain soaked in milk until swollen, and then cooked. It was improved for festive occasions by the addition of dried raisins, currants and prunes – which led to its other common name, plum pudding. In its final festive phase the pudding has become almost solid fruit.

Everyone in the family should take a turn at mixing the pudding. In Victorian times, a silver threepenny piece or two would be put in for good luck. Christmas pudding can be stored for months – or even years: the British often serve a pudding at Christmas which they made the year before.

Prepare at least several months in advance.
Makes 2 medium-sized puddings

4 cups flour, sifted
1 cup fresh white breadcrumbs
10 eggs
2½ cups milk
⅔ cup brown sugar
2 lb raisins
2 lb currants
2 tablespoons brandy
½ cup dark beer or ale
⅔ cup candied peel
½ cup chopped blanched almonds
grated rind and juice of 2 lemons
½ teaspoon apple pie spice

Brandy butter
½ cup butter, softened
1 cup confectioners' sugar
1 tablespoon brandy

Mix all the ingredients together in a large bowl. Spoon the mixture into 2 greased 1-quart steaming molds. Cover with foil and a floured cloth, tied in a knot. Place in boiling water in a saucepan and boil for 8 hours, topping up the water when necessary. When cold, store the puddings in a cool cupboard.

On the day a pudding is to be served, put it in a pan of boiling water, cover and cook for 2½–5 hours. You can't spoil it by overcooking.

To make brandy butter, warm the butter until it almost melts. Remove from heat and mix it to a cream with the sugar. Beat in the brandy.

To serve, unmold the pudding upside-down onto a dish. Plunge a holly leaf in the top. For the final dramatic climax lower the lights. Warm a tablespoon of brandy over a flame, pour it over the pudding and light it. It will burn for a short time with a low blue flame.

CURD TART (GREAT BRITAIN)

Soft cheese curds mixed with egg yolks made a filling for medieval pastries which we now call cheesecakes. From the same origin comes custard tart, in which a thick egg custard replaces the cream cheese mixture.

Serves 6

pie pastry made with 2 cups flour (p. 30)
½ lb cream cheese
3 egg yolks
½ cup heavy cream
¼ cup sugar
a pinch each of ground saffron and grated nutmeg

Line a 6 in greased tart pan with pastry and bake unfilled (covered with a layer of foil weighted with dry beans) for 10 minutes in a hot oven (450°F). Remove and let it cool.

Beat together the cheese, eggs, cream, sugar and flavorings with a fork or in a blender. Pour the filling into the tart shell. Lower the oven temperature to 425°F and cook for 30–45 minutes until slightly brown. Sprinkle with grated nutmeg.

That open sandwiches are not food,
And that love is not hate,
That is what at this time I know
About open sandwiches and love.

Johan Herman Wessel (1742–1785)

Scandinavia encompasses the five Nordic countries Denmark, Norway, Sweden, Finland and Iceland; but this chapter takes you on a culinary journey through the first four countries only, and I beg my Icelandic friends' forgiveness for only mentioning them in passing.

The fortunes of the Scandinavian countries have been interwoven in a turbulent history. The Norwegian kingdom was at its most powerful in the thirteenth century when it ruled the Faeroes, Iceland, Greenland, Shetlands, Orkneys and Hebrides, but the Black Death (1349–50) left the kingdom impoverished. Denmark, Norway and Sweden were then united under the Danish crown, a union which lasted well over a hundred years. It broke up early in the sixteenth century, although Norway remained in voluntary union with Denmark until 1814, when she declared her independence. However, Norway's freedom did not last long: after a brief war with the powerful Swedes, Norway was forced to capitulate and enter into a union with Sweden which lasted until 1905, when she finally regained her independence and became a separate kingdom. The Danes and Swedes in their turn fought several trade wars with each other for control of the Baltic. Eventually, after the Danish–Swedish War (1657–60), Denmark was forced to concede her dominant position to the Swedes.

Finland and Sweden were politically united for more than six hundred years, until 1809, when Finland became a Grand Duchy of the Russian Empire. In 1917, after the Russian Revolution, Finland declared herself an independent republic. Today Finland remains a republic while Denmark and Sweden are both monarchies.

Geographically the Scandinavian countries vary enormously. Denmark, separated from the other three countries by water, is the only one to share a frontier with the rest of Continental Europe. Norway and Sweden form what is known as the Scandinavian peninsula, and to the east of Sweden and northern Norway lies Finland, bordering the USSR.

The landscape of rural Denmark is mildly undulating and pleasing to the eye, but it cannot compare with the spectacular scenery of Norway's majestic fiords and snowclad mountains. Sweden is the biggest and wealthiest of the Scandinavian countries and its capital, Stockholm, built on an archipelago, is perhaps the most beautiful city in the world. Finland is often justly described as 'the land of the thousand lakes'.

All the countries have extensive coastlines, and the sea has played an important part in their history. A thousand years ago the Vikings – Danes, Swedes and Norsemen – were known in far-away countries as brave, adventurous, if barbaric peoples. One still has to marvel at their incredible feats, voyaging in frail longboats across the North Sea and the Atlantic and down Russian rivers to the Black Sea in search of new colonies, trade routes, and strange, rare objects and materials to bring back to their native lands. Shipping and trade are an integral part of the history of Scandinavia and to this day play a vital part in the economic and cultural lives of the four Nordic countries.

The languages of Denmark, Norway and Sweden are similar and have common roots, while Finnish bears no resemblance to any of the others, having originated in central Europe. Finland is the only country with two official languages: Finnish, spoken by the majority of its people, and Swedish.

The cultural and historical links between the countries are obviously very strong, but the peoples of Scandinavia are still quite different from one another, and have succeeded in retaining their national characteristics.

These contrasts are reflected in the literature and music of Scandinavia. The symphonies of Carl Nielsen, the Danish composer, are inspired by the fertile garden island of Funen which was his home; the music of Edvard Grieg conjures up the grandeur of Norwegian fiords and mountains; Bellman's songs evoke the gaiety and charm of eighteenth-century Sweden, and the majestic music of Jean Sibelius echoes the proud history of the Finns. Scandinavian literature ranges from Hans Andersen to Søren Kierkegaard (both Danish); from Norway's Henrik Ibsen to Sweden's August Strindberg; and from Sweden's *Frithjof's Saga*, adapted by Esaias Tegnér from ancient Icelandic legends, to one of the greatest epics of all time, the *Kalevala*, adapted from ballads handed down orally by the Finns for generations and finally transcribed by Elias Lönnrot in the middle of last century.

Denmark, Norway, Sweden and Finland are all famous for their modern architecture and furniture, for their highly developed applied arts – pottery and china, silver and stainless steel – in short their design for living, so it is not surprising to find that each country also takes great pride in its cuisine.

The Danes remain convinced that their meatballs – *frikadeller* – are the best in the world, not to mention their butter, bacon and cheese. They are also famous for their *smørrebrød* (open sandwiches). The Norwegians go dewy-eyed when they offer you a freshly caught salmon, poached with dill and served simply with new potatoes, melted butter and cucumber salad. The Swedes modestly claim that they know more delicious ways to serve the humble herring than all the other countries put together. They have also given the world the splendid marinated salmon – *gravad lax*. The Finns remain aloof from the battle; they simply take a sauna, followed by a dip in an ice-cold lake and afterwards serve smoked reindeer steaks accompanied by vodka.

The Scandinavians all love *akvavit* – the water of life – which is related to vodka, but flavored with caraway seeds, herbs or spices. Each country makes its own *akvavit*, and there are

Scandinavia

numerous varieties distilled from different grains or from potatoes. It is always served ice-cold in small glasses and often accompanied by a chilled lager, the national drink of all the Scandinavian countries. The Scandinavian climate is not suitable for vine-growing; however, cherry orchards in Denmark provide the fruit for the famous Cherry Heering liqueur; the Finns make a strong liqueur called *lakka* from the wild cloudberries which are also found in Norway, and the Swedes make a fruit punch which tastes so innocent it may easily catch you unawares.

All Scandinavian countries claim the Cold Table, now known all over the world by its Swedish name, the smörgåsbord, as their own specialty. This is a sumptuous buffet-style feast composed of a large number of fish dishes, hot and cold meats, salads, pickles and cheeses. A selection of breads and crackers, butter, fresh fruit garnishes and, sometimes, a fruit salad or other dessert complete the feast. It is by no means just an hors d'oeuvre; it is a giant meal.

Although you could prepare a small smörgåsbord with just a few of the following dishes, the smörgåsbord is traditionally prepared for a large number of people. Here are some of the dishes you might find on it.

First the fish: the herring is a great favorite, and the most popular herring dishes, such as marinated herrings with onion rings, herrings in dill, herring salad and herrings in sour cream, are made with raw pickled herrings. Then there are Bornholm smoked herrings, named after the Danish island of Bornholm in the Baltic Sea where many herrings are caught. A freshly smoked *Bornholm sild* served with an onion ring containing a raw egg yolk, and sprinkled with chopped chives, is enough to make you hear angels sing. Unfortunately Bornholm smokies do not travel well, so you seldom find this specialty outside Scandinavia.

The Swedes pickle their Baltic herring and call it *susströmming*. If you have ever come across it, you are not likely to forget the experience as the smell of fermented herring at its ripest is unique. For those who do not like raw herring – and all Scandinavians pity them – there is another great delicacy: marinated fried herring, served with onion rings.

Other smörgåsbord fish dishes include: mackerel in tomato sauce; smoked trout in olive oil; Norwegian brislings (a type of sardine); smoked cod roe; smoked cod liver; Danish or Norwegian-style caviar; Norwegian fishballs and shrimp in mayonnaise; Danish smoked eel with scrambled egg; *gravad lax* with mustard sauce; freshly boiled and shelled fiord shrimp; lobster salad; and fried fillets of flounder served lukewarm with rémoulade sauce.

Hot meat dishes on the smörgåsbord might include: Danish *frikadeller*; Swedish meatballs; small hamburgers with soft onions; Swedish bacon and apple; Danish egg cake with bacon; and Danish pork sausage. The splendid array of cold meats might include: homemade liver pâté (served with crisp bacon and mushroom); beef tongue; smoked Norwegian ham; Norwegian dried, salted and smoked mutton; Danish smoked pork loin with scrambled egg; a selection of salamis from all the countries; Finnish smoked reindeer tongue; roast pork with crackling, prunes and red cabbage; roast beef with cold potato salad; and steak tartare with raw egg yolk, grated horseradish and capers. Tomato salad, hard-cooked

The sources of Scandinavian cooking – the sea and the farm

eggs, pickled cucumber and pickled beets accompany the meat dishes.

On the table there would also be a selection of Scandinavian breads, biscuits and crackers, and finally a large cheeseboard. Each of the Scandinavian countries has its own range of cheeses, including Danish Blue, Samsø and Danbo with caraway seeds, Norwegian Jarlsberg and Gjetost (a sweetish brown cheese made with goats' milk), Finnish Emmenthal (which comes in three grades, the one with the black stamp being the best), and Herrgård from Sweden. The cheese-board will be garnished with grapes, radishes, celery and tomatoes. In Denmark you will also find a bowl of fruit salad near the cheese, made with fresh fruits in season, gently folded into a mixture of whipped cream and stiff homemade mayonnaise.

If you are completely overwhelmed and wonder how anyone can prepare, let alone survive, such a feast, the simple answer is that the smörgåsbord is designed to include foods for all tastes; but you are not meant to eat your way through each and every dish.

How are you to tackle a smörgåsbord? First, you will find that there are always plenty of plates and flatware next to the table, and you are supposed to change plates frequently so that you do not mix the different flavors. Start with a selection of fish dishes, perhaps try the various kinds of herrings first, then come back for more delicate fish such as shrimp, salmon and eel. Do not overload your plate – you will lose your appetite too quickly; whereas frequent visits to the Cold Table give exercise and aid the appetite! Help yourself to the rye bread with a nice thick layer of butter – it is delicious with herrings. Choose white bread for the salmon and shrimp. And then, how about a warm fillet of flounder with rémoulade sauce?

By now you should be ready for a selection of cold meats and hams with their different garnishes, and then you can complete your meal with some cheese and fruit salad. Remember that you are most welcome to go back and forth to a smörgåsbord – indeed you are expected to. Nothing upsets a Scandinavian more than watching the uninitiated piling their plates full at the first go with a bit of everything, thus ruining the whole idea of the feast and playing havoc with their taste buds.

The meal is best accompanied by a chilled lager (or two) and ice-cold *akvavit* (or *schnaps* as we call it) or vodka, served in

small glasses. The rule is that as soon as your *schnaps* glass is empty it will be filled again, so remember that both *schnaps* and vodka are strong drinks and, if you are not used to them, it is best to go slow.

The presentation of a smörgåsbord is an important part of the enjoyment, and often you will be invited to view the feast before it is devoured. Garnishings include fresh dill, parsley, chives, tomatoes, cucumbers, lemons, green and red peppers, hard-cooked eggs and cress.

As the world grows smaller with modern transportation methods, fresh food and vegetables can be moved around the world with speed, enabling such treats as fresh strawberries, tomatoes and new potatoes to be served all year round. The Scandinavians, however, still observe the ritual of the seasons in their home cuisine, especially on the smörgåsbord. At Christmas time the smörgåsbord is more lavish than ever and

The smörgåsbord: a feast to be eaten little by little

COLD DISHES
1 *Spiced herrings*
2 *Marinated herrings*
3 *Herrings in curry*
4 *Eggs and tomatoes with caviar*
5 *Shrimp and fishballs in mayonnaise*
6 *Brislings*
7 *Smoked cod roe with mayonnaise*
8 *Smoked ham*
9 *Fillet of flounder*
10 *Marinated salmon*
11 *Beef tongue with Russian salad*
12 *Salami selection*
13 *Roast beef with crisp onions and rémoulade sauce*
14 *Spiced Danish pork with mustard and parsley*
15 *Cheese and fruit*
16 *Roast pork with apples and jelly*
17 *Bread and crackers*

HOT DISHES
18 *Frikadeller*
19 *Hamburgers with onions*
20 *Bacon and apple*
21 *Bacon and egg cake*

each country has its own traditional fare. Christmas recipes have been handed down from generation to generation – Christmas ham, brawn, liver pâté, spiced pork, black sausage, salamis, cakes and Christmas cookies.

In summer the foods are not so heavy: there are fewer hot dishes, but more fish delicacies such as crayfish and shrimp. Crayfish (called *kräftor* in Swedish) are perhaps the most memorable of all Scandinavian summer dishes. They are cooked in salted water with plenty of dill and served cold, arranged in a beautiful pattern on a large platter and garnished with more fresh dill. Scandinavian crayfish are quite small, and you must allow 10–12 per person. As each guest has to shell his own, you need finger bowls and plenty of paper napkins and, ideally, crayfish parties are held out-of-doors.

The Danes are fond of lobster parties in summer, and another Danish summer treat is a shrimp *smørrebrød* (open sandwich). The recipe is simple: on a slice of *surbrød* (a sour bread made of rye flour with caraway seed) spread evenly with a thick layer of butter, pour a small bowlful of tiny fiord shrimp, caught, boiled and shelled the same day. Serve with a chilled draft lager and an ice-cold *schnaps*.

With all this information about the great Scandinavian invention – the smörgåsbord – you may think that Scandinavian cuisine involves nothing but sumptuous feasts. Of course this isn't true: it is the everyday cooking that tells us most about the lifestyle of other nations and the following recipes have been chosen because they reflect the special character of each of the Scandinavian countries. Some have become part of the repertoire of more than one country and sometimes of them all. If you have been to Scandinavia you will remember many of these dishes, and now you can enjoy cooking them for yourself and your family.

Soups

HYLDEBAERSUPPE (DENMARK)
Elderberry soup

Hot fruit soups, served as an appetizer, are very popular in Scandinavia. This Danish one is made with either fresh elderberries or elderberry juice.

Serves 6

1¼ lb elderberries or
  1 pint elderberry juice
¼ cup sugar
1 tablespoon lemon juice
1 lb apples, peeled, cored
  and cut into eighths
2 tablespoons potato flour
  (or 3¼ tablespoons, if
  using fresh extracted
  juice)

Bread cubes
6 thick slices of white
  bread
butter
sugar

If using fresh elderberries trim and wash them and simmer in 1¼ quarts of water for 10–15 minutes. Press the berries through a fine strainer, extracting all the juice from the fruit.

Reheat the fruit juice, add the sugar, lemon juice and apples, and cook until the apples are tender. Mix the potato flour with a little cold water. Pour this mixture into the soup, stirring all the time, but not allowing it to boil. The final soup should have a velvety finish.

If you are using elderberry juice instead of fresh elderberries, boil the apples in 1 quart of water until tender. Add the elderberry juice and lemon juice and thicken the soup with potato flour as before. Taste to see if it needs more sugar.

To make toasted bread cubes, cut the bread into ½ in cubes. Melt some butter in a skillet and add the bread cubes. Sprinkle them with sugar and brown on all sides, shaking the pan frequently to avoid burning. Remove and allow to cool.

Serve the soup in a tureen, with toasted bread cubes in a separate bowl.

RABARBERSOPPA (SWEDEN)
Rhubarb soup

This is a refreshing summer soup from Sweden, which you may also find in Denmark and Norway. When hot it is served before the main course; but it can also be served cold as a dessert.

Serves 6

1 lb rhubarb
1 cup sugar
2¼ tablespoons potato
  flour

Clean the rhubarb; cut it into 1 in sections and boil in 1 quart of water for about 10 minutes. Purée through a fine strainer and reheat the soup, adding the sugar. Taste to see if it is sweet enough.

Mix the potato flour with a little cold water to a smooth thin paste. Pour slowly into the soup, stirring all the time, but do not allow the soup to boil. Serve hot or cold with toasted bread cubes.

BLOMKÅLSSUPPE (NORWAY AND DENMARK)
Cauliflower soup

This simple soup is popular in Scandinavia in the summer, when cauliflowers are plentiful. Like many Danish soups it is flavored with a *suppevisk*, which consists of a bunch of parsley (with stalks), some greens of leek and a few celery leaves, all tied together with a piece of thread.

Serves 6

1¼ quarts light stock
1 'suppevisk'
1 teaspoon salt
1 medium cauliflower,
  separated into flowerets
3 tablespoons butter
¼ cup flour
2 egg yolks
¼ cup cream
paprika

Make a light stock by simmering some veal or beef bones with a *suppevisk* for about 1 hour. Strain well. Salt the stock and bring it to a boil. Add the cauliflower flowerets and simmer until tender – about 10 minutes. Remove with a slotted spoon and keep warm in a dish.

Melt the butter, stir in the flour and cook for a few minutes, stirring all the time. Add the stock slowly, still stirring. In a separate bowl, mix the egg yolks with the cream, add a little of the soup drop by drop, and return this mixture to the soup. Add the cauliflower pieces and heat gently, but do not let the soup boil or it will curdle. Serve in individual bowls and sprinkle each with a little paprika.

FISKESUPPE (NORWAY)
Fish soup with fishballs

The Norwegians are experts at making fish soup which they often serve with their famous fishballs. The essence of the soup is a good fish stock made from fresh fish trimmings. One version of the soup adds tomato purée.

Serves 6

Stock
2 lb fish trimmings
  (cod, haddock, halibut)
2 carrots, cut into chunks
1 parsnip, cut into chunks
1 onion, quartered
1 large potato, cut into
  chunks
1 bay leaf
1 'suppevisk'
6–8 black peppercorns
1 teaspoon salt

Fishballs
¾ lb cod fillet (or cod
  and pike)
up to 1 cup milk
1 egg
2 tablespoons flour
a little potato flour
  (optional)
1 teaspoon salt
white pepper

Tomato fish soup
1¼ quarts fish stock
2 tablespoons butter
3 tablespoons flour
3 tablespoons tomato
  purée
salt and black pepper
1 tablespoon chopped
  parsley

Put all the ingredients in a large saucepan with 2–3 quarts of cold water. Bring to a boil, skim the surface, cover and simmer for about 30 minutes. Strain through a fine strainer or muslin into a large bowl. Press the liquid out of the vegetables and fishbones, then discard them.

Clean the saucepan. Pour the fish stock back and reheat it. Let it boil for about 20 minutes, then strain it again.

To make the fishballs, grind the fish 4 or 5 times or purée in a blender. Add the milk a little at a time, and then the other ingredients, stirring vigorously. Chill for about 30 minutes, then form into tiny balls with a teaspoon dipped in boiling water. Drop the fishballs a few at a time into a pan of boiling water and poach for 2–3 minutes, until they rise to the surface. Remove with a slotted spoon and set aside.

To make the soup heat the fish stock thoroughly. Melt the butter in a large saucepan, stir in the flour and cook for a few minutes. Gradually add the hot fish stock, stirring all the time. Add tomato purée, salt and pepper. Add the fishballs and heat through. Serve in a soup tureen or individual bowls, with parsley sprinkled on top.

Scandinavia

GULE AERTER MED FLAESK (DENMARK)
Yellow pea soup with pork

This rich pea soup is found all over Scandinavia. Lager and *akvavit* are traditionally drunk with it.

Prepare the peas 24 hours in advance.
Serves 6

2 lb lightly salted pork or bacon
½ lb pearl onions
½ celeriac (celery root) or 3–4 celery stalks
¾ lb carrots, whole
1 'suppevisk'
½ teaspoon dried thyme
1 lb dried yellow peas, soaked overnight in a cool place
salt and pepper
vinegar (optional)

First boil the pork or bacon in 1 quart of water with the whole onions, celeriac or celery, carrots, *suppevisk* and thyme for 1–1½ hours.

Place the peas and soaking water in a large saucepan and bring to a boil. Simmer for 45–60 minutes until soft. Put the peas through a strainer or blender or beat them to a purée. Add some of the liquid in which the pork has been boiled until the pea soup has the right consistency – it should be very thick.

Discard the *suppevisk*, drain the vegetables, slice the carrots and celeriac, and add with the onions to the soup. Season with salt and pepper, and, if you like, a drop of vinegar.

Serve very hot in a large tureen with the pork on a separate serving plate. Boiled potatoes, rye bread and a good, strong mustard should also be on the table.

Humankind is dwarfed by the mountains and the sea of Norway.

HØNSEKØDSUPPE MED BOLLER (DENMARK)
Chicken with meatballs and flourballs

This soup is as old as the kingdom of Denmark itself; it used to be served at every village feast, when the menu was inevitably soup, fish, roast and dessert (*suppe, fisk, steg og dessert*). The soup was always made with a couple of old hens that were past egg-laying, and the meat was roast pork.

You need patience to make meatballs and flourballs. In the old days when there was going to be a feast, the cook and her helpers would start the preparations at least a day in advance, and the meat and flourballs would be stored overnight in the cellar in big earthenware tubs.

Prepare at least 3 hours in advance.
Serves 8

Små kødboller – small meatballs
½ lb finely ground lean pork (about 1 cup)
1 egg, beaten
½–1 cup milk
1 tablespoon flour
1 tablespoon potato flour
salt and pepper

Melboller – flourballs
6 tablespoons butter
1 cup flour, sifted
½ teaspoon salt
3 eggs

The soup
1 large stewing chicken (3–4 lb)
2 carrots, whole
2 leeks, whole
a 'suppevisk'
1–2 teaspoons salt
salt and pepper

Place the pork in a large bowl and add the other ingredients, using just enough milk to make a firm mixture. Mix well: the longer you stir, the better the result. (Use an electric mixer for best results.)

Boil 2 quarts of water with 2 teaspoons of salt. Reduce the heat to simmer. Dip a teaspoon in the water, then form a meatball with it, using another teaspoon to drop it into the water. Continue in this way until there is no more room in the saucepan.

When the meatballs rise to the surface bring the water to a boil 2 or 3 times, pushing them under each time with a slotted spoon. When they are firm, remove with the spoon. Cut one through to check that it is cooked.

Repeat until all the meat mixture is used up. Leave the meatballs to cool. Then place them in a covered bowl and store in a cool place.

Boil 1 cup water with the butter in a saucepan. Add the flour and beat rapidly until the mixture is smooth and cooked through. Add salt, still beating, then remove the pan from the heat. Let it cool a little, then beat in the eggs, 1 at a time, until the mixture is a smooth, soft, dropping consistency.

To cook the flourballs, boil about 2 quarts of water in a large saucepan. Remove from the heat. Form the flourballs with a teaspoon in the same way as you did the meatballs and drop them into the water.

When the whole surface is covered with flourballs, return the pan to the heat. As soon as the water reaches boiling point add a little cold water, for the flourballs will disintegrate if they boil. Repeat the process once or twice until all the balls are cooked. Remove carefully with a slotted spoon and place in cold water. Drain and keep in a covered bowl in a cool place until required.

Place the chicken in a large saucepan, cover with 2 quarts of water and bring to a boil. Skim the surface. Add the vegetables, *suppevisk* and salt. When the vegetables are cooked remove them with a slotted spoon, but leave the chicken to simmer for about 2–3 hours until tender.

Remove the chicken. Strain the stock and skim off the fat. Dice the vegetables and heat them in the soup together with the meatballs and flourballs. Season with salt and pepper to taste. Serve hot.

The chicken itself may be served as a main course: cut up the meat and discard the bones. Make a white sauce, using a little of the chicken soup. Add freshly grated horseradish or mushrooms, asparagus or capers; season with sugar, salt and pepper. Heat the chicken gently in the sauce and serve with potatoes and green peas.

Scandinavia

The Finnish landscape of lakes and pine forests

ÄRTER MED FLÄSK (SWEDEN)

Yellow pea soup with pork

The Finns and the Swedes have served this hearty soup once a week for as long as anyone can remember. The Danes have a slightly different version, which they make in winter.

Prepare the peas 24 hours in advance.
Serves 6

1 lb dried yellow peas, soaked overnight
1 medium onion, quartered
1 teaspoon dried marjoram
½ teaspoon dried thyme
1 lb lightly salted pork or bacon
salt

Bring the peas to a boil in the soaking water. Skim off any husks that come to the surface. Add the onion, marjoram, thyme and pork. Cover the pan and simmer gently for about 1½ hours until the peas are tender.

Remove the pork, slice it and keep it warm. Taste the soup and season with salt. Serve very hot with the pork on a separate plate accompanied by a good strong mustard and dark rye bread.

ØLLEBRØD (DENMARK)

Beer soup

Øllebrød – made of leftover rye bread and non-alcoholic beer – is to the Danes what oatmeal is to the Scots. It is a kind of gruel which is served with cream and eaten as an appetizer. It used to appear in most Danish homes at least once a week. *Øllebrød* is a very nourishing dish and some people like to eat it as a warming winter breakfast.

Prepare the prunes 12 hours and the bread 2 hours in advance.
Serves 6

¾ lb (about 12 slices) dark rye bread
1½ pints water
1½ pints mild ale
a piece of lemon rind
¼ cup sugar
12–18 prunes, soaked overnight (optional)
cream
1 or 2 eggs (optional)

Soak the bread in the water and beer for about 2 hours. Transfer the bread and beer mixture to a large saucepan. Add the lemon rind, bring to a boil and cook for 10 minutes. Pass through a fine strainer. Reheat and add the sugar and prunes. Cook until the prunes are tender and the *øllebrød* is thick and smooth. Serve in individual bowls with cream.

To enrich the soup, you can beat the sugar with 1 or 2 eggs before adding; but do not let the soup boil or it will curdle.

KESÄKEITTO (FINLAND)

Summer vegetable soup

The Finnish summer is short but sweet, and the Finns celebrate the season with this fresh vegetable soup. You can vary the list of vegetables according to what is available.

Serves 6–8

1 small, firm cauliflower, separated into flowerets
4–5 medium carrots, diced
2–3 new potatoes, cubed
½ lb fresh green beans, cut in strips
1¼ cups fresh green peas
4–6 radishes, quartered
2 teaspoons salt
3 cups finely chopped fresh spinach
2 tablespoons butter
2 tablespoons flour
1 cup milk
1 egg yolk
¼ cup heavy cream
¼ teaspoon white pepper
2 tablespoons finely chopped parsley or dill
about 30 fresh shrimp, cooked and shelled (optional)

Place the prepared vegetables, except the spinach, in a very large saucepan that holds at least 3 quarts and cover with cold water. Add salt. Boil for 5–8 minutes until the vegetables are tender, but do not overcook them. Add the spinach and boil for another 5 minutes. Strain the stock into a large bowl, keeping the vegetables warm in a separate bowl.

Melt the butter in the same saucepan, but do not let it brown. Stir in the flour and cook for a few minutes, then gradually add the hot vegetable stock, stirring constantly. Bring to a boil and simmer for a few minutes. Finally add the milk.

Beat the egg yolk in a small bowl with the cream, then add a little of the soup stock, drop by drop, still beating. Pour this mixture back into the soup, stirring all the time. Now add all the vegetables and heat gently, taking care that the soup does not boil or it will curdle. Season to taste with pepper and a little salt.

Serve in a soup tureen with parsley or dill sprinkled on top. For a special occasion, add a few shrimp to this soup at the end when it is almost ready to serve.

Fish

RØGET MED SPINAT (DENMARK)

Smoked salmon with spinach and scrambled egg

This is a typical Scandinavian party dish, often served as an appetizer at a dinner party or on the smörgåsbord.

Serves 4

4 large slices of smoked salmon

Creamed spinach
1½ lb fresh spinach
¼ cup butter
2 tablespoons flour
¾ cup cream
½ teaspoon salt
¼ teaspoon sugar

Scrambled egg
4 eggs
1 cup cream
2 tablespoons butter
¼ teaspoon salt

Remove the stems from the spinach and wash thoroughly; then, without adding any extra water, steam in a covered saucepan. Drain thoroughly.

Melt butter in a saucepan, add the spinach and sprinkle with flour. Slowly stir in the cream and cook for a few seconds. Season with salt and sugar and place in the center of a large serving plate.

Meanwhile beat the eggs with the cream. Melt the butter in a solid saucepan with a thick bottom, being careful not to let it brown. Pour in the egg and cream mixture and stir gently with a wooden spoon over a low heat until it begins to set (about 10 minutes). Sprinkle with salt and remove quickly from the pan before the eggs overcook.

Place a spoonful of scrambled egg on each slice of smoked salmon and roll it up. Arrange salmon rolls around the cooked spinach. Serve at once.

Wafer-thin smoked salmon combines deliciously with scrambled egg and spinach in this light dish.

Fiskefars med fyll: a subtle dish from the northern seas

GRAVAD LAX (SWEDEN)
Marinated salmon with mustard sauce.

This Swedish delicacy is not an everyday dish, but it is ideal for a celebration: it can be served as an appetizer at a dinner party, or on the smörgåsbord.

Prepare the salmon 48 hours in advance.
Serves 6

2 lb fresh salmon, middle-
  cut if possible
¼ cup sugar
3 tablespoons sea salt
¼ teaspoon saltpeter
a large bunch of fresh dill
10 peppercorns, crushed

Scrape and dry the salmon, but do not wash it. Halve it along the backbone and remove this and any other bones. Mix sugar, salt and saltpeter, and rub the fish on all sides with the mixture.

In a shallow dish, make a bed of some of the dill. Place half of the salmon on top, skin down. Sprinkle with more dill and the peppercorns. Place the other piece of salmon, skin uppermost, on top and cover with more dill. Cover with a wooden bread-board and put a heavy weight on top to press the salmon firmly together.

Keep in a cool, dark place for at least 48 hours (this explains the name of the dish: *gravad* literally means buried). It will keep for a week if kept cold.

Arrange the salmon on a wooden board, decorate with sprigs of dill and carve in not-too-thin slices. Discard the skin. Serve with mustard sauce, freshly made toast and butter, lager and a cold *schnaps*, or if you prefer it, a dry white wine.

MUSTARD SAUCE
2 tablespoons German
  mustard
1 tablespoon sugar
2 tablespoons vinegar
1 egg yolk (optional)
7 tablespoons oil
chopped fresh dill
salt and pepper

In a bowl mix mustard, sugar and vinegar (and egg yolk if you wish, to make the sauce smoother). Add the oil slowly, beating all the time until well mixed. Add the dill, season with salt and pepper and keep cool in an airtight container.

JANSSONS FRESTELSE (SWEDEN)
Jansson's temptation

This 'tempting' anchovy pie makes an ideal luncheon dish and is often served on the smörgåsbord. Swedish anchovies are actually smelts, which are pickled in salt, spice and sugar.

Serves 6

¼ cup butter
1 tablespoon vegetable oil
  (or use oil from the
  anchovies)
3 medium onions, thinly
  sliced
6 medium potatoes, cut in
  matchsticks
16 anchovy fillets
white pepper
1 cup cream
chopped parsley

Melt half the butter with the oil in a skillet and cook the onion rings gently until they are soft and transparent, but do not let them brown.

Butter an oblong baking dish, place a layer of potatoes in the bottom, then a layer of onions, then anchovies and finally a layer of potatoes. Sprinkle each layer with a little white pepper. Pour half the cream over the top, dot with the remaining butter and bake in the oven (425°F) until the potatoes are golden brown on top. Then add the remaining cream and continue to bake until the potatoes are tender and the liquid has been absorbed (about 45 minutes altogether).

Sprinkle with chopped parsley and serve hot.

STEGT (RØDSPAETTE (DENMARK)
Fried flounder

There is nothing like a freshly caught Danish *rødspaette*! In Scandinavian delicatessens you can buy a fresh deep-fried fillet of flounder with a spoonful of rémoulade and eat it outside just like fish and chips or take some home for the smörgåsbord.

Serves 4

2 large or 4 small
  flounder, cleaned, or 8
  flounder fillets
1 egg
1 cup dry white
  breadcrumbs
¼ teaspoon pepper
1 teaspoon salt
2 tablespoons flour
6 tablespoons butter
1 tablespoon oil
1 lemon
chopped parsley

If you buy 2 large fish, cut them in half lengthwise, leaving the backbone in 1 half. But cook small ones whole, simply with the heads removed.

Beat the egg with a fork in a flat dish. Mix the breadcrumbs with pepper and salt in another shallow dish. Coat the fish in flour, dip in the beaten egg and then turn them in the breadcrumbs.

Heat the butter and oil in a large skillet until golden brown and frothy. Fry the fish for 10–15 minutes, turning once. Serve immediately on a shallow dish, decorated with lemon boats and parsley. New potatoes, green peas and lightly browned butter complete the meal.

Fillets of flounder may be fried in the same way and often feature on the smörgåsbord accompanied by rémoulade sauce in a separate bowl. Delicious!

Scandinavia

FISKEFARS (NORWAY)
Fish purée

This dish plays an essential part in Scandinavian cooking, especially in Norway, where the household economy is closely linked with the sea. The fishmarket sells ready-made purée, and it is served about once a week in most homes.

A number of varied dishes can be made from a basic fish purée: tiny fishballs for soup; large fishballs to serve with shrimp or tomato sauce; fish pudding; and the renowned *Fiskefarsrand* – fish purée in a ring.

FISKEFARS MED FYLL (NORWAY)
Fish purée with creamed filling

For this you need a tube pan and a blender or a grinder. The filling can be made with either shellfish or creamed vegetables, such as carrots and peas.

Fish purée
6 oz fresh cod fillet
½ tablespoon potato or corn flour
salt and pepper
2 eggs, separated
2 tablespoons butter
2 tablespoons flour
⅔ cup milk

Creamed seafood filling
1¼ cups fish stock
¼ cup butter
¼ cup flour
1 tablespoon cream (optional)
salt and pepper
2 lemons
a pinch of curry powder
1 lb fresh shrimp, shelled
fresh dill or chopped parsley

To make the fish purée, mix together the fish, potato or corn flour and 1 teaspoon salt and pass through the grinder 4 or 5 times, or purée in a blender.

Beat the egg whites until stiff. Make a white sauce by melting the butter in a saucepan over a low heat and slowly stirring in the flour, then gradually add the milk until the mixture is smooth. Add the ground fish and the egg yolks. Season with salt and pepper and gently fold in the beaten egg whites. Place in a well greased tube pan, cover with foil and cook for 1 hour on the lowest rack in the oven at 300°F.

Meanwhile, to make the filling, first prepare the stock in the usual way, using fish trimmings. Melt butter in a saucepan and add the flour, stirring well. Slowly add the fish stock, stirring constantly until the sauce is thick and smooth; add the cream for an extra rich consistency. Season with salt and pepper, 1 teaspoon of lemon juice and just a pinch of curry powder. Fold in the shrimp and warm through gently, but do not allow to boil.

Remove the fish ring from the oven, loosen the edge with a knife and turn it out onto a warmed plate. Fill the center with the shrimp mixture. Serve at once, sprinkled with dill or parsley and decorated with lemon slices.

Fisherman of the Lofoten Islands (Norway) at the turn of the century

KALAKUKKO (FINLAND)
Fish and pork pie

The *kalakukko* is a typical Finnish dish combining meat and fish. It was traditionally cooked in a baker's oven as it cooled down after the bread was baked. With long, slow cooking all the fish bones simply disappeared.

In this dish the pie crust acts primarily to seal in the juices during cooking and only some of it is eaten with the dish.

Serves 4

Pastry
1 pint water
1 tablespoon salt
3 tablespoons melted butter
3¼ cups rye flour
3¼ cups wheat flour

Filling
1½–2 lb perch or other freshwater fish, cleaned but not boned
salt
½ lb pork fat back, sliced
pork drippings for basting

Mix the water, salt, melted butter and flour and knead until you have a smooth, firm dough. Roll out with a rolling pin to an oblong shape about ½ in thick. Clean the fish, wash and dry well.

Sprinkle a little flour in the center of the dough and place a layer of fish on top, lightly salted, then a layer of pork slices and a little more salt and so on until all the ingredients are used up. Moisten the edges of the dough with cold water, fold over the filling and seal firmly. Place on a baking sheet and bake in a hot oven (480°F) for about 2 minutes, then reduce heat to 350°F and cook for another 2–3 hours. Cover with aluminum foil but remember to baste occasionally with pork drippings. Remove the pie from the oven and fold in a damp towel to prevent the crust getting too hard.

To serve, cut off the top of the crust, scoop out the fish and pork mixture and eat it with a little of the crust and plenty of melted butter.

Kogt torsk: *a succulent meal and a half, with the head as a bonus*

KOGT TORSK (DENMARK)
Whole cod as the Danes serve it

Cod is known to be at its best in the months with an R in them. In Denmark whole cod is traditionally served on New Year's Eve. It is best cooked in a fish kettle but it can also be cut in half and cooked in a large saucepan if necessary.

On a cold winter's night it makes a very satisfying meal, while leftovers can be used in a fish pie the following day, served with hot tomato sauce.

The guest who is a true connoisseur of cod will ask for the fish's head, which is considered a great delicacy. He will need a finger bowl and an extra plate for the bones! You could also use this recipe to cook cod fillets.

Serves 8–10

a whole cod weighing 4–5 lb (or use cod fillets)	Rinse the cod well in cold water and place in a fish kettle. Add about 1½ quarts of cold water and the salt, vinegar, onion and peppercorns. Bring slowly to a boil and skim the surface. Simmer gently for 15–20 minutes (fillets will not take as long). Lift the fish out carefully and place on a large oval platter.
¼ cup salt	
1 tablespoon vinegar	
1 small onion	
6 peppercorns	
2 black olives	Remove the eyes and replace with black olives, and fill the mouth with a lemon wedge. Decorate with more lemon wedges and parsley.
1 lemon	
chopped parsley	
	For a truly Danish meal, serve with boiled potatoes, melted butter, chopped hard-cooked eggs and chopped, marinated beets or grated fresh horseradish.

KOKT LUTFISK (SWEDEN, NORWAY AND FINLAND)
Baked ling or burbot

Ling, a member of the cod family, is traditionally served on Christmas Eve throughout Scandinavia, except Denmark. For this recipe the fish are dried outdoors on wooden racks, then soaked, first in water and then in a lye solution for 5–6 days. Nowadays *lutfisk* can be bought ready prepared and just need to be soaked in cold water for 48 hours before use.

Prepare the fish 24 hours in advance.
Serves 4

4 lb dried ling or burbot, soaked overnight	Drain the soaked fish and place it skin down in a buttered baking dish. Sprinkle with salt, cover with foil and bake at 425°F for 30–35 minutes. Drain and serve with boiled potatoes.
4 teaspoons salt	

MARINEREDE STEGTE SILD (DENMARK)
Marinated fried herrings

This is a very popular dish on the smörgåsbord. The vinegar used should preferably be Danish Heidelberg vinegar which is quite mild. If you use a stronger vinegar, dilute with water.

Prepare this dish 24 hours in advance.
Serves 4

2 lb fried herrings, lukewarm (p. 133)	Arrange the herrings in a single layer on a flat dish. Boil the vinegar, sugar and pepper in a saucepan for a few minutes, allow to cool and pour over the herrings. Leave to marinate for a few hours or overnight. Serve the herrings with freshly cut onion rings neatly arranged on top.
1 cup vinegar	
6 tablespoons sugar	
1 teaspoon pepper	
2–3 onions	

Scandinavia

MARINEREDE SILD (DENMARK)

Marinated herrings

Fresh herrings are unsuitable for this recipe; use raw salted herrings out of a barrel from a delicatessen. As a substitute try plain rollmops, unrolled and rinsed under cold water.

Allow one fish per person and soak in water overnight. Drain and fillet the herrings, and wipe them dry with a paper towel. Then prepare one of the following marinades.

Prepare 2–3 hours in advance.

Serves 6

Vinaigrette marinade
1 cup white vinegar (preferably Heidelberg vinegar)
$\frac{1}{2}$ cup sugar
20 black peppercorns
6 salted herrings, soaked overnight
1 or 2 onions or shallots, sliced

Vinegar varies greatly, and you may have to dilute this mixture with a little water if you are using a very strong one. Boil the vinegar, sugar and peppercorns together for a few minutes, then leave the mixture to cool. Pour over the herrings and refrigerate for a couple of hours or more. Serve with onion rings on top. Or drain, cut into thick slices and serve tossed in homemade mayonnaise seasoned with lemon juice and curry powder to taste.

Oil and vinegar marinade
$\frac{1}{2}$ cup olive oil or vegetable oil, or both mixed
$\frac{1}{4}$ cup vinegar
$\frac{1}{2}$–1 tablespoon sugar sugar
1–2 onions, chopped
a small bunch of chives, finely chopped

Mix the oil, vinegar and sugar. Pour over the herring fillets and leave in a cool place for several hours. Serve with chopped onions and chives sprinkled on top.

STEGT SILD MED STUVEDE KARTOFLER (DENMARK)

Fried herrings with potatoes in white sauce

This is a very old, traditional dish. The thrifty Danish cook used leftover potatoes for the sauce, and often fried enough herrings to marinate some for the next day's cold table.

Serves 4

Fried herrings
2 lb herrings, cleaned and boned
flour (or 2 beaten eggs and breadcrumbs)
salt and pepper
1 cup butter
1 teaspoon oil
parsley to garnish
Potatoes in white sauce
$1\frac{1}{2}$ lb firm potatoes (preferably new)
3 tablespoons butter
$\frac{1}{4}$ cup flour
$1\frac{3}{4}$ cups milk or cream
$\frac{1}{2}$ teaspoon salt

Rinse the herrings well, drain and coat in either seasoned flour or beaten eggs and breadcrumbs. Melt the butter in a skillet and add the oil. Fry the herrings for a few minutes on each side. Drain on paper towels and keep hot in the oven.

Boil the potatoes, leave them to cool before peeling, then cut them into slices or cubes.

To make the white sauce: melt the butter in a saucepan, add the flour and stir until it has been absorbed. Add the milk or cream slowly, stirring all the time until the sauce is smooth.

Season with salt. Add the potatoes, turning them gently in the sauce over a low heat until they are heated through.

If you wish you can use floury old potatoes to accompany the herrings: simply peel and dice, then boil them in $1\frac{3}{4}$ cups milk with 3 tablespoons butter and $\frac{1}{2}$ teaspoon salt. The potatoes themselves will thicken the sauce.

Serve the herrings, decorated with parsley, and the potatoes in a separate dish. Serve vinegar as an accompaniment.

STRÖMMINGSLÅDA (FINLAND AND SWEDEN)

Herring and potato pie

This popular luncheon dish makes a wholesome meal in itself. The potatoes should be sliced very thinly, like potato chips.

Serves 4

6 tablespoons butter
$1\frac{1}{2}$ lb potatoes, very thinly sliced
1 lb fresh herrings, filleted
2–3 tomatoes, sliced
1 medium onion, finely chopped
1 tablespoon salt
$\frac{1}{2}$ teaspoon white pepper
2 eggs
$1\frac{3}{4}$ cups milk
1 tablespoon flour
2 tablespoons oil from canned anchovies (if you happen to have it)
$1\frac{1}{2}$ tablespoons dry breadcrumbs

Butter a baking dish and cover the bottom with potato slices. Place the herrings on top, then a layer of tomato slices. Sprinkle with onion, dot with butter and season with salt and pepper. Repeat this again, ending with a layer of potatoes.

Beat the eggs with the milk and flour (and anchovy oil if used), and pour this over. Sprinkle with breadcrumbs, dot with the rest of the butter, and bake in a hot oven (425°F) for 30–45 minutes, until the potatoes are tender.

Serve hot with tomato sauce or a mild vinegar.

GLASMÄSTAR SILL (SWEDEN)

Glassblower's herring

The origin of this dish is uncertain, but it gets its name from the large glass jar that you need to make it.

Prepare 4–5 days in advance.

Serves 4

2 salted Iceland herrings (the big, fat ones), soaked overnight
1 carrot, thinly sliced
1 large red onion, thinly sliced
a piece of fresh horse-radish root, thinly sliced
1 dill flower or a small bunch of fresh dill
$1\frac{1}{2}$ cups white vinegar
3–4 tablespoons sugar
1 cup water
10 black peppercorns
2–3 bay leaves

Clean and scrape the herrings, cut off the heads and tails, but do not remove the backbones or skin. Cut into pieces 1 in wide. Arrange the herring pieces with the vegetables, horseradish and dill in layers in a tall glass jar.

Heat the vinegar with the sugar, water, peppercorns and bay leaves. Boil for a few minutes, remove from heat and allow to cool. Pour over the herrings in the jar and put a saucer on top, if necessary, to keep the herrings immersed in the dressing. Cover and leave in a cool place for 3–4 days.

Serve on the smörgåsbord with rye bread and butter.

The Faeroe Islands – Denmark's windswept outpost between Iceland and the Shetlands

Meat

AEGGEKAGE (DENMARK)

Bacon and egg cake

An egg cake with bacon is a great situation-saver, if you have unexpected visitors: it makes a quick, satisfying and attractive meal. If any is left over you can eat it cold the next day on buttered rye bread.

Serves 4

10 bacon slices
4 eggs
½ cup milk
½ teaspoon salt
a little freshly ground black pepper
1–2 tablespoons finely cut chives

Fry the bacon until crisp in a heavy skillet. Remove and keep warm.

In a mixing bowl beat the eggs, milk, salt and pepper together, using a fork. Pour the mixture into the skillet (if there is too much fat from the bacon, pour a little away). Let the egg mixture set over a low heat, lifting the edges with a palette knife now and again to let the egg run underneath.

When the egg mixture has set, but is still a little damp on top, turn off the heat, and decorate with the crisp bacon slices in a star pattern. Sprinkle generously with chopped chives and serve at once straight from the pan, with rye bread and mustard.

ÄPPEL-FLÄSK (SWEDEN)

Bacon and apple

This light luncheon dish is often found on the smörgåsbord, served with dark rye bread.

Serves 4

about 2 tablespoons butter
1 lb bacon in thick slices
2 large onions, thinly sliced
1½ lb cooking apples, cored and cut into wedges, but not peeled
a pinch of sugar (optional)
freshly ground black pepper
2 teaspoons chopped parsley
a pinch of curry powder (optional)

Melt half the butter in a large skillet and fry the bacon until golden brown. Remove and keep hot in the oven. Clean the pan to prevent the onions burning. On a reduced heat add the rest of the butter and fry the onions in the same pan. When the onions are soft, but not browned, add the apple wedges (and a pinch of sugar if the apples are very tart) and shake the pan. Cover with a lid and cook gently for about 10 minutes. Check occasionally to make sure that the apples do not stick to the bottom.

When the apples are cooked, return the bacon to the pan and turn the mixture gently to heat through. Add black pepper and sprinkle with chopped parsley. Serve straight from the pan.

As a variation on this dish you can add a little curry powder with the apples. You can also broil the bacon if you prefer, and use the bacon fat from the broiler pan to fry the onions and apples.

Danish bacon and egg cake: simple ingredients for a satisfying meal

LEVERPOSTEJ (DENMARK)

Liver pâté

Leverpostej is a must for *smørrebrød.* If you like pâté strongly spiced, then add anchovies and allspice.

Serves 6

1 lb pork liver
½ lb bacon or pork fat back, cut into strips
1 onion, peeled and quartered
3–4 anchovies (optional)
¼ cup butter
½ cup flour
1½ cups milk
1–2 eggs, beaten
1 teaspoon ground allspice (optional)
1 teaspoon salt
¼ teaspoon black pepper

Wash the liver, remove sinews and cut into strips. Put the liver, bacon, onion and anchovies (if used) through the grinder 3 times.

Make a roux with the butter and flour and stir in the milk to make a smooth, thick white sauce. Let it cook for a few minutes, then add the liver mixture, eggs, allspice (if used) and salt and pepper.

Pour the mixture into a well greased oblong baking pan and bake in the lower part of the oven at 350°F for 45–60 minutes, covered with foil to prevent a skin from forming.

KARJALANPAISTI (FINLAND)

Lamb, pork and veal stew

This traditional dish from the region of Karelia is very simple to prepare. The combination of three kinds of meat produces a quite unique flavor. Traditionally it was cooked very slowly, overnight, in a cooling bread oven, so that the meat became especially tender.

Serves 8–10

1 lb boneless beef
1 lb boneless lamb
1 lb boneless lean pork
1 teaspoon salt
boiling water
10 peppercorns

Cut the meat into chunks, place in a deep casserole and season with salt. Pour over just enough boiling water to cover the meat and add the peppercorns. Cook uncovered in a hot oven (400°F) for 30 minutes, then reduce the heat to 325°F, cover the casserole with a tight-fitting lid and cook for a further 2 hours or so. Serve with baked potatoes and Karelian turnovers (page 140).

KÖTTBULLAR (SWEDEN)

Meatballs

Små köttbullar (small meatballs) are a traditional part of the Swedish smörgåsbord, and are often served at cocktail parties. The Norwegians are also fond of these meatballs, and the Danes have their own version, which they boil and serve in soups and stews.

Serves 6

1 cup dry white breadcrumbs
1 cup milk (or half cream and half water)
1 small onion, chopped
⅓ cup butter
1 lb ground beef (or ¾ lb beef, ¼ lb veal)
¼ lb ground pork
1 egg
2 teaspoons salt
¼ teaspoon white pepper
½ teaspoon ground allspice (optional)

Soak the breadcrumbs in the milk. Sauté the onion in 2 tablespoons butter until golden.

In a large bowl combine the meat with the breadcrumb mixture, egg, onion, salt, pepper and allspice, if used. Stir well until smooth. Form into small meatballs with a teaspoon in the palm of your hand. Fry them in the remaining butter, a few at a time, shaking the pan so that they brown on all sides. They will take 3–5 minutes.

The meatballs can also be served as a main course with gravy. They are made larger using a tablespoon instead of a teaspoon, and the gravy is prepared as for hamburgers (see page 136).

KOKT GRILJERAD SKINKE (SWEDEN)
Christmas ham

In Sweden and Finland the *griljerad skinke* takes pride of place at the Christmas dinner. It is cured and salted in the weeks before the festival, served hot on Christmas Eve and cold on the days that follow. The Finns serve baked rutabaga or turnips with the ham, but the Swedes prefer red cabbage and mashed potatoes.

Prepare at least 3 weeks in advance.

½ cup salt
¾ cup sugar
2 teaspoons saltpeter
1 fresh ham on the bone, about 8–10 lb

Brine
1 cup salt
⅔ cup brown sugar, firmly packed
1 tablespoon saltpeter
2 teaspoons whole cloves
4½ quarts boiling water

Seasonings
1 onion, chopped
1 carrot, chopped
2 bay leaves
½ teaspoon ground allspice

Glaze
1 egg white, stiffly beaten
1 tablespoon dry mustard
1 tablespoon sugar
fine dry breadcrumbs

Garnish (optional)
parsley
orange sections
eating apples
prunes or cranberry jelly
creamed butter

Mix the salt, sugar and saltpeter, rub it into the ham. Leave in a cool place for 2–3 days to cure. Then place the ham in a deep container.

To make the brine, add salt, brown sugar, saltpeter and cloves to the boiling water. Cook for a few minutes, then allow to cool and pour over the ham. Cover with a plate weighed down with a heavy object to keep the ham fully immersed in the brine. Leave in a cool place for 2–3 weeks, turning the ham in the brine occasionally.

The day before serving, remove the ham from the brine and wipe dry. Place in a large saucepan, fat side up, and cover with cold water. Bring gently to a boil and skim the surface, then add the seasonings. Simmer for about 4 hours, turning once halfway through, until the ham is tender.

Remove from the pan, trim off the skin and excess fat, return to the pan and leave to cool overnight with the seasonings.

Mix the beaten egg white with mustard and sugar to make the glaze and brush this on the fat side of the ham, then sprinkle with breadcrumbs. Bake in the oven at 350°F for about 50 minutes, until golden brown. Arrange the ham on a large wooden board and trim the bone with a paper frill and sprigs of parsley. It may also be garnished with orange segments or stuffed apples. (Peel and core eating apples and simmer with a little sugar and lemon rind until tender, but not soft. Stuff with prunes or cranberry jelly.) If the ham is served cold, decorate it with creamed butter piped through a pastry nozzle.

BØF À LA NELSON (DENMARK)
Beef à la Nelson

I am not sure how this dish got its name, especially since Lord Nelson, the British naval hero, has a quite different reputation in Denmark. He has never been entirely forgiven for turning his blind eye to the plight of the Danes at the battle of Copenhagen in 1801!

For best results with this dish, use a good quality beef flank steak or veal loin.

Serves 4

1½ lb tender beef or veal, sliced
¼ cup butter
1 lb potatoes, thinly sliced
½ lb tomatoes, skinned and quartered
½ cup stock or water
about 1 teaspoon salt

Pound the meat slices lightly with a meat mallet, then brown them in butter in a skillet. Arrange them in a baking dish in alternate layers with potatoes and tomatoes. Add the stock or water and sprinkle with salt. Cover and cook in a moderate oven (350°F) for about 1 hour until the meat is tender. Adjust seasoning before serving.

HAKKEBØF MED LØG (DENMARK)
Hamburgers with onions

Who knows, maybe the Vikings invented the hamburger? This dish is certainly a Danish classic.

Serves 4

½ cup butter
2 onions, thinly sliced
salt
1¾ cups stock or water
1½ lb best quality ground beef
4–5 tablespoons flour
freshly ground black pepper
a dash of soy sauce
a dash of Worcestershire sauce
1 tablespoon tomato sauce (optional)
a pinch of sugar (optional)
cream (optional)

Melt half the butter in a skillet and fry the onions until golden brown. Remove from pan and sprinkle with a little salt. Keep warm in the oven. Rinse out the pan with a little of the stock or water and reserve this for the gravy.

Divide the beef into 6 or 8 portions. Shape them into balls, and flatten them with the palm of your hand to a thickness of about ½ in. Tidy the edges of the hamburgers with the side of a large knife and make a shallow criss-cross pattern on each side.

Mix the flour, salt and pepper on a flat plate and carefully coat each hamburger with the mixture, covering it completely. Brown the rest of the butter in the skillet and fry the hamburgers on each side for about 4 minutes, turning carefully with a wide spatula. They should still be slightly pink inside. Keep warm in the oven.

Add the onion water and stock to the pan and swirl around. Mix the flour left over on the plate with a little cold water and add to the pan, stirring constantly. Add the soy sauce, Worcestershire sauce, and also the tomato sauce if you like it. Taste and adjust seasoning. A pinch of sugar may improve the flavor; and if you have a little cream to spare, add this too.

Serve the hamburgers with the fried onions on top and either pour the gravy around them or serve in a sauceboat. Boiled potatoes and a sweet-sour pickle like beets or *asier* (Danish pickled cucumbers) are the traditional accompaniments.

SJÖMANSBIFF (SWEDEN)
Sailor's beef

This Swedish favorite is normally made with beef, but you could use horsemeat, reindeer or elk! The Danes have a similar dish, made without the beer.

Serves 4

½ cup butter
4 medium onions, sliced
1 cup stock or water
1½ lb flank steak cut into 8 slices
salt and pepper
8 potatoes, sliced
1 cup light ale
1 tablespoon chopped parsley

Melt half the butter in a large skillet and fry the onions until golden brown. Remove the onions, rinse out the pan with a little of the water or stock to add flavor to it, then pour this into a cup and reserve for addition to the stock.

Melt the rest of the butter in the pan and fry the meat on both sides, 2 or 3 slices at a time. Season with salt and pepper, and set aside. Rinse out the pan with the reserved onion water and add to the rest of the water or stock.

In a deep casserole place layers of meat slices, potato slices and onions, finishing with a layer of potatoes. Pour the beer and the meat stock over the stew. Cover tightly and cook in the oven at 400°F for about 1½ hours. Taste the meat juice and adjust seasoning. Serve in the casserole with chopped parsley sprinkled on top.

Christmas ham: a dish that more than repays the weeks of preparation, here served the Swedish way with red cabbage

Scandinavia

Norwegian farmers work every bit of ground between the mountains and the sea.

SKIPPERLABSKOVS (DENMARK)
Sailor's beef stew

This simple winter dish has a meaty gravy thickened with potatoes.

Serves 4

1½ lb beef stew meat, diced	Boil about 1¾ cups water, add the diced meat and onion, bring back to a boil and skim. Add the potatoes, bay leaves, peppercorns and salt. Simmer for 1½–2 hours until the meat is tender. Serve the stew piping hot with parsley sprinkled on top, and serve Danish rye bread and butter with it.
1 large onion, diced	
1¼ lb floury potatoes, diced	
1–2 bay leaves	
6 whole black peppercorns	
1 teaspoon salt	
1 tablespoon chopped parsley	

DILLKÖTT (SWEDEN)
Lamb in dill sauce

Lamb is expensive in Scandinavia. The lambing season begins quite late and the first roast lamb is awaited eagerly. The Danes serve it with the first cucumber salad of the season, new potatoes and perhaps stewed young rhubarb. In Sweden, lamb is often served with dill sauce.

Serves 4

2 lb breast of lamb	Put the meat into a large saucepan and cover with 1 quart of water. Bring to a boil. Skim, add salt, peppercorns, bay leaf, onion and dill. Cover with a lid and simmer for about 1–1½ hours, until the meat is tender.
2 teaspoons salt	
5 white peppercorns	
1 bay leaf	
1 onion, sliced	
5 sprigs of fresh dill	Melt the butter, add flour, stir and add stock a little at a time, stirring constantly until you have a smooth, thick sauce. Simmer gently for a few minutes. Add dill, vinegar, sugar, salt and lemon juice. Beat the egg yolk lightly in a small bowl with a little of the sauce and pour into the pan. Continue heating the sauce, beating all the time, but do not let it boil or it will curdle. Taste and season as required.
Dill sauce	
2 tablespoons butter	
2 tablespoons flour	
1 pint stock from the meat	
3 tablespoons chopped fresh dill	Cut the meat into pieces and strain the sauce over it. Serve with boiled potatoes or rice. Garnish the meat with sprigs of dill.
1 tablespoon white vinegar	
2 teaspoons sugar	
¼ teaspoon salt	Dill sauce is also delicious with boiled fish: use fish or chicken stock instead of the meat stock.
a dash of lemon juice	
1 egg yolk	

FRIKADELLER (DENMARK)
Danish meatcakes

Frikadeller – isn't that a lovely name – is a national dish served in every Danish home as a main course, on the smörgåsbord, or sliced cold as a topping for a *smørrebrød*.

Serves 4

½ lb boneless veal	Grind the meat with the onion twice, then beat in the eggs, seasoning and flour or breadcrumbs. Add the liquid gradually: if you have time add only half the liquid at first, leave the mixture for 30 minutes and then add the rest. Beat the mixture very thoroughly: the more you stir it, the better it will be. Making *frikadeller* by hand is quite hard work, so it is easier to use an electric mixer on a low speed.
½ lb boneless lean pork	
1 medium onion, quartered	
1–2 eggs	
2 teaspoons salt	
¼ teaspoon freshly ground black pepper	
¾ cup flour or dry breadcrumbs	The finished meat mixture should be light and airy. A Danish cook will taste it at this stage to see if the seasoning needs adjusting.
1¼–1½ cups soda water or half milk and half soda water	Melt the butter in a large skillet and dip a tablespoon in it. Then shape an oblong meatcake with the spoon pressed against the side of the bowl and drop it into the pan. Repeat until the pan is full, but do not let the *frikadeller* touch each other. Shake the pan and fry for 5–6 minutes over a medium heat, then turn them and fry on the other side for a further 5–6 minutes.
¼ cup butter	

The meatcakes should be nicely browned on both sides and cooked through, not pink inside. Keep them warm in a baking dish in the oven while you make the next batch.

For a main course serve *frikadeller* with boiled potatoes and a gravy made in the pan after you have finished frying the meatcakes, or a little browned butter. Pickled beets or cucumber salad often accompany the dish, or spring cabbage in a white sauce, seasoned with nutmeg.

Tiny *frikadeller*, shaped with a teaspoon instead of a tablespoon, are popular with cocktails or at children's parties. You can also vary the seasoning of the meat mixture by adding curry powder, allspice or other spices of your choice.

FÅR I KÅL (NORWAY)
Lamb and cabbage stew

This Norwegian hotpot is traditionally made with mutton or lamb, but you can also use a mixture of lamb and beef.

Serves 6

¼ cup butter	Melt the butter in a large flameproof casserole and brown the meat on all sides. If you wish you can sprinkle a little flour on the meat cubes to thicken the stew. Remove and set aside. Brown the cabbage in the same pan, remove and set aside.
2 lb boned breast of lamb, cut into large cubes	
flour (optional)	
2 lb head of white cabbage, cut into large chunks	In the same casserole, arrange alternate layers of meat, cabbage and potatoes if used, sprinkling salt between the layers. Add the muslin bag with spices and 1 cup water (or 1 pint if you have added potatoes). Cover with a lid and simmer for about 1½–2 hours. Taste and adjust seasoning, remove the muslin bag and serve in the casserole with chopped parsley sprinkled on top.
1 lb potatoes, sliced (optional)	
2–3 teaspoons salt	
10 white peppercorns, slightly crushed, and 1 bay leaf, tied together in a muslin bag	Serve with boiled potatoes and carrots.
1 tablespoon chopped parsley	

Poultry and game

DYRESTEG (DENMARK AND NORWAY)
Roast venison or reindeer

Dyresteg is a great delicacy in all the Scandinavian countries. Finnish reindeer is particularly good, and the Norwegians use venison a great deal. There are no reindeer in Denmark, but the Danes serve venison on special occasions.

The meat has a flavor of its own, but needs careful cooking to avoid being too dry. It is the sauce that makes this dish such a special one.

Serves 8

*5–6 lb saddle of vension
or reindeer
2 teaspoons salt
¼ teaspoon pepper
5 oz fat bacon or lard,
thinly sliced
parsley*

First make the beef stock by boiling a couple of large bones with a small onion, 2 carrots and a little salt for several hours. Add a *suppevisk* (see Glossary) if you have the ingredients.

Wash the saddle of venison or reindeer and remove the membranes. Rub with salt and pepper and cover with bacon or lard. Wrap in foil and place on a rack in the oven preheated to 325°F.

After an hour or so, remove the saddle from the oven and carefully fold down the foil on each side. Return to the oven, increasing the heat to 400°F. Cook for about another hour.

*Sauce
¼ cup butter
4–5 tablespoons flour
1 pint beef stock
½ cup heavy cream
a dash of soy sauce
salt
2–3 teaspoons redcurrant
jelly
1 tablespoon finely diced
gjetost (Norwegian goat
cheese) or 1 tablespoon
tomato catsup, for
extra flavor*

Meanwhile to make the sauce melt the butter in a large saucepan. Add the flour and stir. Add the beef stock a little at a time, stirring vigorously. Add the cream, soy sauce (for coloring), salt, redcurrant jelly and *gjetost* or tomato catsup. Carefully remove the roast from the oven and pour the meat juice in the foil into the sauce.

Carve the meat before serving by loosening the fillets on either side of the back with a sharp knife. Cut them diagonally into ½ in slices, put them back in place and arrange the whole saddle on a large serving platter.

Pour a little of the hot sauce over the meat and serve the rest in a sauceboat. Place French fried potatoes beside the saddle, and garnish with parsley.

STEGT KYLLING (DENMARK)
Roast chicken

This is an old Danish recipe dating from the time when chicken was a delicacy. The birds were stuffed with parsley, pot roasted and served with a delicious cream sauce.

Serves 4

*2 chickens, each weighing
about 2 lb
about 2 teaspoons salt
1 teaspoon freshly ground
black pepper
2 bunches parsley
⅓–½ cup butter
1 cup cream (half light,
half heavy)
flour (optional)*

Rub the chickens with salt and pepper. Wash and dry the parsley, removing stalks. Mix half the butter with half the parsley tops and put inside the birds. Make a stock by simmering the parsley stalks and chicken giblets in a little water.

Melt the rest of the butter in a large heavy pot or casserole until it foams, add the chickens and brown them on all sides. Add about ½ cup stock, cover and let the chickens cook, breasts up, for about 45 minutes. Remove the chickens and keep them warm in the oven.

Make the sauce by adding the cream and a little more water or stock to the pot. If necessary thicken the sauce with a little flour mixed to a thin paste with cold water. Taste and season as required.

Finally cut the chickens in half with a pair of poultry shears. Arrange the birds on a heated platter with a spoonful of sauce on each portion. Garnish with fresh parsley and serve with boiled new potatoes and the remainder of the sauce in a sauceboat, sprinkled with more chopped parsley. Cucumber salad or a green salad with a cream and lemon dressing go well with this dish.

Gathering hay in Norway

Vegetables

AGURKESALAT (DENMARK)
Cucumber salad

Cucumber salad is served all over Scandinavia, particularly in the summer, which is probably why in Denmark that season is called *Agurketid* – cucumber time.

Cucumber salad made in the following way will not give you indigestion. It is at its best when freshly made, but it can be kept covered in the refrigerator for a day or two. It's delicious served with most meat dishes, hot or cold salmon and as a garnish for *smørrebrød.*

Serves 4

1 medium cucumber
1 teaspoon salt
½ cup Danish Heidelberg or other vinegar
½ cup water
½ cup sugar
freshly ground black or white pepper
chopped chives or dill (optional)

Wash the cucumber and, if the skin is very tough, peel it. Slice thinly, place in a large bowl and sprinkle with salt. Toss to spread the salt evenly, then place a heavy weight on top and leave for about 15 minutes.

Meanwhile mix the vinegar, water and sugar together and season with a little pepper. The dressing should taste fairly sweet and not too sharp.

Now squeeze the cucumber in cheesecloth to remove all the liquid. Place the cucumber in a serving bowl and pour on the dressing. Leave for 30 minutes before serving.

If you wish you can add chopped chives or freshly cut dill.

RØDKÅL (DENMARK)
Red cabbage

Sweet-sour red cabbage, an essential feature of a Scandinavian Christmas, is at other times eaten cold on *smørrebrød* with slices of roast pork and crisp crackling. Some Danish cooks add caraway seeds to the cabbage and others sweeten it with a little redcurrant jelly instead of some of the sugar. It can be made a day in advance, as it improves with reheating.

Serves 6

about 3 lb head of red cabbage
5 tablespoons butter
¼ cup brown sugar
½ cup water
½ cup white or brown vinegar
1 teaspoon salt
½ cup beet vinegar or red wine (optional)

Cut the cabbage into 4. Remove the outer leaves and white core, and wash thoroughly. Drain, dry and slice finely. Melt the butter in a large flameproof casserole, add the cabbage and sugar, and stir. Now add the water, vinegar and salt. Cover and cook slowly for 1½–2 hours. Check occasionally to see that the cabbage does not boil dry, and add a little beet vinegar or red wine, if you have it, to give the dish a fine, red color. When the cabbage is tender, taste to see if it needs more seasoning. The flavor should be sweet-sour, not too sharp.

BRUNEDE KARTOFLER (DENMARK)
Caramelized potatoes

Danes are always being asked how they make their delicious *brunede kartofler*; so here is the recipe. Be careful not to overcook the potatoes, or they will break up.

Serves 4

3 tablespoons sugar
3–4 tablespoons butter
1½ lb small, firm potatoes, boiled and peeled

Melt the sugar in a large skillet. When it is light brown, add the butter. Rinse the potatoes well under a cold tap and quickly tip into the pan. Shake the pan so that the potatoes are caramelized all over. Heat through and serve at once.

LÄNTTULAATIKKO (FINLAND)
Rutabaga casserole

This is a popular way of serving rutabaga in Finland as an accompaniment to pork and ham. If you cannot get rutabaga, try the recipe with turnips.

Serves 6

2 lb rutabaga, peeled and cut into cubes
salt
1 tablespoon flour
2 tablespoons butter
½–1 cup milk or cream
pepper
grated nutmeg
sugar
1–2 eggs, lightly beaten
3–4 tablespoons dry breadcrumbs

Cover the rutabaga with slightly salted water and simmer for about 20 minutes until tender. Drain and mash or press through a potato ricer. Add the flour and half the butter, stirring all the time, then slowly beat in the milk or cream until the mixture is light and fluffy.

Season to taste with salt, pepper, nutmeg and sugar. Add the egg and pour the mixture into a well-buttered baking dish. Sprinkle breadcrumbs on top, dot with the remaining butter and bake in the oven at 350°F for about 1 hour, until the top is lightly browned.

KARJALAN PIIRAKKA (FINLAND)
Karelian turnovers

Karelian cooking in general has been greatly influenced by its close proximity to Russia. In fact, today's modern boundaries place the old Finnish province in the USSR. However, many Karelians have settled in other parts of Finland, where they still preserve their ancient traditions. These turnovers, which can be filled with either rice or mashed potatoes, are usually served as an accompaniment to meat stews.

Makes 20 turnovers

Filling
1 cup water
1 cup short-grain rice
¾ pint milk
2 tablespoons butter
1 teaspoon salt

Pastry
1 cup water
1½ cups flour, sifted
1¼ cups rye flour, sifted
1 teaspoon salt

Glaze
1 cup boiling water
2 tablespoons butter

To make the filling, bring the water to a boil and add the rice. Cook slowly, uncovered, for 10–15 minutes, until the water has almost been absorbed. Add milk, cover with a lid and cook slowly until the rice is tender. Stir occasionally. Finally, add the butter and salt.

To make the pastry, mix the water, flour and salt. Knead well until the dough is smooth and pliable. Divide into about 20 small sections and roll them into oblong shapes, as thin as possible.

Spread a thin layer of the filling in the middle of each oblong. Fold the edges over, seal and crimp neatly. Bake in a hot oven (425°F) for 15–20 minutes, until golden brown. Remove from the oven and cover immediately with a damp cloth. While still hot, dip them in the glaze of boiling water and butter. Cover again until ready to serve.

An old Viking settlement in Sweden

Desserts

RØDGRØD MED FLØDE (DENMARK)

Soft berry pudding

This Danish summer dessert with a tongue-twisting name has become famous throughout the world. It is a useful way of making soft fruit go further or of using up imperfect or surplus berries. A *rødgrød* will keep for several days in the refrigerator.

The art of making a *rødgrød* is to add just enough thickening to give the pudding the right consistency, neither too runny nor too firm. Vary fruit according to what is in season.

Serves 6

½ lb redcurrants
½ lb blackcurrants
½ lb raspberries
about 1 cup sugar
2–3 tablespoons potato flour
¼ cup blanched, peeled and sliced almonds (optional)
1¾ cups light cream (or a mixture of heavy and light cream)

Wash the fruit, place in a large pan with 1 pint water and simmer for about 5 minutes. Remove from the heat and press through a fine strainer. Reheat the fruit juice in a saucepan, and add sugar to taste. Do not make it too sweet.

Meanwhile mix the potato flour to a thin paste with a little cold water, remove the hot fruit mixture from the heat and pour this in slowly, stirring briskly to avoid lumps. Cool slightly, stirring occasionally, before pouring into a glass bowl. (If you use a crystal bowl, add a little of the mixture first to allow the bowl to heat up slowly or it may crack.)

Sprinkle sugar on top to prevent a skin forming and decorate with almonds if you wish. Leave to cool, then place in the refrigerator until ready to serve. Serve with cream.

Some whole raspberries or strawberries may be set aside and added to the fruit juice just before you add the thickening. If fresh fruit is not available, *rødgrød* can be made with frozen fruit.

RIS A L'AMANDE (DENMARK)

Almond rice pudding

In the olden days in Denmark a rice pudding (*risengrød*) was always served as the appetizer on Christmas Eve. The huge bowl of piping hot gruel was sprinkled with sugar and cinnamon, dotted with butter and eaten with a glass of sweet beer. It laid a good foundation for the main course and an additional attraction was the 'almond prize' – traditionally a marzipan pig with a red ribbon around its neck – awarded to the person who found the one and only almond in the bowl.

Nowadays many people break with tradition and serve a cold rice pudding called *ris à l'amande* after the main course; but you still have to hunt the almond. The pudding is usually served with a hot cherry sauce.

Serves 6

1 quart milk
½ cup long-grain rice
½ vanilla bean, split lengthwise
¾ cup sweet almonds, blanched and skinned
1 or 2 bitter almonds, blanched and skinned
2 tablespoons sugar
1¾ cups cream, whipped until stiff

Boil the milk in a thick-bottomed saucepan; add the rice and vanilla bean, stirring all the time with a whisk or a wooden spoon in a figure-of-8 movement until the mixture boils. Reduce the heat to a simmer and let the rice cook gently until tender. Leave to cool.

Meanwhile chop the almonds coarsely, keeping aside 1 whole sweet almond, if it is Christmas.

Fold the almonds, sugar and whipped cream gently into the cool rice mixture. When all the ingredients are well mixed, pour into your best crystal bowl and finally put in the whole almond. Keep in the refrigerator until ready to serve.

CHERRY SAUCE

about 1½ cups canned cherries
¾ cup cherry liqueur
1 tablespoon potato flour

To make cherry sauce, heat the drained cherries in a saucepan and add the cherry liqueur. Mix the potato flour to a thin paste with a little cold water and pour slowly into the cherries, stirring gently all the time, but do not let the sauce boil.

Serve the hot sauce in a sauceboat with the *ris à l'amande*. The contrast between the cold pudding and the hot sauce is delicious.

If you prefer a cold cherry sauce, just mix the cherries in syrup with the liqueur and serve as before. Needless to say a small glass of cherry liqueur goes well with this rich dessert.

CITRONFROMAGE (SWEDEN AND DENMARK)

Lemon soufflé

You might think *citronfromage* would be a cheese dish, but *fromage* is in fact the Scandinavian word for soufflé. Scandinavian cooks flavor their soufflés in many different ways, but this fluffy lemon one is the most popular of all. It is very refreshing after a rich main course like roast pork or duck.

Serves 6

4 eggs, separated
6 tablespoons sugar
grated rind of 1 lemon
1 envelope unflavored gelatin
juice of 1 or 2 lemons (according to taste)
½ cup whipping cream

Beat the egg yolks with sugar until light, then add the lemon rind. Beat the egg whites in a separate bowl until stiff.

Dissolve the gelatin in the lemon juice over a very low heat. Allow to cool before adding to the egg mixture, and finally fold in the egg whites. Pour into a glass bowl and allow to set for 1–2 hours in the refrigerator. Just before serving, whip the cream and spread or pipe it on top of the soufflé.

If you use the juice of 2 lemons, the sharp flavor contrasts well with the bland whipped cream.

ROMFROMAGE (DENMARK)
Rum soufflé

In contrast to *citronfromage*, this dessert is very rich. It is usually topped with whipped cream, or it can be served with a lukewarm cherry sauce (see page 141), made without the liqueur.

Serves 6

2 eggs, separated
2 tablespoons sugar
½ cup rum
1½ cups whipping cream
1 envelope unflavored gelatin
12 almonds, blanched, skinned and finely chopped

Beat the egg yolks with sugar until white, and add the rum. Whip two-thirds of the cream, and beat the egg whites until stiff.

Dissolve the gelatin in a little cold water over a low heat, and pour slowly into the rum and egg mixture, stirring all the time. Fold in the cream, almonds and egg whites. Keep turning the mixture over until it begins to set, then pour into a glass bowl or individual glasses. Just before serving, whip the remainder of the cream to decorate the top of the soufflé.

KANELLAGKAGE (DENMARK)
Cinnamon layer cake

Layer cakes filled with cream are very popular in Scandinavia. This is an old family recipe from North Zealand for a most delicious dessert, which is well worth the trouble of making it. There was once a Danish country doctor who would happily eat half a *kanellagkage* at a dinner party if he got the chance. He had a theory that whipped cream was not fattening!

Serves 6–8

1¾ cups sugar
1¾ cups butter
2 whole eggs
2 tablespoons ground cinnamon
3 cups flour, sifted
3 squares semisweet chocolate
12 almonds, blanched, skinned and chopped
1 pint whipping cream

In a large mixing bowl cream the sugar and butter thoroughly, then add the eggs and cinnamon and beat again. Add the flour and mix well until the mixture is smooth.

Grease an 8 in layer cake pan, fill it with a thin even layer of the mixture and bake at the top of the oven at 400°F for 4–6 minutes, depending on the thickness of the layer. (If you have 2 pans you can bake 2 layers at a time.)

These quantities will make 10–12 layers. Remove each layer and turn out quickly onto a flat surface with the aid of a spatula. Press back into shape if any damage occurs, but be quick as the cake cools rapidly, becoming fragile and crisp.

When all the layers have been baked and cooled you can store them in an airtight container, placing circles of wax paper between the layers. They will keep crisp and fresh like this for some time.

Just before you want to serve the cake, melt the chocolate in a bowl over gently boiling water. Spread the melted chocolate evenly with a spatula over one layer, which will eventually be the top layer. Decorate it with chopped almonds around the edge before the chocolate sets, and keep to one side.

Whip the cream until thick and velvety, but not too stiff. Place the first layer of the cake on a flat round serving plate and spread evenly with a layer of cream. Place another layer of cake spread with cream on top and build up the cake in this way, ending with the decorated top. Do not press the layers down too firmly or the cream will ooze out. Chill, then serve at once. You will need a sharp knife and a cake server to cut and serve the cake.

With these quantities you can make 2, 5, or 6-layer cakes or make 1 cake using half the layers and store the rest in an airtight container to use another time.

ÄPPELKAKA (SWEDEN)
Apple cake

Apples grow well in most parts of Scandinavia, and are available almost all year round. Each country has its own apple desserts. This Swedish apple cake is served lukewarm with custard sauce or cream.

Serves 6

1½ lb apples, sliced
½ cup dry white breadcrumbs
5 tablespoons butter
3 tablespoons sugar
2 teaspoons ground cinnamon or ½ cup chopped almonds

Butter a baking dish and arrange in it layers of apples, breadcrumbs, thin flakes of butter, sugar and cinnamon or chopped almonds, finishing with a layer of breadcrumbs. Bake at 350°F for about 30 minutes until the apples are tender.

OMENALUMI (FINLAND)
Apple snow

Finnish apple snow is traditionally served in a glass bowl with a pinch of cinnamon sprinkled on top.

Serves 6–8

1 lb tart apples, peeled, cored and sliced
¾ cup sugar
4 egg whites
a pinch of salt
½ teaspoon lemon juice
a pinch of ground cinnamon

Cook the apples in a covered pan with little or no water, stirring frequently. When they are cooked, add sugar to taste and beat to a smooth purée. If it is too stiff, add a little boiling water. Allow to cool.

Beat the egg whites with a pinch of salt in a large mixing bowl and gradually add ½ cup sugar, beating until the whites form stiff peaks. Add lemon juice to the apple purée in another large bowl. Stir in a little of the beaten egg whites and finally fold in the rest of the whites until well mixed. Pour into a glass bowl to serve, and sprinkle a pinch of cinnamon on top.

AEBLEKAGE (DENMARK)
Applecake

This is a very popular dessert in Denmark; and on Danish farms you will often be served *aeblekage* with Sunday afternoon coffee. Each housewife has her own favorite recipe; for a more luxurious version you can use macaroons sprinkled with sherry instead of breadcrumbs.

Serves 6

1½ lb cooking apples, peeled, cored and sliced
½ vanilla bean
about 3–4 tablespoons sugar or honey
½ cup butter
3 cups breadcrumbs mixed with ½ cup sugar
blackcurrant or other jam (optional)
sherry or Madeira (optional)
1 cup whipping cream
plain chocolate (optional)

Cook the apples in a heavy saucepan with half a vanilla bean, preferably without water (add a pat of butter instead) until you have a thick apple purée. Season to taste with sugar or honey, but do not make the purée too sweet. Leave to cool.

Melt the butter in a large skillet and pour in the breadcrumb mixture. Stir all the time with a wooden spoon, turning the breadcrumbs constantly to prevent burning. When they are golden brown, cool on foil, shaking it gently.

Just before serving, assemble the apple cake in a glass bowl. Put a layer of apple purée at the bottom, then a layer of the crisp breadcrumbs (with a few dabs of jam on top if you like, or a spoonful of sherry or Madeira), then another layer of apples and finally a layer of breadcrumbs. Cover with a layer of whipped cream and decorate with a teaspoon of jam in the center, or grate a little plain chocolate over the top.

Scandinavia

KRAEMMERHUSE MED FLØDESKUM (DENMARK)
Cones with whipped cream

In Denmark these cream-filled cones are traditionally served with a teaspoon of homemade strawberry preserve on top (red and white are the colors of the Danish flag, the *Danne-brog*). In Sweden, where the cones are called *fyllda strutar*, lingonberries are used as a topping. However, you can vary the filling according to your own taste and what you have on hand.

The cones are filled just before serving and each is placed upright in a tall glass, or they are all placed in a glass bowl half-filled with sugar to prevent them from falling over.

Makes 16–20 cones

3 eggs
¾ cup sugar
1 cup flour, sifted
4–5 tablespoons cold
  water
1¼ cups whipped cream

Beat the eggs with the sugar until light and fluffy. Add the flour and a little cold water, until the batter has the right consistency for spreading thinly.

Using a well-greased, lukewarm baking sheet, spread the batter evenly with a spatula into circles the size of a saucer. (You can mark out the shape beforehand by sprinkling flour on the baking sheet and drawing a ring around an upside-down saucer.) You can probably get 5 or 6 cakes on each sheet, but do not try to squeeze too many on or they will be difficult to remove.

Bake in the upper part of the oven at 375°F for about 10 minutes. Open the oven to check the cakes; when they are light brown at the edge and golden in the center, they are ready. Loosen the cakes with a wide spatula before removing entirely from the oven, then quickly shape them 1 by 1 into cones. Place them in bottle tops, to ensure that they keep their shape while cooling. This calls for nimble fingers, as they are very fragile. Grease the sheet well again before making the next batch of cakes.

Once the cones are cooled they will keep crisp in an airtight container, so you can make them well in advance and fill them with whipped cream just before serving.

HJEMMEBAGT KRINGLE (DENMARK)
Homemade Danish pastry

Danish pastries are world-famous, but to prepare them well is an art which even Danes usually leave to the professional baker; or they buy them frozen and ready to bake. However, for special celebrations, Danish housewives make this quick and equally delicious version.

Serves 6–8

2 cakes compressed yeast
1 cup cream, lukewarm
2 whole eggs
6 tablespoons sugar
4 cups flour, sifted
¼ teaspoon ground
  cardamom
⅓ cup butter
1–1¼ cups mixed dried
  fruit (raisins and
  candied peel)
confectioners' sugar

Dissolve the yeast in a little of the cream. In a large mixing bowl beat the eggs with sugar, cream, flour, dissolved yeast, cardamom and the butter, cut in small pieces. Beat the dough with a wooden spoon until smooth and shiny, then cover and leave to rise in a warm place for about 30 minutes. Now add the dried fruit, mix well and shape the dough into a figure of 8 about 2 in long. Carefully transfer to a well-greased baking sheet. Cover and leave in a warm place for another 10 minutes while pre-heating the oven to 375°F. Bake for about 30 minutes. While still warm, glaze with confectioners' sugar mixed to a thick paste with cold water. Serve as soon as the glaze sets.

Cones with whipped cream: topped with delicious strawberry preserve they give a colorful finish to a Danish dinner.

S pain and Portugal tend to be classed together because they are side by side on the same vast peninsula. But in many ways – racially, geographically, and gastronomically – the two countries are very different.

Western Portugal has miles of golden beaches washed by long, slow Atlantic rollers. Although enjoying many hours of hot sunshine, it is often swept by cold wet winds from the sea that soften the landscape with beautiful flowers and lush green vegetation. On the Spanish border are harsh high mountains, sparsely populated and difficult to farm. Portugal's food reflects these diverse climatic conditions. It includes a tremendous variety of seafood and among the special delights are young herrings and sardines, grilled over charcoal or wood fires on the beach, sprinkled with sea-salt and washed down with local red wine. In contrast the dishes from the Portuguese mountains are usually made with sausages, dried beans, vegetables and pork, designed to keep out the cold and sustain hard-working farmers.

Spain is by nature and location a Mediterranean land, influenced by Africa and the East: it is hotter in climate and temperament than Portugal, with a love of strong flavors such as garlic, cumin and saffron, and rich, tasty stews. Spain's vast, arid plateaux and rocky sierras contrast with its fertile valleys and coastland. In this large complex country there are many sorts of regional specialties, such as the famous and piquant sauces of Catalonia, the rice dishes of the eastern coast, the fried fish of Andalusia, and the salt cod and baby eels of the Basque provinces.

Spain and Portugal smell different. Cross the border from the Algarve into Andalusia and this is instantly noticeable. The two countries even sound different: Spain is much noisier. In a Spanish restaurant you can hardly hear yourself speak; but in Portugal the silence is broken only by the lilt of the *fado*, the wistful traditional songs. Compare the *fado* with the harsh earthiness of the flamenco and you will have compared Portugal with Spain.

The Portuguese, and the Galicians from northwest Spain, are probably descended from nomadic Celts who came to the peninsula in the fifth century BC. (They share with their Irish cousins the love of the potato, which they eat with almost everything.) It was the Greeks who colonized the Mediterranean coastlands, and the rich valley of the river Guadalquivir in southern Spain. Here they bred horses and cattle and produced wheat, honey, and some of the finest olive oil in the world. The Romans came to Hispania, as they called it, at the end of the first century BC; and in many ways their influence still survives. They planted olive groves and vineyards as far north as the Rioja district, the home of some of Spain's best wines. The olive trees and vines we see today are probably descended from those far-off times. Earthenware cooking pots with small handles and rounded bases for cooking over charcoal or wood fires have not changed their shape since the Romans introduced them nearly two thousand

*A friend in the market place
is worth more
than gold in a coffer.*

Portuguese proverb

Portuguese goods carried to market the traditional way

Spain and Portugal

years ago. Other legacies are the popular Spanish sauces: the garlic-flavored all-i-oli and romesco, hot and pungent, which the Romans ate with roast meats and fish.

Gradually, over the course of two centuries, the whole peninsula came under Roman rule. But it was really the Moorish occupation, lasting for over five hundred years, that fully developed the agricultural potential of the land; and it is the strong Moorish influence which makes Iberian cooking so different from that of the rest of Europe.

Compared to the hot, dry deserts of northern Africa, the Moors found the Iberian peninsula fertile. But they soon began to irrigate the land more expertly and planted vast *huertas* or fruit gardens in the south to grow melons, pomegranates, figs, peaches and apricots, as well as rice and cotton. They brought with them Eastern spices – coriander, cumin, cinnamon and aniseed – and planted huge groves of lemons, oranges and almonds all over southern Spain and Portugal. The Algarve in particular is at its most beautiful in spring, with its acres of perfumed almond blossom. Here you still see white lacy chimney pots, of Moorish origin, and hands of Fatima nailed to the doors of village houses; and smell the sweet-sour carob trees, brought from northern Africa.

Portugal became a nation in her own right in 1143 and Spain was finally united in 1479 under the Christian reign of Ferdinand and Isabella. In the fifteenth century both nations embarked on expeditions to distant corners of the world. The Portuguese were by nature a maritime people, and their voyages of discovery, to the East Indies and to the New World, were greatly motivated by their natural skill and pleasure in seamanship. Their return brought a rich infusion of new flavors to Portuguese cooking – precious spices to preserve and season food, and fruit such as the pineapple from the Indies. The Spanish were more warlike and sought to enlarge their empire and conquer new lands, to gain a greater wealth of gold and silver. Among the booty they brought back from the New World were such homely and useful items as the potato, the tomato, hot and sweet peppers, and chocolate. Spain and Portugal were rich indeed in those days, both gastronomically and financially, and they remained among the most powerful nations in the world for nearly two hundred years.

Two countries with this common heritage are bound to have affinities; and the cooking of modern Spain and Portugal reveals both similarities and striking differences. For example, both the Spanish and the Portuguese use a great deal of olive oil; but the two oils taste different, and are made by slightly different processes. Spanish cooks use the earthy-red *chorizo* sausage, made with pork, garlic and paprika, as the basis for many soups and stews; the Portuguese have their own version, the *chouriço*, which is similar, but not quite the same. Both the Spanish and the Portuguese make little cakes from almonds, eggs and sugar; but their names, shapes and flavors are different.

Neither the Spanish nor the Portuguese use much butter or cream in cooking: few of their pastures are rich enough to support large dairy herds, and cattle are often bred for the bull ring rather than for milk and even as recently as ten years ago it was hard to find good butter in Spanish shops, although now it is as common as in any country. That famous

An abundance of fresh food displayed in the spring sunshine of the Algarve

and delightful sauce, mayonnaise, is said to have been invented by a French chef in the town of Mahon in Menorca when he had to use olive oil instead of butter. Cheese made from cows' milk is rare in both Spain and Portugal, although Spain boasts several excellent cheeses made from ewes' or goats' milk: *Manchego* from the plains of La Mancha, *Queso de Mahon* from the island of Menorca, and *Majorero* from Fuerteventura in the Canary Islands. In fact, every region of both Spain and Portugal has its own local type of soft goats' or ewes' milk cheese, which is usually made into a flat round cake shape. These cheeses are often eaten as *tapas*, the delightful snacks served with a glass of wine in all Spanish and many Portuguese bars.

Portuguese cooking is traditionally handed down from mother to daughter. It is difficult to find a Portuguese cook book in Portugal, for no self-respecting girl would leave home to be married without having considerable skill in the culinary arts. Perhaps this is one reason why Portuguese cooking has stayed mostly inside Portugal, for there are surprisingly few Portuguese restaurants in other countries. In contrast there are plenty of books describing the classic dishes of each region of Spain; for although Spain is in many ways a modern country (perhaps *because* it is more modern) the Spanish people take great pride in cultivating and preserving their regional traditions.

The kitchen in an ordinary Portuguese home will often have no oven; meat tends to be boiled rather than roasted. Soups that make a meal in themselves are very common; and many stews will be strained so that pasta can be cooked in the broth and served after the stew 'to fill you up'. Brisket on the bone boiled with cabbage, potatoes and rice is a popular everyday meal. But Portugal's favorite national dish is undoubtedly dried salt cod. There are at least three hundred and sixty-five ways of preparing it. Cod was first discovered by the Basque whalers when they went to Newfoundland in the fourteenth century, and it was later introduced into France and Portugal. At that time the only way to preserve fish, both in ships' holds and at home during the long winter months, was to dry and salt it. Both Spanish and Portuguese explorers were able to eat dried salt cod throughout their long voyages. But even now, when fresh and frozen fish are plentiful, dried salt cod is as popular as ever.

One of Portugal's strangest and most delicious combinations is pork and clams, often cooked in a kind of primitive pressure cooker called a *cataplana*, which consists of two rounded halves that fit together like a clam shell and seal in the flavor. *Cataplanas* are used mainly in the Algarve: there are tin ones, which can be bought quite cheaply, and copper ones, which are more expensive. A meal of clams and pork *na cataplana* served straight from the freshly opened pan, with crusty bread and a glass of *vinho verde*, will ensure that you never forget Portugal.

The combination of meat and seafood is also typical of the famous Spanish paella. The paella is a favorite Spanish picnic dish: the whole family will set off on a fine morning with rice, oil, a *paëllera* and an assortment of good things to go in it. They will build a wood fire and cook the dish over it, the flames cooking the rice very evenly, as they lick the side of the pan. The traditional time for eating paella in Spain, whether indoors or out, is on Sunday, as the appetizer for lunch. Another regional dish which has become a classic favorite all over Spain is *fabada asturiana*, a strong stew made with beans, smoked blood sausage and *chorizo*, which originated in the rocky northern province of Asturias.

Whether you cook paella, *fabada asturiana* or pork and clams *na cataplana* in your own home, they will evoke the pleasures of Spain and Portugal, making those who have been there long to return and luring the uninitiated to their shores.

Iberian contrasts: an Arab fortress, Granada province; farmlands near Cordoba; and port wine vineyards of the Douro valley

Two prepared tables *by the sixteenth-century painter Francisco de Zurbaran.*

Hors d'oeuvre and tapas

ANGULAS (BASQUE COUNTRY)
Baby eels

In their season these tiny elvers are caught in millions in the coastal reaches of Spain's rivers. They are considered to be a great delicacy, and are eaten with wooden forks. Smelts can be cooked in the same way.

Serves 4

¾ cup olive oil
4 cloves of garlic, chopped
4 small pieces of fresh hot red chili or green pepper
1¼ lb baby eels (or smelts)

Heat the oil in 4 individual-sized earthenware dishes with a chopped garlic clove and a piece of hot pepper in each. Wash and pat dry the eels – which look like silvery threads – and stir them into the hot oil. Cook for a few seconds only (cook smelts a little longer) and serve sizzling hot.

VIERAS GUISADAS (GALICIA)
Baked scallops

A specialty of Santiago de Compostela. The scallop shell is a symbol of St James himself.

Serves 4

1¼ lb sea scallops
2 cloves of garlic
2 medium onions, finely chopped
2 tablespoons chopped parsley
ground black pepper
salt to taste
2 pinches of ground cloves
a good sprinkling of grated nutmeg
2 tablespoons fresh breadcrumbs
2 tablespoons olive oil

Wash and pat dry the scallops. Chop the pieces of scallop and the garlic, and mix together with the onion, parsley, pepper and salt, cloves and nutmeg. Scrub four scallop shells and pile some of the mixture into each one. Scatter with fresh breadcrumbs, a little more parsley, sprinkle with olive oil and bake in a hot oven (400°F) for about 15–20 minutes. Serve hot.

CALAMARES FRITOS (SPAIN)
Fried squid rings

This appetizer is popular throughout Spain.

Serves 4

1 lb small squid ⅓ cup milk 1 cup well salted flour oil for deep frying 2 lemons	Wash the squid thoroughly and remove the ink bags, central bone and tentacles. Cut into rings and soak in milk for an hour or so. Dip in flour and deep fry until crisp. Serve hot with lemon quarters.

DÁTILES CON JAMÓN (SPAIN)
Dates with ham

In Spain you would use *jamón serrano*, that delicious raw ham cured in the sun and snow of the Sierra Morena mountains; but you could use ordinary ham as an alternative.

For each person

2–4 pieces of cooked ham 2–4 pitted dates	Simply roll a piece of ham around each date and secure with a cocktail stick.

ATUM CON ARROZ (PORTUGAL)
Tuna fish with rice

This summer dish may be eaten either as an hors d'oeuvre or as the main course for a light meal. Ideally, fresh tuna should be used, but canned tuna is almost as good. Home-made mayonnaise makes this dish particularly delicious.

Serves 4

⅓ lb tuna fish
2 cups cold cooked rice
⅔ cup home-made
   mayonnaise
1 small crisp head of
   lettuce, chopped
about 4 small firm
   tomatoes, skinned
   and chopped
12 black olives
2 hard-cooked eggs
	To cook fresh tuna, poach in a little water in a covered pan for about 20 minutes. Allow to cool.
	
	Mix the cold rice with the tuna, mayonnaise, lettuce and chopped tomatoes. Press down well into a bowl and chill. Turn out when ready to use and decorate with the olives and sliced hard-cooked eggs. For hors d'oeuvre small individual molds may be used.

SALSA MAHONESA (BALEARIC ISLANDS)
Mayonnaise sauce

Mayonnaise is said to have been invented by a French chef in the town of Mahon in Menorca when he had to use olive oil instead of butter. It is perfectly simple to make at home, as long as all the ingredients are at room temperature.

Serves 4

2 egg yolks
salt
1 cup olive oil
1–2 tablespoons
   vinegar or
   lemon juice
	Place the egg yolks in a large, slightly warmed mixing bowl with a little salt, and stir vigorously with a wooden spoon. Add literally a few drops of olive oil, stirring all the time until the oil is incorporated. (Spanish cooks use an *aceitera* for pouring the oil drop by drop, but you can manage with an ordinary jug.) Continue adding the oil in very small amounts, so that the mixture thickens to a smooth emulsion, and add a few drops of lemon juice or vinegar now and then. When half the oil is added you can begin to add the rest in a thin stream, still stirring all the time.
	
	If the mayonnaise curdles, start again with another egg yolk in a clean, warmed mixing bowl. When the new batch is well established the curdled sauce may be added gradually.

Soups

SOPA DE ALMENDRAS (ANDALUSIA)
Almond soup

This rather glamorous soup is served chilled and milky white, with a few peeled halved grapes and a red rose petal floating in each bowl.

Serves 4

1 cup blanched almonds 1 clove of garlic 2½ cups water ⅓ cup dry white wine 2 tablespoons mild olive oil salt about 20 white grapes ice cubes	Crush the almonds and garlic together in either a mortar or an electric blender. Gradually add the water, wine, olive oil and salt to taste. When you have a smooth consistency your soup is ready. Add the peeled, seeded and halved grapes, some ice cubes, and don't forget the rose petals. (You could add ground cinnamon instead, but it doesn't look as pretty.)

CALDO GALLEGO (GALICIA)
Bean and sausage soup

This soup is almost a meal in itself and is often served alone. In Galicia it is the custom to add a piece of aged, rancid fat bacon called *unto*, which gives the dish a strong distinctive flavor. Galician food in general is very rich and warming to counteract the cold wet climate. In this land where everyone carries a black umbrella, and the women wear high wooden stilted clogs to keep their feet out of the mud, you are reminded of the mystic 'Celtic twilight' of Ireland.

Prepare the beans 24 hours in advance.
Serves 4–6

⅓ lb dried white navy
   beans, soaked
   overnight
1 piece of chorizo,
   about ⅓ lb
1 ham bone
1 lb potatoes, peeled and
   roughly chopped
1 lb kale or cabbage,
   shredded
1 onion, chopped
2 tablespoons flour
1 tablespoon olive oil
1 teaspoon paprika
	Drain the soaked beans. Put them into a large pot with about 1½ quarts fresh water, bring to a boil and add the *chorizo* and the ham bone. Simmer for about 1½ hours, then add the potatoes, the greens and the onion. Cover and cook slowly for about another 2 hours, until all the vegetables have disintegrated except the beans, which should keep their shape. Just before serving, mix the flour with the olive oil and paprika and stir this in. Cook for another 5 minutes. Cut up the *chorizo*, scrape any remaining meat off the ham bone and return these to the soup. Serve very hot.

Spain and Portugal

CALDO VERDE (MINHO)
Potato and cabbage soup

This soup comes from the Minho region in the north, but is pretty well known throughout Portugal. Large dark green leaves are used, from an especially large cabbage known as a *couve*, but good kale or collard greens would do equally well. The tough stalks and any fibrous bits should be removed, the leaves washed thoroughly, and shredded as finely as possible. Special gadgets are sold in Portugal specifically for this purpose, otherwise the best way to do it is to bunch up the leaves tightly and use a very sharp knife.

Serves 4–6

1 lb potatoes
salt and pepper
2 tablespoons olive oil
1 lb cabbage or kale
4 slices of chouriço
　sausage

Peel and cut up the potatoes, and boil them in about 1 quart of salted water until very soft. Remove with a slotted spoon, mash thoroughly and return to the liquid in the pan, together with the olive oil. Add the shredded cabbage and boil quickly for about 3 minutes, then add the slices of sausage and simmer for another minute or so to heat through. Season to taste. Serve with crusty bread. In Portugal this would be *broa*, a delicious crumbly corn bread.

Two chilled soups from Andalusia: Sopa de Almendras *and* Gazpacho

GAZPACHO (ANDALUSIA)
Iced vegetable soup

Gazpacho was originally a humble peasant soup that used up any available leftovers. Its name probably comes from the pre-Roman word *caspa*, meaning bits and pieces. There are many variations of this iced salad soup; the following recipe from Seville is both simple and delicious.

Serves 4

2 tablespoons stale
　white breadcrumbs
1 tablespoon olive oil
1 tablespoon vinegar
4 large tomatoes,
　skinned and chopped
½ cucumber, peeled
1 green pepper,
　seeded and chopped
1 onion, finely chopped
salt and white pepper
8 almonds, ground
stock

Soak the breadcrumbs in the oil and vinegar for about 1 hour, then squeeze dry. Crush all the vegetables (reserving just a little of each for the garnish) to a purée, either in a mortar, which is the traditional way, or in an electric blender. Add the seasoning and the crushed almonds and breadcrumbs, and dilute with fat-free stock to the desired consistency, making about 1 quart of soup. Cover and put in a cool place, or a refrigerator, to chill. Ice cubes may be added just before serving.

Serve with diced cucumber, red and green pepper, chopped tomato, chopped hard-cooked egg and finely sliced onion – any or all served separately in small bowls.

SOPA GADITANA DE PESCADO (ANDALUSIA)
Fish soup from Cadiz

The word *Gaditana* is probably a corruption of *Cádizana*, from Cadiz, and this soup uses almost any fish a fisherman might find caught up in the fine mesh of his net.

Serves 4–6

2 lb assorted fish,
　including bass,
　halibut, hake
any shellfish, such
　as shrimp, mussels,
　clams or small crabs
3 tablespoons olive oil
2 cloves garlic, peeled
　and chopped
1 onion, finely chopped
salt and pepper
juice of 1 lemon (or
　sour Seville orange)
¼ cup sherry or white
　wine

Clean and cut up the fish, scrub the mussels. Heat the oil in a *cazuela* or heavy earthenware casserole and gently fry the garlic and onion for about 10 minutes. Add the pieces of fish (not the shellfish), and about 1 quart of water. Season well and cook covered on low heat for about 15–20 minutes. Strain the soup and remove any bones or pieces of skin. Put the fish and soup back into the *cazuela* and add the shellfish, the lemon or orange juice and the sherry. Cook for another 5 minutes and serve in the same dish with a slice of oven-toasted bread in each person's bowl, or serve croûtons separately.

Harvesting almonds in the Algarve

Rice, pasta and eggs

ARROZ A LA MARINERA (VALENCIA)
Sailor's rice

In the waterfront cafés of the Valencian coast, this dish is served to the sailors and fishermen with a whole unpeeled head of young garlic placed in the center of the rice. In this recipe only two cloves of garlic are used, but you may add as many as you like.

Serves 4

*¼ lb each of any 3 of
these fish: hake,
turbot, halibut,
squid
fish heads and
trimmings
1 bay leaf
a sprig of fresh thyme
¼ teaspoon salt
¼ cup olive oil
1 onion, peeled and
sliced
2 teaspoons paprika
2 cups short-grain rice
2 cloves garlic,
chopped
2 pinches saffron
threads soaked in 1
tablespoon boiling
water, or ¼ teaspoon
powdered saffron
12 shrimp in their shells
12 mussels or clams,
cleaned and scrubbed*

Clean and wash the fish and cut it into small pieces. To make stock place fish heads and trimmings, bay leaf, thyme and salt in a saucepan with 1 quart of water and bring to a boil. Leave to simmer for about 30 minutes, and strain.

Heat the oil in a *paëllera* or large skillet. Add the onion slices and pieces of fish and cook gently until lightly colored. Sprinkle with the paprika. Add the rice, spreading it evenly over the pan. Cook for 1 minute, then carefully stir in 1½ pints fish stock and bring to a boil. Add garlic and saffron, and arrange the shrimp and mussels on top.

Cook on a fairly high heat for a few minutes, then lower the heat and cook gently for 15 minutes or until all the liquid has been absorbed. Transfer the dish to a hot oven (425°F) and bake for about 5 minutes to give a slight crust to the surface. Discard any shellfish that do not open.

Serve in the same dish.

*Oxen on a Basque
farm*

PAELLA VALENCIANA (VALENCIA)

The paella almost certainly originated along the banks and lagoons of the Albufera river near the town of Valencia, the district where much of Spain's rice has been grown since Moorish times. Many variations of this now internationally famous Spanish dish have since evolved, and the recipe given here uses a little bit of everything.

Serves 6–8

*¼ cup olive oil
3 cloves garlic,
peeled and roughly
chopped
1 chicken (about
2½ lb), cut in pieces
2 tomatoes, skinned and
chopped
1 red pepper, seeded
and cut into strips
1 cup shelled peas
¼ cup chopped green beans
1 teaspoon paprika
2 cups long- or short-
grain rice
2 pinches of saffron
threads, soaked in
1 tablespoon
boiling water, or
¼ teaspoon saffron
powder
1½–2 pints chicken
stock
12 shrimp or 8 crayfish
in their shells or 1
lobster, boiled and
cut up
12 mussels or clams,
cleaned and scrubbed
1 lemon, cut in wedges*

Heat the oil in a *paëllera* (the shallow two-handled iron pan from which the dish takes its name) or a large skillet at least 14 in in diameter. Add the garlic and cook for a few minutes to flavor the oil. If you prefer just a hint of garlic, remove it with a slotted spoon. For a stronger flavor leave it in. Stir in the chicken pieces, tomatoes, pepper, peas and beans, sprinkling with the paprika as you do so. Cook gently for 10 minutes, stirring frequently.

Spread the rice evenly over the pan. Raise the heat, and stirring constantly, allow to brown slightly.

Meanwhile, in a separate saucepan add the saffron to the stock and bring to a boil. Pour carefully into the *paëllera*. Stir briefly to mix the ingredients, then bring to a boil. Reduce heat and simmer for 15–20 minutes or until most of the stock has been absorbed and the rice is tender.

When almost ready add the shrimp, crayfish or lobster pieces, stirring the rice as little as possible. Push the clams down into the rice or place the mussels on top. Cover and cook for a further 5 minutes. The shellfish should open in the steam; discard any that do not. Put the lemon wedges around the rim of the pan and allow the paella to stand for 1–2 minutes to settle before serving.

Spain and Portugal

CANALONES (SPAIN)
Cannelloni

Pasta of all kinds is extremely popular in Spain, and to a lesser extent in Portugal. Perhaps the best loved dish of all is cannelloni – in Spanish *canalones*. This has become a traditional favorite for St Stephen's Day (December 26); but it is often served in small individual dishes as a prelude to an everyday meal. The following recipe uses a spinach stuffing but many other stuffings may be used including tuna fish, or ground cooked chicken.

Serves 4

2 lb fresh spinach
salt
8–16 cannelloni tubes
olive oil
a little grated cheese

Tomato sauce
2 tablespoons olive oil
1 onion, finely
  chopped
¼ lb ground beef
½ lb tomatoes,
  skinned and chopped
2 tablespoons tomato
  purée
2 cloves garlic,
  crushed
2 teaspoons oregano
1 teaspoon sugar
2 teaspoons wine
  vinegar
salt and pepper

White sauce
¼ cup butter
¼ cup flour
1 pint milk
salt and pepper

First make the tomato sauce. Heat the oil in a saucepan and sauté the onion for a few minutes. Stir in the ground beef and let it brown. Add the chopped tomatoes and tomato purée, stir well, and add a little water if necessary. Add the garlic, oregano, sugar, vinegar, salt and pepper. Cover and simmer gently for 45 minutes.

Meanwhile, wash the spinach and discard thick stalks; cook until soft with a little salt (no water). Boil the cannelloni in salted water with a teaspoon of olive oil added to prevent them sticking together. When they are tender, after about 15 minutes, transfer them to a bowl of cold water to cool, then drain and stuff with the drained spinach.

To make the white sauce, melt the butter in a small saucepan, stir in the flour and cook for 3 minutes, stirring well to form a roux. Bring the milk to a boil in a separate saucepan; away from the heat, pour it gradually into the roux, stirring well until combined and thickened. Add salt and pepper to taste.

Take a large shallow baking dish – rectangular if possible – or 4 small dishes. Put a layer of tomato sauce in the bottom, arrange the stuffed cannelloni on top, and cover with a second layer of tomato sauce. Finally cover with white sauce, sprinkle with grated cheese, and either bake in the oven (350°F) or put under the broiler for about 10 minutes, until browned.

Garlic, lemon juice and fresh herbs – essential staples in a Spanish kitchen

HUEVOS A LA FLAMENCA (ANDALUSIA)
Eggs flamenca

This very typical Spanish recipe is said to have been invented by the gypsies of Andalusia. It makes a flamboyant-looking dish using basically humble ingredients. You need some *chorizo* sausage, which ideally is Spanish, or you could substitute a good garlic sausage. Smoked lean ham may be substituted for *jamón serrano*, and a small can of asparagus for the wild asparagus the gypsies use.

Serves 4

2 medium potatoes
¼ cup olive oil
1 medium onion,
  chopped
1 red pepper, seeded
  and cut in strips
4 slices of jamón
  serrano or other ham
1¼ cups shelled peas
1 cup sliced green
  beans
¼ lb fresh asparagus
4 tomatoes, skinned
  and chopped
2 tablespoons tomato
  purée
pepper
¼ teaspoon salt
8 eggs
8 thin slices chorizo
1 tablespoon chopped
  parsley

Peel and dice the potatoes; heat the oil in a large saucepan or skillet and fry them until golden on all sides. Remove and reserve. Fry the onion and pepper with 2 slices of the ham until the onion is transparent. Then add the peas, beans and asparagus tips, the tomatoes and tomato purée. Stir in the fried potatoes and about ½ cup water. Season with pepper and salt and stir everything well together. Cook gently for about 10 minutes, stirring occasionally.

Select a large, preferably oval, baking dish, or use 4 individual ones, and brush with a little oil. Pour in the vegetable mixture and make 8 hollows on the surface. Carefully break each egg in turn into a cup and pour into each hollow. Arrange slices of *chorizo* and the remaining ham cut into triangles over the top as decoration and sprinkle with chopped parsley and/or peas. Cook in a moderate oven (350°F) for about 15 minutes, or until the whites of the eggs are just set. Serve at once.

Arroz à la marinera

TORTILLA ESPAÑOLA (SPAIN)
Spanish omelette

This simple and delicious omelette is one of Spain's most popular and versatile dishes. It is wonderful eaten either hot or cold. Cold *tortillas* are a favorite addition to a picnic, children take them to school for packed lunches, and hungry workmen eat them as a *bocadillo* – sandwiched between two pieces of bread. More elaborate versions include a kind of cake arrangement, using three omelettes with tomatoes and white sauce between the layers. It is essential to use olive oil to get the full characteristic flavor of the *tortilla*.

Serves 4

2 large potatoes
2 large onions,
 preferably Spanish
¼ cup olive oil
¼ teaspoon salt
4 eggs

Peel the potatoes and onions and chop them into roughly ½ in cubes. Mix together. Heat the olive oil in a large-sized frying pan, about 10 in in diameter, until it just starts to smoke. Lower the heat and carefully stir in the chopped vegetables, adding the salt. Stir well and cover the pan with a lid (it doesn't have to fit exactly). Gently stew the potatoes and onions in the oil for about 20 minutes, making sure they do not stick or burn.

Meanwhile beat the eggs together in a large bowl. When the vegetables are tender, carefully remove them from the pan with a slotted spoon, leaving behind as much oil as possible, and stir them into the egg mixture. Drain most of the oil from the pan and remove any vegetables that may have stuck to the bottom. Leave just enough oil to cover the bottom of the pan, and reheat. Pour in the egg mixture. Lower the heat and flatten the mixture down with a fork into a thick even layer to fill the pan. Shake the pan to prevent sticking and cook very gently until the omelette starts to come away from the sides, about 10 minutes.

Spanish cooks then invert a heatproof plate over the pan, and quickly tip the *tortilla* out and slide it back into the pan to cook the other side. A simpler way is to put the pan under the broiler for 5–10 minutes, to cook the top. It should turn out like a solid cake when ready. There are many ways of varying this basic recipe – vegetables such as red or green peppers, peas, mushrooms or spinach may be added, or a little cooked chicken or ham.

Tortilla *sandwiched in bread and a flask of wine make a perfect workman's lunch, but this is only one version of Spain's most versatile dish*

ish

AMÊIJOAS NA CATAPLANA (ALGARVE)
Clams cooked in a cataplana with piri-piri sauce

A *cataplana* is a metal cooking vessel made in two rounded halves, rather like the two sides of a shell, which fit tightly together with metal clamps. It is used mostly in the Algarve (the southern region of Portugal), and is usually made of tin or aluminum, or sometimes copper. It works on the same principle as a pressure cooker, the steam and juices being sealed in for a short period of cooking. A flameproof casserole with a heavy, well fitting lid could be used as an alternative. The following recipe is typical of the Algarve, and combines shellfish with *presunto* ham and *chouriço* (spicy red garlic-flavored sausage). Any garlic sausage may be used.

Prepare piri-piri sauce at least 24 hours in advance, if used.
Serves 4

3 lb either clams,
  cockles or mussels
1 tablespoon olive oil
2 tablespoons butter
4 medium onions, finely
  sliced
1 cup chopped cooked
  ham
1 cup chopped
  chouriço
2 cloves garlic, crushed
1 teaspoon paprika
2 tablespoons chopped
  parsley
1 tablespoon piri-piri
  sauce or Tabasco
1 cup white wine
¼ teaspoon salt

Scrub shellfish thoroughly. Heat the oil and butter in the *cataplana* or casserole and cook the onions until slightly soft. Remove and reserve. Place a layer of mixed meats at the bottom, then some shellfish, then onions, garlic, paprika and parsley, more meat and so on until it is all used up. Add the piri-piri sauce and wine, and sprinkle with salt. Cover and cook on a moderate heat on top of the stove for 15–20 minutes. If using a *cataplana* it should be shaken or turned over once during cooking. Serve at once, bringing the *cataplana* or casserole hot to the table.

PIRI-PIRI SAUCE

Piri-piri sauce is a favorite addition to many Portuguese dishes. It is made by soaking small hot dried chili peppers in olive oil and allowing them to stand in a sealed bottle for about a month, or more quickly by heating in a slow oven, but even so it should be prepared at least a day in advance.

6 chili peppers
1 bay leaf
a piece of lemon rind
1 cup olive oil

Put the chilies in a small airtight bottle or jar with bay leaf and lemon rind. Pour in the oil. Either seal and leave for 1 month or stand unsealed in a warm place (very slow oven – 225°F – or even in the noon-day sun) for about 3 hours. Leave to stand at least 24 hours – and use with caution.

Lisbon harbor c. 1900

ZARZUELA DE MARISCOS (CATALONIA)
Catalonian fish opera

This celebrated Catalonian dish, literally called a 'light opera' or 'musical comedy' of fish, is a sumptuous concoction of shellfish cooked in a rich red sauce.

Serves 4

1 lobster, lightly boiled
3 tablespoons olive oil
1 onion, finely chopped
1 green pepper, seeded
  and chopped
1 red pepper, seeded
  and chopped
2 cloves garlic, chopped
4 baby squid, cut into
  thin rings (optional)
4 tomatoes, skinned
  seeded and chopped
a few chopped almonds
2 pinches saffron
  threads soaked in
1 tablespoon boiling
  water or ¼ teaspoon
  saffron powder
1 bay leaf
salt and pepper
6 tablespoons dry white
  wine
¼ cup brandy
1 cup water
juice of 1 lemon
12 shrimp in their shells
8 mussels
12 clams
parsley

Cut open the body of the lobster lengthwise. Discard the head, stomach sac, spongy grey-green lungs and intestinal thread which runs along inside the body. Twist off the claws and crack them.

Heat the oil in a heavy casserole. When it is very hot add the onion, peppers, garlic and squid. Cook gently for 5 minutes. Stir in the tomatoes, almonds, saffron, bay leaf, salt and pepper to taste, and cook for a few more minutes, stirring constantly.

Add the wine, brandy, water and lemon juice, stir well and bring to a boil. Simmer for 1 minute, then add the shrimp, mussels, clams and lobster. Cover and simmer for 10–15 minutes. Discard any mussels and clams that have not opened.

Serve in the same dish, garnished with parsley.

PASTEIS DE BACALHAU (PORTUGAL)
Dried salt cod turnovers

The Portuguese have a rather unusual method of making turnovers, which is also found in parts of Spain. They may be filled in a variety of ways, but the following recipe which uses dried salt cod is one of the most delicious.

Prepare salt cod 12 hours in advance.
Serves 4

Pastry
2 cups water
4 tablespoons butter
2 cups plain flour
¼ teaspoon salt

Salt cod filling
¼ lb dried salt cod,
  soaked overnight
1 bay leaf
1 onion, very finely
  chopped
4 tablespoons butter
1 tablespoon flour
juice of 1 lemon
1 egg
about ¼ cup dry
  breadcrumbs
about 1 cup olive oil

To make the pastry, bring the water to a boil in a saucepan, add the butter, and when it has melted remove the pan from the heat. Stir in the sifted flour and salt. Work into a dough and turn out onto a floured board. Allow to cool slightly and then roll out as thinly as possible. Cut into circles of about 4 in in diameter.

To make the filling, poach the cod with the bay leaf gently for 30 minutes. Fry the onion in the butter until soft. Stir 1 tablespoon flour into the onion and cook until it thickens. Drain the cod, remove all skin and bones and flake finely, reserving some of the liquid. Stir the fish into the onion mixture, add the lemon juice and enough of the fish liquid to give a thick oatmeal-like consistency. Cool a little. Put 1 tablespoon of the filling onto each circle of pastry, dampen the edges and fold over to make a turnover. Brush with beaten egg and coat with breadcrumbs. Heat the oil in a skillet and fry the turnovers, a few at a time, until they are crisp and golden. Serve hot with tender lima beans.

Harvesting the sea from the sweeping beaches of the Atlantic in southern Portugal

MERO AL JEREZ (SPAIN)
Grouper in sherry sauce

The grouper is a large fish in the same family as sea bass and abundant off the African banks, near the Canary Islands, where it is justly considered a great delicacy. There is a Spanish saying: '*del monte el cordero, de la mar el mero*' – as lamb is the best meat from the mountains, so the grouper is the finest fish in the sea. It is usually simply fried or broiled, or cooked in the oven in the following way. Halibut is the nearest substitute.

Serves 4

2 tablespoons olive oil
4 fresh grouper steaks
 (or halibut steaks)
1 teaspoon salt
a little pepper
1 cup blanched slivered
 almonds
½ cup medium or dry
 sherry
2 tablespoons chopped
 parsley

Brush a shallow baking dish, large enough to take the fish in a single layer, with oil. Arrange the fish steaks in it, sprinkle with salt and pepper, pour on the rest of the oil and sprinkle with almonds. Pour in the sherry and cook in a moderate oven (350°F) for about 30 minutes, basting frequently. Add the finely chopped parsley before the fish is quite done. Serve in the same dish.

SALMONETES A LA PARRILLA (CATALONIA)
Broiled red snapper

This fish dish was much favored by the Romans, who are said to have invented the very hot romesco sauce and the garlic-flavored all-i-oli sauce that usually accompany it.

Prepare the fish 2 hours in advance.
Serves 4

4 small red snapper
2 teaspoons salt
2 tablespoons olive oil
2–3 lemons
parsley
romesco sauce and/or
 all-i-oli sauce

Slit the fish and clean them, leaving the liver inside (or buy them already cleaned). Wash the fish thoroughly and scrape off the scales. Sprinkle with salt, olive oil and lemon juice and leave in a cool place for 1–2 hours.

Broil the fish, turning once, until they are cooked through to the bone, about 10–20 minutes depending on the size.

Serve sprinkled with chopped parsley and covered with the juices from the broiler pan, with the romesco and/or all-i-oli sauce in separate bowls.

Spain and Portugal

ALL-I-OLI SAUCE

The name of this strong garlic sauce from Catalonia is derived from the Latin words for garlic and oil, *allium* and *oleum*. In its various forms it is said to be one of the oldest sauces in the world and is even mentioned in the writings of Virgil. Popular all over eastern Spain, it is often served with romesco sauce, as the two complement each other. Two versions of the sauce are given: the first, without egg yolk, is the classic Catalan version.

Serves 4

5 large cloves garlic, chopped
¼ teaspoon salt
¼ slice white bread, without crust
1 cup warm olive oil
1 teaspoon lemon juice or wine vinegar

All of the ingredients should be at room temperature. Crush the garlic with the salt in a mortar until a paste is formed. Pound in the bread. Add half the oil drop by drop, beating constantly. Add the lemon juice or vinegar also drop by drop, then slowly add the remaining oil. This will form a thick sauce which may be thinned with a little cold water, if desired. Serve in the mortar.

All-i-oli sauce made with egg yolk

3 cloves garlic
¼ teaspoon salt
1 egg yolk
1 cup warm olive oil
1 teaspoon lemon juice or wine vinegar

Crush the garlic in a mortar. Add salt and stir in egg yolk. Add half the oil drop by drop, beating constantly. Add some of the lemon juice or vinegar, then a little more oil, then the rest of the lemon juice or vinegar. Slowly add the rest of the oil to form a thick sauce.

If all the ingredients are at room temperature the sauce should not curdle. If it does curdle, start again with another egg yolk and more garlic. Add the oil very slowly and also add the sauce that curdled.

ROMESCO SAUCE

This sauce takes its name from the small, hot peppers that grow in Tarragona, a province of Catalonia, where contests are held to find the chef who can produce the best sauce. It is usually served with fish, but goes equally well with some meats, lamb especially, and vegetables. Catalan chefs use a traditional pestle and mortar to make the sauce but an electric blender will produce equally good results.

Serves 4

2 tomatoes, skinned and seeded
4 dried romesco or small chili peppers, seeded, or 1–2 teaspoons cayenne pepper or chili powder
10 almonds, blanched
10 hazelnuts, toasted
3 cloves garlic, chopped
2 tablespoons chopped mint
¼ teaspoon salt
¼ cup olive oil
2 tablespoons vinegar
¼ cup dry sherry (optional)
chopped parsley

Pound and blend together the tomatoes, peppers, almonds, hazelnuts, garlic, mint and salt. Then gradually add the oil, drop by drop, as if making mayonnaise. When you have used half the oil, the remainder may be added in a steady stream. Stir in the vinegar and the sherry to make a fairly thick consistency. Sprinkle with parsley before serving.

SARDINAS FRESCAS AL HORNO
Baked fresh sardines

Fresh sardines are a great feature of Spanish and Portuguese life. Eaten in the open air, grilled over charcoal on beaches and in seafront cafés, they are a delight to locals and tourists alike. The cry of *sardinas frescas* is a familiar one, echoing through the streets of a seaside village or town. Housewives appear bearing plates or plastic bags to buy gleaming fresh sardines from the fishermen, who hawk them round in huge baskets. The sardines are fried or broiled, or baked as in the recipe given here. In parts of Spain, large outside leaves of lettuce are used instead of foil to 'seal' the dish and add extra flavor. These are discarded after the dish is cooked.

Serves 4–6

2 lb fresh sardines
2 tablespoons olive oil
2 large onions, cut in rings
2 teaspoons salt
freshly ground black pepper
2 lb tomatoes, skinned and sliced
2 tablespoons chopped parsley
2 cloves garlic, chopped
1 tablespoon wine vinegar
juice of ¼ lemon

Cut the heads off the sardines and clean them. Wash them under a running tap. Brush a large, shallow baking dish with oil. Cover the bottom of the dish with onions. Place the sardines neatly on top and season with salt and pepper. Cover the fish completely with the sliced tomatoes and sprinkle with chopped parsley and garlic. Mix together the olive oil, vinegar and lemon juice and pour over the tomatoes. Cover with foil and bake in a moderate oven (350°F) for about 30 minutes. Remove the foil and cook for another 10 minutes.

right *A fishwife of Lisbon, seventy years ago*

Bacalhau à Gomes de Sá:
*salt cod is almost the
national food of Portugal.*

SANCOCHO CANARIO (CANARY ISLANDS)
Salt fish with garlic and cumin sauce

Sancocho literally means something like 'boiled saint'. This dish may indeed take its name from such an unfortunate incident, but no one knows for sure. At any rate it is one of the most popular of all Canary Islands dishes, and is equally well known on Gran Canaria, Tenerife and Lanzarote. It is really more like a whole meal than a dish, consisting of fish, potatoes, sweet potatoes, and a special sauce. Traditionally the fish used is *vieja* ('old woman'), a locally dried fish of the bream family. But dried salt cod may be used instead.

The people of the Canaries salt and dry many varieties of fish themselves, including moray eels, *vieja* and flying fish. As soon as the fish are caught they are cleaned, salted, and laid out in the sun on specially prepared beds of porous lava, which allow air to circulate freely.

Prepare the fish 24 hours in advance.
Serves 4

2 lb dried vieja or
  salt cod
2 lb small potatoes,
  scrubbed or peeled
1 lb sweet potatoes,
  peeled and cut up
  (optional)

Garlic and cumin sauce
3 large cloves garlic
1 teaspoon cumin seeds
1 teaspoon paprika
¼ teaspoon salt
a pinch of thyme
⅓ cup olive oil
2 teaspoons vinegar

Soak the fish overnight in the usual way. When ready to cook, divide it into fairly large pieces and put in a cooking pot with the whole potatoes and the sweet potatoes, if used. Cover with water and poach gently for 30–45 minutes, until the fish and vegetables are tender. Drain thoroughly. Put a clean folded cloth over the fish and potatoes and replace the lid. (This will ensure that the contents of the pot remain hot and perfectly dry.)

To make the sauce, pound the garlic with the cumin seeds in a mortar. Add the paprika, salt and thyme, and continue pounding until well pulped. Beat in the oil gradually, then the vinegar, as if making mayonnaise. Transfer the sauce to an earthenware serving bowl and add about ¼ cup warm water or more, if you think the sauce is too strong. Allow to cool thoroughly before serving. Arrange the fish and potatoes together on a heated plate to serve. Traditionally this is served with dried figs and a salad of crisp lettuce, tomatoes and cucumber, and cubes of goats' milk cheese.

BACALHAU Á GOMES DE SÁ (PORTUGAL)
Dried salt cod à Gomes de Sá

Portugal has at least two dried salt cod recipes for each day of the year. Here's just one of them, named after the nineteenth-century General Gomes de Sá, who invented it.

Prepare the fish 24 hours in advance.
Serves 4

1 lb dried salt cod
1 lb potatoes, peeled
1 bay leaf
5 tablespoons olive oil
2 cloves garlic,
  finely chopped
1 lb onions, sliced
⅔ cup black olives
pepper
4 eggs, hard-cooked
  and sliced
chopped parsley

Soak the cod in cold water for 24 hours, changing the water once. Drain and place in a saucepan with the potatoes and bay leaf. Cover with fresh water and bring to a boil. Simmer for about 20 minutes, until the potatoes are tender but still whole. Drain. Remove the skin and bones from the fish and flake it. Cut the potatoes into 1 in cubes. Meanwhile, heat the oil in an earthenware or flameproof casserole that will later go in the oven. Add the garlic and onions and cook gently until the onions are tender. Add the fish and potatoes, stirring well to mix the ingredients. Stir in the olives and add pepper to taste. Transfer the casserole to a fairly hot oven (375°F). Bake for about 5 minutes, or until the top is lightly browned.

Transfer to a serving dish and garnish with the hard-cooked egg slices and chopped parsley.

BESUGO AL HORNO (ASTURIAS)
Porgy baked in the oven

Variations of this dish are traditional Christmas Eve fare all over Spain.

Serves 4

1 porgy of about
  2–2½ lb
2 lemons (1 sliced
  thickly, juice of 1)
⅓ cup olive oil
1 teaspoon salt
½ teaspoon freshly
  ground black pepper
6 tablespoons dry white
  wine or sherry
2–3 cloves garlic,
  chopped
chopped parsley
1 bay leaf, crumbled

Clean the fish, trimming the tail and fins but leaving the head on. Scrape off scales. Make several diagonal slits in one side of the fish and insert a thick piece of lemon in each.

Put 3 tablespoons of the oil in an oval baking dish just large enough to hold the fish. Put in the fish with the cut side uppermost. Season well and pour over the remaining oil, the wine or sherry and the lemon juice. Sprinkle with garlic, plenty of chopped parsley and the bay leaf.

Bake in a moderate oven (350°F) for 45 minutes to 1 hour, or until the fish is cooked. Add a little more wine if too dry, and baste frequently.

Serve in the same dish.

Meat

BIFE À PORTUGUÊSA (PORTUGAL)
Portuguese steak

This simple and delicious way of cooking steak is very popular in Portugal, where both beefsteak and other meat is often topped with a fried egg. In this recipe the eggs are optional. Also, the ham need not be inserted in the steak; it can quite simply be placed on top instead.

Serves 4

4 thick sirloin steaks
salt and pepper
¼ cup butter
2 tablespoons olive oil
4 slices of smoked ham
  (preferably presunto)
½ cup cream
6 tablespoons dry
  white wine
2 tablespoons chicken
  stock (optional)
4 eggs (optional)

Season the steak with salt and pepper. Slit each piece open horizontally like a sandwich, without cutting right through. Heat the butter and oil in a skillet and fry the steaks quickly on both sides. Open them out and press down into the fat to fry the center. Keep hot. Turn the ham slices (which should be just smaller than the steaks) in the fat, remove and keep hot. Pour the cream and wine into the pan and stir over a low flame until it thickens to form a sauce; add a little chicken stock if you like it thinner. Season with a little salt and freshly ground black pepper. Fry the eggs in a separate pan.

To serve, insert a slice of ham into each piece of steak like a sandwich and put an egg on top (if liked). Pour over the sauce and serve with either fried potatoes and mushrooms or rice.

LOMO DE CERDO ALMENDRADO (BALEARIC ISLANDS)
Pork tenderloin with almonds

Pork tenderloin is popular all over Spain. This dish is a particular favorite in Mallorca, where vast quantities of very high-quality almonds are produced.

Serves 4

2 long pieces of
  pork tenderloin, about
  2 lb
½ teaspoon salt
1¼ cups broken almonds
  lightly toasted
pepper
1 tablespoon flour
1 tablespoon lard or
  drippings
1 cup chopped scallions
  or shallots
½ cup dry sherry
1 cup stock
1 tablespoon cream

Make 2 incisions along the length of each tenderloin without cutting right through. Sprinkle in a little salt and press some crushed almonds evenly into each incision. Tie the tenderloin neatly with string and roll in well seasoned flour. Heat the lard in a heavy, shallow pan. Brown the tenderloin carefully, turning them gently, then add the chopped scallions (use the green parts as well) or the shallots, and cook for a few minutes. Add the sherry and the stock and cover the pan. Cook on a low heat for about 1 hour, turning the meat once.

When the meat is quite tender, remove and cut off the string. Slice neatly and arrange on a hot plate. Stir the cream into the sauce in the pan, without boiling, and pour it over the meat slices.

Garnish with small triangles of fried bread, and serve with mashed or baked potatoes.

Windmills haven't changed since Don Quixote.

JABALÍ ESTOFADO (ASTURIAS)
Stewed wild boar

There are many wild boar in the more mountainous and remote parts of Spain. Often the owner of a large estate will organize a hunt – a ritualistic affair, involving the wearing of leather 'chaps', cowboy style, and large cloaks. The principal members of the hunt are mounted, but the villagers are invited to join in on foot. Eventually the boar are driven from cover and shot. The following recipe is also suitable for venison or even pork.

Prepare 1 day in advance.
Serves 4

2 lb wild boar (or
  substitute venison),
  cut into 4 slices
¼ cup olive oil
salt
freshly ground black
  pepper
a bunch of fresh
  mountain herbs
  (thyme, rosemary,
  fennel and oregano),
  or use 1 teaspoon of
  each dried herb
2 bay leaves
6 peppercorns
1 cup white wine
  (with venison use
  red wine instead)
2 tablespoons wine
  vinegar
2 large onions,
  finely chopped
4 large cloves garlic
2–3 tablespoons
  chopped parsley
2 celery stalks, chopped
2 carrots, sliced
about ½ cup stock or
  water

Rub the meat well with some of the olive oil, place in a large shallow dish and sprinkle with a little salt and pepper. Add the herbs, bay leaves and peppercorns. Mix the wine and vinegar and pour over the meat. Leave to marinate overnight in a cool place.

To cook the meat, remove and dry it with paper towels. Reserve the marinade. Heat the rest of the olive oil in a heavy saucepan and lightly brown the meat. Add the onions, garlic, parsley, celery and carrots, and cook for a few minutes, stirring gently. Pour in the marinade, including the herbs and peppercorns. Add enough stock or water to ensure the meat is covered and season with salt and pepper. Cover the pan tightly and cook very slowly on top of the stove until the meat is tender, or transfer to a tightly covered casserole and cook in a slow oven (300°F). The cooking time will vary, but it will be at least 2½–3 hours.

To serve, arrange the meat on a hot plate and pour the liquid over it.

COCIDO MADRILEÑO O OLLA PODRIDA (MADRID)
Madrid stew, or 'rotten pot'

This is one of Spain's oldest dishes. It is a very accommodating dish, infinitely stretchable and easy to cook: all you need is a very large pot and a fire of some sort. Some of the ingredients may be left out, if they do not happen to be available. Also it improves with keeping for a day at least and does not easily spoil.

Prepare the chick-peas one day in advance.
Serves 6–8

1 lb chick-peas
  (garbanzos), soaked
  overnight
½ stewing chicken,
  about 2 lb
1 pig's foot
½ lb fresh or salted
  beef stew meat, with
  bone if possible
¼ lb bacon
¼ lb tocino (salted
  pork fat), cut into
  cubes
1 morcilla (black
  blood sausage)
¼ lb chorizo
1 large onion, sliced
¼ small head of cabbage,
  shredded
2 carrots, chopped
2 leeks
2 turnips, chopped
½ head (not clove)
  garlic
salt and pepper

Half fill a large (4 quart) pot with cold water and put in the chick-peas, chicken, pig's foot, beef, bacon, *tocino* and sausages. Bring to a boil and skim, then simmer half-covered on a low heat for 2–3 hours, skimming occasionally. Add more (hot) water if necessary.

Put the prepared vegetables, and the garlic in 1 unpeeled piece, in the pot, add more boiling water if necessary, and pepper and salt to taste. Bring back to a boil and simmer for 1 hour at least.

When ready to serve, remove the garlic and throw it away. Remove meats and sausages with a slotted spoon and cut into serving pieces. Pile the chick-peas and vegetables into a large hot dish, arrange the meats and sausages around them and pour a little broth over the top. The rest of the broth should be served first as soup with either fried bread cubes or pasta added. You can keep the stew hot while eating this, though it is the Spanish custom to let it stand and eat it lukewarm.

RIÑONES AL JEREZ (ANDALUSIA)
Kidneys in sherry sauce

Sherry takes its name from Jerez de la Frontera in Andalusia, where the special sherry grapes are grown. In Andalusia, and in southern Extremadura, cool sherry is drunk at mealtimes, like wine. This recipe combines sherry with tender young veal kidneys, another specialty of this bull-fighting region, to make a light and delicately flavored dish.

Serves 4–6

2 lb veal kidneys
salt and pepper
1 onion, finely
  chopped
1 clove garlic, finely
  chopped
1 bay leaf
¼ cup olive oil
1 tablespoon flour
about 1 cup
  beef stock
1 tablespoon
  tomato purée
½ teaspoon
  grated nutmeg
2 tablespoons
  chopped parsley
1 cup dry sherry

Remove the skin and gristle from the kidneys and cut them into thin slices. Sprinkle with salt and freshly ground pepper.

To make the sauce, fry the onion, garlic and bay leaf in half the oil, stirring frequently until the onion is soft. Stir in the flour and about 1 cup stock or water. Add the tomato purée and keep stirring until the sauce thickens. Season to taste with salt, pepper and nutmeg, and stir in the parsley. Keep warm on a low heat.

In a separate skillet, quickly fry the pieces of kidney in the remaining oil, turning them over to avoid burning. Lower the heat a little and continue to cook for about 4 minutes. Remove the kidneys and set aside. Pour the sherry into the pan and let it bubble, scraping up all the brown bits with a wooden spoon. Return the kidneys to the pan, and then add the prepared sauce. Heat through thoroughly, stirring gently. Serve on a hot plate, with triangles of fried bread and rice.

Fabada Asturiana

ISCAS DE LISBOA (LISBON)
Liver Lisbon style

This simple but delicious way of cooking liver is a specialty of Lisbon.

Prepare several hours in advance, or the night before.
Serves 4

1½ lb calf or lamb liver,
  sliced very thinly
1 cup dry white wine
2 tablespoons wine
  vinegar
4 cloves garlic, crushed
1 bay leaf
½ teaspoon salt
6 peppercorns
¼ cup olive oil
¼ lb bacon, diced

Put the liver slices into a shallow dish. Combine the wine, vinegar, crushed garlic, bay leaf and seasoning to make a marinade, and pour it over the liver. Cover the dish and leave to stand in a cool place for several hours, or overnight.

To cook, remove the pieces of liver and pat dry. Reserve the marinade. Heat the olive oil in a large skillet and quickly fry the pieces of liver and the bacon, turning once. Remove and keep hot. Pour the marinade into the pan and boil, stirring well, until slightly reduced. Remove the bay leaf. Pour the sauce over the liver and serve at once, with fried sliced potatoes.

Spain and Portugal

Serves 4–6

¾ lb dried beans,
  soaked overnight
1 bay leaf
1 ham bone
1 pig's foot (optional)
2 oz tocino, diced
¼ lb beef stew meat,
  cubed
1 onion, peeled and
  roughly chopped
¼ small hot chili
  pepper, seeded
6 cloves garlic
1 piece cooking-quality
  chorizo sausage
  (about ¼ lb)
2 morcillas de Asturias
  or blood sausage
  (about 5 oz)
salt

Drain the beans and put in a large pot with about 1½ quarts fresh water, and the bay leaf. Bring to a boil and add the ham bone, pig's foot, *tocino*, beef, onion, chili pepper and whole unpeeled garlic. Simmer gently for at least 2 hours, skimming when necessary.

Add the sausages, whole, and salt and simmer for a further 2 hours. The beans should not break up.

Cut up the sausages and return to the pot. Remove the meat from the ham bone; it should fall off the bone easily. Discard the bone and return the meat to the pot. Discard the garlic and pig's foot.

Serve the *fabada* immediately, or allow to cool and chill overnight. The next day, remove the fat from the surface of the dish and reheat. Serve with fresh crusty bread and dry hard cider or a *vino verde* (rough young wine).

RABO DE TORO (SPAIN)
Bull's tail (oxtail)

The Spanish like to eat their beef freshly killed, not aged as is the custom elsewhere. Perhaps this has something to do with the warmer climate of Spain. The day after the *corrida* or bullfight, the carcasses of the bulls killed in the ring appear for sale in the local market. The meat is of excellent quality – the animals are three or four years old and in fine condition. The tail makes a good nourishing stew. As an alternative, oxtail may be used. Choose a tail with plenty of gristle between the joints, as this is what gives the dish its flavor.

Serves 4

1 bull's tail (or
  oxtail), cut in
  joints
1 teaspoon salt
¼ cup flour
¼ cup beef drippings
  or lard
3 onions, cut in rings
3 tablespoons olive oil
1 lb carrots, sliced
¼ lb mushrooms, whole
2 celery stalks,
  chopped
1 clove garlic

Dip the joints in salted flour. Heat the fat in a flameproof pot and gently brown them all over.

Fry the onions separately in hot oil. When they start to brown, tip them into the pot with the tail and add the rest of the vegetables, including the whole peeled garlic clove. Stir well and add a little salt if necessary, but no pepper. Add about 1 cup water and cover the pot tightly. Cook in a slow oven (300°F) for at least 2 hours. Check occasionally to make sure it does not dry up, and add a little more water if necessary.

Serve in the same pot with plenty of fresh crusty bread and dry red wine.

FABADA ASTURIANA (ASTURIAS)
Asturian beans

This is one of Spain's best loved dishes, from the rocky northern province of Asturias. Warming and sustaining, it keeps out the winter chill of the wet Cantabric seaboard. For the non-Spanish cook, there is one disadvantage: it relies for complete success on the smoked black blood sausage, *morcilla de Asturias*, made in Asturias, but available everywhere in Spain. Specialist Spanish food stores do stock it, but if you are planning a trip to Spain it is well worth bringing some home. It will keep for up to a year, well sealed in the refrigerator or hung in a cool place, although it dries out eventually. Make sure you get the smoked variety. To substitute, use blood sausage.

The beans traditionally used are called *alubias*. They are slightly smaller and fatter than lima beans, and are said to have a stronger flavor, but lima beans will do as well. Long, slow cooking is the secret of this delicious dish.

Wheat brought to the threshing floor, Portugal

Poultry and game

CONEJO CON CEBOLLITAS (MALLORCA)
Rabbit with little onions

Small evenly sized pearl onions should be used for this Mallorcan recipe; or shallots would do.

Serves 4

*1 young rabbit
salt
¼ cup olive oil
5 oz tocino or fat
  bacon, diced
¼ cup dry sherry
a sprig each of thyme
  and parsley
1 bay leaf
16 pearl onions
2 tablespoons seasoned
  flour
1 cup water or stock*

Cut up the prepared rabbit and rub with salt. Heat the oil in a heavy saucepan and fry the *tocino* lightly, turning over and over. Add the pieces of rabbit and brown on all sides. Lower the heat and pour in the sherry. Tie the herbs together and add these to the pan. Cover and cook gently for 15–20 minutes.

Meanwhile peel the onions, leaving them whole. Roll them in seasoned flour and fry in a separate pan in a little olive oil, rolling them around until lightly golden. Remove and put into the pot with the rabbit. Add about 1 cup water or stock and simmer gently, covered, for about 1 hour, until the rabbit is tender. Remove the herbs and check for seasoning.

Place the rabbit pieces in the center of a hot plate, arrange the onions around them and pour the liquid from the pan over them. Serve with new potatoes.

POLLO EN CHILINDRÓN (ARAGON)
Chicken in chilindrón sauce

Chilindrón is a piquant sauce made with red, or sometimes green, peppers, onions and tomatoes, in which chicken, rabbit, pork or lamb may be cooked. It is native to the northern province of Aragon, but is popular throughout Spain.

Serves 4

*1 tender chicken,
  about 2–2½ lb
1 teaspoon salt
¼ cup olive oil
1 clove garlic
1 large onion, sliced
1 red and 1 green
  pepper, seeded
  and cut into strips
a pinch of toasted saffron
  threads or powdered
  saffron
2 teaspoons paprika
¼ lb smoked ham
  (preferably serrano)
¼ lb tomatoes, skinned
  and chopped
1 small hot dried red
  chili pepper, seeded
1 tablespoon chopped
  parsley
6 pitted olives, cut
  in half (optional)*

Cut the chicken into serving pieces and rub with salt. Heat the oil in a large saucepan and fry the chopped garlic. Add the chicken pieces and brown well on all sides. Remove and set aside. Put the sliced onion and peppers into the oil, cover and cook gently until soft, about 10 minutes. Stir in the saffron, paprika, ham cut into cubes, and the tomatoes. Put in the pieces of chicken and the chili pepper. Add a little more salt if necessary. Stir gently, cover the pan and cook on a low heat for about 1 hour, or until the chicken is tender. If it dries up add a little water or chicken stock.

To serve, arrange the chicken pieces on a hot plate and pour the sauce over them. Sprinkle with chopped parsley and garnish with halved olives.

A peasant kitchen, Majorca, with a floor of pebbles from the beach

Spain and Portugal

CONEJO EN SARMOREJO (TENERIFE)
Rabbit cooked in white wine

This is a favorite dish in the Canary Islands. It goes well with the purplish red wine of Tacaronte, which leaves an effervescent feeling on the tongue.

Prepare this dish several hours to one day in advance.
Serves 4

1 medium-sized rabbit
salt
at least 2½ cups dry
white wine
⅓ cup vinegar
2 sprigs of fresh wild
thyme (or 2 teaspoons
dried thyme)
2 teaspoons oregano
1 bay leaf
¼ cup olive oil
2 large cloves of garlic
2 teaspoons paprika
1 small hot dried chili
pepper, seeded and
chopped, or ⅓
teaspoon cayenne
pepper

Cut up the rabbit, sprinkle well with salt and put into a shallow dish. Make a marinade to cover the rabbit using half the wine, the vinegar, the thyme, oregano and bay leaf. Allow to stand in a cool place for several hours, or better still overnight.

When ready to start cooking remove the pieces of rabbit from the dish, reserving the marinade. Dry them on paper towels. Heat the olive oil gently in a saucepan and brown the pieces of rabbit. Take the pan off the heat, pour in the marinade, and add the rest of the wine. Partially cover the pan and cook slowly. Meanwhile crush the peeled garlic cloves in a mortar with the paprika, cayenne or chili pepper and a little salt. Add this to the saucepan, stir well and taste. It should be slightly hot. Continue to simmer gently for 1½–2 hours or until the rabbit is really tender. Add a little more wine if necessary. This dish improves with reheating and is even better if cooked the day before it is needed. Serve with fried or boiled potatoes and crusty bread.

CODORNICES EN SALSA (MENORCA)
Quails in sauce

These tiny game birds used to be abundant throughout Spain, especially in the Balearic islands. Although their numbers are much reduced they are still a popular dish. Allow one large or two small quails per person.

Serves 4

¼ cup butter
4 or 8 quails according
to size, or 4 young
tender pigeons
1 tablespoon finely
chopped summer
savory (optional)
1 tablespoon finely
chopped parsley
a sprig of mint, finely
chopped
a pinch of thyme
¼ teaspoon salt
pepper
4 or 8 slices bacon
¼ cup white wine
¼ cup chicken stock
1 tablespoon flour

Place a pat of butter inside each prepared bird and fit them into a greased earthenware dish or roasting pan. Spread a little butter over each one, sprinkle with the mixed chopped herbs, salt and pepper, and cover each with a slice of bacon. Mix about two-thirds of the wine with the stock and pour over the birds. Roast in a moderate oven (350°F) for about 45 minutes, basting frequently; then remove the bacon, and finish cooking at a higher temperature (400°F) for about 10 minutes, or until browned. Put them onto a hot plate and keep warm.

Stir 1 tablespoon flour into the juices left in the pan and cook on top of the stove, stirring all the time, until thickened. Add the rest of the wine and a little stock or water and allow to boil, still stirring. When the sauce is smooth, taste for seasoning and add more salt and pepper if necessary. Pour the sauce over the quails and serve decorated with triangles of fried bread.

left Codornices en Salsa
below *The household vine provides shade for sewing in Castille.*

Brazo de gitano

Desserts

ANANÁS COM MADEIRA (MADEIRA)
Fresh pineapple with Madeira wine

This simple dessert successfully combines pineapples, which in Portugal come from the Azores, and the famous fortified wine which takes its name from the island where it is made – Madeira.

Prepare several hours in advance.
Serves 4

*4 thick slices of fresh
  pineapple with skin
  removed
about 1 cup dry
  Madeira wine
sugar*

Place a slice of pineapple in each of 4 shallow glass bowls and cover with Madeira. Sprinkle with sugar and allow to stand for several hours. Serve chilled if preferred.

BRAZO DE GITANO (SPAIN)
Gypsy's arm

This decorated roll may have flavored custard or fresh whipped cream as a filling.

Serves 4–6

*Sponge cake roll
4 eggs
¾ cup sugar
½ cup self-rising flour
a pinch of salt
butter frosting and sugar
  flowers for
  decoration*

To make the sponge cake roll: grease and flour a jelly roll pan (15½ × 10½ × 1 in). Beat the eggs and sugar together well and fold in the sifted flour and salt. Pour the mixture into the pan and bake in a fairly hot oven (375°F) for about 15 minutes or until the cake is well risen and golden. Turn it out onto a sheet of sugared paper, put more paper on top and roll up lengthwise while still hot; this will ensure the roll keeps its shape. When nearly cool unroll and spread the filling quite thickly along the center. Roll up again. The result should be a cream-filled tube, rather than a jelly roll. Smooth butter frosting over the outside and decorate with sugar flowers or rosettes.

*Custard filling
1 cup milk
1 vanilla bean or a few
  drops vanilla extract or
  coffee flavouring
2 egg yolks
¼–½ cup sugar
1 tablespoon cornstarch*

To make the filling, bring the milk to a boil with vanilla bean or other flavoring, then allow to cool slightly. Beat the egg yolks and sugar together thoroughly. Remove vanilla bean and pour egg and sugar mixture into the milk. Dissolve the cornstarch in a little cold milk and pour into the pan. Cook gently for 5 minutes or so, stirring all the time until it thickens. Cool before use.

MANZANAS ASADAS ASTURIANAS (ASTURIAS)
Baked apples

The province of Asturias in northern Spain is famous for its apples. They include both eating and cooking varieties, and also cider apples. This is the only part of Spain where cider takes precedence over wine. Anise is also made in Asturias.

Serves 4

*4 large cooking
  apples of equal size
½ cup sugar
¼ cup butter
½ cup sweet white wine
2 egg whites
a few drops of anise oil
2 tablespoons apricot
jam*

Wash the apples and remove the cores. Place in a buttered shallow baking dish. Sprinkle with sugar, and add a pat of butter to the center of each apple. Pour the white wine over them and bake in a moderate oven (350°F) for about 10 minutes until almost tender.

In the meantime beat the egg whites with the rest of the sugar, adding the anise drop by drop, until it forms stiff peaks. Take the apples from the oven and spread a little apricot jam on each one. Top with a large spoonful of egg white, sprinkle with a little more sugar and put back into the oven for a further 10 minutes, or until the apples are tender and the meringue brown on top.

Spain and Portugal

CAVACAS ZAMACOÍS (PORTUGAL)
Small light cakes

Portuguese cake recipes tend to be prodigious in their use of eggs, but this produces very light and delicious results. The original recipe for these cakes suggested beating the eggs by hand for two hours, but this can be overcome with the use of an electric mixer. You will also need kitchen tongs – an essential item in every Spanish and Portuguese kitchen – to dip the cakes in the syrup.

Makes 16 cakes

5 eggs
½ cup mild olive oil
¾ cup flour
whipped cream
  (optional)

Beat the eggs thoroughly for 2–3 minutes on high speed. Slowly add the oil, beating on a slightly lower speed. Add the sifted flour, 1 teaspoon at a time, and beat for another minute. A thick foamy batter should result. Preheat the oven to 425°F and grease either a large baking sheet or shallow muffin tins (which is generally better as the mixture is fairly runny). Spoon out the mixture (1 tablespoon for each cake on the baking sheet, or 2 in each muffin tin) and bake for 10–15 minutes, or until the cakes are well risen and golden brown.

Syrup
1 cup sugar
½ cup water

Meanwhile for the syrup, dissolve the sugar in the water in a saucepan and boil for 30 seconds. When the cakes are cooked let them cool a little, then dip each one in the cooled syrup using kitchen tongs. Place a layer of paper under the rack on which the cakes are cooled to catch the sticky drops of syrup which inevitably run down. A personal addition to this recipe is a blob of thick cream on each cake. It is not strictly traditional, but makes them extra delicious.

QUESEDILLAS DE HIERRO (CANARY ISLANDS)
Cheesecakes from the island of Hierro

In the Canaries, *gofio* – toasted ground wheat or corn – is used in many recipes for cookies and cakes, and also added to the thick *potajes* or soup-stews so beloved of the Canary Islanders. It is also used as a breakfast food, mixed to a paste with a little milk and sugar. In this recipe lightly toasted wholewheat flour could be used instead of *gofio*.

Serves 4

½ cup butter
½ cup sugar
3 eggs
½ lb soft Hierro
  cheese (or cottage
  cheese)
2 teaspoons gofio
1 cup blanched ground
  almonds
juice and grated rind
  of 1 lemon
Pie pastry made with 2 cups
  flour (p. 30)

Cream the butter and sugar until light and fluffy. Separate the eggs and beat the yolks one by one into the mixture. Stir in the cheese, the *gofio* or flour, the almonds and the juice and rind of lemon. Beat the egg whites as stiffly as possible and fold in. Roll out the pastry fairly thickly and line some greased shallow muffin tins. Put some of the mixture into each and bake in a moderate oven (350°F) until the filling is set, about 30 minutes. One large pie pan could be used instead, and the cheesecake cut into wedges when cool.

CREMA DE CHOCOLATE (SPAIN)
Chocolate mousse

Chocolate was first brought back from Mexico by the Spanish *conquistadores* in 1519 and it was soon used throughout Europe. Apart from its more conventional role as a confection or hot drink, the Spanish use it in an unusual way. They add a few squares of dark chocolate to a meat sauce, or even to a lobster dish, which gives an exquisite smoothness and a subtle bitter-sweet tang. In this recipe, however, chocolate is used in a more familiar way: as a delicious, rather unsweet dessert.

Serves 4

3 tablespoons strong
  black coffee
8 squares semisweet
  chocolate
¼ cup butter
a few drops vanilla
3 eggs
½ cup whipped cream
½ cup split toasted
  almonds

Put the black coffee in a small saucepan over a low heat and add the chocolate broken into pieces. Melt slowly, stirring all the time. When the chocolate has completely melted, remove from the heat and stir in the butter and vanilla. Separate the yolks from the whites of the eggs and beat them 1 at a time into the chocolate. Beat the whites until very stiff and fold well into the chocolate mixture. Pour into 4 glass bowls and chill for 3–4 hours. When ready to serve, cover with whipped cream and stick the pieces of almond upright all over the top.

Spanish exterior

FLAN
Caramel custard

This dessert is popular throughout both Spain and Portugal, and is most often served in the classic original form given here. There are many variations, however: some add a little shredded coconut, orange juice, or coffee flavoring.

Serves 4

1 pint milk
¾ cup sugar
¼ teaspoon vanilla
  or 1 vanilla bean
4 eggs
½ cup sugar for caramel

Heat the milk, sugar and vanilla bean if used until the sugar dissolves. Set aside to cool and remove the bean. Beat the eggs well together in a bowl and add the vanilla, if this is what you are using. Pour the sweetened milk into the eggs, and beat again very thoroughly.
  To make the caramel, heat the sugar in a dry, heavy saucepan until it dissolves and starts to brown, remove from heat, and carefully add 2 tablespoons water. It will bubble up, so take care. Pour a little caramel into 4 dampened individual molds or 1 large one. Fill the molds with the custard mixture and stand in a baking dish with water coming about halfway up the molds. Put into a moderate oven (350°F) for about 30 minutes. To test, stick a small knife into the custard: if it comes out clean, the custard is done. Allow to cool and serve chilled. Turn out onto plates at the last minute.

The stomach is the teacher of the arts and the dispenser of invention.

Persius (34-62 AD)

Italians adore modern life; they have embraced it in all its aspects with an almost simple-minded fervor. Their cities are noisy, dirty and packed, full of skyscrapers and smart stores, crammed with chic clothes and avant-garde furniture. But when it comes to food Italians have not changed their standards at all, and in Italy today, provided you follow your nose to the places where the locals eat, whether they be businessmen or truck drivers, you are likely to eat some of the finest food in the world.

It's best to search around until you find a nice little restaurant, with some really *fresh* looking things, like green bulbs of fennel, a few large pears, ripe figs, and perhaps some newly made green and yellow noodles piled up on a shelf by the window, clean white cloths on the tables, old mirrors on the walls and an old wooden stand to hang up your coat. Choose carefully from the menu and you will be given a whole succession of treats, particularly if you are with Italians, who like to try some of everybody's dish to reassure themselves that they have chosen well. If you have hit on the right place, all the food will have been cooked with an unselfconscious, generous hand, and will be far more appetizing than all those exquisitely careful dishes, which result from hours of experimentation in a celebrated three-star kitchen.

Of course what you find to eat in each place will vary enormously according to the region you are in. Italy was united in 1870 by King Emmanuel. Until then it had developed over the centuries, not as a single nation, but as a group of separate neighboring states. These states were rarely friendly, and frequently hostile to one another; consequently the people of each state cultivated a tremendous pride of possession, jealousy and love for everything of their own – families, traditions, and of course food. The result was that cooking, although defined to a large extent by the limitations of local climate, soil and situation, varied immensely from state to state; while the rich traveled about carrying new cooking ideas from town to town, the people of the countryside kept their local dishes, and handed them on proudly to the next generation.

Eating is always a great event in Italy. Lunch is important: everybody devotes two hours to it; factories and stores close down and people rush home, or, if they live too far away, they go to a small homey restaurant with a few tables and a big dominating patron-chef, who simply serves you whatever he has cooked, without the formality of presenting a menu.

Lunch consists of several courses, and they are all equally important. Bread is served with the meal, but there is usually no butter. Wine is a must, often sent down the table with a carafe of water in case there are some who want to drink a lighter mixture. The food is generous (although the meat is often served in very small quantities, since it is, after all, only part of the meal). The occasion brings everybody together, from the youngest of the children to the oldest of the grandparents.

It is very difficult to generalize about Italian meals, because they vary so widely from place to place; but as you pass from one region to another you will notice some broad differences between the north and the south of the country. In the south, for example, where durum ('hard-grain') wheat grows best, pasta in all its delightful variety forms the basis for most meals; corn and rice grow in the rich, fertile plains of the Po valley in the north, so here risotto and *polenta* are common staples. In the north people often cook with butter, while in the south olive oil is more frequently used, since an olive tree costs less to maintain than a cow, and can live off poorer soil. The people of the south eat less meat than their more well off cousins of the north. This is because they keep their cattle for the farm-work and for milk, rather than for meat. But there are many variations within this broad outline, and the following comments on the character and specialties of each region are offered as a guide to what you can expect as you travel through this delightful country.

Piedmont means white truffles to anyone deeply interested in food matters. If you are in Piedmont in the late autumn, try them grated to clay-colored paper-thin wafers and sprinkled over local dishes such as *fonduta*, or over risotto or chicken breasts. They are delicious and addictive.

Turin, the industrial center of Piedmont, appears dull to all who do not live there; but it does have very good restaurants, where you will find local specialties such as braised beef in red wine, hare cooked with its own blood (like jugged hare), risotto with salami and beans and *vitello tonnato*, a delicious combination of veal and tuna fish, served cold. Italy's most famous wines, Barolo and Barbaresco, and fizzy Asti Spumante – very delicious if you can obtain a dry one – also come from this region.

Valle d'Aosta in the Italian Alps has many dishes based on the celebrated local cheese, Fontina, which is mild, soft and fragrant. When you see the cows grazing knee-deep in flowers in the alpine fields in spring, it's easy to imagine why the cheese tastes so sweet.

Alto Adige, which lies east of Lombardy, is another mountainous area, dominated this time by the grand and jagged Dolomites. Austrian influence is strong here; skiers are likely to be instructed in German as well as Italian, and fed on sauerkraut and dumplings when they arrive back at their hotels tired and cold. *Polenta* – the cornmeal staple of northern Italy – and game are favorite dishes. At certain times of the year small migratory birds can be seen in rows on the large wood-burning stoves that many restaurants still have. The famous mushrooms that appear here in all shapes, colors and sizes are broiled. (In these mountains there are over sixty edible varieties of *funghi*.) Another local specialty is *canderli*, a dumpling similar to *gnocchi*.

Italy

color of flowers – red speckled with cream, or the shade of deep wine with white stems; green-tinted cream-frizzled chicory; and long, tender yellow stems which turn out to be dandelions.

Not far away, the ancient city of Padua boasts another superlative market, where in May wild strawberries and asparagus are piled up in red and white mountains beneath large square white umbrellas. Padua is also the home of delicious sausages, black risotto and chicken livers with rice. Other specialties of Veneto include salt cod cooked in olive oil with onions; *risi e bisi* – rice with peas; sirloin steak served raw in thin slices with mustard sauce; and small fried fish of all sorts.

Emilia-Romagna is the home of Bolognese sauce and the cradle of some of the best food – certainly some of the richest food – in Italy. Parmesan cheese, mortadella sausages and egg noodles all have their birthplace in Emilia-Romagna, as well as dozens of succulent sausages and salamis. The local pasta dishes are rich and creamy, with meat sauce and béchamel sauce combined; the pasta itself is made with eggs, and rolled out fresh daily. Butter – and plenty of it – is used for cooking.

Parma, a great gastronomic center and the home of Parmesan cheese, once had a flourishing royal court of its own and a marvelous opera-house, the *Teatro Reggio*, where the audience – true devotees of the arts of music and eating – used to dine in their boxes between the acts. Specialties of this area include eels cooked with peas; lasagne *al forno*; and *tortellini* – little pockets of pasta stuffed with turkey breast and mortadella.

Liguria is the most French-influenced area of Italy; its cooking is excellent, making use of green vegetables, tomatoes, and delicious seafood. Specialties include whitebait salad; ravioli stuffed with cheese and herbs and served with nut sauce; and a large flat pie of thin pastry filled with all sorts of greenery – spinach, artichokes, lettuce – as well as cheese, rice and eggs.

Tuscany with its warm, neatly farmed slopes is regarded by many as the most fascinating of all Italian regions. The home

A Florentine cartload of Chianti

Lombardy has many dreary miles of industrial landscape, but in their center lies Milan, one of the most elegant of all Italian cities. Even the grocery stores are the most glorious you will ever see: the dewy freshness of the cheeses, the size of the multi-layered, multi-colored omelette-pies, the pink plumpness of the sausages are unequaled anywhere. Milanese customers require an exceedingly high standard when it comes to food.

Lombardy specialties include *carbonata* – a beef and red wine stew; *costoletta Milanese* – veal chop in breadcrumbs; and *ossobuco* – veal shin cooked with saffron rice. By all means eat the *risotto Milanese*, but try the bean soup too, and the kidney and liver dishes and the sweetbreads – the Milanese are unrivaled at cooking variety meats, and treat them with a rare respect.

Veneto encompasses Venice with its astonishing food market. Visit it in the morning, reasonably early and, when you have admired all the stacked-up cheeses, olives and dried mushrooms, turn into the fish market. Nowhere else will you see such a variety of weird crustaceans, mollusks and slippery, boneless fishy things, scarlet, pale and black, each with a definite place in the scheme of Venetian cooking.

Then there is the locally grown salad: *radicchio* lettuces the of Dante, Leonardo da Vinci, Boccaccio, and Botticelli, this is also the land of olive oil, wine, beefsteak and vegetables: simple cooking of the highest quality. Tuscan specialties include young pork roast with garlic and rosemary and *cacciucco*, a fish soup from Livorno.

Rome has so many culinary specialties that it is hard to single out one or two, but *fettuccine alla Romana* – thin noodles in generous amounts of melted butter and freshly grated Parmesan – is superb. Fried baby artichokes with garlic is another memorable treat; and young lamb cooked with rosemary is smaller, paler, and more tender than anything you can imagine.

The Marches, a mountainous, rugged region along the Adriatic coast, about halfway down the leg of Italy, is inhabited by farmers and fishermen. Their food is mainly based on fish, squid and lobsters. Local specialties also include black olives preserved in a special brine, and pork braised in white wine. The wine of the region is Verdicchio, which is worth drinking wherever you are.

Umbria is where Saint Francis was born; and it is true that the locals are fond of animals and birds – especially pigs and wild pigeons, which they eat in large quantities. They also make an excellent straw-colored wine called Orvieto, which can be sweet, dry or fruity, and is excellent with fish.

The rolling countryside, covered with pretty olive slopes and grassy folds, is shaded by oaks. These feed the pigs and provide the people with black truffles similar to the 'black pearls of Périgord'. One local dish not to be missed is spaghetti *alla spoletina* – spaghetti with truffle sauce. Other dishes include: *paglia e fieno* – 'straw and grass' – a mixture of green and yellow noodles served with *prosciutto* and cream; and trout broiled in a coating of breadcrumbs.

Abruzzi e Molise is Italy's problem area, with hard land, few industries, and relatively few visitors. The food here is chiefly remembered for being eaten in gigantic quantities.

Tuscan harvest

If you sit down to one of these large meals, be sure to have *maccheroni alla chitarra* – noodles cut on a frame like a guitar with wires strung across. They are served with a sauce made of either lamb and green peppers or smoked pork and tomatoes. Local cheeses play an important part in the Abruzzi diet – particularly a hard sheep's cheese called *pecorino*, not quite as salty as the Sardinian version, and *scamorza*, a little bag-shaped cheese that is roasted on a spit before being eaten around the fire. Other dishes are fish soup with chili peppers and lamb with egg and lemon sauce.

The food of Apulia, the harsh treeless southeastern corner of Italy, is strong and colorful, with excellent vegetables and tremendously varied pasta and pizza. Local dishes include: *orecchiette* – tiny *gnocchi* made to look like shells; *laganelle* – small stuffed lasagne; and piquant mushroom or squid salads sharpened with anchovies, capers and black olives.

Naples, the center of Campania, may at first seem an atrocious place: filthy, overcrowded, hideous in all its modern aspects. But in the old part of the town the everyday business of living goes on, not behind curtains or doors, but all over the streets. Lively bustles and smells and noises and crowds – a terrific experience. Eat in Naples and you eat fast: you find pizza everywhere, a convenient way of eating your bread, tomatoes and sausages or anchovies without bothering about knives and forks. Spaghetti is another of the staple dishes – served *al dente* with mussels or clams, or a fiery sauce of chili peppers and black olives.

Not far away from Naples are the pretty vacation resorts of Amalfi, Ravello, Positano, Capri and Ischia. Here's where you should sample the tomato salads, the cannelloni, pizza, and the marvelous ice creams. You should also drink the local wine – Caruso.

In Calabria and Basilicata the soil is poor and ungenerous, but the sun beats down and ripens the peppers and eggplants, and the sea provides plenty of fish and salt. Although the grass is never more than sparse, and the sheep and pigs are thin and muscular, fruitful olive and orange groves, fig trees and almond orchards flourish in the more fertile plains.

Since life is harsh for the few inhabitants of this area the food is simple, austere and often rather salty; but it is a pleasure to sit by the sea and eat spaghetti with tiny clams, or *fusilli* – a spiral pasta – with red pepper and tomato sauce; eggplants stuffed with mozzarella cheese, and peppers cooked in oil and bathed in tomato sauce.

It is quite difficult to find traditional Sardinian cooking in Sardinia now that the island has been developed as a vacation resort; but one or two families still make the strange bread called *carasau* – 'music paper' – with its thin white sheets of dough baked crisp like paper. Other specialties include meat cooked in a pit with aromatic branches of juniper or myrtle, and *pecorino sardo*, a sheep's milk cheese, hard and dry and excellent for cooking. Then there are stuffed squid, *culingiones* – ravioli stuffed with cheese and chopped beet leaves – and lamb braised with tomatoes and fennel.

The one thing all the regions of Italy do have in common is a joyful approach to food and cooking – none of the solemn, heavy ritual attached to so much French cooking, but a freshness, a way of playing many light-hearted variations on well known, well loved themes.

Hors d'oeuvre

INSALATA DI FUNGHI E FORMAGGIO (TRENTINO)
Mushroom and cheese salad

Wild mushrooms abound in the Alps: in autumn over sixty different varieties are to be found, and only three are said to be poisonous. The people here are expert at finding the most delicious varieties, which they preserve in oil, ready to use in the winter when fresh vegetables are scarce.

The mushroom most often used for this salad is egg-shaped and brilliant glowing orange; sometimes a few slices of raw *cèpe* may be added too. It makes a very pretty dish, and tastes exquisite. However, cultivated white button mushrooms can easily be used instead.

Serves 4

$\frac{1}{4}$ lb white button
  mushrooms
juice of $\frac{1}{4}$ lemon
$\frac{1}{4}$ lb Gruyère cheese
salt and pepper
olive oil
white truffles (optional)

Slice the mushrooms very thinly and immediately sprinkle them with lemon juice. Cut the Gruyère into the thinnest slices and then cut these into strips about 1 in long by $\frac{1}{4}$ in wide. Sprinkle them over the mushrooms, season with salt and pepper, and pour on a fine thread of the very best olive oil. Lastly, if you are in Italy, scatter on a few paper-thin flakes of white truffle.

Milking cows for customers in the streets of Naples

UOVA IN TEGAME CON PROSCIUTTO E MOZZARELLA (CAMPANIA)
Eggs baked with ham and mozzarella cheese

Every country in the world seems to have its own version of bacon and eggs; this is the Italian one. Somewhat akin to French *oeufs sur le plat*, it includes lovely strands of melted mozzarella to add to its succulence.

Serves 6

6 slices of smoked ham
  or prosciutto
1 lb mozzarella cheese,
  thinly sliced
6 eggs
butter
salt and freshly ground
  pepper

Preheat the oven to 400°F. Butter an oval gratin dish and lay the slices of ham over the bottom. Cover with slices of mozzarella, then break the eggs carefully into the dish. Dot with butter, season lightly with salt and pepper and bake in the oven for about 6 minutes, until the eggs are just set and the cheese melted.

SCRIPPELLE IMBUSSE (ABRUZZO)
Cheese and ham crêpes

Unlike other Italian stuffed crêpes these are moistened with stock before their final cooking in the oven. In Abruzzo – where the people have notoriously large appetites – this dish would be served as only one course among many but it makes an appetizing lunch on its own.

Serves 4

Crêpes
3 eggs
1$\frac{1}{4}$ cups flour
$\frac{1}{4}$ teaspoon salt
oil for frying

Filling
1 cup freshly grated
  cheese – Parmesan or
  pecorino if possible
4 slices of prosciutto or
  smoked ham, finely
  chopped
1$\frac{1}{4}$ cups chicken stock
2 tablespoons butter

First make the crêpes. Beat the eggs in a bowl and gradually add the flour, sifting it in and beating until it is a thick paste; now add salt and just enough water to make a thin flowing batter, the consistency of cream. Pour the mixture into a measuring jug.

Heat a small 8 in skillet and coat the bottom very lightly with oil. Pour in about 2 tablespoons of the batter. Let it cook for roughly 1$\frac{1}{2}$ minutes; turn it over with a spatula and cook 1 minute longer. The crêpes can be made in advance and stacked up with wax paper between them.

When you want to eat the *scrippelle* spread them out on a board. Sprinkle each one generously with a mixture of grated cheese and chopped ham and roll them tightly. Lay them in a large but shallow dish and pour on the stock. Sprinkle with more cheese, dot with butter and place under the broiler for a few minutes until the stock is absorbed.

CROSTINI DI FEGATINI DI POLLO (TUSCANY)
Chicken livers on toast

In Tuscany the consumption of chickens is simply enormous, and this is just one of the little dishes made with chicken livers. Served hot with a glass of wine, it makes a delicious appetizer. The dish can be prepared in advance and re-heated just before serving.

Serves 4

4 chicken livers, finely
  chopped
1 tablespoon butter
$\frac{1}{4}$ tablespoon chopped
  parsley
1 teaspoon flour
4 anchovy fillets, chopped
$\frac{1}{4}$ cup chicken stock
a pinch of salt
a squeeze of lemon juice
2 tablespoons freshly
  grated Parmesan cheese
8–12 small pieces of
  freshly made toast or
  fried bread

Fry the chicken livers in the butter until they are just brown. Stir in the parsley, flour and chopped anchovies. Add the stock and salt and cook down to a paste.

Stir in the lemon juice and Parmesan cheese and spread the mixture on the hot toast or fried bread. Serve hot.

Seafood salad: a delicate delight of the Mediterranean

INSALATA DI MARE (CAMPANIA)
Seafood salad

Seafood was until quite recently one of the greatest delights of a visit to the bay of Naples; unfortunately it's now unobtainable because of the unclean water there. However, if you have the patience, you can still make one of these extremely intricate but wonderfully good salads at home, using all or some of the shellfish mentioned.

Prepare 2 hours in advance.
Serves 6

36 mussels
6 tablespoons olive oil
8–10 baby squid
2¼ lb shrimp
1 tablespoon lemon juice
¼ dried red chili pepper, flaked very small
salt
2 tablespoons coarsely chopped parsley
freshly ground pepper

Scrub and wash the mussels thoroughly, and shake dry. Heat 2 tablespoons olive oil in a large pan with a lid; when it is hot put in the mussels, cover the pan and shake them over the heat until they open. Remove the mussels, reserving the liquid in a bowl, and allow them to cool.

Clean and skin the squid and cut off the tentacles. Wash all the pieces well under running water and put them into the liquid from the mussels, diluted with a little water. Bring to a boil and simmer for 20 minutes or until the squid are tender. (This varies according to their size.) Add the shrimp and cook for 10 more minutes.

Shell the shrimp and mussels and put them in a shallow dish with the squid bodies cut into rings and the tentacles.

Mix the remaining olive oil with 1 tablespoon lemon juice. Add the flaked chili and a pinch of salt. Stir this dressing into the seafood salad. Sprinkle with parsley and a little freshly ground pepper and chill lightly for 2 hours before serving.

LA BAGNA CAUDA (PIEDMONT)
Hot anchovy sauce

La bagna cauda is a warm anchovy sauce often served in a big communal pot into which the guests, seated around the table, dip raw vegetables. Served like the French *crudités*, the sauce substitutes oil, butter, garlic and anchovies for the thick garlic-laden mayonnaise of Provence. The Piedmontese country people serve it with raw broccoli (you could substitute cauliflower), spinach, tiny tender zucchini, cardoons, red or green peppers, celery, carrots, radishes, cucumber, and crisp leaves of chicory – in fact whichever vegetables are freshest and best according to the season. *Bagna cauda* is also poured over a dish of broiled red peppers and sliced tomatoes, and served as an hors d'oeuvre.

Serves 6

¼ cup olive oil
¾ cup butter
5–6 cloves of garlic, finely chopped
2 oz can of anchovies, chopped
salt if needed

Heat the oil and butter in an earthenware pot or chafing dish until foaming. Stir in the garlic and cook gently without browning.

Add the anchovies and stir over a very low heat until they melt. Add a small pinch of salt and keep warm at the table over a plate warmer or alcohol lamp. Heap the prepared vegetables on a huge plate and let the guests help themselves.

If there is any sauce left over, you can scramble an egg or two in it, as an extra little treat.

FAGIOLI FRESCHI AL TONNO (TUSCANY)
Dried navy beans with tuna

This salad of creamy white beans freshened with raw onion and tuna fish is familiar to most visitors to Italy. It makes a most satisfying lunch, or a delicious appetizer.

Canned tuna is usually used and if necessary the salad can be prepared in an instant using canned beans as well, although these can be slightly on the soft side.

Soak the dried beans for 24 hours.
Serves 6

1¾ cups dried white navy beans, soaked overnight
2 small mild onions (preferably red ones)
salt
½ lb can tuna fish
⅔ cup olive oil
3 tablespoons red wine vinegar
freshly ground pepper
flat parsley

Place the beans in a pan of cold water with a peeled whole onion, bring them to a boil and simmer gently for 30 minutes. Add ½ teaspoon salt and continue cooking for a further 30–45 minutes, adding more water if necessary to keep the beans just covered.

When they are tender and creamy – the time varies very much according to the quality of the beans – let them cool in their liquid.

Slice the other onion thinly and soak the rings in cold water for 1 hour to modify the flavor.

Drain the beans and put them in an earthenware bowl. Flake the tuna fish and mix lightly into the beans, adding any oil that remains in the can. Make a plain oil and vinegar dressing seasoned with salt and pepper, and add this to the beans.

Drain the onion rings and scatter them over the salad. Add a few sprigs of flat parsley and serve.

Soups

MINESTRA DI RISO E FAGIOLI (FRIULI-VENEZIA GIULIA)
Rice and bean soup

This soup is traditionally made with local beans, which are red mottled with black, and a ham bone from the famous San Daniele ham; but red kidney beans and other ham bone may be used.

Soak the beans for 24 hours.
Serves 8

1¼ cups dried beans, soaked overnight
1 ham bone
1 carrot
1 celery stalk
1 large onion
¼ lb bacon
1 small onion
2 oz mortadella sausage
3 tablespoons olive oil
1 cup rice
salt and pepper

Drain the beans and put them in a pan with the ham bone and the carrot, celery and large onion, all coarsely chopped. Pour on 3 quarts of water. Bring to a boil, skim and cook for 2½ hours. Remove the ham bone, let it cool, and take off any meat.

Chop this meat, the bacon, the small onion and the mortadella very, very finely and fry them in the oil in a large pan. Pour in the beans and their cooking liquid, return to a boil, and then add the rice. Season to taste and cook for another 20 minutes.

The soup should be fairly thick and the rice just nicely cooked.

The serenity of the Mincio river in the Po valley, Italy's rice growing district

MINESTRA DI POMODORI ALLA TORINESE (PIEDMONT)
Tomato soup

The Piedmontese prefer to start a meal with soup. Their soups are delicious, based on chicken stock and thickened with rice from the rice-fields of the Po, or vegetables from the hills surrounding Turin. This smooth, velvety tomato soup should be made with a well flavored homemade chicken stock.

Serves 4

1 lb large ripe tomatoes, skinned and coarsely chopped
1 clove of garlic, finely chopped
5 leaves of fresh basil
1 tablespoon fresh lemon juice
1 teaspoon salt
freshly ground black or white pepper
2 tablespoons butter
¼ cup flour
1 quart homemade chicken stock
1 tablespoon tomato purée

Put the tomatoes in a large pan with the garlic, basil, lemon juice, salt and pepper. Cover the pan and bring to a boil, then lower the heat and simmer for 10 minutes. Liquidize in a blender or put through a food mill. Melt the butter in a saucepan and add the flour. Let it cook for 2 minutes, then gradually add the chicken stock, stirring all the time to keep the mixture smooth and lump free. Add the liquidized tomatoes. Cover the pan and simmer for 10 minutes. Dissolve the tomato purée in a little of the soup, add this to the pan, and taste for seasoning. Cook for 10 minutes more and serve hot.

MINESTRONE ALLA GENOVESE (LIGURIA)
Vegetable soup

This is an entirely vegetable soup: no meat, no pig's feet or skin, no stock. Nonetheless it is rich and comforting, and it improves with reheating. Since long cooking sometimes exhausts vegetable flavors, the soup can be flavored at the last moment with the famous Genoese *pesto* – basil and garlic paste – which gives it an extra lift.

Prepare the beans 24 hours in advance.
Serves 8

1 cup dried navy beans, soaked overnight
1 onion, chopped
2 leeks, chopped
2 celery stalks, chopped
3 potatoes, chopped
2 carrots, chopped
¼ cup olive oil
salt and pepper
3 zucchini, chopped
3 tomatoes, skinned and chopped
¼ cup chopped green beans
6 oz noodles, broken into short lengths
¼ cup pesto (optional: p. 175)

Put the drained navy beans into a very large pan with 3½ quarts of cold water. Bring slowly to a boil and simmer for 1 hour.

Add the coarsely chopped onion, leeks, celery, potatoes and carrots with the olive oil and ½ teaspoon salt. Cook for 1 hour longer.

Now add the zucchini and the tomatoes. Cook for 30 minutes or longer until the broth begins to thicken nicely from the starch in the beans and potatoes. Add a further ½ teaspoon salt and some pepper.

Throw in the green beans and the noodles, and cook until both are tender. Taste for seasoning. Serve with *pesto* stirred into the soup at the last moment if you wish.

ZUPPA ALLA PAVESE (LOMBARDY)
Egg soup

This soup, widely liked throughout Italy but originally a specialty of Lombardy, is said to have been invented in 1525 after the battle of Pavia. The exhausted King of France suddenly appeared at a tiny cottage just outside the town. He was in a hurry, as the Spaniards were hot on his heels; and the ingenious peasant woman quickly made something special out of her lunch-time broth by breaking into it pieces of toast and a couple of eggs.

Serves 4

1 quart chicken stock, preferably homemade
4 thick slices of bread, preferably French
¼ cup butter
¼ cup freshly grated Parmesan
4 eggs
pepper

Heat the stock in a wide flameproof casserole. Spread the slices of bread on one side with half the butter and some grated Parmesan, and fry them to a golden brown on both sides in the remaining butter.

Crack the eggs carefully into the stock, taking great pains not to break them. Season each with a few turns of the pepper mill, and cook in a moderate oven (350°F) or under the broiler until the eggs are just cooked.

Slip in the slices of bread, cheese side up (beside the eggs, not on top of them) and serve at once, handing a bowl of grated cheese separately.

Rice and pasta

POLENTA (VENETO)
Cornmeal

Polenta has been the staple food of the northeastern regions of Italy for several centuries, and many rituals have been built up around it. It had to be made daily, stirred with a wooden stick in a copper pan, then poured out to form a great golden disk on the wooden table-top. Alessandro Manzoni, the nineteenth-century Italian novelist, described the circle of polenta shrouded in steam as 'a harvest moon coming out of the mist'.

Serves 4

2 quarts cold water
1¼ teaspoons salt
3¼ cups coarse yellow cornmeal

Bring salted water to a boil and turn down the heat until it is simmering steadily. Take a handful of cornmeal and pour it slowly into the pan in a thin stream, letting it trickle out between your fingers. At the same time keep stirring it continuously with a wooden spoon. The stream of cornmeal should be so thin that you can see the individual grains as they fall. Keep stirring all the time or you may get lumps. If they do form you can crush and dissolve them against the side of the pan with the wooden spoon. Keep the water at a slow steady simmer.

When the mixture thickens keep stirring it over a low heat for 20 minutes. The polenta is done when it pulls away from the sides of the pot.

Wet a large clean board – a chopping board or a wooden platter – and pour on the polenta in a large golden pool. It will spread out and set. Serve it piping hot with melted butter, or let it cool and slice it for frying.

Curtains of macaroni at an old-style pasta factory

The sheer enjoyment of fresh pasta

RISOTTO ALLA MILANESE (LOMBARDY)
Ham and saffron risotto

The rice grown in Lombardy is the large round-grained variety, *arborio*. It can be either white or yellow, but in this recipe it is dyed a beautiful pale gold with saffron, a legacy from medieval times. This is a simple dish but justly famous; its flavor is subtle and superb as well as being very comforting to a tired spirit.

Serves 6

1 quart stock, preferably homemade
¼ cup butter
2 tablespoons oil
2 shallots or 1 onion, finely chopped
¼ cup diced prosciutto or lean smoked ham
1 lb Italian round-grain rice
¼ teaspoon powdered saffron
salt and freshly ground pepper
plenty of freshly grated Parmesan

Bring the stock to a boil in a large saucepan.

Heat half the butter and the oil in a heavy-bottomed pan, and soften the shallots or onion together with the ham (about 10 minutes). When they are half-cooked and transparent add the rice, stirring until it is well-coated and glistening. Add enough of the boiling stock to cover the rice and allow to simmer until it is almost all absorbed. Add more stock, stir well and keep adding small quantities of stock and stirring until the rice is almost cooked (about 15 minutes).

Now add the saffron, dissolved in a little of the remaining stock. Continue to add stock and stir for about 5 minutes more until all the stock is absorbed and the rice is tender but still firm. Add water if you run out of stock.

Remove from the heat and season to taste. Stir in the rest of the butter and about ½ cup grated Parmesan. Serve immediately; the cheese is melted by the heat of the rice and becomes creamy. Serve with more freshly grated cheese in a bowl.

PIZZA RUSTICA (APULIA)
Pizza with tomatoes, anchovies and olives

The history of pizza goes back a long, long way: Neolithic man probably devised it as a way of cooking meat, vegetables, cheese and fish without a cooking pot. In the Middle Ages, when bread was customarily used instead of plates, pizza continued to be popular, requiring neither plates nor tableware. But it was not until the arrival of the tomato in the sixteenth century that the pizza really came into its own.

There is a vast number of different *pizze* – sweet ones, fruit ones, tiny thin *pizzette* made to be eaten as hors d'oeuvre, and these hefty rustic pizzas that enclose the filling completely, handy for a packed lunch and taking out to the fields.

Serves 6

Dough
¼ cake compressed yeast
2 cups strong bread flour
1 teaspoon salt
2 tablespoons olive oil

Filling
1 small onion, chopped
¼ cup olive oil
1 lb tomatoes, skinned,
* seeded and coarsely*
* chopped*
salt and pepper
8 anchovy fillets, coarsely
* chopped*
¾ cup black olives, pitted
* and halved*
1 egg, beaten with
* 1 teaspoon water*

Mix the yeast with ⅔ cup warm water and let it dissolve. Mix in a quarter of the flour and leave it, covered with a cloth, to work for 15 minutes.

Sift the remaining flour onto a board (to be authentic) or into a bowl, and make a well in the center. Pour in the yeast mixture and add the salt and olive oil. Mix and knead to a smooth and supple dough. Cover with a cloth and leave to rise in a fairly warm place for about 1 hour until doubled in size.

Meanwhile, brown the onion in the olive oil in a small saucepan. Add the chopped tomatoes, season with salt and pepper and cook briskly for 20 minutes. Mix in the anchovies and the olives. Allow to cool.

When you are ready to use the dough knead it again; then, on a floured board or table, roll out 2 sheets of dough about ¼ in thick. Oil a large baking sheet and put on one of the sheets of dough. Spread the sauce over it, leaving a border of dough around the edge. Cover with the second sheet of dough and press the edges together. Brush the top with beaten egg and prick it all over with a fork. Now let it rise for a further 20 minutes, covered with a cloth.

Bake in a fairly hot oven (425°F) for 30–40 minutes, until the pizza is well risen and brown. Serve very hot.

Italy

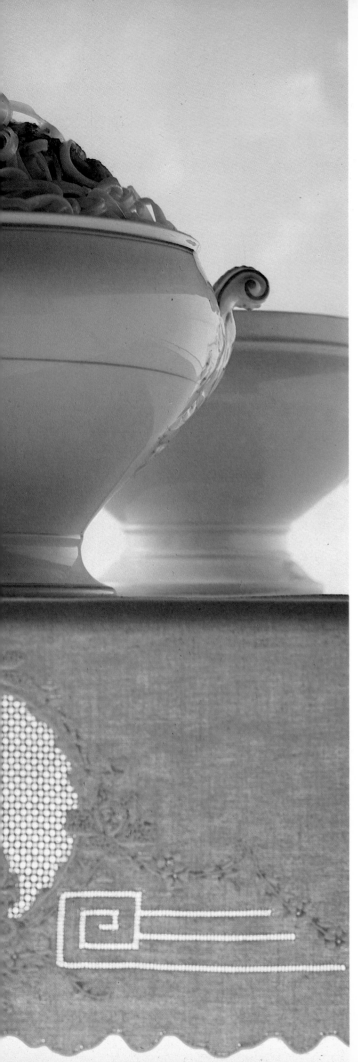

Trenette col pesto:
*delicious noodles with
an aromatic basil sauce*

TRENETTE COL PESTO (LIGURIA)
Noodles with basil sauce

This aromatic sauce, made with basil, pine nuts and garlic, is one of the most distinctive and appetizing sauces for pasta. The basil of Liguria is usually the small-leaved pot variety, but large-leaved basil makes a very delicious *pesto* too.

Serves 4–6

3¼ cups basil leaves
2 tablespoons pine nuts or walnuts
2 cloves of garlic
¼ teaspoon coarse salt
¼ cup grated Parmesan
¼ cup olive oil
¼ cup softened butter
¾ lb trenette (narrow noodles), or ordinary noodles

Put the basil leaves, pine nuts, garlic and salt in a mortar and pound to a fine purée with a pestle. Stir in the grated cheese and then add the olive oil gradually, a few drops at a time, beating it in with a wooden spoon, until you have a green emulsion. Lastly stir in the softened butter. (*Pesto* can also be made in a blender, in which case stir in the cheese by hand at the end.)

Cook the *trenette* or noodles in a very large pan of boiling salted water for 10 minutes. Test frequently and when they are just tender drain and toss quickly with the *pesto*. Serve with freshly grated Parmesan in a separate bowl.

BUCATINI ALLA MARCHIGIANA (THE MARCHES)
Pasta with tomato and vegetable sauce

The tremendous advantage of this simple sauce for pasta is that all its ingredients are available in winter. The wine which local cooks would use might be either the greenish *verdicchio*, or *vino cotto*, a syrup made by simmering grape juice over a gentle heat for several hours until it is thick.

Serves 4

1 small onion, chopped
1 celery stalk, chopped
1 carrot, chopped
2 tablespoons oil or lard
¼ lb cooked ham, cut in little strips
¾ cup white wine
2 tablespoons tomato purée
1 lb ripe tomatoes, skinned and chopped
marjoram
thyme
salt
pepper or chili powder
1 lb bucatini (ribbed elbow macaroni)
1 cup grated Parmesan

Make a *trito* by cooking the onion, celery and carrot together in a medium saucepan in the oil or lard. Add the ham and stir together for a few minutes. Pour in the wine and let it reduce until almost evaporated. Add the tomato purée, tomatoes and herbs. Season and bring to a boil. Turn down the heat and simmer for 30 minutes.

Meanwhile, drop the *bucatini* into a large pan of boiling salted water. Cook for about 12 minutes until just tender. Drain and mix in a heated bowl with 3–4 tablespoons grated Parmesan, then stir in half the sauce.

Serve the remaining sauce and cheese in separate bowls.

Street cooks of Naples, with an admiring audience

SPAGHETTI AL SUGO DI VONGOLE BIANCO (CAMPANIA)
Spaghetti with clams

In the area south of Naples, where the fields and hillsides are positively overburdened with lemon and orange groves, vines, nut groves and curious tall cabbages which seem to grow all year round among the trees, one of the nicest experiences is to sit by the sea and eat spaghetti with tiny clams. These are usually served in their shells; Italians seem to relish eating things that take a long time, and it certainly makes the dish more memorable.

Serves 4

36–40 tiny fresh clams or cockles in their shells, or 1 lb can of clams
1 small onion, finely chopped
3 tablespoons olive oil
2 cloves of garlic
2 tablespoons chopped parsley
¼ teaspoon chopped or flaked dried red chili pepper
1 lb spaghetti
salt and pepper

If you are using fresh clams or cockles wash and scrub them meticulously in 2 or 3 changes of water. Put them in a large pan, cover and shake over a high heat for several minutes until they have opened.

Now remove the shells if you wish, and put the shellfish in a bowl with their juice.

Soften the onion in the olive oil until it is translucent. Add the garlic and let it brown lightly. Now add the parsley, chili pepper and clam liquid (filtered through a cloth if it is gritty) and boil the sauce until it has reduced by half. Finally add the clams and let them just heat through. Keep warm.

Put the spaghetti into a large pan of boiling salted water and let it cook for 12 minutes. As soon as it is cooked but still *al dente*, drain it and put it in a heated bowl.

Taste the sauce for seasoning and stir it into the pasta. Serve immediately without any cheese if you want to be authentic, or with grated Parmesan if you prefer.

LASAGNE AL FORNO BOLOGNESE (EMILIA-ROMAGNA)
Baked lasagne

This well known oven-baked pasta dish contains all the things prized by the residents of Bologna: rich meat sauce, creamy *besciamella*, homemade pasta and mozzarella cheese. It takes a time to prepare but is one of the world's great dishes when carefully done. *Porcini* are dried mushrooms; they are available at most Italian delicatessens.

Serves 6–8

Meat sauce
1 onion
1 carrot
1 celery stalk
1–2 cloves of garlic
4–5 tablespoons olive oil
¼ lb ground beef
¼ lb ground pork
1 cup red wine
2 tablespoons tomato purée
1¾ cups stock or water
salt and pepper
3 sprigs of parsley, finely chopped
grated nutmeg
3 tablespoons dried porcini, soaked in a little warm water

Besciamella sauce
¼ cup butter
¼ cup flour
1 quart boiling milk
salt and pepper
grated nutmeg

Pasta (p. 32)

Cheese layer
¼ lb mozzarella cheese, coarsely grated and mixed with ¼ cup grated Parmesan

First make the meat sauce. Chop the fresh vegetables and garlic finely and soften them in the olive oil in a skillet. When they are translucent turn up the heat and add the meat. Fry it briskly, breaking up the lumps from time to time until it starts to stick to the pan in a dark brown crust. Now add the wine and let it boil fiercely until it has all but evaporated. Stir in the tomato purée, stock, seasoning, parsley, nutmeg and *porcini* with their soaking liquid. Stir and simmer gently for 1 hour, adding more stock or water if the sauce becomes too dry.

Meanwhile make the *besciamella* sauce. Melt the butter in a medium heavy pan and stir in the flour. When it starts to seethe and leave the sides of the pan clean, remove it from the heat and pour on all the boiling milk. Stir, return to the heat, simmer for 10 minutes. Season well with salt, pepper and nutmeg and allow to cool.

While the sauces are cooking, prepare the pasta. Divide the dough into 3. Roll it out into transparently thin sheets and cut these into rectangles about 8 by 6 in, preferably using a fluted pasta cutter.

Bring a very large pan of salted water to a boil. Have ready a large bowl of cold water with a teaspoon of oil in it (to prevent the *lasagne* sticking together), and 3 or 4 clean dry dish towels spread out on a table.

Drop a few sheets of the pasta into the boiling water. If it is transparently thin it can be taken out as soon as it rises to the surface; if rather thicker, boil for 2 minutes. Transfer to the bowl of cold water, then drain and lay flat on a cloth. Continue until all the pasta is used.

When you are ready to assemble the dish, butter a large ovenproof baking dish. Put in a tablespoon of meat sauce, then a layer of sheets of pasta, which should come up the sides of the dish and hang over the edge by about 2 in. After another thin layer of meat sauce add a thin layer of *besciamella* sauce, then a sprinkling of cheeses, and more pasta – not over-hanging the edge this time. Continue layer by layer until everything is used up. Place 2 sheets of *lasagne* on the top and bring the sides over to enclose the stuffing. Dot with butter and a last sprinkling of cheese.

Bake at 375°F for 30–35 minutes. Allow to sit in a warm place for 15 minutes before serving. Slice the *lasagne* right through with a knife and serve in square wedges like a cake.

Fish

SARDINAS AL FORNO (APULIA)
Baked sardines

Fish of all kinds form an important part of the diet in the southeastern region of Apulia. There are bass, red mullet and grey mullet, swordfish, octopus, squid, shrimp and prawns, mussels and cultivated oysters. The fish are cooked simply with olive oil and served with lemon or olives; and the shellfish are fried or baked, or served in a hot 'stew' with chili peppers. In this recipe sardines are baked in the oven and eaten very hot as an hors d'oeuvre.

Serves 4

16 small sardines
  (or smelts)
3 slices white bread,
  crusts removed
3 cloves of garlic, chopped
a handful of parsley,
  chopped
juice of ⅓ lemon
salt and pepper
olive oil

Clean and scale the sardines and cut off their heads. Slit them open along the belly and lift out the backbone as you would if you were filleting a herring.

Grate the bread on the coarse side of the grater to make rough crumbs. Mix the garlic and parsley with the crumbs. Add a light sprinkling of lemon juice, salt and pepper and just enough olive oil to bind the mixture.

Brush the bottom of a medium-sized baking dish with olive oil. Put in a third of the sardines, cover with a third of the crumbs, and repeat the layers twice more.

Sprinkle the top with olive oil and bake in a moderately hot oven (375°F) for about 20 minutes until the sardines are cooked and the top is golden brown.

Early morning: gondolas wait near the Piazza San Marco, Venice

SCAMPI ALLA GRIGLIA (VENETO)
Broiled scampi

The local Venetian prawns and shrimp look most appetizing heaped up on the market stalls. For this dish use scampi or jumbo shrimp. Ideally they should be grilled over charcoal, when a delicious smell rises from them.

Serves 4–6

2 lb raw scampi in their
  shells
olive oil
salt
freshly ground pepper
juice of 1 lemon
chopped parsley

Preheat the broiler. 'Butterfly' the scampi by slitting them lengthwise down their undersides and opening them out, still in their shells, leaving the two halves joined down the middle of the back. Brush them with olive oil, season with salt and pepper, skewer them in pairs and cook for 3–4 minutes on each side.

Sprinkle with lemon juice and parsley and eat very hot, shelling them and savoring the juices from the shells.

TROTE MARINATE (VALLE D'AOSTA)
Trout marinated in vermouth

The ice cold Alpine streams of Valle d'Aosta abound with trout famous for their fine, delicate flesh. They are traditionally eaten freshly cooked over a wood fire; and any left over from the day's catch are bathed in a rich marinade, ready for another day.

Prepare this dish at least 3 days in advance.
Serves 6

6 small trout, cleaned
flour
oil for frying

Marinade
⅓ cup oil
2 onions, sliced
2 cloves of garlic, sliced
3 tablespoons white wine
  vinegar
⅓ cup dry vermouth
2 strips of lemon rind
a few sage leaves
a sprig of rosemary
salt
black peppercorns

Wash the trout, dry them with paper towels and coat them lightly with flour. Fry in hot oil until they are golden and just cooked through, about 5 minutes on each side. Arrange them side by side in an earthenware dish.

To prepare the marinade heat the oil in a small pan and sauté the onion and garlic for a few minutes until tender but not brown. Add all the other marinade ingredients, bring the mixture to a boil, and pour it, hot, over the trout. Allow to cool and leave the fish in the marinade for at least 3 days, turning them from time to time.

As a variation, the marinade can be made with strips of orange rind instead of lemon, and if you want a sweet-sharp flavor, 1–2 tablespoons of raisins can be added.

Shimmering fish in a Venetian market

Liver, onions and kidneys the Venetian way: fried lightly to bring out their delicate flavor and subtle aroma

M*eat*

ROGNONE DI VITELLO TRIFOLATO ALLA ROMANA (LAZIO)
Sautéed kidneys

In Italy variety meats are treated with great respect and seen as an ideal way of adding to the variety of meat dishes. Kidneys are considered one of the greatest delicacies, particularly when fried as in this recipe, but they must be cooked briskly, to seal the outsides so that the juices do not run out.

Serves 4

2 calf kidneys, each weighing about ¼ lb
a little flour
¼ cup butter
salt and freshly ground pepper
1 tablespoon chopped parsley
juice of ½ lemon

Skin the kidneys and remove the cores. Slice them on the bias into small scallops, and coat them lightly in the flour.

Melt the butter in a heavy skillet, throw in the pieces of kidney and season them with salt and pepper. When they have browned very lightly add a sprinkling of lemon juice and the chopped parsley. Turn them out onto a hot dish and serve with pieces of fried bread. Follow with a green salad.

FEGATO ALLA VENEZIANA (VENETO)
Liver and onions the Venetian way

Northern Italy produces marvelous milky veal; the liver for this Venetian dish should come from a very young animal and be cut (preferably by the butcher) into the thinnest possible slices. The thinner the liver and the more quickly it cooks, the better the flavor: in restaurants it is on and off the stove in a flash. In Venice the calf liver is pale and finely textured and almost melts in your mouth.

Serves 4

5–6 tablespoons olive oil
3 onions, thinly sliced
salt and white pepper
1 lb calf liver, thinly sliced and cut into small strips 1 by 1¼ in
1 lemon, quartered

Heat the oil in a large skillet and stir in the onions. Season with a little salt and a pinch of white pepper. Cover the pan and cook over a very low heat for 30 minutes, turning from time to time until the onions are limp and nicely browned. Remove them with a slotted spoon and keep hot.

Turn up the heat and put in the slices of liver 1 at a time so that they do not overlap. Fry them very quickly for about 1 minute on each side. As soon as the slices change color, return the onions to the pan. Add a pinch of salt and pepper and cook for 1 minute, stirring to combine the liver, onions and seasoning.

Serve immediately with quarters of lemon and spinach, or simply with a green leafy salad.

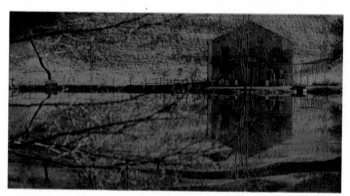

Spring comes to the south and colors Calabria green

FEGATELLI DI MAIALE ALLA FIORENTINA (TUSCANY)
Broiled liver parcels

Fegatelli are little pieces of liver grilled on skewers with bay leaves. This classic Tuscan dish is quite wonderful cooked over charcoal. The caul – which may be difficult to obtain – is used for basting the liver as it cooks.

Serves 4

a large piece of caul fat weighing about 1 lb
4 tablespoons olive oil
1–2 teaspoons fennel seeds
1½ lb beef liver
bay leaves
salt and freshly ground pepper

Soak the caul in warm water for 2–3 minutes in order to soften it. Then stretch it out on a cloth on the kitchen table and cut it with scissors into pieces about 5 by 7 in.

Put the oil on a plate and sprinkle it with the fennel seeds. Cut the liver into pieces the size of a large walnut, roll them in the fennel seeds and oil, add ½ a bay leaf, and wrap each one in a piece of caul, enclosing it completely. Season with salt and pepper.

Skewer each little parcel with a wooden toothpick. Cook under the broiler, or over glowing charcoal, turning the skewers after 2–3 minutes. They do not need more than 5 minutes' cooking altogether.

COSTOLETTE ALLA VALDOSTANA (VALLE D'AOSTA)
Veal chops with cheese

Valle d'Aosta is famous for its beautiful cheese, Fontina, which is made in the mountains in large cartwheel shapes. It is indisputably one of the world's great cheeses. Traditionally made from ewes' milk, though nowadays cows' milk is more likely to be used, it is soft and buttery and has a sweetish, nutty flavor. It also melts easily, so it is excellent for cooking. Locally it is used to make *fonduta*, an Italian version of fondue. This is eaten with large hunks of bread and liberally poured glasses of local red wine, either Barolo or Barbera. Sometimes it is sprinkled with finely slivered white Piedmontese truffles – a dish not to be missed if you travel through this region. If you cannot obtain Fontina the next best thing is Gruyère; but any melting cheese, Edam, or Emmenthal, Gouda or Jarlsberg can be used instead.

Serves 4

flour
salt and pepper
4 veal chops, boned and beaten flat
1 egg
fine dried breadcrumbs, preferably homemade
⅓ cup butter
4 small slices of smoked ham, preferably prosciutto
¼ lb Fontina cheese

Mix the flour with salt and pepper and use to coat the chops. Dip them in the beaten egg using a pastry brush, and sprinkle with breadcrumbs, taking care to cover all the surfaces.

Melt the butter in a large skillet, and when it ceases to foam (it stops singing and becomes silent at this point) slip in the chops and cook fairly gently for about 5 minutes on each side until they are an even golden brown. Place them in an earthenware dish. Cover each chop first with a slice of ham, the edge snipped with scissors to prevent it curling up, then a slice of cheese. Cook under the broiler until the cheese melts and begins to bubble, but not brown. Serve immediately.

MAIALE UBRIACO (TUSCANY)
Drunken pork

Tuscan cooks have many good ways of cooking pork; this quickly prepared dish, that blends the flavor of pork with fennel seeds and red wine, is one of the best, especially with fennel salad or braised fennel.

Serves 4

4 pork chops
3 tablespoons olive oil
salt and pepper
¼ lemon
3 cloves of garlic, finely chopped
a few fennel seeds
a few sprigs of parsley, finely chopped
¾ cup red wine (Chianti)

Beat the chops gently with the side of a meat cleaver to flatten them a little. Heat the oil in a large skillet and brown the chops over a brisk heat for about 1 minute on each side. Season them with salt and pepper, lower the heat and cook for a further 8–10 minutes, turning them from time to time.

Transfer the chops to a hot serving dish and squeeze some lemon juice over them. Throw the garlic, fennel seeds and parsley into the skillet, allow them to brown and then add the red wine, letting it bubble up. Turn up the heat and reduce the wine to about half, scraping up the juices from the bottom of the pan. Pour the sauce over the chops and serve immediately.

CODA DI BUE ALLA VACCINARA (UMBRIA)
Oxtail in red wine

Umbria, although not well known to foreign visitors, has a very great deal to disclose. The home of several of Italy's finest Renaissance painters, it provides excellent food for the stomach as well as for the mind and is famous in a quiet way for its black truffles, suckling pigs and fine cattle. This dish is the good familiar oxtail with a spicy sauce. It tastes just as delicious when reheated.

Prepare this dish 8 hours in advance.
Serves 4

4 lb oxtail, cut in pieces
3 tablespoons coarse salt
1 carrot, chopped
1 leek, chopped
1 celery stalk, chopped
a sprig of thyme
1 bay leaf
2 tablespoons olive oil
¼ lb bacon, 1 small onion, and a few leaves of marjoram, all chopped together
1 cup red wine
1 lb tomatoes, skinned
fine salt
freshly ground pepper
a generous pinch of grated nutmeg
3 celery hearts
a generous pinch of ground cinnamon
1 tablespoon pine nuts
1 tablespoon raisins, soaked in water for 10 minutes

Soak the oxtail in a large bowl of cold water for 4 hours. Put the pieces in a very large saucepan or casserole, cover with fresh cold water and bring to a boil. Simmer for 10 minutes, then drain and dry on paper towels.

Wash and dry the casserole, return the oxtail, and add 3½ quarts of cold water and the coarse salt. Bring to a boil, skim, add the carrot, leek, celery (but not the celery hearts) and herbs, and allow to simmer gently for 3 hours. Drain the oxtail thoroughly, reserving the stock.

Heat the olive oil in a separate pan and brown the chopped bacon, onion and marjoram. Add the pieces of oxtail and stir until they are coated with oil; then add the wine and let it evaporate to half. Add the tomatoes, season with salt, pepper and a pinch of nutmeg, and allow to cook for a further hour until the meat comes away from the bones. If the sauce becomes dry, add some of the stock.

Meanwhile cook the celery hearts in the remaining oxtail stock for 15 minutes. Drain in a colander, and 10 minutes before serving add the hearts and the cinnamon to the oxtail.

Remove the pan from the heat and add the pine nuts and raisins. Let them mingle with the sauce for a further few minutes, and then transfer to a heated serving dish.

A Calabrian shepherd with his flock

The pig is an enduring feature of country life

BISTECCA A LA FIORENTINA (TUSCANY)
Charcoal-grilled steak

Like all Tuscan recipes, this one for charcoal-grilling steaks is simple and makes the most of good ingredients.

The cattle breeders of Chiana, near Florence, are world-famous for their beef; but as their meat is scarce even in Italy any good T-bone steaks may be used.

Serves 4

4 T-bone steaks
olive oil
coarse salt
the juice of 1 lemon
lemon wedges

Make the fire well ahead so that it is really glowing, and heat the metal rack.

Rub the steaks lightly with oil. Place them on the rack and cook for 3 minutes. Turn them over carefully without piercing the meat, and while the undersides are cooking sprinkle the tops with coarse salt. After 3 minutes turn the steaks again – some of the salt will fall off but enough will remain. After another 2 minutes the steaks will be cooked – they should be rare.

Sprinkle with a little lemon juice and serve immediately. Have a plate of lemon wedges on the table, as well as a simple green salad, dressed with plenty of oil and very little wine vinegar.

BOLLITO MISTO (PIEDMONT)
Mixed boiled meats

Bollito misto is a splendid dish, despite its rather boring name. It is a mouth-watering mixture of creamy pink-scarlet sausage, pearly poached chicken, velvet-textured pale-brown beef and succulent tongue, served all together just sliced on a huge platter and accompanied by two piquant sauces – a marvelous, if somewhat extravagant, dish for a winter lunch party. You may need to order the beef tongue a day or two in advance.

Serves 10

3–4 carrots
2 onions
1 green pepper
2 celery stalks
1 beef tongue, about
  2 lb, preferably fresh
1½ tablespoons salt
1 long piece of lean
  top round or toprib
  of beef, about 2½ lb
1 chicken, 3–3½ lb
1 boiling sausage
  (cotechino or zampone)

Prepare the vegetables and put them in a casserole large enough to hold all the meat at once. (Otherwise you will have to boil the sausage separately.) Fill the pan with enough water to cover all the meat eventually and bring to a boil. Add the tongue, return to a boil, skim and add the salt.

Simmer gently for 1 hour, then add the beef, skim again and continue simmering for a further hour. Lastly add the chicken and the sausage and skim thoroughly. Simmer very gently for another hour. Remove the tongue and skin it, leaving the rest of the meat in the pot.

Slice all the meats just before serving – they can be kept in the hot liquid away from the heat for at least 30 minutes, until you are ready to carve.

Lay overlapping slices of pink sausage down the middle of the dish and flank it with the sliced beef on one side and the tongue on the other. Pile the pieces of chicken – skinned if you prefer – at each end of the dish and serve immediately with the following sauces.

SALSA ROSSA
Piquant tomato sauce

2–3 onions, sliced
¼ cup oil
2 red peppers, seeded and
  cut into strips
¼ fresh green chili pepper,
  or ¼ teaspoon chili
  powder
1 lb ripe red tomatoes
a pinch of salt

Soften the onions in the oil. When they are transparent add the peppers. Let them cook gently until tender, then add the chili, tomatoes and salt.

Cook for a further 20 minutes until well reduced, and serve hot.

SALSA VERDE
Green sauce

1 hard-cooked egg
3 anchovies
2 handfuls of parsley
1 tablespoon capers
1 clove of garlic
salt and pepper
a good squeeze of lemon
  juice, or ¼ teaspoon red
  wine vinegar
¼ cup olive oil

Chop the egg yolk, the anchovies and parsley and pound to a paste or blend briefly in a blender. Add the capers, garlic and seasoning and pound or blend briefly again. Add the lemon juice or vinegar, and then add the oil a little at a time, blending it in with a wooden spoon. The white of the hard-cooked egg should be chopped and stirred into the sauce just before serving.

Poultry and game

PALOMBACCI ALLA PERUGINA (UMBRIA)
Pigeon with olives

Between March and October, wild pigeons or *palombacci* are in season in Umbria, and they are considered a particular delicacy. They are roasted on a spit and served with *la ghiotta*, a sauce made with the drippings from the spit, olives, lemon rind, sage, anchovy, vinegar, wine, oil and salt. This recipe is a variation.

Serves 4

3 tablespoons olive oil
4 pigeons
1¼ cups red wine
10 black olives, pitted
4 fresh sage leaves
a squeeze of lemon juice
12 juniper berries, crushed
salt and freshly ground pepper

Preheat the oven to 325°F. Heat the olive oil in a large casserole and brown the pigeons all over, turning them frequently. Now add the rest of the ingredients and cook, covered, in the oven for 1 hour until the pigeons are tender. Remove, keep warm and reduce sauce; pour over pigeons.

PETTI DI POLLO ALLA VALDOSTANA (VALLE D'AOSTA)
Chicken breasts with cheese

This rich dish should be flavored with the incomparable white truffles of Albi, but alas, these are not found outside Italy, so mushrooms may have to be substituted.

Serves 4

¼ cup butter
¼ cup olive oil
4 large half chicken breasts, lightly flattened
flour
salt and pepper
¼ lb tiny button mushrooms, thinly sliced
¼ lb mozzarella cheese, thinly sliced
¼ cup white wine
¼ cup chicken stock
1 tablespoon brandy
pat of butter

Heat the butter and oil. Coat the chicken breasts with flour and fry them in the butter for about 3–4 minutes on each side. Remove and place them in a shallow flameproof dish. Season with salt and pepper.

In the same butter cook the mushrooms very gently until they are barely tender. Put them on top of the chicken breasts, then cover with the slices of cheese.

Pour the white wine, stock and brandy into the skillet and scrape up the chicken and mushroom juices. Simmer for 10 minutes until the liquid becomes slightly syrupy. Season and stir in a small piece of butter.

Put the chicken breasts under the broiler just long enough to melt the cheese, and pour the sauce into the dish. Serve very hot.

LEPRE ALLA TRENTINO (TRENTINO)
Hare in pine nut sauce

Game with polenta is a popular winter dish in northern Italy when the snow is thick. Since Italian game is not always very tasty it tends to be cooked with all sorts of complicated ingredients to improve the flavor.

Marinate the hare 4–5 hours in advance.
Serves 6

1 hare, cut in 6 pieces
¼ cup butter
¼ lb bacon, cut in small cubes
a pinch of ground cloves
⅔ cup stock
salt and freshly ground pepper
2 teaspoons flour
grated rind of ¼ lemon
a large pinch of ground cinnamon mixed with
¼ teaspoon sugar
pat of butter
the hare's liver, chopped
1 tablespoon crushed seeded grapes
1 tablespoon pine nuts

Marinade
2¼ cups red wine
1 onion, chopped
2 sprigs of parsley
1 bay leaf

Place the pieces of hare in an earthenware dish, combine all the ingredients for the marinade and pour this over the hare. Allow to stand for 4–5 hours, turning the hare from time to time.

Remove the hare and wipe it dry. Strain and reserve the marinade.

Melt the butter in a casserole and fry the bacon to a light golden brown. Add the pieces of hare and let them brown on all sides.

Combine the strained marinade with the cloves, stock, salt and pepper. Sprinkle the meat with flour and pour in the marinade. Bring it to a boil, stirring constantly until it has absorbed the flour. Cover the casserole and allow to simmer on a gentle heat for 45 minutes, or until the pieces of hare are tender.

Remove the hare and keep it hot. Add the lemon rind and the cinnamon mixed with sugar to the stock, together with a pat of butter, and allow the sauce to reduce for 30 minutes more. Check the seasoning.

Ten minutes before serving add the liver, grapes and pine nuts, together with the hare. Cook gently for 10 minutes, then serve at once with polenta (page 173), which should be moist and very hot.

Moorish-style houses punctuate the patchwork fields of Taranto

Vegetables

ACCIUGHE CON PEPERONI (CALABRIA)
Salad of anchovies with red or yellow peppers

In Calabria this salad is often served as an appetizer on its own or with a shellfish salad or a few stuffed squid. It might then be followed by kid or sausages cooked on a spit.

Serves 4

3 red or yellow peppers
1 can of anchovy fillets
4 hard-cooked eggs
1 tablespoon capers
salt and pepper
olive oil

Broil the peppers under a fierce heat until the skins are blackened and puffed. Remove the papery outside skin either under the cold tap or, if you can stand burning your fingers, dry. Remove the cores and cut the peppers into halves.

Put a layer of peppers in a shallow dish, cover it with anchovy fillets, halved hard-cooked eggs and capers. Sprinkle with a very little salt and pepper, and moisten the whole dish with good olive oil.

INSALATA DI POMODORI (CAMPANIA)
Tomato salad with basil and oregano

The tomatoes of southern Italy are so well flavored that they hardly need any added seasoning. This salad is made by simply sprinkling an olive oil dressing on slightly unripe sliced tomatoes.

Serves 4

2 lb large tomatoes,
  firm and very slightly
  green
1 clove of garlic
¼ cup olive oil
salt and pepper
several leaves of basil
a pinch of oregano

Put the tomatoes either under running water or in the refrigerator to harden and refresh them. Dry them, cut them in half and take out the hard part of the stalk.

Cut the tomatoes into slices and mound them in a salad bowl. Crush and pound a clove of garlic and stir this into the oil with a little salt and pepper, the basil and oregano, and pour this dressing over the tomatoes. Since the tomatoes are astringent, fresh and cold, no vinegar or lemon is required.

Anchovies with red and yellow peppers: a piquant salad to whet the appetite

GNOCHETTI ALLA PIEMONTESE (PIEDMONT)
Baked potato dumplings

This recipe combines comforting potato *gnocchi* with the exquisite flavor of Fontina cheese. Allow plenty of time to prepare the dumplings – perhaps an hour. They can be prepared several hours in advance.

Serves 4

2 lb potatoes
2 cups flour, sifted
salt
¼ lb Fontina (or
  Emmenthal) cheese
¼ cup butter

Peel the potatoes and boil them in plenty of boiling salted water. When they are cooked, even somewhat over-cooked, drain them and mash them thoroughly with a potato masher or ricer, whipping them to keep them light and dry.

Now add the flour and a pinch of salt, and make a dough by working the mixture with your hands. Break off small pieces of this dough and roll it up into little sausage shapes about 1 in by ½ in.

Press each shape against the tines of a fork with your forefinger so that the back is ridged and the front has a shallow indentation, like a little shell. Place them well apart on a floured board so they don't stick together. Cover with a cloth.

When you are going to eat, bring a large pan of salted water to a boil and poach the *gnocchi*, a few at a time, for about 2 minutes.

Heat the oven to 350°F. Put a layer of cooked *gnocchi* in a gratin dish, cover with thin slices of cheese and sprinkle with melted butter. Repeat the layers until all the ingredients are used up, ending with a layer of cheese. Bake until melted and bubbling, about 5 minutes, and serve immediately.

ZUCCHINI E PEPERONI AL FORNO (SARDINIA)
Zucchini baked with peppers

Anchovies are frequently used as a seasoning in southern Italy. In this vegetable dish from Sardinia, they are combined, as they often are, with mozzarella, a cheese originally made with buffalo milk, that melts beautifully to a rich cream when it is baked in the oven.

Serves 4

4 zucchini
salt and pepper
olive oil
2 cloves of garlic, chopped
4 yellow or red peppers
1 lb ripe tomatoes,
  skinned and chopped
4 sprigs of fresh basil
¼ lb mozzarella cheese
8 anchovies

Trim the zucchini and blanch until crisp tender in boiling salted water. Drain, and slice in half lengthwise. Fry the slices gently in olive oil, together with a clove of garlic. Broil the peppers until the skins are puffed and blackened. Peel off the skin, remove the core and seeds, and cut into strips.

Make a simple sauce by cooking the tomatoes, remaining garlic and basil in the oil for 20 minutes. If it is very watery drain off some of the liquid through a strainer. Season with salt and pepper.

In an oiled baking dish put a layer of zucchini, then strips of pepper. Cover this with a layer of tomato sauce and finish with a layer of sliced mozzarella. Sprinkle the top with olive oil and chopped anchovies, and finally bake in a moderate oven (350°F) for 20–25 minutes until the whole dish is heated through and the cheese is melted.

ZUPPA DI FINOCCHIETTI SELVATICI (SARDINIA)
Fennel baked with cheese

Although you may have to substitute hard cows' milk cheese for *pecorino sardo* – a salty sheep's cheese – and cultivated fennel bulbs for wild fennel roots, this savory lunch-time dish is still well worth making.

Serves 4

1¼ lb fennel
salt
6 slices of bread, cut in
   strips
olive oil
¼ lb pecorino sardo, or any
   hard cheese, cut in
   thin slices
butter

Preheat the oven to 425°F. Wash the fennel and boil it in plenty of lightly salted water until crisp tender. Drain thoroughly. Fry the bread in olive oil until golden brown.

Line the bottom of a casserole with the fried bread strips. Lay the fennel on top and cover with the slices of cheese. Dot the top with small pats of butter and bake in the oven for 10 minutes or until the top is lightly browned.

Fennel, a true native of Italy, gives a distinctive flavor and texture to many dishes

MELANZANE PARMIGIANA (EMILIA ROMAGNA)
Baked eggplant

Parmesan cheese is the pride of Emilia Romagna; but this dish in fact gets its name from Parma, where it originated, and not from the cheese. It is the luxurious sort of dish that the inhabitants of Emilia Romagna like best: rich, melting eggplant and mozzarella cheese baked in a fresh tomato sauce.

Serves 4

4 eggplants
salt
⅔ cup olive oil
¼ lb mozzarella cheese,
   thinly sliced
¼ cup grated Parmesan

Tomato sauce
1 lb ripe tomatoes,
   skinned and chopped
1 tablespoon olive oil
a few leaves of basil or
   marjoram
1 teaspoon tomato purée
salt and freshly ground
   pepper

Wash and slice the eggplants, sprinkle them with salt and leave them to drain in a colander for 30 minutes. They will exude their bitter juices and become softer.

Meanwhile put the tomatoes in a saucepan with the oil, basil, tomato purée, salt and pepper. Simmer for 15 minutes, mashing with a wooden spoon, then remove from the heat.

Rinse the eggplant slices in cold running water and dry with paper towels. Heat about 3 tablespoons of olive oil in a skillet and fry the eggplant slices a few at a time until they are golden on both sides. Add more oil as it is needed – they absorb a large quantity. Drain on paper towel.

Now assemble the dish. Butter a baking dish. Spread a tablespoon of tomato sauce over the bottom. Put a layer of eggplant on top, cover with a layer of mozzarella and sprinkle with Parmesan. Now add another layer of tomato sauce. Continue with layers of eggplant, cheese and tomato until everything is used, ending with a layer of cheese.

Bake for 25 minutes at 375°F. Allow to rest for 10 minutes before serving.

This dish can also be eaten cold.

CAVOLFIORE A VASTEDDA (SICILY)
Sicilian cauliflower

Sicilian cauliflowers are sometimes white, sometimes deep purple, and are cooked and served with strong cheese or anchovies which offset their bland flavor. In this recipe the cauliflower is dipped in a *pastella* or fritter batter and deep fried, to give it a coating which is astonishingly crisp and light.

Serves 4

1 large head cauliflower,
   divided into flowerets
salt and pepper
1¼ cups flour
2 anchovy fillets, finely
   chopped
2 eggs
oil for deep frying

Drop the cauliflower flowerets into boiling salted water and cook for 10 minutes until just tender but still firm. Drain them well.

To make the fritter batter put 1¼ cups of water in a bowl and gradually add the flour, sifting it in and beating the mixture constantly with a fork until all the flour has been added. The resulting white cream is your *pastella*, or batter. Now add the finely chopped anchovies.

Beat the eggs in a separate bowl and season with salt and pepper. Heat the oil in a deep fat fryer. Dip the pieces of cauliflower first into the *pastella* and then into the beaten egg, and fry. This dish is delicious hot and even better cold.

A simple *pastella* without the anchovies or the subsequent egg dip can be used to dip and then deep fry many different prepared vegetables.

*The beauty of eggplants:
with melting mozzarella and
rich tomato sauce they blend
to form a luxurious dish*

The domed hills of Tuscany have inspired many artists

Desserts

FICHI IN SCIROPPO (CALABRIA)
Fresh figs in rum syrup

The figs of southern Italy are small and full of intense flavor. They ripen in the baking sun without much moisture and are concentrated to a delicious sweetness.

Prepare 1 week in advance.
Serves 8

1¾ cups sugar	Dissolve the sugar in ⅓ cup rum in a large saucepan.
1 cup rum at least	Add the lemon juice. Put in the figs and simmer for
a squeeze of lemon juice	1½ hours. Transfer the figs to a glass jar and pour
2 lb green figs	on the syrup with enough additional rum to cover
	the figs completely. Keep for a week before eating.

CASSATA ALLA SICILIANA (SICILY)
Ice cream mold

Sicily is famous for its extremely sweet and highly colored confectionery and crystalized fruits, and its ice cream is among the best in the world. This *cassata* combines fruits and ice cream together, and is one of the prettiest of all desserts.

Prepare several hours in advance.
Serves 8

1 pint vanilla ice cream	With a metal spoon dipped in hot water line the
¾ pint chocolate ice cream	inside of a 1½ quart freezerproof mold with a layer of the vanilla ice cream. Freeze solid.
⅔ cup heavy cream	Now cover with a layer of chocolate ice cream,
¼ cup confectioners' sugar	leaving a well in the center for the cream, and then freeze again.
¼ lb mixed crystalized fruits, cut in small pieces	Meanwhile, make the light foamy filling. Whip the cream to a soft snow and stir in the confectioners' sugar and crystalized fruit. Beat the egg white until
1 egg white	fairly stiff and fold it thoroughly into the cream.

Pile the mixture into the ice cream mold, tapping the mold to avoid air bubbles. Smooth the top, cover with foil and freeze again for several hours until the whole *cassata* is firm.

When ready to serve, dip the mold quickly in hot water and turn the *cassata* out onto a dish. Serve by cutting in wedges.

GRANITA DI ARANCIA
Orange sherbet

A *granita* is a sherbet which is frozen to a granulated texture, like crushed ice, but not so hard. It is a delicious, very cold dessert and perfectly refreshing on a hot day.

Prepare at least 3 hours in advance.
Serves 4

3 tablespoons sugar	Dissolve the sugar in the orange and lemon juice
1 pint freshly squeezed orange juice (about 10 oranges)	and put in a container which will fit into the freezer. Let it start to set into crystals, then break it up by raking it with a fork. Put it back to set and
juice of 1 lemon	repeat the breaking up process every 30 minutes for 3 hours. The *granita* is now ready, but it can be kept for 1–2 days in the freezer.

By substituting 1¼ cups strong black coffee for the orange and lemon juice you can make *granita di caffè*, which is served with whipped cream.

ZABAIONE (SICILY)

This delicious foam, the most famous of all Italian desserts, and so rich that it is best accompanied by fresh fruit, was once prescribed by Italian doctors as a pick-me-up. It certainly does produce a warm benevolent feeling in those who eat it.

For each person	In the top of a double boiler, away from the
1 egg yolk	heat, beat together the egg yolks and sugar. When
1 tablespoon sugar	they start to turn thick and creamy place the pan
2 tablespoons Marsala	over hot water, just below simmering point, and add the Marsala, beating continuously until the mixture becomes a lovely creamy amber foam. When it is thick and hot, spoon it into glasses and serve at once.

Cassata alla siciliana: *ice cream and rainbow-colored fruits combine in this perfect finale to an Italian meal*

**Food – like a waltz in the skillet,
peppered with charm
and sprinkled with high spirits.**

Austrian saying (anon)

*Czechoslovakia – the
apple harvest*

*A patchwork of terraced
orchards and vineyards in
Krems, Austria*

The cooking of the former Austro-Hungarian Empire is as interwoven as the pattern of a wickerwork basket. It mingles the native cooking of many countries: Austria, Hungary, Bohemia, Slovakia, Moravia, parts of Yugoslavia and Poland, and a corner of Italy.

The region which fell within the boundaries of the Austro-Hungarian Empire of the nineteenth century comprised, as well as what we now know as Austria, Trentino-Alto Adige and Istria in the west; in the north lay Bohemia, Moravia, Slovakia and Polish Galicia; to the east stretched the kingdom of Hungary, embracing Transylvania, and to the south were Dalmatia, Croatia, Slovenia and the endless cornfields of the Bacska and the Banat. It was a region of mountains and forests, rivers and fertile valleys dominated by the mighty Danube; vast plains yielded a harvest so rich that it earned the name 'the bread basket of Europe'.

For six hundred years the Habsburg monarchs reigned over these lands; but it was not until 1867, with the establishment of the Dual Monarchy, that the name Austria-Hungary was born. Dual power existed in name only for the Empire was jealously governed from Vienna, the capital, which had already gained a reputation for gaiety, good food and wine; and for that imponderable thing called *Gemütlichkeit*, which is almost untranslatable, but means something close to a special kind of sentimentality. This the Austrians have harnessed and even injected into their cuisine. They have cheerfully adopted dishes from their early invaders and their neighbors alike, added a little touch of *Gemütlichkeit*, made them their own and styled them Austrian.

To consider the many influences which helped to evolve the cuisine of the Austro-Hungarian Empire perhaps one should start with Hungary. This enchanting country with plains that appear to stretch like a mirage into infinity has created cooking that is a mixture of flavors and techniques. Some were inherited from invaders: Attila the Hun chose to settle in northeast Hungary even when he had the whole of Europe to choose from, and later so did the Turks. It was the latter who introduced peppers into Hungary. At first these were known as Turkish peppers and then paprika peppers. In the mid-nineteenth century the Palffy family of Szeged developed a technique for producing ground paprika pepper, a new spice which was red and sweet, but not hot. Today most Hungarians are unaware that paprika pepper is of such recent origin but many of their savory dishes have a characteristic flavor and color from this versatile seasoning.

It could be argued that in the realm of food the Hungarians were more dominant than the Austrians; many famous dishes claimed today as Austrian, and in particular Viennese, are in fact of Hungarian origin. There's the famous paprika-flavored goulash; and *Dobòs torta*, a chocolate cake named after the Hungarian chef who invented it; the world-famous strudel is of Hungarian descent.

The Hungarians claim the secret of their cooking is the

A common sight in Hungary or Czechoslovakia – the goose girl with her flock

freshness of their ingredients, their partiality for the good things of the table and their natural gift for cooking. They boast it is easier to find a white raven in Hungary than a bad cook.

Throughout the early centuries of Hungarian history cooking was robust country fare; the great Magyar families of Transylvania rejected outside influences in their kitchen, maintaining the tradition of the genuine ancient dishes of Hungary. Typical is an immense mixed broil piled on a large wooden platter which is still served in restaurants today.

Under the rule of King Matthias, Hungarian cooking increased in refinement. In 1475 he married Beatrice d'Este of Italy, who brought her Italian cooks with her, who in turn brought cheese, dill and garlic. Nevertheless Hungary kept its own style of cooking with its strong Magyar influence and robust recipes including bandit or robber roasts, and gypsy-style stews.

During the eighteenth century under the reigns of Maria Theresa and her son Joseph II of Austria, French eating habits were adopted at the royal court in Vienna. Nobles from Poland, Czechoslovakia, Italy and Hungary, who all had palaces in Vienna, returned to their estates and instructed their cooks in the newly discovered French techniques. In this way the art of French cooking spread throughout the Empire. These same nobles also introduced their national dishes to the Austrian Court: the Italians brought their pasta, which in Vienna became noodles, the Bohemians their pastries and dumplings, the Hungarians their paprika dishes,

and the Poles their sour cream and horseradish sauce. *Wiener Schnitzel* came from Spain, via Milan, and *Pischinger cakes* from Czechoslovakia. This mixture developed into what is now known as traditional Viennese cooking.

Food is a favorite topic of conversation among Czechs, in particular the rival merits of their sausages and dumplings, and the quality of their famous Prague ham. They may tell you at great length that they do not consider themselves great cooks; yet having made this point clear they will spend endless time explaining what a fine cuisine theirs is, so rich, so full of meat and game, and with plenty of dumplings too. Their dumplings are as light as a goose feather; and then what marvels they can work with a goose. No bird is more beloved by the Czechs (or Hungarians) than the goose. All through the long summer peasant women ply these birds with food until they can hardly waddle; and goose girls make their way along dusty country roads, bare of foot, guiding their cackling flock with long thin sticks.

Throughout most of Czechoslovakia there is a marked Slav influence in the cooking, most noticeable in the use of sour cream, vinegar and pickles. In Bohemia there are overtones of German influence, and in Slovakia with its spices and liberal use of paprika there are traces of neighboring Hungary. But the cakes and pastries of Prague have no rivals.

One thing is certain in Czechoslovakia, you never leave the table hungry. It is no joke when they say the Czechs have only one meal a day which starts at breakfast time and continues

The hills of Austria . . .

. . . and the great Hungarian plain

until evening. Breakfast alone is a hearty meal – a so-called 'peasant' breakfast consists of broiled meats, sausages, fried eggs, mushrooms and potatoes.

In Austria they candidly admit to six meals a day. They start with a roll and coffee for breakfast, maybe an egg or perhaps bread with honey or jam. At 11 o'clock there is a concerted rush for a second breakfast (*Gabelfrühstück*), a meal in itself. There is a brief break until the midday meal of meat, vegetables and, of course, a dessert. An hour or so later hunger again rushes in, and it is time for the mid-afternoon *Jause* (tea). This is called a snack, but an enormous number of pastries are downed. However, the day is still not complete. Around 6 o'clock the time has come for dinner, the so-called first substantial meal of the day. Then there is also supper for, after all, one might feel hungry in the middle of the night. The Hungarians have a similar pattern but they lunch later, especially in the summer, and have a very late dinner.

The Galician Poles, the Slovenes, Croats and Italians were on the edge of the Empire. Austrian influence was very strong – Zagreb looks like a miniature Vienna – yet all these people retained their local customs and their own traditional cooking.

The Austro-Hungarian Empire collapsed in 1918 at the end of World War I. Many boundaries were re-drawn to provide territory for the 'liberated' countries. The great days of the Empire were over. But, although an Empire may be abolished by the stroke of a pen, you cannot so easily demolish an atmosphere or a way of life. Austria still danced to Strauss waltzes, and Hungary listened to the haunting tones of her gypsy violins. The atmosphere of the old Austro-Hungarian kitchen still lingers in Vienna's *Naschmarkt*, the former purveyor of the old Empire's specialties, almost as old as the Habsburgs themselves. Although the city encroaches on it more and more, and it is now scheduled to be moved to another site, here you can still find all the necessary ingredients for the wide range of Austro-Hungarian cooking. And here too you can make a round of the numerous national restaurants and eat and drink your way gracefully into the past, as you can in your own home when you invite your guests to taste these traditional dishes.

Soups

GOMBA LEVES (HUNGARY)
Mushroom soup

The Hungarians share with their neighbors a great love of mushrooms of all kinds, and some of the finest are to be found in the Carpathian mountains. When cooking mushrooms, you should always use either butter or a good margarine; lard or oil spoils their delicate flavor.

Serves 4

½ lb mushrooms
¼ cup butter or margarine
½ small onion,
   finely chopped
a little parsley or dill,
   finely chopped
¼ cup flour
1 quart white stock
½ cup heavy cream
a squeeze of lemon juice
salt and pepper

Clean but do not peel the mushrooms, then slice them, keeping the sliced caps and stems separate. Melt half the butter. Add the onion, mushroom stems and parsley, and cook gently for a few minutes. Add the caps. Continue cooking for 15 minutes. In another pan melt the remaining butter. Stir in the flour and, stirring all the while, slowly add the stock. Cook this for about 10 minutes. Stir in the mushrooms and onion, then the cream and the lemon juice. Do not let the mixture boil after the lemon juice has been added or it will curdle. Season with salt and pepper just before serving.

KORHELY LEVES (HUNGARY)
Sauerkraut soup

Like *cesnecka* in Czechoslovakia, both this soup, which literally translated means 'dissipated soup', and *bableves* in Hungary are served to offset the results of having indulged well but not wisely the night before. There was a time in Hungary when a party was not considered a success unless the guests remained until the early hours of morning, and before leaving ate a bowl of soup. Some might even drive to Csepel, a small island downstream in the Danube, to get their soup. The island, like London's old Covent Garden, was a huge market for fruit and vegetables; and one or two eating houses catered for the early morning workers and the late night revellers.

In Hungary *Debrecen* sausages are used. But failing these you could use Spanish *chorizo* or Italian smoked sausages.

Serves 4

1 lb sauerkraut
2 quarts stock
2 tablespoons fat
1 small onion, finely chopped
¼ cup flour
1 lb Debrecen sausages
salt
2 tablespoons medium-strong paprika or chili powder paste
1 teaspoon caraway seeds
¼ cup sour cream or yogurt

Squeeze and save the liquid from the sauerkraut and put the sauerkraut aside. Combine the liquid with an equal quantity of stock taken from the measured stock, put into a large pan and bring to a boil. In another pan heat the fat and fry the onion until soft but not too brown. Stir the flour into the onion and cook, stirring all the time, for a minute or so without letting it brown. Gradually add the remaining water, still stirring, then pour in the diluted sauerkraut liquid and cook gently. Skin and thinly slice the sausages, and add these to the pan. Then add the salt, paprika pepper or chili powder, caraway seeds, and finally the sauerkraut. Stir well and cook over a gentle heat for 45–60 minutes. Just before serving, add the sour cream.

Korhely leves: *the perfect pick-me-up after a night's revelry*

TERLANDER WEINSUPPE (AUSTRIA)
Wine soup with stock and cream

There are several different versions of this ancient wine soup from Austria. An eighteenth-century recipe flavors the soup with sugar and nutmeg or mace. Failing beef stock, an equally clear chicken or turkey stock may be substituted.

Serves 4

4 egg yolks
1 cup heavy cream
1 pint very clear beef stock
1 cup dry white wine
croûtons from 2–3 slices of black bread
cinnamon

Beat the egg yolks until thick and smooth, then gradually add the cream, stock and wine, beating all the time. Cook gently in a heavy pan on top of the stove until the mixture is smooth.

Make the croûtons from black or very dark brown bread sprinkled lightly with cinnamon. Serve the soup hot with the croûtons passed separately.

CESNECKA OR OUKROP (CZECHOSLOVAKIA)
Bohemian garlic soup

This soup is reckoned by knowledgeable Czechs to be a supreme cure for a hangover. In the old days you ordered it at a bar in the wee hours or took it from a roadside stall on the way home. It makes a good cold-weather soup even without a hangover. However, the Czechs warn that, when you have consumed a bowl of *cesnecka*, you should keep your distance from others, unless they too have eaten some – and definitely no kissing.

Serves 6–8

4 large cloves of garlic, chopped
salt and pepper
2 quarts stock
½ lb potatoes, peeled and coarsely chopped
1 teaspoon caraway seeds
½ teaspoon dried marjoram
½ teaspoon ground ginger
2 tablespoons lard, shortening or goose fat
fat for frying
4 thick slices rye bread, cut into large cubes

Mix the garlic with a little salt and mash until smooth, almost like a thick paste. Put the stock into a large pan and add the garlic, potatoes, caraway seeds, marjoram, pepper and ginger (this last gives the soup an unusual flavor and assists digestion). Finally add the measured quantity of fat, stir gently and cook over a moderate heat until the potatoes are soft, even slightly mushy. While the soup is cooking heat enough fat to fry the bread cubes until brown and crisp – this is what the Czechs call *oukrop*. Divide these among 4 soup bowls, preferably of earthenware or brown pottery, add the hot soup and serve after about 1 minute, when the soup has begun to soak into the bread.

Threading peppers for drying

Austrian peasants setting off for the fields

GULYÁS LEVES (HUNGARY)
Goulash soup

This is the classical goulash soup, usually served with small dumplings which are cooked in it.

Serves 4

2 tablespoons fat
1 small onion, finely chopped
1–2 teaspoons mild paprika
1 lb brisket of beef, wiped and cubed
1 cup dry white wine
salt
1 lb potatoes, peeled and quartered
1 red pepper, seeded and coarsely chopped (optional)

Heat the fat, add the onion and let it cook until golden brown. Sprinkle with paprika, stir well, then add the meat. Stir again and cook gently until it browns, but watch carefully, for paprika pepper often burns. Pour in the wine, sprinkle with salt and cook slowly until tender. Meanwhile, boil the potatoes in salted water until just cooked. (Many Continental cooks contend that all potatoes should be dropped in boiling water, never cold, as the flavor is ruined.) Add the potatoes to the meat with as much of the potato liquid as is needed to make a soup. Cook the meat and potatoes together for a short time until both are soft and their flavors are intermingled. If using the red pepper, add it just after the meat.

Austria–Hungary

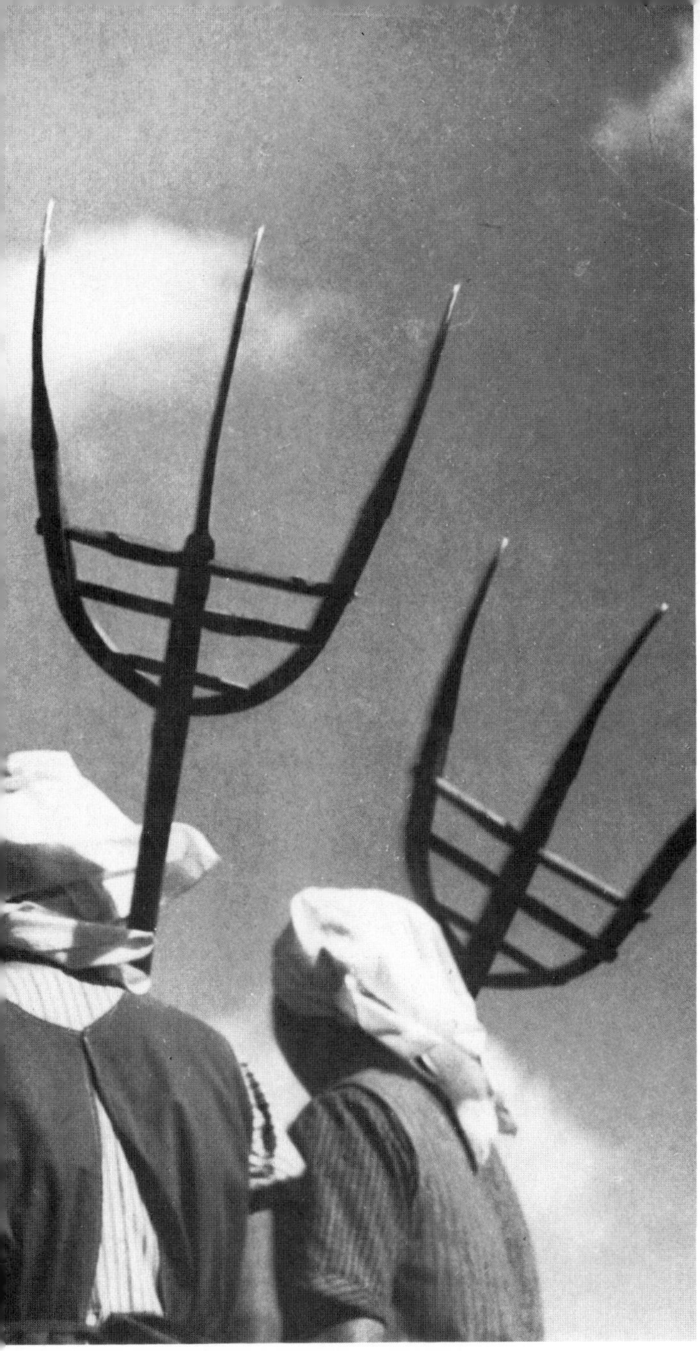

APRIKOSEN KALTSCHALE (AUSTRIA)
Cold apricot soup

Cold fruit soups often were and still are served at the beginning of the main Christmas Day meal in many parts of the old Austro-Hungarian Empire.

The Hungarian version is rather sweeter than the Austrian one with milk and cream added.

Serves 4

½ lb fresh apricots
1 pint dry white wine
¼ cup sugar
juice of ½ lemon
plain cookies

Take 2–3 apricots, pit them carefully and cut the flesh into thin slices. Put aside. Pit the remainder, then coarsely chop and purée in a blender together with the wine, sugar and lemon juice. Chill until required. Serve in deep glass bowls, garnished with the sliced apricots. Serve with plain cookies.

BABLEVES (HUNGARY)
Bean soup

This substantial Hungarian soup is often served as a main dish as well as being very popular after a night out. There is some controversy as to whether white or brown beans should be used.

Prepare at least 36 hours in advance.
Serves 4

1 cup dried white or brown beans, soaked overnight
¾ lb smoked ham
1 large onion, coarsely chopped
¼ cup chicken or goose fat
2¼ quarts water
½ cup flour
2 tablespoons mild paprika
¼ cup sour cream or yogurt

Drain the soaked beans and put them with the remaining ingredients (except the sour cream) into a large pan. Cover and simmer for as long as possible – at least 12 hours (some recipes insist on 24 hours). Stir in the sour cream immediately before serving or add a tablespoonful to each plate.

Fish

PASTRMKA (SLOVENIA – YUGOSLAVIA)
Blue trout

The mountains, rivers and lakes of Slovenia are filled with trout, salmon, pike and many other freshwater fish. The Slovenes are renowned for their fish dishes and particularly for their method of cooking trout and salmon. Continental cooks prepare blue trout in many different ways, but whatever the recipe the fish must be absolutely fresh.

Soup greens or 'pot herbs' are used throughout the area: market women and grocery stores sell these bunches of mixed vegetables and herbs, which include celery, carrots, parsley and leeks, when in season.

Serves 4

1 pint water
1 cup red wine
vinegar
soup greens
4 trout
butter

Heat the water and red wine in a deep pan. Add a little vinegar and the soup greens. Boil for 10 minutes, take the pan from the heat and carefully drop in the trout. They will turn blue immediately.

Return the pan to the heat and cook very gently for 20 minutes. On no account must the stock boil, but bubble gently so that the fish is not spoiled. Take the trout from the pan, place them on a hot oval dish and rub them with butter so that they shine. Serve with mayonnaise or *maître d'hôtel* butter.

MAÎTRE D'HÔTEL BUTTER
finely chopped parsley
¼ cup butter
salt and pepper
lemon juice

Beat the parsley into the butter, and add salt, pepper and enough lemon juice to flavor it. The butter should be softened, but still firm.

Austria–Hungary

FOGAS BETYÁR MÓDRA (HUNGARY)

Pike betyár style

The *betyárs* were bandits who still roamed the Hungarian countryside as late as the nineteenth century, stealing from the rich and giving to the poor. What is known of them comes from folk songs and legends; their exploits caused the Hungarian authorities considerable trouble.

Most of the *betyárs* were peasant lads who took to the hills and forests out of bitterness. Some were avoiding military service which in those days, as they sang, was 'twelve years hard labor for a king who is not our own'. Affecting a romantic style of dress, they wore jackets covered with silver buttons, linen shirts, wide pleated trousers, silken stockings and leather boots.

When the *betyárs* felt safe, they prepared extravagant feasts. There is evidence of their culinary influence in many rural Hungarian dishes, such as this pike cooked in a paprika and sour cream sauce, which is named after them.

Serves 4

3 lb pike
salt
¼ cup butter
1 large onion, finely chopped
½ lb mushrooms, sliced
2 tablespoons medium-strength paprika
¼ cup flour
1 pint sour cream
chopped parsley

Skin and bone the fish, and wash it under cold running water. Pat dry. Generously butter a shallow baking dish and lay the fish in it. Set aside.

Simmer the fish skin and bones in 1 cup salted water to make stock. Melt the butter in a skillet, add the onion and fry until soft but not brown. Add the mushrooms, simmer for 5 minutes, then stir in the paprika. Strain the fish stock and gradually pour it into the onion-mushroom mixture, stirring all the time. Continue to cook gently.

Combine the flour and sour cream, stir this into the fish sauce and bring slowly to a boil, stirring continuously. Pour the hot sauce over the fish and bake until tender in a moderate oven (350°F) for 15–20 minutes. Garnish with parsley and serve with boiled potatoes.

Other firm freshwater fish can be cooked in the same manner.

HERINGE VOM ROST (AUSTRIA)

Baked herrings

As Austria is far from the sea, fish is apt to arrive in rather a tired state, and most Austrians turn up their noses at the mere mention of fresh sea fish. The only variety they have any use for is the herring, which they cook in a dozen or more different ways. Herrings are considered an antidote for carnival excesses, and in the old days there was a so-called Herring Feast when all the restaurants served different herring dishes.

Serves 4

4 large herrings, cleaned
salt
2 tablespoons butter, melted
juice of ½ lemon
chopped parsley

Sprinkle prepared herrings lightly with salt and rub them with the butter. Place in a shallow dish and bake in a moderate oven (350°F) until tender (10–12 minutes). Sprinkle with lemon juice, garnish with parsley and serve hot with boiled potatoes or a green salad, or cold with *maître d'hôtel* butter (p. 193).

KAPR NA ČERNE (CZECHOSLOVAKIA)

Carp with black sauce

Carp were introduced to Europe centuries ago from China, and today they are bred in special ponds. They are a favorite Central European dish, served on Christmas Eve and Good Friday, and often prepared in three different ways at the same time (fried, cooked in black sauce, and boiled and served in aspic). In Prague, housewives used to crowd the streets leading to the Moldau river to buy the live carp that were kept in huge tubs or vats. Today carp comes to the Czech markets almost exclusively from southern Bohemia, where there are a number of carp ponds.

Generally speaking the carp is cooked the day before serving as its flavor is considered much improved that way, but unless served in aspic, the fish must be reheated. This recipe uses Hamburg parsley – a root vegetable which is botanically a true parsley. Its flavor lies between celery root and parsley. Its white fleshy tap root can be eaten raw or cooked in the usual manner of root vegetables.

Prepare 24 hours in advance.
Serves 4

3 lb carp, cleaned and scaled
vinegar
¼ cup butter
1 onion, thinly sliced
1 pint dark beer
1 carrot, sliced
celery root, chopped
peppercorns and salt
a pinch each of ground allspice, mace and dried thyme
½ teaspoon ground ginger
1 bay leaf
2 good strips of lemon rind
2 cups crumbled gingerbread
2 tablespoons redcurrant or cranberry jelly
¼ cup flour
2½ teaspoons brown sugar
a few prunes, pitted and chopped
a few blanched almonds and raisins
½ cup red wine

Soak the fish in 2 or 3 changes of water and finally rinse it in vinegar-flavored water.

Heat half the butter in a large pan; add the onion and cook gently until golden brown but still soft. Add the beer, vegetables, seasonings, spices, bay leaf, and 1 strip of lemon rind. Stir well and bring almost to a boil, then lower the heat and simmer for 20 minutes. Add the gingerbread, redcurrant jelly and finally the fish. Cover the pan and cook the fish gently for 20 minutes. Carefully lift the fish from its pan; put it aside and keep warm. In another pan heat the remaining butter. Add the flour and cook, stirring, to a dark brown roux. Add half the sugar and stir well, then gradually pour in enough hot water to make a thin sauce.

Stir the sweet sauce into the beer sauce and cook for 5 minutes. Add the fish, the remaining strip of lemon rind, and the prunes, almonds and raisins. Sprinkle lightly with the remaining sugar and add the red wine. Cook gently for another 10 minutes or until the carp is very tender and the head and fin can be pulled off easily. Place the carp in a deep dish, cover it with the sauce and leave until the next day. Reheat and serve with boiled potatoes.

Freshly caught carp for a favorite European dish – Kapr na černe

Meat

SZTUKAMIES Z CHRZANEM (GALICIA – POLAND)
Boiled beef with horseradish sauce

A specialty of Galicia, where it is considered an important dish, this is served at formal as well as informal dinners.

Serves 4

*a 2 lb boneless fresh
  brisket of beef*
1 onion
1 carrot
1 stalk celery
1 bay leaf
salt
6–8 large potatoes
2 tablespoons butter
*finely chopped
  parsley*
4 dill pickles, sliced

Choose a pan which will just hold the meat and vegetables and fill with enough water to come half-way up the side of the meat. Bring to a rapid boil, then add the meat, onion, carrot, celery, the bay leaf and salt. Reduce the heat immediately and continue cooking slowly until the meat is tender, about 1½–2 hours. Do not let the water boil as this will toughen the meat.

While the meat is cooking, boil the potatoes. As soon as the meat is tender, take it from the pan and slice it. Drain the vegetables and slice them too. Arrange a layer of the sliced beef in a shallow casserole, add a layer of the vegetables, cover these with the rest of the meat and finally smother in horseradish sauce. Dot with butter and put into a hot oven (425°F) for 10 minutes so that the meat absorbs the flavor of the horseradish. Arrange the meat on a hot platter. Along one side, place the potatoes sprinkled with the parsley and along the other side, the sliced pickles.

HORSERADISH SAUCE
2 tablespoons butter
¼ cup flour
*about 1 cup stock
  or water*
*⅔ cup grated
  horseradish*
salt
juice of ¼ lemon
a little sugar
1 egg yolk, well beaten
¼ cup cream

Melt the butter, add the flour, stir well, then gradually add the stock to make a thick sauce. If too thick, add more liquid. Add the horseradish, salt, lemon juice and sugar. Beat the egg yolk into the cream, add to the pan and stir well. Remove from the heat.

MAGYAR GULYÁS (HUNGARY)
Hungarian goulash

Many Hungarian dishes originated on the Puszta, a wide plain that lies between the Danube and the Carpathian mountains in the east. Here worked the herdsmen (*gulyás*) who at night cooked their beef in large cast-iron cauldrons called *bogrács* in the open air alongside their cattle. During the days of the Austro-Hungarian Empire these herdsmen did their military service in Austria, often in Vienna. They took their recipe with them. It changed considerably and in Austria is usually cooked with veal rather than beef. This recipe, however, is an original Hungarian version.

Serves 4

¼ cup lard or other fat
*2 large onions,
  preferably red ones,
  sliced*
*2 lb lean beef stew meat,
  cut in cubes of equal size*
salt
4 teaspoons paprika
*about 2 tablespoons
  tomato purée*
*1 teaspoon caraway
  seeds*
warm stock or water
6–8 large potatoes
1 tablespoon butter

Thoroughly warm a thick pan (earthenware, copper or iron if possible), add the fat and, when it has melted, the onions. Fry these until they begin to change color and soften, but do not let them brown. Add the meat, shake the pan and cook, stirring all the time, until the meat changes color and the onions are soft (about 15 minutes). Add the salt, 1 tablespoon paprika, tomato purée, caraway seeds and just enough warm liquid to cover. Cook gently, covered, until the meat is very tender.

Meanwhile boil the potatoes in their skins. Cool, peel and quarter them. When the meat is quite tender, add these to the pan, mix well, then continue cooking gently for another 10 minutes. Just before serving, melt the butter in a small pan, add the remaining paprika, stir well and add this to the pan immediately before serving. This is what gives a goulash its traditional bright red color.

*The back-breaking
work of the harvest in
Hungary*

Magyar gulyás: *this internationally renowned dish originated among the herdsmen of Hungary*

ESZTERHÁZY ROSTÉLYOS (HUNGARY)
Eszterhazy beefsteak

The Eszterhazys, one of the most prominent families in Hungary, must have been great supporters of gastronomy, for a large number of dishes have been named after them. There are several recipes for this steak and no two cooks agree on how to cook it. The recipe does not give very precise measurements for ingredients, probably because it comes from a family where quality was the only important detail.

Serves 4

2 lb beef round steak
2 tablespoons butter
2–3 celery stalks, cut into thin strips
1 large carrot, cut into thin strips
1 medium-sized onion, cut into thin strips
1 teaspoon paprika
salt and pepper
¼ cup heavy cream

Broil the meat for 15 minutes, or until browned on both sides. Melt the butter in a pan, add the celery, carrot and onion and cook them for a few minutes. Take the steak from the broiler, put into a thick pan and add the vegetables, any drippings from the broiler pan, and the paprika, salt and pepper. Cook over a moderate heat for 15–20 minutes or until tender. From time to time add cream. Cut the steak into thick slices for serving and garnish with the vegetables.

Cooking time varies not only with the quality of the meat but also according to how it is preferred: rare, medium or well done.

TAFELSPITZ (AUSTRIA)
Boiled beef

This was a favorite dish of the long reigning Emperor, Franz Josef, and, because of his royal patronage, was elevated from popularity among the peasantry to a noble household dish. Now it has become a part of the Austrian way of life. It requires good quality prime beef cut from the leg, a fine-grained tender meat.

Serves 4

1 carrot, cut in lengths
1–2 celery stalks, cut into 2–3 pieces
1 large onion, quartered
2 tomatoes, halved
1 small parsnip, cut into thick slices
a 1¼ lb beef pot roast
salt
1½ quarts water
chopped chives

Put the vegetables into a large pan and add the meat, salt and water. Bring gently to a boil, lower the heat and let the water simmer so that it scarcely moves for 2–3 hours or until the meat is very tender. To serve, take the meat from the pan, cut it into medium-thick slices and sprinkle with the chives. This can be served with horseradish sauce and hot vegetables, such as spinach and cabbage; with a cold chive sauce, creamed apple sauce, lettuce, red cabbage salad or cole slaw; or with fried or sautéed potatoes, roast potatoes or roast onions – the choice is unlimited.

BÀRÀNY PÖRKÖLT (HUNGARY)
Braised lamb

This dish is a cousin to a *gulyás*. The word *pörkölt* means scorched or singed, referring to the quality of paprika used. Beef, veal or poultry may be used, instead of lamb.

Serves 4

2–3 slices bacon, chopped
3 onions, preferably
　red, sliced
1 tablespoon paprika
1 teaspoon vinegar
salt
2 lb boneless lamb, in
　cubes
stock or water, warmed
¼ cup skinned and
　finely chopped tomatoes
1 tablespoon butter

Fry the bacon until the fat runs freely. Add the onions and fry until they begin to soften and change color. Add three-quarters of the paprika and the vinegar, salt and meat. Cook until the meat starts to brown, stirring from time to time, then add enough stock to cover. Cover and cook gently for about 1 hour or until the meat is tender. Add the tomatoes. Just before serving, melt the butter in a small pan, add the remaining paprika and stir well. Then add 1 tablespoon of warm water. Pour this mixture over the top of the stew without stirring. This will give the stew its coveted color and flavor which are so important in Hungarian cooking.

ŠPECKOVÉ KNEDLÍČKY (CZECHOSLOVAKIA)
Potato dumplings with smoked ham

In days gone by, a good dumpling recipe formed part of a Czech girl's dowry, and would be handed down through generations of a family. Occasionally villages would organize a dumpling eating competition, where up to forty or fifty dumplings might be consumed.

Even today it is said that the favorite topic of conversation in Prague is not politics, as one might think, but how to prepare dumplings. This topic is as popular in Czechoslovakia as the weather in Britain, or women in France.

Serves 4

2 lb floury potatoes
¼ cup butter
3 egg yolks
salt
1 cup fine breadcrumbs
½ lb smoked ham,
　diced
3 egg whites, stiffly
　beaten

Boil the potatoes in their skins until tender. Drain, cool, peel and rub them through a ricer into a mixing bowl. Soften the butter, mix into the potatoes and beat until both are well mixed. Add the egg yolks, 1 at a time, beating well after each addition. Put in the salt and the breadcrumbs, again beat well, then stir in the ham. Fold the egg whites into the potato and meat mixture. Rinse a large linen napkin in hot water and squeeze it dry. Place the mixture in the middle, shape it into a fat sausage and wrap in the cloth. Tie tightly at each end but allow room for expansion. Put into a pan of boiling water and boil for 20 minutes. Take the dumpling from the pan, unwrap it and place on a hot plate. Cut into thick slices and serve with sauerkraut or a green salad.

Instead of smoked ham, cold cooked pork may be used.

WIENER SCHNITZEL (AUSTRIA)

This famous 'Viennese' dish is not by origin Viennese or even Austrian. It came to Vienna via Milan, where it was brought by the troops of Charles V from Spain. It is recorded that Field Marshal Radetsky, reporting on the progress of the Italian campaign to his Emperor, also wrote enthusiastically of the *Costoletta alla Milanese*. On the Emperor's orders, he personally taught the royal chefs how to prepare and cook it, and so well was the lesson learnt that the *costoletta* found itself naturalized and renamed.

Only very tender veal round steak should be used, pounded until it is very thin, but not wafer-thin. Over-pounding spoils the flavor. It is not possible to give exact quantities of either flour or breadcrumbs. Different cooks coat lightly or thickly, as their tastes dictate.

Serves 4

4 veal scallops, 4–5 oz
　each
salt
flour for dredging
1 egg
fine breadcrumbs
oil for frying
4 slices lemon
　(optional)
anchovy fillets
　(optional)

Pound the scallops with a meat mallet and make a few cuts around the edge to prevent curling. Sprinkle each fillet lightly with salt. Have ready 3 shallow bowls. Into the first put flour, in another beat the egg, and in the third put the breadcrumbs.

Heat the oil in a skillet; it should come up to about ½ in in the pan. Dip each scallop first in the flour, then in the egg, and finally the breadcrumbs. Do not press down the breadcrumbs too much. Cook the scallops one by one. When brown on the underneath, turn the scallop and brown the other side. Let the fat reheat between cooking each scallop. Drain them on paper towels.

Some people like to garnish the *schnitzels* with a slice of lemon topped with an anchovy fillet. If you do this, do it quickly and serve immediately, otherwise the *schnitzels* will become cold and soggy.

Serve with wedges of lemon, sautéed potatoes and a green salad.

Stacking the golden wheat in Austria

Špeckové knedlíčky: *the Czech girl's dowry of pork-flavored dumplings*

Poultry and game

WATROBICA BUZZONA MADERA (GALICIA–POLAND)
Chicken livers in Madeira sauce

A light dish, this is usually served for lunch with rice.

Serves 4

3 tablespoons butter
1 onion, chopped
1 lb chicken livers, sliced
flour
2–3 tablespoons stock or water
¼ cup cream
salt
¼ cup Madeira

Melt the butter in a pan, add the onion and cook gently until soft but not brown. Add the livers, sprinkle lightly with flour and fry over a good heat, turning them over and over until brown. Pour in the stock, stir well, then add the cream, salt and Madeira. Cover the pan and cook for 5 minutes.

CSIRKE PAPRIKÁS (HUNGARY)
Paprika chicken

Hungarians say a chicken should be slaughtered only an hour before being cooked; otherwise it is not fresh. There is a saying that choosing your piece of chicken from the pan is like choosing a wife – you never know what you are getting.

Serves 4

2 small chickens, quartered
salt
¼ cup butter
1 large onion, thickly sliced
2 teaspoons mild paprika
1 tablespoon mild vinegar
1¼ lb small potatoes
⅔ cup thick sour cream

Sprinkle the chicken pieces lightly with salt and leave them in cold water until required. Heat the butter in a thick pan, and when it is hot add the onion and stir well. Cook until the onion begins to change color, then add the paprika and vinegar and stir well. Drain but do not dry the chickens, add them to the pan and cook until they begin to brown, shaking the pan from time to time to prevent burning. Pour in a little water (enough to prevent sticking or burning), cover the pan and cook until the chickens are tender (40–45 minutes).

While the chickens are cooking, boil the potatoes in their skins. Cool and peel them. Add to the chicken before serving, together with the sour cream.

Serve with small dumplings or noodles if you prefer them to potatoes.

FAZAN NA PODVARKA (SLOVENIA–YUGOSLAVIA)
Roast pheasant

In Slovenia pheasant is not quite the luxury bird that it is considered to be elsewhere.

Serves 2

1 young pheasant
salt and pepper
juice of 1 lemon
6 tablespoons melted butter
1 lb cooking apples

Rub the pheasant inside and out with salt, pepper and lemon juice and place, breast upwards, in a roasting pan. Add the butter. Core but do not peel the apples and either leave them whole or cut them into halves, depending on their size. Surround the pheasant with the apples and bake, covered, at 375°F for 30 minutes. Uncover, and bake until the bird is tender. Baste frequently.

Serve with the apples and also with sauerkraut.

PEČENÁ HUSA (CZECHOSLOVAKIA)
Roast goose

A Czech adage runs: 'The goose is an awkward bird, too much for one, not enough for two', which provides an insight into the Czech appetite. In Czechoslovakia goose fat is used for baking throughout the year, and goose feathers provide the softest down.

Serves 4

a 5 lb goose
salt
1 teaspoon caraway seeds
about 1 cup boiling water

Lightly rub the goose all over with salt, then place it breast-side down in a roasting pan and sprinkle with caraway seeds. Add the boiling water to the pan (this helps the skin to release the fat, important if it is a fatty bird). Roast in a moderate oven (350°F) for about 1½ hours, basting often and pricking the skin occasionally to let the fat flow.

After the goose has been roasting for 30 minutes, turn it over and continue roasting until tender and a good golden color. If there is too much fat in the pan, take it out and add more boiling water. If the goose should brown too quickly, cover the top lightly with foil but do not press it down. Make gravy from the liquid in the pan and serve it with the goose.

Serve with sauerkraut and dumplings.

PRELICE SA PRINICEM (SLOVENIA–YUGOSLAVIA)
Quail pilau

Slovenia is a rich hunting region and wild quail is considered among its finest birds. Although most game birds are laid on ice for some days before being cooked, quail are cooked as soon as possible after they have been shot or caught. Farm bred quail can also be used for this recipe.

Serves 4

1 red pepper
⅔ cup butter
8 quail
1 small onion, finely chopped
1 cup long-grain rice
1–2 medium-sized tomatoes, sliced
finely chopped parsley
salt

Discard the stalk, core and seeds from the pepper and chop the flesh. Melt the butter, add the quail and brown them all over. Take them from the pan, put aside but keep warm. In the same butter fry the onion until it begins to change color, add the pepper and rice, stir well and continue frying for 5 minutes. Add the tomatoes, quail, parsley and salt and let this cook for 10 minutes. Add warm water to barely cover, put the lid on the pan, place in a preheated moderate oven (350°F) and cook for 25–30 minutes or until the rice is dry.

Serve with a green salad.

ZAJAC W ŚMIETANE (GALICIA–POLAND)
Saddle of hare with sour cream sauce

Hunting in Poland was a national sport as well as a practical pastime. Thus, it is not surprising that the Poles have a large repertoire of game recipes of all kinds, from wild boar to small, so-called game birds. Hare, being a gamier meat than rabbit, should be well washed but not soaked under running water. Remove as much as possible of the tendons and membranes. For this dish the best part of the hare is that behind the shoulders.

Prepare this dish 24 hours in advance.
Serves 4

⅓ cup vinegar
1 pint water
8 peppercorns
10 juniper berries
a sprig of thyme
1 saddle of hare
salt
2 oz speck or bacon for larding (see Paprika potatoes, p. 202)
6 thin slices bacon
1 cup sour cream
2 tablespoons flour

Bring the vinegar, water, peppercorns, juniper berries and thyme to a boil. Leave until cold, then pour over the saddle. Leave for 24 hours, turning the saddle from time to time. Take from the pan, pat dry and rub with salt about 30 minutes before roasting. Make a number of slits in the flesh and into these push the pieces of *speck*.

Line a roasting pan with bacon. Add the saddle and cover with the remaining bacon. Add about ½ cup boiling water and bake in a hot oven (425°F) for about 45 minutes or until tender, basting frequently with the drippings. Combine sour cream and flour, stir this into the gravy in the pan, mixing it well, and continue roasting for another 15 minutes.

Serve with mashed potatoes and a refreshing grated beet salad.

GRATED BEET SALAD
1 lb beets
salt
juice of ⅓ lemon
1 teaspoon sugar
1 tablespoon gravy (from the hare)

Wash the beets thoroughly and carefully, taking care not to break the skins. Their green tops hould be cut off, leaving about 2½ in of stems. Cover them with boiling water, add the salt and cook until they are tender (½–1 hour, depending on age). Do not prick them with a fork to test for tenderness but pinch the skin and, if it is loose, the beet is done. Take from the pan and leave until cold before removing the skin, tops and root. Grate them and add the lemon juice, salt and sugar, plus the gravy which in this case will be from the hare.

PECENJE OD ZECA (SLOVENIA–YUGOSLAVIA)
Roast hare

This recipe is designed for a young hare which does not require marinating, as does an older animal.

Serves 4

2 oz dried mushrooms
1 saddle of hare
⅔ cup butter
1 tablespoon flour
1 pint dry white wine
¼ lb bacon, cut into strips
coarsely chopped parsley
salt and pepper
⅔ cup sour cream

Soak the mushrooms in warm water for 20 minutes before using. Wipe the hare with paper towels. Melt the butter in a roasting pan on top of the stove, add the saddle and brown it all over. Sprinkle with flour, let this brown, then pour the wine over the top of the saddle. As the wine begins to cook, add the bacon, parsley, salt and pepper. Put the pan in a preheated moderate oven (350°F).

Drain the mushrooms, pat dry, add to the pan and continue cooking for about 1½ hours or until the hare is tender. Take the hare from the pan, cut into 4 portions and return it to the oven to keep hot. Put the roasting pan on top of the stove, stir the sour cream into the gravy and heat gently. Strain the sauce and pour over the saddle before serving.

ZAJÍC NO ČERNE (CZECHOSLOVAKIA)
Rabbit with black gravy

It was Confucius who, it was said, declared rabbits to be among those animals worthy of being sacrificed to the gods. This recipe suggests that the Czechs share his high opinion of rabbit.

Serves 4

1 rabbit, cut up
4 slices bacon, chopped
3 tablespoons butter or other fat
1 large onion, finely chopped
1 bay leaf
sprig of thyme
6 peppercorns
6 allspice berries
1 strip of lemon rind
salt
1¼ tablespoons flour
1 tablespoon brown sugar
2–3 tablespoons dark vinegar

Wipe the pieces of rabbit with a damp cloth. Fry the bacon in a large pan until its fat begins to run. Add one-third of the butter and when this has melted put in the onion and fry gently. Add the bay leaf, thyme, peppercorns, allspice, lemon rind, salt and rabbit pieces and cook gently until the rabbit changes color. Pour over enough warm water just to cover the rabbit, cover the pan and cook slowly until the rabbit is tender, 1–1½ hours.

Towards the end of cooking, melt the remaining butter in a small pan, add the flour and cook to make a roux, stirring all the while. Take enough of the liquid from the simmering rabbit and mix it into the roux to make a thick gravy. Add the sugar and vinegar, stir well and cook gently for a few minutes. Take the rabbit from the pan, place it on a warmed dish and keep it hot. Strain off any remaining gravy from the rabbit into the small pan of gravy, stir well, then pour this over the rabbit.

Serve with dumplings or with boiled potatoes.

After the hunt

egetables

ZELÍ PO ČESKU (CZECHOSLOVAKIA)
Bohemian cabbage

This is an important Czech dish; and even more important is the unanswerable question, which tastes the better, the Bohemian or the Moravian way of serving cabbage? This rivalry creates clashes between the two provinces. Moravians have especially strong feelings on the subject, and one is warned never, but never, to ask for Bohemian cabbage in a Moravian restaurant. The Czechs serve this dish with roast goose or duck; but it may be served with boiled pork or ham.

Serves 4

2 lb head of white cabbage *salt and pepper* *½–1 teaspoon caraway seeds* *1 small onion, finely chopped* *½ cup sour cream*	Pull off any bruised leaves from the cabbage and discard with the thick tough stalks. Wash the cabbage and cut it into quarters, then shred it finely. Put it into a large pan and add the salt, pepper, caraway seeds and onion with enough water to cover the bottom of the pan to prevent burning. Cover and cook the cabbage over a low heat until tender (30–45 minutes), stirring from time to time. The cabbage should be very soft. Just before serving, add the sour cream, stir again and continue cooking until the cream is hot.

KELKÁPOSZTA FASIRT (HUNGARY)
White cabbage pancake

This pancake can be served as a main dish with a thick home-made tomato sauce, yogurt or sour cream, or (as it is in some parts of the country) with stewed apples or pears.

Serves 4

1 bread roll *3 tablespoons milk* *2 lb head of white cabbage* *1–2 cloves of garlic, peeled* *¼ cup butter* *2 eggs, well beaten* *about 2 tablespoons soft breadcrumbs* *salt and pepper* *oil for frying*	Soak the roll in the milk until soft. Wash the cabbage, pull off the bruised leaves and discard any thick stalks. Cut into quarters and shred. Put the cabbage into a pan with the garlic, and just enough water to cover the bottom of the pan. Cook for about 20 minutes, until the cabbage is soft, and drain it well. Melt the butter in the same pan, return the cabbage to it and cook over a low heat until the cabbage is dry. In the meantime, squeeze the roll dry and mash it until smooth. Mix together with the eggs, breadcrumbs, salt and pepper. Stir this mixture into the cabbage. Heat just enough oil to cover the bottom of a skillet. Add the cabbage and spread it thickly over the bottom of the pan. Fry the 'pancake' until brown underneath, then put the pan under the broiler and cook until brown and crisp on top, unless you prefer the hazardous business of turning it. Serve cut into wedges.

PAPRIKÁS BURGONYA (HUNGARY)
Paprika potatoes

This is a typical Hungarian dish; the quantity and strength of paprika used varies according to taste. Some Hungarians like to use a large quantity of fairly strong paprika, justifying no doubt the Hungarian proverb: 'Give a dying man paprika pepper and he will live, as death cannot stand too much paprika pepper.'

Speck is thick white pork fat, one of the traditional Hungarian cooking mediums, generally available in good delicatessens and some supermarkets.

Serves 4

3 tablespoons speck *1 medium-sized onion, finely chopped* *2 teaspoons mild paprika* *salt and pepper* *½ cup fresh or sour cream, or tomato juice* *2 lb potatoes, peeled and cut into thick slices or quarters* *garlic (optional)* *caraway seeds (optional)*	Heat the *speck* until the fat runs, add onion and cook slowly until soft and transparent. Add the paprika, salt and pepper and mix thoroughly. Take the pan from the heat, stir in the cream, then add the potatoes. Cover the pan and cook over a very low heat until the potatoes are tender, 30–45 minutes. Turn the potatoes carefully from time to time and do not let them brown. Tomato juice may be used instead of cream, and garlic and caraway seeds may also be added.

KLUSKI (GALICIA–POLAND)
Potato dumplings

These potato dumplings are an essential part of Galician cooking, and there are several ways of preparing them.

Serves 4

1 lb floury potatoes
2 tablespoons butter
1 medium-sized onion, finely chopped
¾ cup flour
1 egg yolk, well beaten
1 egg white, beaten until stiff
milk, if needed
	Boil the potatoes in their skins until soft. While they are cooking, heat the fat and gently fry the onion until soft but not brown. Peel and mash the potatoes in a potato ricer. Combine with the flour, onion and fat, add the egg yolk, then fold in the egg white. Knead to a paste, neither too soft nor too stiff; if the latter, cautiously add a little milk. Roll this on a floured board into a long sausage about 1 in in diameter. Slice into rounds roughly ½ in thick and make a dent in the middle of each one.
	  Bring plenty of water to a boil in a large pan, add the dumplings and cook them for about 5 minutes, until they are tender and rise to the surface.
	  Remove them with a slotted spoon, drain and serve with melted butter or, better still, with diced, crisply fried bacon or fried mushrooms and finely chopped parsley.

GERÖSTEL (AUSTRIA)
Fried potatoes with onions and bacon

This peasant dish has become an Austrian specialty beloved by all, especially in Vienna.

Serves 4

2 lb potatoes
3 tablespoons pork or
  poultry fat
2–3 onions, finely
  chopped
2–3 slices bacon, diced
salt and pepper
finely chopped parsley
caraway seeds
  (optional)

Boil the potatoes in their skins until soft. Peel and slice thickly. Heat the fat, add the onions and fry until soft and golden brown. Add the bacon and cook for a few minutes, then put in the potatoes and mix well into the onions. Stir gently and continue cooking until the potatoes are tipped with brown but not as brown as for sautéed potatoes. Add salt and pepper, and sprinkle with parsley and with caraway seeds, if liked.

Geröstel can be varied by adding diced cooked meats, sausages etc. The dish should never be allowed to get dry. Serve it, as they do in the Tyrol, with a green or tomato salad and pickles.

PAPRIKÁS-PARADICSOMOS LECSO (HUNGARY)
Sweet peppers with tomatoes

They say that red peppers and paprika – which is made from red peppers – belong to the Hungarians as a stamp belongs to a letter. Peppers in fact came to Hungary only a century or so ago from the New World; yet paprika is so popular in Hungary today that it seems there could be no Hungarian cuisine without it. The following dish, which is reminiscent of Provençale *ratatouille,* is also claimed by both the Czechs and Yugoslavs, while some Austrians add caraway seeds, thus making it 'typically' Viennese.

Serves 4

1¼ lb ripe tomatoes
1¼ lb green or yellow
  peppers
¼ cup lard or other
  fat
1 large onion, finely
  chopped
1–2 teaspoons paprika
salt and pepper

Scald the tomatoes, skin and cut into quarters. Cut the peppers lengthwise into 4 or 6 strips, discarding the cores and seeds. If the peppers are very long, cut the strips into halves. Heat the fat, add the onion and cook it gently until it begins to change color. Stir the paprika well into the onion, then add the tomatoes and peppers. Season lightly, cover the pan and cook over a low heat for 30–40 minutes, or until the peppers and tomatoes are soft and well mixed. Stir from time to time.

Serve with rice, with scrambled eggs or omelettes, or with diced bacon and fried sausages.

Tyrolean children at the farm

DŮSENÉ HOUBY (CZECHOSLOVAKIA)
Mushrooms cooked in cream and wine

This dish makes an excellent hors d'oeuvre which can be prepared with all types of mushroom. In Czechoslovakia and many parts of Central Europe there is a vast variety of edible mushrooms. People know which are edible and which are not, and make mushrooming in the fields and forests a kind of national sport.

Serves 4

¼ cup butter
2 lb mushrooms, sliced
2–3 tablespoons finely
  chopped parsley
salt and pepper
1 teaspoon caraway
  seeds
2 tablespoons flour
¼ cup red wine
¼ cup sour or fresh
  cream

Melt the butter in a shallow pan; add the mushrooms, parsley, salt, pepper and caraway seeds. Cook slowly for 15 minutes. Mix the flour with a little of the wine to make a thin paste and stir this into the mushrooms, making sure the mixture is smooth. Add the rest of the wine and the cream and continue cooking for another 10–15 minutes. Stir gently from time to time. Serve hot.

Desserts and cakes

GESZTENYEPÜRÉ (HUNGARY)
Chestnut cream

In Budapest and other parts of Hungary chestnuts are very popular. In this recipe they are creamed to make a delicious dessert.

Serves 4

2 lb sweet chestnuts
milk
1 cup sugar
1 cup water
a little vanilla sugar
or extract
1 pint cream, whipped
until thick

Make a slit with a small sharp knife in each of the chestnuts, then boil them until both their outer and inner skins can be removed. Drain the nuts and return them to the pan, cover with milk and continue cooking, rather more gently, until very soft. Blend to a smooth purée.

While the chestnuts are cooking, boil the sugar with the water to make a syrup. Combine this with the puréed chestnuts, add the vanilla, and cool. Mix half the cream into the chestnuts. Pile the mixture into a conical shape on a plate and top with the rest of the cream, letting it fall like snow down the sides. Chill before serving.

ŠVESTKOVÉ KNEDLÍČKY (CZECHOSLOVAKIA)
Fruit dumplings

These dumplings are so popular in Czechoslovakia that a well known painter, Josef Lada, uses them in an illustration for a book of fairy tales taken from the Hana region of Moravia. This shows a heavenly landscape with little angels on clouds preparing the dumplings; lower down other angels are immersing them in a lake of melted butter. Then they are rolled down the slopes of hills, one made of grated pumpernickel, another of sugar, one of poppy seeds, and finally one of grated cheese. At the bottom of the slopes is a *Hanak* (a man from Hana) lying on his back, his mouth wide open to receive the dumplings as they roll down.

The fruits used in these dumplings vary according to the season; but favorites are fresh apricots, chopped peaches, pitted cherries and plums.

Serves 4

1 egg
2 tablespoons butter,
melted
1 pint milk
4¾ cups flour
¼ lb fresh fruit
more melted butter
sugar (preferably brown)

Beat the egg well and mix into the butter and milk. Add the flour to the egg and milk mixture. Make a firm dough, adding more flour if required. Knead until smooth. Break off small pieces, roll into rounds and on each place a little fruit. Wrap the dough around the fruit and make sure it is well sealed.

Have ready a pan of boiling water, drop in the dumplings and cook quickly for 8 to 10 minutes, or until they rise to the surface of the water. Take them from the pan and put into a colander until all are ready. Transfer them to a hot plate, coat with melted butter and sugar, and serve at once. They are delicious garnished with crumbled cottage cheese, or buttered breadcrumbs with crushed poppy seeds.

REIS TRAUTTMANSDORFF (AUSTRIA)
Rice mold

The Trauttmansdorff family is an ancient one, coming from the Vienna Woods. One Trauttmansdorff fought in the battle of Marsfeld in 1278 and another in the Thirty Years' War (1618–48). However, this very sweet rice mold was dedicated to Ferdinand, Count of Trauttmansdorff, an Austrian diplomat. He served as his country's ambassador in several countries for many years, and returned eventually to become President of the Austrian House of Representatives.

Serves 4–6

1¼ pints milk
½ cup short-grain rice
⅓ cup sugar
a good piece of
vanilla bean
2 envelopes unflavored
gelatin
1 cup stiffly whipped
cream
2 tablespoons
Maraschino liqueur
⅔ cup coarsely chopped
candied fruit

Put the milk into a pan, add the rice, sugar and vanilla and cook over a low heat until the rice has absorbed all the liquid. Remove the vanilla bean.

Soften the gelatin in cold water, then dissolve in hot water in a double boiler. Combine the gelatin with the cream and Maraschino. Leave until cold. Put aside some of the candied fruit to be used as a garnish and mix the rest into the rice. Add the gelatin mixture.

Rinse a decorative mold with cold water. Add the rice mixture and leave in the refrigerator until set. Unmold to serve, garnished with the reserved candied fruit, and with a fruit sauce served separately.

SERNIK (GALICIA–POLAND)
Cottage cheese pudding

This Galician recipe is a cross between the little French *coeur à la crème* and the rich Russian *paskha*.

Serves 4

3 egg yolks
1 cup less 2 tablespoons
sugar
1 lb cottage cheese
3 tablespoons diced
candied orange peel
¼ cup unsalted butter,
softened, not melted
3 egg whites,
stiffly beaten

Beat the egg yolks until fluffy. Add the sugar and continue beating until the mixture is thick. Push the cheese through a strainer, then beat it into the eggs and sugar. Add the candied fruit and butter and continue beating. Fold the egg whites into the cheese. Pile the mixture into a mold and leave in the refrigerator for a couple of hours or longer. Turn out to serve.

This pudding is delicious on its own, but can be served with sweetened whipped cream or strawberries.

Austria–Hungary

MAKOVÝ KOLÁČ (CZECHOSLOVAKIA)
Poppy seed cake

Poppy seeds come from a large poppy grown in Holland, and they are used extensively in European cooking. The seeds may be either gray or black, without fragrance but with a distinctive flavor. They are so tiny that there are said to be 900,000 seeds to the pound. Before starting on this recipe, either grind the seeds in a blender or coffee grinder, or pound them in a mortar.

Serves 4–6

breadcrumbs for sprinkling
¾ cup unsalted butter
2 tablespoons sugar
6 egg yolks
⅓ cup raisins
1¾ cups poppy seeds
juice and grated rind of 1 lemon
about ½ teaspoon ground cinnamon
¼ teaspoon ground cloves
6 egg whites, stiffly beaten
apricot, strawberry or raspberry jam
stiffly whipped cream for decoration

Grease two 10 in layer cake pans, then sprinkle with breadcrumbs. Cream the butter and sugar. Beat the egg yolks until pale and fluffy, beat them into the butter and sugar, and continue beating until the mixture is thick. Add the raisins, poppy seeds, lemon juice, rind and spices. Mix well.

Using a metal spoon, fold the egg whites gently into the batter. Pour the batter into the prepared pans and bake in a preheated moderate oven (350°F) for about 30 minutes or until the cake is firm to the touch. Remove from the oven but leave to cool in the pans. Unmold gently, spread 1 layer with jam and place the other on top. Serve topped with whipped cream.

PIŠINGRUV DORT (CZECHOSLOVAKIA)
Oblaten cake

Oblaten or wafers were once the specialty of the town of Karlovy Vary, formerly Carlsbad, in Czechoslovakia. There are several varieties, some very small and crisp, others with a chocolate flavor. In Vienna some of the smaller bakeries still produce fresh, hot *oblaten*, but usually they are bought in delicatessens. For this recipe, the round plain wafers are essential.

Prepare 48 hours in advance.
Serves 4–6

½ cup unsalted butter
1 cup sugar
8 squares unsweetened chocolate
a little vanilla sugar or extract
1 cup finely chopped hazelnuts
4 egg whites, stiffly beaten
8–10 round oblaten, 8 in in diameter
1¾ cups confectioners' sugar

Beat the butter until creamy and gradually beat in the sugar. Melt 5 squares of the chocolate in a bowl over boiling water and beat it until smooth, then add the creamed butter. When mixed, put in the vanilla sugar and nuts and again beat well. Fold the egg whites into the chocolate mixture with a metal spoon. Place a wafer on a round plate. Spread this with some of the chocolate mixture and cover with a second wafer. Spread this with more chocolate mixture, cover with a third wafer and continue in this fashion until all the *oblaten* and chocolate are used up. The top wafer should be left plain.

Melt the remaining chocolate over boiling water, add the confectioners' sugar, vanilla sugar or extract and about 2 tablespoons of lukewarm water. Beat until smooth and spread it over the top wafer. Leave for 48 hours at room temperature before serving.

PALACSINTA (HUNGARY)
Crêpes

In Hungary it is the custom to add wine, beer or brandy to crêpes to make them especially light. It also gives them that extra little alcoholic flavor. Crêpes are often served with a stuffing of cottage cheese or finely chopped or grated walnuts, but they may also be served with almost any other stuffing.

Makes 12 crêpes

1½ cups plain flour
2 eggs
a pinch of salt
3 tablespoons sugar
1 pint milk
1 tablespoon wine, beer or brandy
butter for frying
sugar to sprinkle

Sift the flour into a mixing bowl. Make a well in the center. Add the eggs, one by one, then the salt, sugar, milk and wine. Mix in the flour, working from the center gradually toward the edges; beat thoroughly to a smooth batter. This can be used immediately or left to stand for 30 minutes.

Heat a thick pan 8 in in diameter. Test the pan: sprinkle a few drops of water into it, and when they dance in small beads on the surface, it is ready. Very lightly rub the bottom with butter, turning the pan round and round so that it is coated with butter.

Pour 1 to 2 tablespoons of batter into the middle of the pan, tilting it back and forth to make the batter flow evenly. Fry over a medium heat until the crêpe is lightly browned underneath. Do not peek under the crêpe to see if it is brown, as this causes it to toughen. Turn the crêpe over carefully, loosening the edges with a spatula, and cook the second side. Stack the finished crêpes on a heated plate and keep them warm in the oven. Sprinkle with sugar before serving, or stuff with your favorite filling.

KAISERSCHMARRN (AUSTRIA)
The Emperor's crêpe

There are many stories about the origin of this dish. One story relates how this crêpe, which had humble beginnings, finished grandly in an Emperor's kitchen. It is said that the Emperor Josef, while hunting, found himself lost and alone in a forest (strange for an emperor), and stopped exhausted and hungry at a peasant's cottage. He was given a crêpe, which tasted good but had evidently come adrift in the cooking, for it was served broken. The Emperor enjoyed it and thought it was meant to be cooked this way, so he instructed his own chefs to make crêpes in the same manner. However, it seems more likely that the word *Kaiser* is a corruption of a word meaning a cowherd or alpine dairy maid.

Serves 4

4 egg yolks
⅓ cup sugar
1⅔ cups flour
½ cup milk
6 tablespoons melted butter
salt
⅔ cup sultanas or raisins
4 egg whites stiffly beaten
extra sugar to sprinkle

Beat the egg yolks with the sugar until the mixture is fluffy, then add the flour alternating with the milk, all but 2 tablespoons of the butter and the salt. Fold the egg whites into the batter.

Melt the rest of the butter in a skillet and pour the batter into this pan; it should be very thick. Let the batter begin to cook, then sprinkle the raisins on top. When the underside is brown, turn the crêpe and brown the other side – if it breaks it does not matter. When the crêpe is brown on both sides, sprinkle it with sugar. Using 2 forks break it into small pieces and let it stay in the pan to become almost dry.

Serve with stewed cranberries, apple sauce or stewed dark plums.

TVAROHOVÝ KOLÁČ (CZECHOSLOVAKIA)
Cheesecake

When the Czechs are not extoling the joys of poppy seed cake, they are fulsomely praising their special brand of cheesecake which, indeed, is not like the usual versions of this favorite dessert.

Serves 4 (say the Czechs)

1 cup shelled hazelnuts
  or walnuts
¼ cup fine breadcrumbs
½ cup unsalted butter
½ cup sugar
4 eggs, separated
½ cup cottage cheese

Garnish
warmed raspberry or
  apricot jam
grated chocolate
finely chopped nuts

Put the nuts into a thick, dry pan and roast quickly over a good heat until they begin to brown. Stir to prevent burning. Crush coarsely and set aside.

Grease an 8 in springform cake pan and sprinkle lightly with 1 tablespoon breadcrumbs. Cream the butter and sugar and add the egg yolks 1 at a time, beating vigorously after each addition. Rub the cheese through a strainer, add to the butter mixture and beat thoroughly. Beat the egg whites until stiff. Fold them gently into the mixture with a metal spoon, adding the remaining breadcrumbs. Finally add the nuts.

Turn the mixture into the prepared cake pan and bake in a preheated moderate oven (350°F) for 45 minutes or until the top feels firm and a knife inserted into it comes out clean. Remove the cheesecake from the oven but leave it in the pan to cool. Unmold carefully. When ready to serve, spread lightly with jam and sprinkle generously with chocolate and nuts.

SALZBURGER NOCKERLN (SALZBURG)
Salzburg dumplings or soufflé

These dumplings were first made at the beginning of the seventeenth century under the instruction of Agide von Raitenau, Archbishop of Salzburg, who, we are told, loved pomp, power and puddings. It is said in Salzburg that those who do not like these dumplings have no taste, and Austrian women who cannot cook them have no talent for cooking.

Salzburg dumplings will collapse, if not correctly handled; also if the right heat is not applied or there is a slight draft, they will flop. So when serving, make sure there is no draft and that there is no great difference in temperature between the kitchen and the dining room.

Serves 4

½ cup butter
½ cup sugar
4 eggs, separated
½ cup flour
½ cup milk
vanilla sugar

Beat the butter until creamy, add the sugar and continue beating until fluffy. Add the egg yolks, one by one, and beat until they are completely integrated into the butter. Beat the egg whites until stiff. Very carefully fold these into the creamed mixture, at the same time adding the flour. Put the milk into a casserole (one that can be used on top of the stove and in the oven) and bring it to a boil. With the utmost care spread the mixture over the top, put the casserole cautiously but swiftly into a preheated hot oven (425°F) and bake until it is a golden brown (a matter of a few minutes). As it bakes the milk is absorbed. Take the dish from the oven, scoop out large dumplings of the mixture, dust with vanilla sugar and serve immediately.

APFELSTRÜDEL or ALMÁS RÉTES (AUSTRIA AND HUNGARY)
Apple strudel

A strudel is a pastry of paper thinness with either a sweet or a savory filling, although it is the apple filling which has become synonymous with strudel. This is generally considered to be an Austrian dish, but it belongs to Hungary, as even some Austrians grudgingly admit.

Making strudel pastry is not easy. In Austria they say you must start young and work with love and a prayer if you want to be successful in this art. Also, in order to stretch the dough so thin that, as they say in Vienna, you can read a love letter through it, four hands are required and six are even better. Apart from that there are two essentials: bread flour with a high gluten content and a large kitchen table.

Serves 4

1 cup flour plus extra
  for dusting
1 tablespoon olive oil
a pinch of salt
a few drops of vinegar
  or lemon juice
6 tablespoons butter
¾ cup fresh breadcrumbs
1½ lb tart apples
about 2 tablespoons
  raisins
1 teaspoon ground
  cinnamon
1 teaspoon grated
  lemon rind
¼ cup sugar

Sift the flour onto a wooden board, make a well in the center, and add the oil, salt, vinegar and just enough warm water to mix to a smooth dough – elastic, but softish rather than very firm. Brush with oil, then cover with a warm cloth or bowl and leave for 20–30 minutes to rest.

While the dough is resting, make the filling. Melt ¼ cup of the butter in a small pan, add the breadcrumbs and fry quickly until just brown, stirring all the time. Peel, core and thinly slice the apples. (Keep them covered or, if you are not going to use them immediately, drop them into lemon-flavored water, but drain and dry them before using.)

Melt the remainder of the butter. Spread a large white cloth over the kitchen table; it should be large enough to come down the sides. Sprinkle with flour. On this roll out the dough as thinly as possible and as far as it will go. It will go a long way, especially if you are using a long thin Continental rolling pin. When you have rolled it as far as possible, work the dough from underneath with the floured back of your hand, pulling and easing the dough until it gets thinner and thinner and extends just beyond the cloth. Cut off the thick edges; if you have any holes in the dough, patch them with cut-off pieces.

Brush the dough with melted butter, then spread with the fried breadcrumbs. Arrange the apples over the top and sprinkle with the raisins, cinnamon, lemon rind and sugar. Lift up the cloth and roll the dough (rather as you would a jelly roll) as tightly as possible. Close the ends carefully – otherwise the filling will ooze out. Roll the strudel off the cloth onto a baking sheet – greased if you wish.

Brush the strudel with the rest of the melted butter and bake in a preheated hot oven (425°F) for about 15 minutes or until golden brown and the pastry is flaky, brushing with melted butter 2 or 3 times more. The strudel can be sprinkled lightly with sugar before serving either hot or cold, or sugar can be served separately, but you should still be able to taste the rather tart flavor of the apples. Cut into thick slices to serve.

Apple strudel: the art of pastry-making perfected over centuries

Balkan in Turkish means a mountain and it was the Turks who gave the Balkans their name. The Balkan Peninsula is a block of five countries enclosed in a rough square. It runs from the Danube on the Black Sea to Trieste on the Adriatic and south to the Aegean, and it includes Greece, Yugoslavia, Rumania, Bulgaria and Albania – all mountainous countries and thus well named. It encompasses many nationalities – Greeks, Serbs, Bulgarians, Rumanians, some Hungarians and some Germans – and many religions: Islam, Greek Orthodox, Roman Catholic, Jewish and Protestant. In the north-east corner of the Balkans we find a part of European Turkey, a country not included in this chapter, but whose influence is felt throughout the region, especially in the cooking. This polyglot multi-racial mixture has combined to produce a cuisine that some people call the most fantastic in the world. Certainly over the centuries such a combination had to produce the exceptional.

To begin at the beginning, Greece is considered not only the father of civilization but also of European cuisine. Ancient Greece was famous for its cooking. Indeed, it has been claimed that you are practically in Greece when in Marseilles eating *bouillabaisse* – a development of the Greek mixed fish dish *caccavia*; or tasting *boudin noir*, the blood sausage which originally came from Sparta.

A cook is as useful as a poet, and as wise.

Euphron (c. 200 BC)

An army of sunflowers reviewed by a Rumanian farmer

Greece and the Balkans

Many famous Greek dishes found their way to Rome. In an attempt to improve their cultural and gastronomic image, the Romans took not only Greek teachers into their homes but Greek cooks also. They even set up warehouses to store the spices essential for Greek cooking such as balsam, nutmeg, cinnamon and cloves. Lucullus, whose name is synonymous with fine eating, founded his reputation on Greek cooking while Roman philosophers blamed the increasing decadence of the younger generation on the over-consumption of rich Greek food.

After the Turks conquered Constantinople in 1453 they adopted the dishes of their Byzantine captives, gave them Turkish names and served them to their own Sultans. In this way Greek cooking was kept alive, and when the Turks expanded their territory throughout the following centuries, they also spread these cooking techniques. Turkish domination of the Balkans lasted several centuries and many Greco-Turkish dishes, with their Turkish names, became an integral part of the cooking of this region. Other nations have also left their mark on the cuisine of the Balkans: Austrian dumplings, strudels from Hungary, and southern German food from the Swabs for example.

Whatever its origin, Balkan food is most distinguished by the unusual and often subtle combinations of vegetables, fruits and meats. Also, with the exception of present-day Greece, the people of the Balkans tend to have a taste for highly seasoned food, using plenty of garlic, hot peppers, fennel, cumin and dried mushrooms, which they collect in pounds from forests and fields, and dry at home.

At first the puzzled visitor to the Balkans may feel that there is little difference between the food served in Greece and that in Bulgaria and the other Balkan countries. But there are differences throughout the Balkans, acquired over the centuries by local usage and a touch of chauvinism, and these variations are most noticeable in the cooking medium: the Greeks cannot conceive of a cuisine without olive oil; the Bulgarians prefer sunflower oil; while the Yugoslavs and Rumanians use lard and sometimes butter. The Rumanian cooks are perhaps the most individual of all, partly because they use a great deal of dill and lovage, and partly because, without abandoning their own Turkish-influenced kitchen, they adopted many of the French techniques which were fashionable all over Europe.

Since sheep can thrive in alpine country where extremes of heat and cold make it difficult to provide fodder for cattle, it is not surprising that lamb is used most in Balkan cooking. Broiling and roasting in the Balkans are practiced to virtuosity, and in spring the air is filled with the appetizing aroma of barbecued kabobs, sausages, even whole lamb on festive occasions. Generally speaking, lamb, goat and kid are the main meats. Pork is prohibited in the areas where the Turks were successful in imposing the Moslem faith; but the non-Moslem regions, especially those in Yugoslavia and Rumania, make up for this with their consumption of pig. Veal is popular with the people of Hungarian or German descent. The Rumanians eat a lot of meat: one of their most famous and spectacular dishes consists of steak, lamb chops, sausages, sweetbreads, liver and kidneys, pork chops and any other meats available, all cooked together over charcoal and

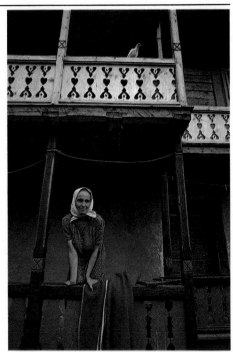

Two aspects of village life: Rumania (above) and Greece

served on a wooden platter with sauerkraut, red peppers and spicy pickles or relishes.

Poultry, game and fish abound throughout the area. Albanians have a predilection for small birds, such as thrush and blackbirds; Bulgarians and Rumanians have good fish from the Black Sea, while the Yugoslavs claim that there are three hundred and sixty-five different species of fish along the coast of Dalmatia, one for each day of the year. Greece has octopus, squid, mussels, and mullet.

Bulgaria is the market-garden of Europe. The ubiquitous *givech*, a vegetable and meat casserole, which owes its name to the heavy iron casserole in which it simmers for hours, is found throughout the area. It is usually served with yogurt, which the Bulgarians insist only they know how to make.

In winter the presence of the stove meant that living, eating and sleeping were all confined to one room in this farmhouse in Bosnia, Yugoslavia.

The Bulgarians consume vast quantities of yogurt daily; it is used for every possible cooking purpose and appears at every meal. They maintain that it is of paramount importance to health and responsible for their amazing longevity. However, although they have made a cult of yogurt, preparing it with a mixture of water-buffaloes' and goats' milk, it is not of their invention: *The Old Testament* has several references to asses' and goats' milk soured, Genghis Khan waged his wars on a diet of soured mares' milk mixed with yaks' milk, and the Mongolians, Armenians and Persians have always produced soured milk or types of yogurt.

Balkan longevity is attributed not only to the consumption of yogurt, but also to the eating of sauerkraut. This came to the Balkans via the Tartars who discovered it when fighting in China, where it was already well established. They liked it so much and it kept so well that, when they journeyed through southern Europe, they carried it with them.

Vegetables of all kinds grow in profusion throughout the Balkans and are used extensively in their cooking. In Yugoslavia they are particularly fond of sweet and chili peppers, introduced from the New World by the Turks. The Bulgarians would find life insupportable without onions: apart from putting them into almost every savory dish, they consume vast quantities raw. The Greeks love to stuff their vegetables, and all Balkan cooks show imagination in the mixing of raw vegetables in salads. The Greek housewife uses lemon juice to make her salad dressing and many vegetables are marinated in lemon juice before being cooked.

Cereals are of great importance: Yugoslavia produces a considerable quantity of good quality rice, excellent for pilau, and all five countries grow maize. The favorite dish of the Rumanians is *mamaliga*, cornmeal mush as we Americans say; and no Rumanian, whatever his station in life or his shade of politics, would consider life worth living without his precious *mamaliga*. Yet, curiously, cornmeal only came to the Balkans in comparatively recent history, for it was taken there from the U.S. in the eighteenth century.

If nothing else unites the Balkan peoples, then the long list of sweet dishes certainly does. For Balkan desserts are really sweet, whether they are cakes soaked in syrup or honey, rose-petals in syrup, or any one of their numerous fried doughnut-type fritters coated with sugar. And there is no doubt that the favorite sweet of all is the many-layered, very sweet baklava which is served with *kaimak*, a thick clotted cream. Apart from these, there are fruit *compotes* made with fresh and dried fruits and vast quantities of fruit jams and conserves. There is also a delightful age-old custom of offering guests a tray with a small bowl of preserves, a glass of water, a spoon and sometimes a liqueur.

Wines are made throughout the Balkans; many are very pleasant though they vary considerably, from red and white wines of some distinction to the *retsina* of Greece, flavored with pine resin, which was originally a preservative. Most regions have their own beer, which is light like lager and served ice-cold. There are also many fruit spirits such as Yugoslavian *slivovitz*, which is made from plums and Greek *ouzo*, flavored with aniseed.

Balkan cooking has a special flavor, a seductive aroma that one remembers long after the taste has been forgotten. This combines with the hazy, smoky aroma of charcoal cooking mingled with the smell of garlic and, in Yugoslavia, the scent of *pekmez*, a thick fresh prune jam. Throughout the Balkans, people love eating outdoors and, as soon as the weather is warm, out come all the chairs and tables into the gardens and on to the sidewalks; they sprawl into the street, where people sit for hours on end, gossiping, eating, drinking and relaxing.

You remember the many summer meals eaten in villages, often little more than a wide, long, sunbaked road flanked on each side with color-washed houses surrounded by beautiful giant sunflowers; in the cool shade of woods or by the waters of quiet quaysides; under pines or by mountain streams; in old rambling houses and courtyards under the shadow of walnut trees with freshly picked walnuts offered with the many glasses of delicious wine.

These recipes will perhaps revive pleasant memories for those who know the Balkans, and provide an introduction to others still to discover the cooking of this romantic and historic region.

Hors d'oeuvre

PATLAGELE VINETE TOCATE (RUMANIA)
Eggplant purée or 'caviar'

The great shiny purple eggplant is beloved by all the Balkan people; and eggplant purée, prepared throughout the region, is so popular and so good that it has been dubbed 'poor man's caviar'. It is served with a glass or two of *tzuica*, a plum brandy often so potent that it has earned the nickname *apa chiora*, or 'cross-eyed' water.

Serves 8

1–2 large eggplants
¼–⅓ cup olive oil
juice of 2 lemons
salt and pepper
1 clove garlic, crushed (optional)
chopped onions and black olives to garnish

There are many recipes for 'poor man's caviar' but for all of them the eggplant must be roasted, preferably over a glowing charcoal fire, until the skin becomes black and well blistered. To do this on a gas ring, hold the eggplant on the end of a toasting fork and turn for 5–10 minutes. Alternatively, broil the eggplant until thoroughly black, or bake in a very hot oven (450°F). Do not boil, since this merely results in a rather bland flavor. When the eggplant is burnt and blistered it is also tender. Allow it to cool, then pull off the black skin and chop and mash the flesh to a smooth purée. Transfer to a mixing bowl and beat well, using a wooden spoon (do not use metal since this blackens the flesh). Add the olive oil gradually, still beating continuously. When the oil and purée are well mixed, add just enough lemon juice to give a mayonnaise consistency. Add salt and pepper, and garlic if desired, and transfer the purée to a cool place.

Serve chilled in a pile garnished with onions and olives, and eat it using soft brown bread as a scoop.

Taramosalata *with hot peppers and olives*

SRPSKA SALATA OD PAPRIKE (YUGOSLAVIA)
Serbian sweet pepper salad

In regions where sweet peppers grow in abundance 'large' can mean enormous, in which case one pepper makes enough salad for four. Cooks must use their own judgment.

Serves 4

2–3 large sweet peppers (red or green)
oil and wine vinegar
plenty of chopped garlic (optional)

Spike the peppers on the end of a toasting fork and hold over a high gas flame until their skins are black and blistered; or bake in a very hot oven (450°F). Let them cool, discard the stalks, cores and seeds, and pull off the blackened skin. Cut the flesh into wide strips and place on a shallow dish. Make a dressing of oil and vinegar – 2 parts oil to 1 of vinegar is the local taste – and while the peppers are still warm pour the dressing over them. Add the garlic, although this is not absolutely necessary, and serve either warm or cold.

MASLINE FRECATE (RUMANIA)
Black olive pâté

As Rumania is not a great olive-growing country, it is odd to find this unusual little recipe tucked in here. But it is nevertheless one of the favorite national dishes.

Serves 4

1 cup large black olives
olive oil, if required
1 cup unsalted butter
sweet pepper, chives or onions, fennel and parsley, all finely chopped and to taste

Pit the olives, chop them finely and rub through a coarse strainer, or purée in a blender with a little olive oil. Soften but do not melt the butter. Combine the olive purée with the softened butter and continue beating until the mixture is absolutely smooth. Add the remaining ingredients.

This purée is particularly good served on black bread; or it can be shaped into a square and chilled in the refrigerator to a firm pâté, which is both unusual and delicious.

Greece and the Balkans

TARAMOSALATA (GREECE)
Fish roe salad

This is a type of caviar traditionally made from the roe of either mullet or tuna fish. The prepared roe of the mullet has a unique rich flavor, is as thick as fudge, and clings to the roof of the mouth. In Rumania a similar salad, *icre de crap*, is made with carp roe and served garnished with tomatoes and black olives. Nowadays, taramosalata is often prepared with smoked cod roe.

Serves 4

¼ lb mullet roe
  or smoked cod roe
4 slices white bread,
  crustless
1 cup olive oil
juice of 1–2 lemons
1 clove garlic, crushed
  (optional)

If using cod roe, remove the skin. If using mullet roe, soak in water for 1–2 hours to abate its saltiness. Soak the bread in water until soft, then squeeze dry and place in a mixing bowl. Crumble the roe, add it to the bread and pound the mixture thoroughly until smooth. When these two ingredients are well mixed, gradually add enough olive oil to make a soft purée (but not too soft). Then add enough lemon juice to loosen it. Some people add a little water to make the purée lighter, others a crushed clove of garlic, or even more oil.

To make taramosalata in a blender, place the bread in the goblet and add just enough oil to keep it moving. Gradually add the roe and the oil alternately to the bread. If the mixture is too stiff, add a tablespoon or so of water. Finally, add the lemon juice.

Serve chilled as an appetizer with soft country bread.

TZATZIKI (GREECE)
Cucumber and yogurt salad

The difference between a salad, a soup and an appetizer is not always easily defined in the Balkans. For example, *tzatziki* is served in Macedonian Greece as a soup, but elsewhere as a salad or an hors d'oeuvre. It is closely related to Bulgarian *tarator*.

Serves 4

1 pint plain yogurt
1 small cucumber, peeled
  and coarsely grated
1 tablespoon olive oil
1 tablespoon lemon juice
crushed garlic to taste
salt to taste

Beat the yogurt, add the remaining ingredients and chill. Serve in bowls, and eat with spoons.

The traditional design of Aegean fishing boats has not changed for centuries.

ANGINARES ME KOYKIA (GREECE)
Artichoke hearts and lima beans

For this recipe very large artichokes are required, but if these are not available you could use canned artichoke hearts instead.

Serves 4

1 lb podded lima beans
4 large fresh artichokes
  or 1 can artichoke hearts
juice of 1 lemon
3 tablespoons olive oil
1 tablespoon cornstarch
1 pint bean liquid
handful finely chopped
  parsley
salt and pepper

Cook the beans until tender, drain and reserve the liquid. To prepare the artichokes, cut off most of the stalk and trim the tips of the leaves to make a neat shape. Place in boiling salted water, stalk up, and simmer for about 20 minutes, or until an outside leaf pulls off easily when tested – over-cooking spoils the flavor. Take them out by the stalk and carefully drain upside down, squeezing to remove some of the water. Pull off the outer leaves until you are left with the choke and base. Remove the choke, or flower, and drop the hearts immediately into a bowl containing the juice of 1 lemon and enough water to cover them. This will preserve their color. Heat the olive oil in a wide shallow pan, add the cornstarch and stir well. Add the bean liquid, stirring all the time to make a thin, almost transparent sauce. Add the parsley, salt and pepper to taste, and stir the mixture well. Add the drained artichoke hearts and beans and simmer until the artichokes are warmed. Serve cold in the same dish.

Soups

SOUPA AVGOLEMONO (GREECE)
Egg and lemon soup

This everyday, yet elegant soup is one of the best known of Greek dishes and a favorite throughout the Balkans. Even the Albanians regard it as one of their national dishes.

Serves 4–5

1¾ quarts chicken stock
salt and pepper to taste
⅓ cup long-grain rice
2 eggs
juice of 1 lemon

Bring the stock to a boil, test for seasoning, and add salt and pepper only if required. Add the rice and continue cooking until it is tender, about 15 minutes. Meanwhile, prepare an egg and lemon sauce by beating the eggs well, then gradually beating in the lemon juice. When they are well mixed, very slowly add about 1 cup of the hot stock in which the rice is cooking.

Just before serving, add the egg and lemon sauce to the rice and stock, stirring all the time. Continue to cook slowly until the soup is reheated, then cover the pan, turn off the heat and leave the soup to rest for 5 minutes. Serve hot.

The open, rolling farmlands of southern Rumania

SUPA DE AGRISA (RUMANIA)
Gooseberry soup

The charm of this fruit and vegetable soup lies in its unusual flavor and its delicate pale green color.

Serves 4–6

1 large carrot
1 celery stalk
1 small onion
1 tomato
1 lb gooseberries
1¾ quarts chicken stock
1 teaspoon chopped chives
salt and pepper
2 eggs
⅔ cup sour cream or yogurt
finely chopped parsley to garnish

Dice the carrot and celery, finely chop the onion, skin and chop the tomato, and top and tail the gooseberries. Put these ingredients into a pan together with the stock, add the chives, salt and pepper and cook gently until all the vegetables are tender. Remove from the heat and leave to cool. Beat the eggs together with the sour cream, either in a soup tureen or in a deep serving bowl. Gradually pour in the soup, stirring all the time. Chill, and immediately before serving sprinkle with parsley.

HIADNA JUHA OD JABUKE (YUGOSLAVIA)
Cold strawberry soup

This fresh, pale pink soup is served ice-cold on long hot summer days.

Serves 4

1 lb garden or wild strawberries
⅜ pint red wine
⅓ cup milk
⅓ cup water
1 teaspoon salt
about 2–3 teaspoons sugar
1 cup sour cream or yogurt
1 tablespoon flour
2 egg yolks
2 tablespoons unsalted butter

Wash and hull the strawberries and combine with the red wine in a saucepan. Simmer gently until soft, and pass through a strainer. Return the strawberry purée to the pan and continue cooking gently. Mix the milk and water together, add salt and sugar. Combine the sour cream with the flour, egg yolks and butter and beat well. Stir into the milk and water. Pour into the strawberry purée, stirring all the time, and continue cooking until the mixture is thick. Chill and serve ice-cold. If during chilling the soup thickens more than you like, thin it down with more wine.

TARATOR (BULGARIA)
Yogurt, cucumber and walnut soup

It is to a Russian, Professor Mecknikov, that we owe the introduction of yogurt, and also this soup, to the western world. Visiting Bulgaria towards the end of the nineteenth century, the professor idly watched the peasant women in the fields eating their midday meal, which appeared to be bowls of white soup. He was told that this dish kept one healthy and active for a hundred years. It was *tarator* or yogurt soup.

Serves 4–5

1 medium cucumber
salt
1¼ pints plain yogurt
1 cup iced water
3–4 cloves garlic, finely chopped
about 12 walnuts, shelled and chopped
2 tablespoons olive oil

Thinly peel and dice the cucumber, sprinkle lightly with the salt and put aside for about 30 minutes. Beat the yogurt and mix with the iced water. Wash the salt from the cucumber and pat dry. Rub a large bowl generously with garlic, add the cucumber, the diluted yogurt, the remaining garlic and the walnuts. Mix well, beat in the oil and continue beating until the oil is well mixed into the soup. Divide into soup bowls and chill before serving.

As a variation, omit the walnuts and garlic, and instead add finely chopped mint and currants.

Three cold soups: Yugoslavian hiadna juha od jabuke, tarator from Bulgaria, and Rumanian supa de agrisa (bottom)

Cornmeal and rice

MAMALIGA (RUMANIA)
Cornmeal

Rumania has been described as 'the land of *mamaliga*'. This cornmeal mush is the national dish – the staple food of the country people, and in days gone by 'the delight of the upper classes'. Considered a gift from heaven, its full name is *mamaliga de aur*, or bread of gold.

Usually *mamaliga* is cooked to a firm mass, like a pudding, then combined with other foods. The variations are endless: it can be sprinkled with grated cheese or chopped onions; or served with fried eggs, fried bacon and sour cream, or small broiled birds. The average Rumanian cook book contains dozens of suggestions.

Leftover *mamaliga* is cut into slices and fried in butter, or rubbed generously with melted butter flavored with garlic, or wrapped in fat bacon and baked in a shallow pan in a moderate oven (350°F) until the top is golden brown. In the old days, when cooks had more time and doubtless more patience than we have today, it took several hours to make *mamaliga*. Today most people cook it by what is known as the 'modern' method to save time.

Serves 4–6

1 quart water
2 teaspoons salt
1⅓ cups cornmeal

Heat the water and salt in a large saucepan until boiling furiously. Put the cornmeal into a shallow bowl, take out a handful and let it dribble slowly, like rain, into the boiling water, stirring all the time with a long wooden spoon (the Rumanians use a long wooden stick not unlike a thin rolling pin, with a decoratively carved handle). Continue dribbling in the cornmeal until it is all in the pan and the mass begins to thicken. The reason for adding the cornmeal slowly is to keep it soft. If it is added all at once it becomes hard. A word of warning: keep as far away from the pan as possible, as the cornmeal has a tendency to spit out suddenly when cooking, and burns can result.

When the mixture is smooth and has reached the desired thickness – and this is a matter of individual taste – cover the pan, lower the heat and continue cooking for a further 30 to 40 minutes. Take a wet spatula and run this around the sides of the pan to loosen the mush from the sides. Turn out on a wooden board and shape it like a cake, either with a spoon dipped in water or, if you have such a thing, a wooden knife. Cool and cut into slices like a bread and serve with stews, soups and ragoûts. Or serve it straight from the pan in which it was cooked, spooning it into mounds on the wooden board, or directly on to plates.

Here is a typical method of serving *mamaliga*.

MAMALIGA FELEI PRAJITA
Fried mamaliga slices

mamaliga
1 beaten egg
grated cheese
butter, for frying
yogurt or sour cream,
* for serving*

Let the *mamaliga* mush get quite cold and then cut into slices. Dip them into well beaten egg, then coat generously on both sides with grated cheese, patting it on well (a piquant ewes' cheese is used in Rumania). Melt some butter and fry the slices on both sides until brown. Serve very hot with yogurt or sour cream, well chilled.

KABUNI (ALBANIA)
Sweet raisin pilau

This is one of Albania's national dishes, a sweet rice cooked in chicken stock.

Serves 4

¼ cup butter
1 cup long-grain rice
2 cups hot chicken stock
⅜ cup raisins
about ¼ teaspoon
* ground cinnamon*
¼ cup sugar

Melt the butter and fry the rice until it looks transparent. Slowly pour in the stock, stirring all the time, and cook the rice for 10 minutes. Add the raisins, stir once, cover the pan tightly and continue cooking over a very low heat until all the liquid has been absorbed and the rice is tender. Combine the cinnamon and sugar and stir into the rice just before serving.

Serve with boiled chicken as a main course, or alone as a dessert with brown sugar and melted butter.

Greek fishermen display a mammoth catch of octopus.

Fish

PASTRMKA NA OHRIDSKI NAČIN (YUGOSLAVIA)
Trout Ohrid style

In Lake Ohrid there are fish not generally found elsewhere, even in other local lakes and rivers, and many are famed for their unique flavor. Ohrid trout are especially popular, as are the eels which start out from the lake on their marriage journeys along the Black Drin, through Albania into the Adriatic, and finally to the Atlantic.

This recipe mixes trout with prunes, and prunes are extremely popular in the Balkans. In Yugoslavia they are used to make the famous drink slivovitz as well as a thick, dark jam called *pekmez*.

Serves 4

*2 large trout
  or 4 small ones
1 cup prunes, pitted
plenty of parsley, finely
  chopped
3–4 cloves garlic, finely
  chopped
¼ cup oil
2 tablespoons vinegar
4 eggs, well beaten
2 lemons
salt and pepper*

Clean the fish, and stuff with some of the prunes. Place in an oiled baking pan and cover with the rest of the prunes. Cover with parsley, sprinkle with garlic, add the oil, vinegar and finally water to cover. Bake small trout for about 25 minutes, large ones for up to 45 minutes, in a hot oven (400°F) until tender.

Take the fish and prunes out of the pan and arrange them on a hot platter. Leave the parsley and garlic in the pan, stir in the beaten eggs, add the juice of 1 lemon, salt and pepper and cook gently on top of the stove until the eggs are set. Spread the eggs, which are more or less scrambled, around the trout and serve with wedges of lemon.

RIBA S CHERVENO VINO (BULGARIA)
Fish cooked in red wine

The red wine of Bulgaria is so dark that it is often called 'black wine'. If the real thing is unobtainable, use the darkest red table wine you can find.

Serves 4

*2 lb fish fillets – bream,
  cod, hake, etc
salt
1 bottle dark red wine
handful parsley
peppercorns
2–3 cloves garlic,
  coarsely chopped
¼ cup butter
2 tablespoons flour*

Wipe the fish fillets and sprinkle lightly with salt. Put the wine with the unchopped parsley, peppercorns and garlic into a pan and simmer for 5–10 minutes. Add the fish and cook until tender (15–20 minutes depending on the type of fish). Remove the fish from the pan, place on a hot serving dish and keep hot.

Strain the wine, return it to the pan and continue cooking until it is reduced by about two-thirds. In a small pan melt the butter, add the flour, stir to a roux, gradually add the wine, stirring all the time to make a thick sauce – but do not let it boil. Pour the sauce over the fish immediately before serving.

SMUD SA PECURKAMA (YUGOSLAVIA)
Pike-perch with mushrooms and yogurt sauce

This is a dish of completely local origin, owing nothing to Turkish influence: the Turks never use yogurt with fish, considering it positively harmful, and they seldom use mushrooms in cooking. Other freshwater fish can also be prepared in this manner.

Serves 4

*2 lb pike, cut into
  steaks or fillets
salt
¼ cup olive oil
½ lb mushrooms
¼ cup butter
yogurt or sour cream*

Rub the fish steaks lightly with salt. Put the oil in a baking dish, add the pieces of fish and turn them over several times to coat them with the oil. Bake in a fairly hot oven (400°F) until tender, about 15 minutes.

While the fish is cooking, clean the mushrooms, pull off the caps (the stalks can be used for a soup) and slice them thinly. Melt the butter, add the sliced mushrooms and fry gently until soft. By this time the fish should be tender. Cover it with the mushrooms, pour the yogurt over the top and continue cooking for about 10 minutes.

'PIJANI' ŠARAN IZ SKADARSKOG JEZERA (YUGOSLAVIA)
'Drunken' carp

The firm sweet flesh of the carp is popular throughout the Balkans, where it is a traditional Christmas Eve dish. This Montenegrin recipe uses carp from Lake Scutari, but if carp is unobtainable other large freshwater fish may be used.

Serves 4

*1 small carp, about 2 lb
a little vinegar
salt and pepper to taste
3–4 cloves garlic
¼ cup olive oil
1 cup dry white wine*

Clean the carp thoroughly, keeping it whole, and wash it in vinegar-flavored water. Sprinkle lightly with salt and put aside in a cool place for about 2 hours. Wipe off the salt. Peel the garlic and push it inside the fish. Sew up the opening in the belly, rub the fish generously with oil, and sprinkle with pepper. Put into a baking pan, add the remaining oil and cook in a hot oven (425°F) for 30 to 40 minutes, or until tender, basting frequently with the wine.

TARAMO KEFTETHES (GREECE)
Fish roe cakes

A popular dish in Greece, eaten a great deal during Lent. Ideally roe from the mullet should be used in this recipe, but smoked cod roe makes a good substitute.

Serves 4

1 small onion
¼ lb smoked cod roe
2 large potatoes, cooked and mashed
2–3 cloves garlic, crushed (optional)
finely chopped mint
finely chopped parsley
salt and pepper
flour
oil for deep frying

Scald the onion to modify the flavor, and grate finely. Remove the skin from the roe. Pound the roe in a mortar, add the potatoes, garlic if used, onion, mint, parsley, salt and pepper, and beat the mixture thoroughly. Leave for about 2 hours. Shape into small cakes, coat lightly in flour and deep fry until crisp and brown on the outside but soft inside.

JACHNIA A RIBA (BULGARIA)
Fish ragoût with onions

A *jachnia* can best be described as a type of ragoût. It can be prepared with meat, fish or poultry, and any seasonal vegetables. A large bowl of yogurt is the usual accompaniment.

Serves 4

2 lb fish fillets – bream, cod, hake, etc
salt and pepper
1 lb onions
¼ cup olive oil
4–5 tablespoons tomato purée
1 cup dry white wine
paprika
2–4 cloves garlic, finely chopped

Wipe the fish and sprinkle lightly with salt and pepper. Cut into pieces, not too small. Peel and finely chop the onions. Heat the oil in a pan, add the onions and fry until soft and golden brown. Add the tomato purée, stir well, then add the wine (water or beer if preferred) and cook gently to a thick sauce. Add the fish and continue to cook gently for about 15 minutes. Sprinkle with paprika and garlic and serve hot with a bowl of yogurt.

Meat

FICAT DE VITEL FLORA (RUMANIA)
Calf liver casserole

Liver casseroles should be cooked very slowly, otherwise the liver can become tough. Soak the liver overnight in milk before using, to improve the flavor and color.

Serves 4

1 lb calf liver, in one piece
6 bacon slices
salt and pepper
chopped parsley, chives and fennel
1 large clove garlic
2–3 onions, sliced
1 large carrot, sliced
1 bay leaf
1 cup dry white wine
warm meat stock or water
¼ cup cream

Wash the liver in warm water and cut away any tubes or fat. Drain and dry thoroughly on paper towels. Wrap half the bacon round the liver and fix it firmly. Put this into a bowl, add salt and pepper and half the chopped herbs. Cover and put aside until required.

Cut the garlic in half and rub it over the bottom and sides of a frying pan; fry the remaining bacon until the fat runs (if the bacon is not sufficiently fat, add additional cooking fat). Add the onions, carrot, bay leaf, salt, pepper and the liver with the rest of the herbs, and finally the wine. Cover the pan and cook gently until tender. Remove the liver from the pan, set aside but keep hot.

Skim off any surplus fat from the gravy in the pan and add just enough stock or water to make a thick sauce. Bring it slowly to a boil, stir in the cream and cook gently until the sauce is reheated.

Thinly slice the liver and arrange the slices in a ring on a hot serving plate, leaving the center free. Pour the sauce into the center, garnish with the pieces of bacon, and serve at once with creamed potatoes and triangles of crisply fried bread.

COTLETE PORC CU BERE (RUMANIA)
Pork chops with beer sauce

This Rumanian dish adds beer to a traditional pork and apple combination. Use light lager beer to avoid drowning the other delicate flavors.

Serves 4

¼ cup pork fat or drippings
2–3 onions, finely sliced
2–3 large tart apples, peeled and sliced
1–2 cloves garlic, chopped
4 thick pork chops
salt and pepper

Heat the fat in a pan, spread with half the onions, add the apples, the remaining onion and garlic. Cook gently on top of the stove until the onions are soft and the apples cooked. In the meantime prepare the chops. With a small knife score them in two or three places around the edges to prevent curling, and cook them quickly in a dry pan, or under the broiler until brown on both sides. When the chops are brown, place them on top of the simmering onions and apples. Sprinkle with salt and pepper, cover and cook over a low heat until the chops are tender (about 30 minutes). Meanwhile prepare the sauce.

Beer sauce
2 tablespoons butter
2 tablespoons flour
1 cup mild beer
salt, cayenne pepper
finely chopped parsley or chives
1 tablespoon brown sugar

Melt the butter, add the flour, stir well to make a roux, then gradually add the beer to make a thickish sauce. Add salt and pepper, parsley or chives, and sugar; stir well.

Serve the chops with the onion and apple mixture on a hot dish; and serve the beer sauce either separately or poured over the chops.

Greece and the Balkans

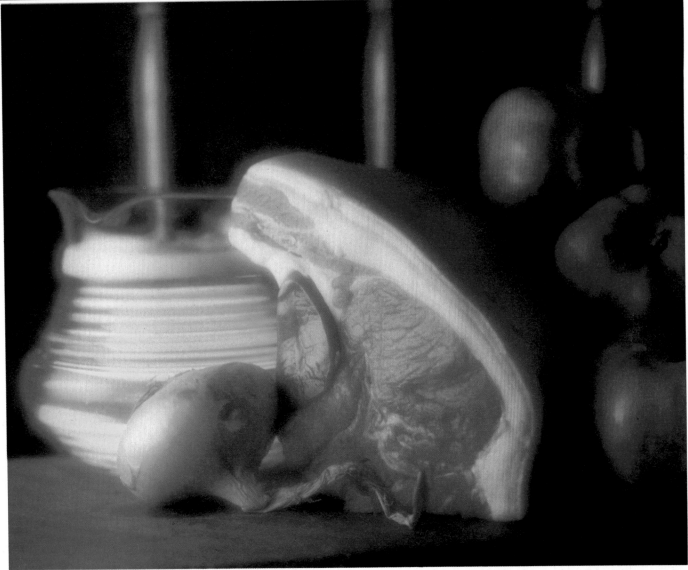

Beer adds an edge to the universal combination of pork and apples in this Rumanian recipe.

KREAS ME KASTANA (GREECE)
Veal or beef with chestnuts

This is delicious and unusual, and it is worth noting that in many Greek recipes chestnuts and potatoes are interchangeable. When fresh chestnuts are not available, use dried ones. They require a long preliminary soaking, but have an excellent flavor.

Serves 4

2 lb veal or beef stew meat
1 lb chestnuts
¼ cup butter for frying
1–2 onions, finely chopped
1 pint beef stock
salt and pepper

Cut the meat into small pieces. Cut a slit in each of the chestnuts and boil them for about 20 minutes or until their skins can be pulled off easily. Melt the butter and fry the onions until just brown, then add the meat. When it is brown, add the stock, salt and pepper and cook slowly for 1–1½ hours, until the meat is tender. Add the chestnuts and continue cooking for a further 10 minutes until they are soft but not broken. Serve with Brussels sprouts – a popular Balkan vegetable.

TELESHKO SAS SLIVI (BULGARIA)
Veal with prunes

Plums grow well in most parts of the Balkans, and recipes using them as prunes and combining them with meat in a main dish are by no means uncommon. This dish is extremely rich as no liquid is added. Really slow cooking is important.

Serves 4

½ lb prunes, pitted
1 lb veal stew meat
* (or beef)*
¼ cup butter for frying
2 medium onions, coarsely
* chopped*
1 teaspoon sugar
salt and pepper
1–2 cloves

Soak the prunes if necessary and pat absolutely dry. Cut the veal into small pieces. Melt the butter in a pan, add the prunes and fry lightly for about 5 minutes. Remove from the pan, put aside, but keep hot. In the same fat fry the onions for 5 minutes, add the meat and fry it until it changes color. Return the prunes to the pan, add sugar, salt, pepper and cloves, cover the pan and cook gently for 1–1½ hours, until the meat is tender. Serve with rice or pasta, and a bowl of yogurt.

MITITEI (RUMANIA)
Barbecued beef 'sausages'

Mititei means 'smaller than small', and these skinless sausages are great favorites among Rumanians. They are usually cooked over charcoal in the open air.

Prepare at least one day in advance.
Serves 6–8

1 lb chuck steak
1 lb brisket
3–4 cloves garlic, crushed
a little ground allspice and cloves
fresh chopped thyme
salt and pepper
⅛ cup beef stock
beef suet (optional)

Pass the meats with the garlic through a grinder. Put the mixture into a large bowl, add spices, thyme, plenty of salt and pepper and knead it well; gradually add half of the stock and continue kneading. If the meat is very lean, a little beef suet may also be added. When the mixture is thoroughly kneaded and smooth, take a small portion and roll it in the hands into a sausage about 4 in long and a little less than 1 in thick. Repeat this process until all the mixture is made into sausages, wetting the palms of the hands from time to time to prevent the meat sticking. Arrange the sausages on a platter and leave them in the refrigerator until the following day. (They may be kept for up to 3 days.)

Take the sausages out of the refrigerator at least 2 hours before they are required, to let them dry in the air. Cook over charcoal, turning frequently until they are brown. Baste from time to time with the rest of the beef stock. Do not dig at them with a fork or anything sharp as this will release their natural juices. Serve very hot.

To be absolutely correct, *mititei* should be served with *ardei*, slender, fiery hot peppers. You can also serve them with sweet pepper salad, sour pickles and plenty of red wine.

QOFTE ME MENTE (ALBANIA)
Mint-flavored meat balls

Mint is the national flavor of Albania, used in almost all lamb dishes, in salads and in cold drinks. The following recipe is very typical.

Prepare 1–2 hours in advance.
Serves 4

1 lb boneless lamb
2 eggs, well beaten
2 cloves garlic, crushed
⅛ cup finely chopped mint
a large pinch of ground cinnamon
salt and pepper
oil for deep frying

Grind the meat twice. Combine in a mixing bowl with the remaining ingredients (except the oil), mix thoroughly and knead until smooth. Leave covered in the refrigerator for 1 or 2 hours, longer if required. When ready to cook, break off pieces of the meat mixture, shape into balls and roll these round and round in the hand until smooth. Heat plenty of oil and deep fry the meat balls, a few at a time, until they are brown all over. As the meat balls are cooked, put them on a hot serving dish and keep warm. Serve with a rice pilau.

ÇEVABÇIÇI, PLJESKAVICA AND RAZNIÇI (YUGOSLAVIA)
Barbecued meat cakes, hamburgers and kabobs

Yugoslavia has three kinds of barbecues: *çevabçiçi*, small cakes of ground meat, *pljeskavica*, larger and shaped more like a hamburger, and *razniçi*, small pieces of meat threaded on to skewers. They are all cooked over charcoal, which is what gives them their distinctive flavor. These three most popular Serbian foods are often cooked in the open, and the night air of late spring and summer is laden with the appetizing smell of barbecued meats. Chopped or sliced onions, usually in vinegar, are served with them all, as well as small, very hot green chili peppers which can take the roof off the mouth.

To help pronounce them, remember that the Yugoslav *ç* is pronounced 'ch'.

Barbecued meat cakes (çevabçiçi)
Serves 6

1 lb boneless pork
1 lb boneless veal
⅛ lb boneless fat beef
salt and pepper

Çevabçiçi literally means little kabobs. The Yugoslavs consider about 10 *çevabçiçi* a portion for 1 person. The given quantity makes about 50. They are usually prepared in the morning and kept in a cold place all day so that they 'set' before being cooked.

Pass all the meat through a grinder, add salt and pepper and grind again, 3 or 4 times if possible. Then knead the mixture until it is absolutely smooth. Break off small pieces and shape them into small fat 'sausages'. Cook over charcoal for about 15 minutes, turning from time to time to ensure that they brown evenly.

Barbecued hamburgers (pljeskavica)
Serves 6

1 lb boneless pork
1 lb boneless veal
salt and pepper
⅛ lb onions
finely chopped sweet pepper (optional)

One *pljeskavica* is considered the equivalent of 10 *çevabçiçi*.

Pass the meat through a grinder. Add salt, pepper and onions, and the sweet pepper, if used. Pass this mixture once more through the grinder, then knead for as long as possible and finally leave to stand for several hours. Break off pieces of the meat and shape into hamburgers. Cook over charcoal, turning from time to time to ensure even browning. They will take 20 to 30 minutes to cook.

Kabobs (Razniçi)
Serves 6–8

1 lb boneless veal
1 lb boneless pork
salt and pepper
⅛ lb onions, thickly sliced

These kabobs are usually served together with *çevabçiçi*, and 2 skewers are considered enough for 1 person. They are seldom made in small quantities.

Cut the meat into small cubes. Flatten lightly with a meat mallet. Thread pieces of veal and pork alternately on to small oiled skewers and cook over charcoal, turning them frequently. Sprinkle with salt and pepper and serve very hot with a garnish of sliced onions.

A Bulgarian farmhouse, photographed between the wars

Poultry and game

PECENJE OD ZECA (YUGOSLAVIA)
Roast hare

This recipe is suitable for a young hare which does not require marinating, as does an older animal. A Yugoslav cook prefers to soak a hare in cold water in the open for a few days before cleaning and skinning it.

Serves 4

1 cup dried mushrooms
1 saddle of hare
⅔ cup butter or other fat
1 tablespoon flour
1 cup stock
1 cup dry white wine
¼ lb very fat bacon, cut into strips
coarsely chopped parsley
salt and pepper
¼ cup sour cream or yogurt

Soak the dried mushrooms in warm water for 20 minutes before using. Dry the hare with paper towels. Melt the butter in a roasting pan on top of the stove, add the saddle and brown it all over. Sprinkle with flour, let this brown, then pour in wine and stock over the top of the saddle. As it begins to cook, add the bacon, parsley, salt and pepper and put the pan in a preheated moderate oven (350°F).

Drain the mushrooms, pat dry, add to the hare and continue cooking for about 1½ hours or until the meat is tender. Take the hare out of the pan, cut into 4 serving pieces and return it to the oven to keep hot. Put the roasting pan on top of the stove, stir the sour cream into the gravy and cook until the sauce is hot. Strain and pour this over the saddle immediately before serving.

The rugged hillsides of Greece

RATZA CU VARZA (RUMANIA)
Duck with cabbage

This recipe can be used with farmyard or wild duck. Duck shooting is a favorite sport in the Balkans, and wild duck is extremely popular.

Serves 3

1 duck, about 4 lb
salt and paprika
⅔ cup butter or other cooking fat
1 large firm head white cabbage
6–8 peppercorns
1 tablespoon tomato purée

Rub the duck liberally inside and out with salt, paprika and half the butter. Place the duck, breast up, on a rack in a roasting pan, and cook uncovered in a preheated moderate oven (350°F) for 30 minutes. Prick the skin from time to time to release the fat.

While the duck is cooking, wash and shred the cabbage, discarding any old leaves and hard stalk. Melt the remaining butter in a saucepan and add the cabbage, turning it from time to time until it browns. Add salt and peppercorns. Dilute the tomato purée with a little water or, better still, stock and add this to the cabbage. Leave to cook over a moderate heat until the cabbage is soft. Take the duck from the oven and out of the roasting pan. Remove the rack and pour off excess fat. Spread the cabbage on the bottom of the pan, place the duck on top, return the pan to the oven and continue roasting until the duck is tender (about another hour, or longer if a larger duck is used).

KOTOPOULO TIS SKARAS ME SALSA (GREECE)
Broiled chickens with a lemon sauce

The Greeks rub the flesh of the chicken with lemon, which adds to its flavor and also whitens it. Another Greek tip is to pour a kettle of boiling water over the chicken. This plumps it out and prepares it for any type of cooking.

Rice and a fresh watercress salad make the perfect accompaniments to this dish.

Serves 4

2 small chickens
salt and pepper
garlic
¼ lemon
olive oil or butter

Sauce
2 tablespoons olive oil
1 tablespoon lemon juice
¼ teaspoon dry mustard
fresh or dried thyme
salt and pepper

Split the chickens down the center and flatten gently. Rub each piece with salt, pepper, garlic and lemon. Brush them with oil and put on a rack in a shallow pan under the broiler, but not too near the heat. Do not have the broiler too hot. Turn the chickens from time to time and baste with the sauce until they are tender and browned all over (about 15–20 minutes).

To make the sauce, mix the oil and lemon in a small pan, add the remaining ingredients and cook gently for 3 minutes. Pour the sauce over the chickens, and serve at once.

PULE MEDROP (ALBANIA)
Stuffed chicken

This recipe originated in Turkey, but it is now one of the most popular national dishes of Albania.

Serves 4

salt and pepper
1 large roasting chicken
1 tablespoon butter,
 softened
¼ cup hot water

Stuffing
¼ cup butter
3½ cups soft breadcrumbs
¾ cup mixed dried fruit –
 currants, raisins
1 cup mixed nuts –
 walnuts, pine nuts,
 almonds, hazelnuts, etc
1 tablespoon sugar
¼ cup chicken stock
salt and pepper

First prepare the stuffing. Melt the butter in a pan, add the breadcrumbs and fry for a few minutes, stirring to prevent over-cooking. Add the remainder of the ingredients and, if the stuffing seems dry, add a little more stock. Set aside.

Mix the salt and pepper together and rub into the chicken, inside and out. Pack the stuffing into the chicken and close the openings with thread or small skewers. Spread the chicken with the softened butter, put it into a preheated hot oven (425°F) and roast until tender, about 1½ hours depending on the size and tenderness of the bird. Baste the chicken from time to time and, after about 1 hour of cooking, add the hot water.

To test whether the chicken is done, insert a fork or skewer between the thigh and the body and let the juices run. If they are still streaked with blood let the chicken continue roasting for a little longer. When the chicken is done, take it out of the pan, remove the thread or skewers and serve.

PUI CU CAISE (RUMANIA)
Chicken with apricots

A recipe very typical of Rumania, where apricots are produced in abundance, this dish can be served on the day it is cooked, but its flavor is better if it is served the day after cooking, gently reheated.

Dried apricots may be used if fresh ones are not available, and the liquid in which they are soaked used instead of the warm water. Even canned apricots, well drained of their sweet syrup, may be substituted for fresh ones.

This dish may be served alone, or with sautéed potatoes and a green salad.

Serves 4

oil for frying
3 lb chicken, cut into 4
1¼ tablespoons flour
1 pint chicken stock
1 medium onion, minced
1–2 teaspoons brown
 sugar
salt and pepper
1 lb fresh apricots,
 pitted

Heat just enough oil in a large pan to fry and brown the chicken pieces. Remove them from the pan, but keep hot. Pour off all but about 1 tablespoon of the oil, add the flour to the pan, stirring all the time, and, still stirring, gradually add the stock. When the sauce has thickened, add the onion and continue cooking until it has almost disappeared. Return the chicken pieces to the pan, add the sugar, salt, pepper and apricots, cover and cook gently until the chicken is tender.

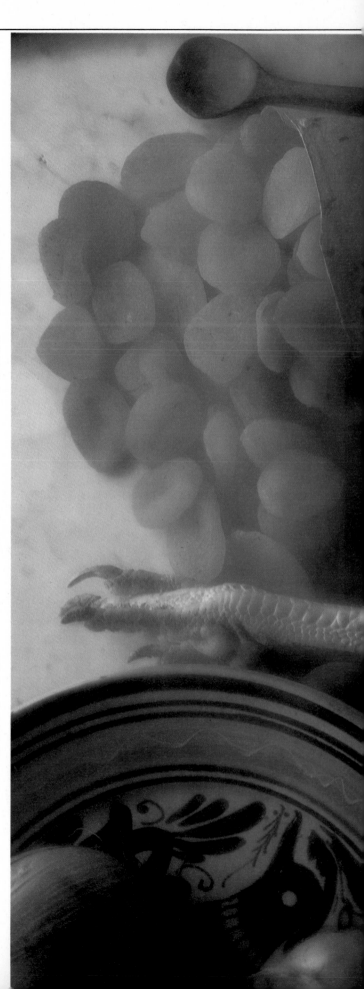

Pui cu caise: apricots lend their sharp sweetness to chicken.

Greece and the Balkans

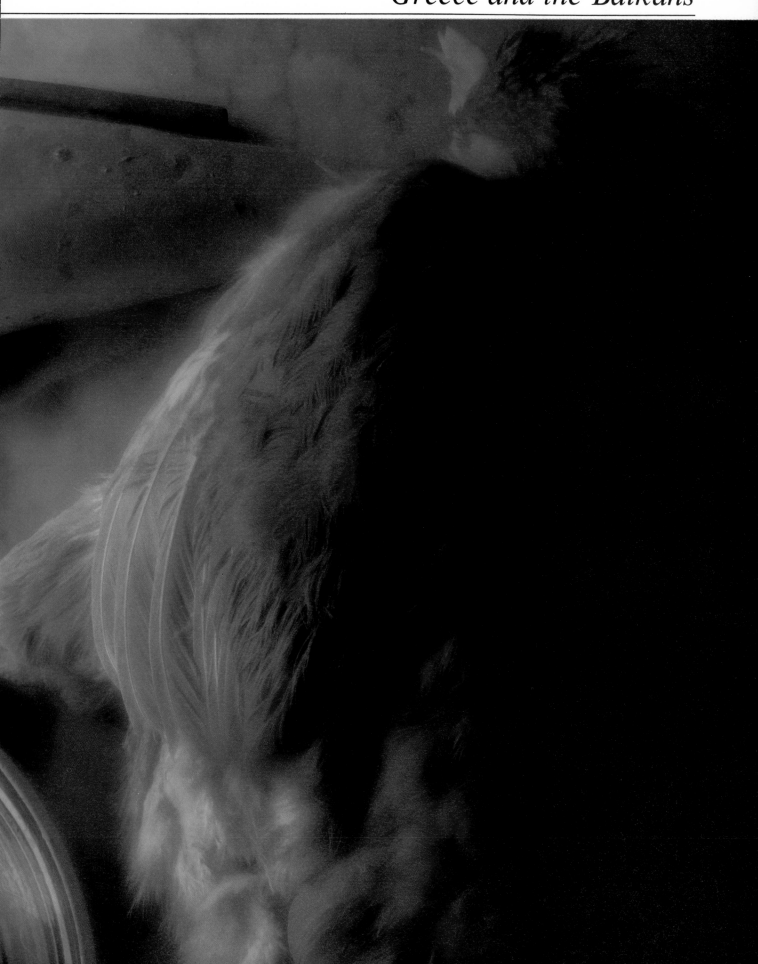

Vegetables

MUSAKA KARTOFI (BULGARIA)
Potato pie

Musaka is probably the best known of traditional Balkan dishes. There are many versions, but they usually consist of layers of meat and seasonal vegetables. This one is different, more of a Lenten dish, since it uses no meat. For a less rich dish, the potatoes can be boiled instead of fried.

Serves 4–5

2 lb potatoes
olive oil
2 medium-sized onions, coarsely chopped
3 tablespoons tomato purée
1 cup dry white wine
fine breadcrumbs
salt and pepper

Peel and thinly slice the potatoes. Heat some oil in a frying pan, add the potatoes and fry gently. Take from the pan with a slotted spoon as they begin to brown. Put aside, but keep hot. Drain off most of the oil, add the onions to the pan and fry lightly until soft but not brown. Add the tomato purée, the wine and enough breadcrumbs to make a thick but soft paste.

Rub a baking dish with oil and at the bottom arrange a layer of potatoes, sprinkle lightly with salt and pepper, and spread with a layer of the onion and tomato mixture; add another layer of potatoes and so on until all the ingredients are used up, with a final layer of onion and tomato at the top. Each layer should be sprinkled with salt and pepper. Sprinkle the top layer with about 1 tablespoon of warm water, no more, 1 tablespoon of olive oil and a thin layer of dry breadcrumbs. Bake in a moderate oven (350°F) for 30 to 40 minutes, and serve hot with a green salad and chilled yogurt.

SPARANGEL CU SMANTANA (RUMANIA)
Asparagus au gratin

This dish can be served as a main course or as a side dish with roast meat. Canned or frozen asparagus, or cauliflower, broken into flowerets, can be cooked in the same manner.

Serves 4

2 lb asparagus, green or white
juice of ¼ lemon
butter
1 pint sour cream
about 1¼ cups soft breadcrumbs
salt and pepper

Cut off all the hard stem from the asparagus, wash the spears thoroughly but carefully to avoid breaking them. Cook in lightly salted water flavored with lemon juice for 15 minutes. Drain, set aside but keep warm. Generously butter a casserole and cover the bottom with 2 or 3 tablespoons of sour cream, then sprinkle with breadcrumbs. Cover with a layer of asparagus, sprinkle lightly with salt and pepper, dot with butter, sprinkle with breadcrumbs and a few tablespoons of sour cream. Continue in this manner until the asparagus is finished. Sprinkle the top with breadcrumbs, dot with butter and bake in a hot oven (425°F) for 30 to 35 minutes.

GUIVECIU DE CIUPERCI (RUMANIA)
Ragoût of mushrooms

In Rumania this ragoût is served as a main dish, often with the cornmeal staple, *mamaliga*. All types of mushroom can be used and if scallions are not available, use coarsely chopped onion.

Serves 4

5 bacon slices, chopped
bunch of scallions, trimmed and chopped
chopped parsley
salt and pepper
2 lb whole mushrooms
1 tablespoon flour
1 cup sour cream or yogurt

Heat a shallow pan, add the bacon and fry it until the fat runs freely. Add the scallions, parsley, salt and pepper. Cover and simmer for a few minutes, then add the whole mushrooms, cover again and continue simmering for 10 minutes.

Beat the flour into the sour cream and gradually pour this mixture over the mushrooms. Stir gently and cook until the mushrooms are tender.

MELITZANES YEMISTES (GREECE)
Stuffed eggplants

It is essential to use large long eggplants to make this Greek dish. Serve as a main course with rice and a crisp green salad.

Serves 4

4 large long eggplants
2 tomatoes, skinned and chopped
1–2 cloves garlic, crushed
1–2 onions, finely chopped
finely chopped parsley
salt and pepper
3 tablespoons olive oil
chicken stock

Cut off and discard the stem end of the eggplants. Drop the eggplants into a large pan of water, cover and bring to a boil. Cook for 5 minutes, drain and pat dry. Cut 3 or 4 lengthwise slits in each eggplant.

Mix the tomatoes, garlic, onions, parsley, salt and pepper and push this mixture into the slits. Rub the eggplants with oil and place them in a baking pan. Add enough hot chicken stock to come about 1 in up the sides of the pan, bake in a moderate oven (350°F) for 1½ hours, or until tender. This dish may be cooked on top of the stove.

CIUPERCI CU VIN (RUMANIA)
Mushrooms cooked in red wine

This unusual, deep red dish is ideal for a cold buffet; it can also be served as a main course, alone or with creamed potatoes or rice, and a fresh green salad.

Serves 4

2 lb large firm mushrooms
lemon juice
olive oil for frying
1 onion, finely chopped
¼ cup red wine
salt and pepper
finely chopped parsley
black olives and radishes to garnish

Clean the mushrooms and slice fairly thinly. Sprinkle generously with lemon juice and leave for 15 minutes. Heat a frying pan and add enough olive oil to cook the mushrooms (it must be olive oil as the mushrooms are to be eaten cold and fat would congeal). Fry the onions gently until golden, add the mushrooms and continue cooking until they are soft. Add the wine, salt, pepper and parsley, and continue cooking for a few minutes longer. Stir gently once or twice. Cool, then turn into a serving dish. Leave until quite cold, and garnish just before serving.

Musaka kartofi *is a vegetarian version of musaka from Bulgaria.*

Greece and the Balkans

LAHANA DOLMATHES ME HIRINO KE SALTSA AVGOLEMONO (GREECE)
Stuffed cabbage leaves with egg and lemon sauce

In ancient times the Greeks as well as the Romans credited cabbage with the power to cure a hangover. Erasistratus, who founded a school of medicine in Samos in about 220 BC, went further and considered the cabbage a cure for paralysis. In those early days it was cooked with many spices, always including cumin, pepper and coriander.

Serves 6–8

¼ cup butter
1 onion, chopped
2 lb ground pork
⅔ cup long-grain rice
salt and pepper
a large pinch of aniseed or cinnamon
1 large head cabbage

Melt the butter and lightly fry the onion. Add the pork, rice, salt, pepper and aniseed and cook gently for 10 minutes. Remove from the heat.

Cook the cabbage in boiling salted water long enough to soften the leaves, about 5–10 minutes (the tenderness of cabbage leaves is variable). Drain and, when cool enough to handle, separate the leaves. Lay them flat on the table and trim down the thick center vein, to make the leaves easier to fold. Place a little of the meat stuffing on each leaf, more or less depending on the size of the leaf. Roll each leaf carefully into a neat package. Arrange these in a large shallow pan in neat rows, very close together. If a second layer of cabbage rolls is required, put 1 or 2 spare cabbage leaves on top of the first layer, then arrange the remaining rolls on top of this. Add water to cover and then put a plate on the rolls to prevent them moving. Cover the pan and cook gently for at least 1 hour. Remove the rolls carefully from the pan and use the liquid to make the sauce.

SALTSA AVGOLEMONO
Egg and lemon sauce

This is the national sauce of Greece. It can be served with almost any savory dish, as long as the dish has enough liquid in it from which to take the hot broth.

4 egg yolks
¼ cup lemon juice
1 cup hot broth

To make the egg and lemon sauce, beat the egg yolks over a very low heat until fluffy and light, then slowly add the lemon juice, beating all the time. Gradually add the hot broth. On no account must the sauce be allowed to boil, or it will curdle.

Instead of 4 yolks, 2 whole eggs may be used, but this will make a slightly thinner sauce.

KOUNOUPITHI YAHNI (GREECE)
Cauliflower cooked in tomato sauce

The tomato sauce for this popular Greek dish can be deliciously thickened with fresh or sour cream.

Serves 4

¼ cup olive oil
2 large onions, finely chopped
1–2 cloves garlic, crushed
1 cup tomato juice
1 cup water
salt and pepper
finely chopped parsley
1 large cauliflower, cut in flowerets

Heat the oil and fry the onions until they are golden brown, add the garlic and stir well. Combine the tomato juice with the water and add to the pan with the salt, pepper and parsley. Stir well and bring to a gentle boil. Add the cauliflower flowerets and cook until tender. Remove with a slotted spoon and serve hot. Serve the sauce separately, thickened with cream if you like.

FASSOLIA YIYANDES PLAKI (GREECE)
Ragoût of lima beans

Alexander the Great is said to have brought the bean to Greece from India when returning from his conquests; and beans have subsequently become more popular in Greece than they are in India.

Prepare 12 hours in advance.
Serves 4

1 lb dried lima beans
salt and pepper
1 lb onions, coarsely chopped
1 cup olive oil
1 lb tomatoes, skinned and finely chopped
2–3 cloves garlic, chopped
a little sugar
finely chopped mint or parsley

Soak the beans overnight and next morning cook them rapidly in unsalted water for 5 minutes. Drain, return them to the pan with fresh, salted water and cook until tender. Remove from the pan with a slotted spoon, drain well and put aside. Add the onions to the liquid in the pan and cook for 5 minutes, then drain off the liquid leaving the onions in the pan. Add ¼ cup of the olive oil and cook the onions in this until they begin to brown. Add the beans, tomatoes, the remaining oil, salt, pepper, garlic, sugar and mint or parsley and continue cooking slowly for another 30 minutes. Serve as a main dish with a green salad.

Traditional painted pottery displayed on the wall of a Greek kitchen

Fassolia yiyandes plaki and kounoupithi yahni: rich vegetable accompaniments to a taverna meal.

DOVLECEI CU BRINZA (RUMANIA)
Zucchini au gratin

Delicious by themselves, zucchini are further enhanced when cooked in layers with grated cheese, the Rumanian way. To vary the dish, add thinly sliced tomatoes to each layer.

Serves 6–8

2 lb zucchini
salt and pepper
butter
about ¼ cup fine breadcrumbs
¾ cup grated cheese
plenty of parsley, finely chopped
slightly sweetened heavy cream or sour cream

Wash and trim the zucchini, but leave them whole. Put in a pan with water to cover, add salt and cook over a moderate heat until just tender. Cool and cut lengthwise into halves. Generously rub a casserole with butter and sprinkle all around with breadcrumbs. Place a layer of zucchini, cut side up, at the bottom of the dish, sprinkle with grated cheese, dot generously with butter, then sprinkle with parsley, salt and pepper. Repeat this procedure until all the zucchini are used up. Cover the top layer of zucchini with grated cheese and breadcrumbs and bake in a moderate oven (350°F) for 30 minutes. Serve with slightly sweetened thick fresh cream, or sour cream.

KUNGULL ME COS (ALBANIA)
Zucchini fritters with a sour cream sauce

This rather special Albanian dish is in fact of Turkish origin – a reminder of the Ottoman Empire, to which Albania belonged for centuries. In Albania zucchini fritters are a popular main course.

Serves 4

1 lb firm zucchini
1 cup flour
salt
1 large egg
¼ cup water
oil for deep frying
1 pint sour cream or yogurt
1–2 cloves garlic, crushed

Cook the zucchini whole, without peeling, in boiling water for 10 minutes. Drain and cool. Mix together the flour and about ½ teaspoon of salt, and make a well in the center. Beat the egg with the water and pour this into the well. Mix thoroughly, then beat until the mixture is smooth.

Heat the oil. Peel and cut the zucchini into medium-thick rounds, or, if they are very small, slice them lengthwise. Dip the slices in the batter and deep fry in the oil until they are golden brown. Drain on paper towels and keep warm.

Beat the sour cream or yogurt, add salt and garlic and spread this sauce over the fritters just before serving.

Yugoslavian lake fishermen from Bosnia

Desserts

ZHIDZHI-BIDZHI (BULGARIA)
Rose-water cream pudding

Bulgaria is world famous for its roses and rose essence, from which perfumes are made. The road winding down from the Rhodope mountains is unforgettable, with the first glimpse of the shimmering pale pink rose valleys below, and the heavy scent of roses carried on the wind. The best time to visit the valleys is in May, for by June the petals have already been picked and piled into sacks ready to be taken to the Kazanlŭk distilleries, where they are processed.

Roses are also used to make rose-water for flavoring rice and cornstarch puddings, and rose-petal jam, and this traditional cream pudding is served throughout the Balkans.

Serves 4–6

¾ cup cornstarch
1 cup water
1 quart milk
about 3 tablespoons sugar
2–3 tablespoons rose-water
ground almonds

Mix the cornstarch with the water in a large mixing bowl. Bring the milk to a boil. Pour the milk into the cornstarch, stirring all the while. Add at least 3 tablespoons sugar – Balkan puddings are usually very sweet. When the cornstarch cream is thick, remove it from the heat and beat until it is cool. Pour the rose-water into a shallow plain mold or bowl and swirl it round and round. Sprinkle generously with ground almonds. Add the cornstarch cream, sprinkle lightly with sugar to prevent a skin forming, and chill. Turn out to serve, either alone or with rose-petal jam.

SALAMI (YUGOSLAVIA)
Walnut and chocolate roll

This sweet roll looks uncommonly like a salami and is served with morning coffee. It is soft, with the texture of fudge and, apart from being extremely good to eat, is very simple to prepare. The given quantity makes a salami about 12 inches long.

Serves 4

1 cup cold water
¾ cup sugar
3 cups finely ground walnuts
juice of 1 lemon
¾ cup unsweetened chocolate powder or cocoa
confectioners' sugar, sifted

Mix the cold water with the sugar and cook to a thickish syrup. Add the walnuts, lemon juice and chocolate powder and cook this mixture until it forms a thick mass, stirring all the while. Sprinkle a pastry board generously with confectioners' sugar and turn the walnut mixture on to it. Roll into a long sausage shape. Wrap it in a clean napkin or thick paper towels and keep it in a cold place until it has hardened. Serve cut into thin slices which will look like slices of a very dark salami.

Other nuts may be used instead of walnuts, such as almonds or hazelnuts, and quite often chopped dried fruits are added. The salami will keep well for quite a long time in a refrigerator.

The delicate flavor of rose-water permeates this sweet cream pudding from Bulgaria.

OMLETTE CU FRAGI (RUMANIA)
Strawberry soufflé omelette

If you use wild strawberries for this light, summer recipe, marinate them for several hours beforehand in a dry white wine, or in sugar and kirsch. If using garden strawberries, cut them in half after hulling, and marinate them in the same manner. Rum or brandy may be used if preferred.

Serves 4

butter for greasing
fine cake crumbs
dry white wine or kirsch
about ½ lb strawberries,
  preferably wild
4 egg yolks
⅓ cup vanilla-flavored
  sugar
salt
6 egg whites

Before making the omelette mixture, prepare the baking dish. This should be oval, but a round one will do. Rub it with butter, sprinkle lightly with cake crumbs and then add the marinated strawberries, thoroughly drained. Put aside.

Mix the egg yolks with the sugar and a pinch of salt. Beat the mixture thoroughly until it becomes a pale lemon color and very thick. Beat the egg whites until stiff but not dry and gently fold into the egg yolks, using a metal spoon. Pour this mixture over the strawberries and shape with a spatula into a smooth high mound with a deep gash cut in the top. Cook for about 10 minutes in a moderate oven (350°F), until golden brown.

Asparagus tips can also be cooked in this manner, but without sugar, and with breadcrumbs instead of cake crumbs.

Forget philosophy. Vodka is for drinking, sturgeon for eating, women for visiting . . .

Chekhov 'The Breakdown' (1860-1904)

The rich farmland of Poland

The Russian Empire grew over the centuries from its small beginnings in Eastern Europe, to a massive nation that stretched from Poland to the Pacific, from the Arctic to the Caucasus. In the nineteenth century it included Finland, Estonia, Latvia and Lithuania, the Duchy of Warsaw, Eastern Poland, Bessarabia and parts of Armenia. Today the USSR covers one-sixth of the total land surface of the earth, over eight million square miles, almost three times the size of the USA, of which nearly three-quarters is in Asia.

While the northern arctic territories have similarities with Canada, the south of Russia stretches over steppes and hot Asian deserts. The terrain includes everything from tundra to sub-tropical forests, and the climate ranges from freezing in the north, to warm in the Crimea where palm trees and magnolias fringe the coast, to sub-tropical in the Caucasus where there are vineyards, citrus fruits, tea and tobacco plantations. Russian cuisine reflects this immense variety, and every region has its own ingredients and cooking methods.

Some of Russia's regional delicacies were refined by French chefs who came to work in the kitchens of Russian households in the eighteenth century. These chefs also enriched their own repertoires and took back with them to France such splendid inventions as the *coulibiac*, the Russian way with caviar and above all a variety of Russian *zakuski*.

Russia and Poland

Zakuski are the mixture of assorted dainty morsels and very substantial dishes with which a Russian meal begins. (There is no English word to translate the name, the nearest equivalent being the French hors d'oeuvre.) *Zakuski* are eaten with aperitifs, which in Russia means vodka, chilled so that the bottle 'sheds a tear' on being brought to the table. Russians drink it, in small gulp-size glasses, in one go, and have a bite of food – a *zakuska* – immediately afterwards.

Russian classical literature – Leskov, Tolstoy, Turgenev, Chekhov – abounds in splendid accounts of lavish *zakuski*: they were often so abundant that a whole room was set aside to display them. Only after the superb selection of delicacies had been properly sampled would the hostess consider leading her guests to the dining table.

The range of *zakuski* – they can be cold or hot – is endless, from a spoonful of caviar to sterlet in aspic, from a slice of herring to a whole roast suckling pig stuffed with mushrooms. But the greatest *zakuska* of all is caviar. Outside Russia, caviar has long been considered a luxury and an acquired taste. Not so in Russia. Here it is called *ikra*, which simply means 'roe'; and to this day a caviar sandwich can be enjoyed in most bars, a truck drivers' stop, or a *zabegalovka*, the kind of dive you sneak into for a quick vodka.

In the days before refrigeration and the development of modern processing methods, caviar was especially cheap, somewhat like oysters in Pepys' England. In small fishing villages along the Volga, near Astrakhan, caviar was used not only as food: the day's catch was sealed in jars on the spot and any leftover caviar was slapped on the roofs of the cottages – it was said to make perfect waterproofing.

The Russians are not only famous for their *zakuski*: they and the Poles make particularly good soups based on meat or fish stocks simmered gently for many hours. In the countryside these soups are often so substantial that they form a meal in themselves. They are often accompanied by side dishes such as the delicious meat-filled *pirozhki*, the cheese-filled *vatrushki* – or the more substantial 'crêpe pie' – *blinchaty pirog*. *Kasha*, a buckwheat oatmeal often served as a side dish, is also eaten with soup. It has an agreeable texture, an interesting nutty flavor, and is full of protein.

The Russians make delicious fish dishes. The USSR has the longest coastline of any country: two-thirds of its borders are defined by water. Both the seas and the great rivers provide an abundance of seafood and fish, from Kamchatka crab, exported to all parts of the world, to the famous caviar-yielding sturgeon.

In Russia, as elsewhere, the sturgeon is highly prized for its flesh as well as its roe. There are many different fish in the sturgeon family, but the real caviar comes only from the *osetr*, *sevryuga* and *beluga*. The flesh of the *osetr* is excellent for steaming, boiling and broiling; the *sevryuga* is smaller and more delicate; the *beluga*, which provides the very best caviar of all, is the biggest of the three: it reaches from five to six yards in length and can be over two thousand pounds in weight.

Sturgeon are found in the Caspian, Azov and Black seas as well as many rivers, particularly the Volga, the longest river in Europe. Red caviar is the roe of various members of the salmon family, such as the *keta* and the *gorbusha*. Along

A solitary traveler through Russia's vast expanses

the Volga the local cooks make excellent pies and *coulibiacs* using sturgeon and caviar. They also make a superb salmon *ukha* which is the Volga boatmen's answer to the famous French *bouillabaisse*.

Each region of Russia has its favorite meat, from reindeer in the cold tundra to camel in the hot desert, while dense forests all over the land abound in every kind of furred and feathered game. Russian cooks also have a genius for supplementing their diet with vegetables. In the north, root vegetables and cabbage are the favorites. Russians know how to make many magnificent cabbage dishes including *coulibiacs* and *pirozhki*. However, no one in Russia has ever come across the concoction of overcooked vegetables bound together with a synthetic mayonnaise which for some reason is called 'Russian salad' in the West. A salad of cooked vegetables dressed with mayonnaise on Russian menus is often described as 'vinaigrette'.

Russian desserts reflect the contrasts in her climate: cherries, cranberries, grapes, pomegranates, strawberries, orange blossom, walnuts and poppy seeds are used to flavor creams, mousses and cakes. Ice cream is popular all year round: but many desserts, like Easter *paskha* and *kulich*, mark religious festivals and holidays.

The recipes given in this chapter come from many of the regions of the former Russian Empire. Poland has been included since most of it fell within the Empire and each of the Romanovs from the time of Alexander I was styled 'Emperor of all the Russias, King of Poland, Prince of Finland etc'. But Polish cooking really deserves a chapter of its own.

The Poles are hearty but discriminating eaters. Like most

Russia and Poland

Slavs, they like food unashamedly and are clever at producing delicious dishes from simple and inexpensive ingredients. They can turn a piece of boiled fish into a dish to be proud of by dressing it with nicely seasoned melted butter mixed with chopped hard-cooked egg. The Poles have adopted several Russian dishes, notably *borshch* which is now their national soup, and transformed them to their liking. Polish preserves, whether jams or pickles, are second to none, as are Polish mushrooms; and *bigos* is a unique dish that makes a satisfying meal in itself.

Each of the national minorities of the Empire (now known as Union republics) still has its own dishes, reflecting local tastes and cooking methods.

In the south the Central Asiatic peoples are largely the descendants of nomadic tribes who learned to cook without the benefit of a kitchen. Here barbecuing has always been the favorite cooking method, and Uzbekistan and Azerbaijan in particular are famous for their spicy barbecued dishes and great variety of breads.

Nomadic life is responsible not only for the tradition of barbecuing but also for the popularity of Russian adaptations of the Chinese dumpling. These little envelopes of dough with meat were easy to carry and no more trouble to cook than boiling water. In Siberia they are called *pelmeni* and are boiled and served in soup; in the south they are steamed, as in China, and called *manty*, from the Chinese *mantou*.

The landscape of Trans-caucasia (Armenia, Georgia and Azerbaijan) ranges from mountains and fertile valleys to marshes and arid steppe-lands. It is ideal for raising sheep, horses and cattle and also for cultivating orchards and vineyards. The Georgians marinate their meat in red wine for *shashlyk* and other dishes. They love sauces made with walnuts, almonds and pistachio nuts, and add barberries and pomegranate juice to many fish and meat dishes. Freshly made natural yogurt is an important part of their diet.

The area known as Central Asia includes Kazakhstan, Kirgizia, Tadzhikistan, Uzbekistan, and Turkmenistan. It stretches from the Caspian to the frontier of China and is one long shallow basin, consisting mainly of desert and semi-desert, with very little water and marked extremes of temperature. The area has always been unsettled, with nomadic peoples pushing from the north and northeast and the more settled civilizations of the south attempting to extend their area of control northward.

The nomadic, or 'black water' people – the Kirgiz, Turkmen and Kazakhs – used to depend on wells and underground springs for their water. From March to October their diet consisted almost entirely of milk and its derivatives, and green tea. In the autumn, when the animals were slaughtered, the people would eat meat: mainly sheep but also some camel and goat, either roasted or boiled. The rich might also eat smoked horsemeat sausage. They ate no bread or any other cereal food, no fruit and almost no vegetables. In contrast the 'white water' people lived in settled villages by the rivers and oases. They raised animals and farmed the land. Their diet included meat, fruit and vegetables, and a great deal of bread. The people of this area, as befits the descendants of herdsmen, know all there is to know about sheep, and use every bit of the animal to delicious advantage. The Uzbeks in particular are famed for their cooking, which resembles that of Turkey.

Turkish influence can also be seen in the cooking of Moldavia, which borders on Rumania. It was part of the Ottoman Empire for three centuries until captured by Russia in the war of 1806–1812. It has a mild climate, and its two large rivers, the Dniester and the Prut, provide water to irrigate the good black soil. Vegetables, fruits – including excellent wine grapes – and cereals, especially maize, grow here in profusion. Moldavian cooks make good use of their vegetables, and many of their most delicious dishes include eggplants, tomatoes, red peppers and corn. They use maize to make a very good Moldavian version of *polenta*.

The Ukraine, a vast flat region to the east of Poland, extending south to the Black Sea, is the center of Russian wheat production. In the south, in the sunny climate of the Crimea, excellent wine is produced. Ukrainian cooks have always been famous for delicious and copious dishes: their *borshch* is more substantial than the Russian or Polish versions, and pork sausages similar to frankfurters are often added to it. Ukrainian chicken à la Kiev has been the cause of many arguments. Russians say it was their invention, because they claim Kiev used to belong to Russia; Poles claim it because in the sixteenth century the Ukraine belonged to Poland; and naturally Kievans say that they invented it.

The rulers of Russia and Poland have disputed ownership of Byelorussia ever since the Middle Ages. In this country of rolling hills and vast forests there are mild, damp winters and cool, rainy summers: altogether, the perfect climate for growing mushrooms, the local favorite. The soil here is mainly peat – which, combined with the damp climate, makes Byelorussia ideal for growing potatoes; and the area is rich in delicious potato dishes. Pork is the local meat; the dense forests provide excellent foraging ground for pigs, and harbor the rare wild pig and boar.

Karelia and the Baltic States – Estonia, Latvia and Lithuania – have always been strongly influenced by their Scandinavian neighbors. Karelia, which borders on Finland, has a comparatively cold climate; its main cereal crop is rye, which does not need as much continuous warmth as wheat, and rye flour is used to make the excellent Karelian pies. Forests cover a large part of the country, providing the many varieties of berries which local cooks use so imaginatively, and sheltering the deer whose meat is a local specialty.

Estonia, Latvia and Lithuania were formerly ruled by Germany, then Sweden, and became part of the Russian Empire at the beginning of the eighteenth century. The large estates and peasant smallholdings in the area concentrated on dairy farming. Estonians have a variety of milk soups which are served with interesting garnishes. The sea has always been a major factor in Latvian life, and Latvian, like Scandinavian, cooks are extremely versatile with herrings, which are caught in droves along the coast. Many pigs are raised here, and the local version of beef Stroganov uses pork.

This brief survey has covered only some of the areas of the vast former Russian Empire, whose cuisine is as diverse and contradictory as its components. The following recipes will enable you to try just some of the many excellent regional dishes it has to offer.

Blini with caviar: *the perfect start to a Russian meal*

Hors d'oeuvre

IKRA (RUSSIA)
Caviar

Caviar – the roe of the sturgeon – is the queen of hors d'oeuvre. As the quantities which you can afford are usually minute, it is as well to make the best of its presentation. Whether pressed or soft, caviar should be served cold, garnished with lemon sections and parsley, and butter should be served separately to be spread on *blini* or bread.

Although *blini* are traditionally considered the best foundation for caviar, there are people who maintain that the only way to eat black caviar is with a spoon; in more recent times a distinguished weight-conscious Russian poet started a fashion in Moscow of eating it on cucumber slices.

Red caviar is best served on thin slices of rye bread, with fresh unsalted butter and finely chopped scallions passed separately.

BLINI S IKROI (RUSSIA)
Blini with caviar

These small light pancakes are among the best of Russian inventions and are a time-honored way of serving red or black caviar. They are also delicious served with thin slices of smoked salmon or other smoked fish – even with kippers.

Makes about 12 blini

Blini
1 cake of compressed
  yeast
1 cup lukewarm water
1 cup lukewarm milk
2 cups buckwheat flour
2 eggs, separated
¼ teaspoon salt
1 teaspoon sugar
1 tablespoon melted butter

Filling
caviar
¼ cup melted butter
1 cup sour cream
scallions, chopped
  (for red caviar)

Alternative fillings
¼ lb smoked salmon
or 2 plump kippers, boned
and 2 hard-cooked eggs

In a large mixing bowl dissolve the yeast in the water and ½ cup warm milk. Add half the flour and mix well. Cover with a cloth and leave in a warm place for 2–3 hours.

Beat the egg yolks with salt and sugar and beat in the rest of the milk. Add the melted butter and mix again. Add this to the yeast mixture and stir thoroughly. Incorporate the rest of the flour.

Beat the whites until stiff and fold them into the batter. Cover and allow to stand undisturbed for 45–50 minutes. The final batter should have the consistency of thick cream.

It is important to make all the *blini* an equal size, not more than 4 in in diameter. Lightly grease and heat the pan. Drop in some batter and brown the *blini* on both sides. Stack the cooked ones on a plate and keep warm until all the batter is used up. Serve the *blini* with caviar (or salmon or kipper), the melted butter and the sour cream in separate dishes. If using red caviar sprinkle with scallions. If using kipper, add the chopped hard-cooked eggs to the butter.

EKLERI S IKROI (RUSSIA)
Caviar éclairs

Another delicious way of serving caviar. Fill any leftover pastry with cream cheese, or keep it for dessert and add a sweet filling.

Makes about 40 small éclairs

Choux pastry
1 cup water
a pinch of salt
½ teaspoon sugar
½ cup butter
1 cup flour, sifted
3–4 eggs (or 2–3 eggs and 2 tablespoons milk or cream)

Filling
1 oz caviar
2 tablespoons heavy cream
¼ cup softened butter
2 tablespoons whipped cream
a few tablespoons fish fumet (p. 240)

Pour the water into a large saucepan with a thick bottom. Sprinkle in the salt and sugar, add the butter in small pieces, and bring to a boil. Remove from heat and add the flour all at once. Mix well. Cook, stirring with a wooden spoon, until the mixture comes away from the sides of the pan.

Remove from the heat and, stirring constantly, add the eggs one by one. Then add the milk or cream, if used. (The number of eggs used depends on their size.) The amount of milk indicated would replace 1 egg and make a smoother mixture. Beat the mixture vigorously until it is very light, or use an electric mixer.

Pipe about 40 very small éclairs onto a baking sheet and bake in a hot oven (400°F) for 35 minutes until well risen and crisp. Leave until quite cold.

Prepare the filling by mixing the caviar with the heavy cream and butter. Rub through a strainer and incorporate the whipped cream. Fill the éclair shells with the caviar mixture. Brush each with a little melted fish fumet to give a nice gloss. If you have no fumet, dissolve a pinch of unflavored gelatin in ordinary fish stock. Serve chilled.

RUTLETY SO SHPINATOM PO-IMERETINSKI (IMERETIA)
Spinach rolls

In the Caucasus Imeretian white cheese from goats' milk is used for this dish. Good substitutes would be either the Turkish *beyaz peynir* or the Greek *feta*. Soak these salted cheeses in water before use, to rinse away excess salt.

Serves 4

Pastry
2½ cups flour
¼ teaspoon salt
5–6 tablespoons water
½ cup butter

Filling
2 tablespoons butter
2 medium-sized onions, chopped
2 tablespoons chopped parsley
1 lb spinach, freshly cooked, chopped and squeezed dry
½ lb cheese, crumbled
3–4 beaten eggs
salt and pepper

Sift the flour into a mixing bowl, season with salt and, adding the cold water little by little, work into a pliable, non-sticky dough. Knead the dough, cover with a cloth and leave for 25–30 minutes.

Melt the butter. Divide the dough into 4 pieces and shape them into balls. Roll out each piece very thinly, brush each with butter and fold in half. Press the edges together and roll out the pieces again. Brush again with butter, fold each four times, seal the edges and leave to rest for 15 minutes.

Melt the 2 tablespoons butter and gently fry the onions until transparent. Add the parsley and spinach and cook, stirring, for 3–4 minutes. Add the cheese and eggs; season to taste with salt and freshly ground pepper. Remove from heat and leave to cool, but do not chill.

Roll out the 4 pastries very thinly, brush each with melted butter and put a quarter of the spinach mixture on each. Roll up each sheet like a jelly roll. Place them on a lightly greased baking sheet and brush with butter. Bake for 30 minutes in a preheated 400°F oven. Serve hot.

Soups

KASHA (RUSSIA)

Kasha is made from buckwheat, the staple of the northern provinces. It is served as a side dish with soups, and often replaces rice or potatoes with a main dish.

The amount of butter added may be increased ad lib. The grains absorb it, and the Russian equivalent of 'you can't have too much of a good thing' is 'you can't spoil *kasha* with too much butter.'

Serves 6–8

1 lb buckwheat
1 teaspoon salt
¼ cup butter
water

Sort the buckwheat and pick out any black grains – these husked ones are perfectly wholesome but are unsightly. Roast the buckwheat in an ungreased skillet, stirring so they do not burn, until the grains are a pale golden color.

Put in a baking dish, season with salt, stir in the butter and pour in enough boiling water to cover. Bake in a slow oven (275°F) for 2½–3 hours.

BORSHCH (RUSSIA AND POLAND)

This substantial soup is cooked in various ways all over Russia and Poland. The Polish version is often a clear beet soup which can be served hot or cold with a spoonful of sour cream in each bowl. Borshch can be served with *pirozhki*, *vatrushki*, rolled pancakes or *kasha*.

Serves 8

1½ lb beef stew meat
2½ quarts beef stock
3–4 small beets
1 head white cabbage, shredded
2 carrots, cut into 'matchstick' strips
1 parsnip, cut into 'matchstick' strips
2 celery stalks
1 large onion, diced
½ lb tomatoes, skinned and strained
1 tablespoon red wine vinegar
1 tablespoon sugar
1–2 bay leaves
1½ teaspoons salt
½ teaspoon black pepper
4–5 allspice berries
1 tablespoon lemon juice
1 tablespoon dill
1 tablespoon chopped parsley
sour cream

Wash and dry the meat and trim off surplus fat. Cut into pieces and put in a saucepan with stock. Bring to a boil, skim, reduce heat, cover and simmer for 45 minutes.

Reserve 1 beet and cut the rest into 'matchsticks'. Add all the chopped vegetables, apart from the reserved beet and the tomatoes, to the stock and continue to simmer for 20–25 minutes. Add the tomatoes, vinegar, sugar, bay leaves, salt, pepper and allspice. Cook gently for 15 minutes.

To achieve the characteristic rich color of *borshch*, grate the reserved beet finely. Put in a small pan with 1 cup of the stock, simmer for 5 minutes and strain the liquid into the *borshch*.

Check the seasoning, sharpen with lemon juice, sprinkle with dill and parsley. Serve the sour cream separately; each person adds some to his bowl.

SIBIRSKIYE PELMENI (SIBERIA)
Noodle dumplings with meat filling

This Siberian version of Chinese *wun tun* can be prepared days in advance and kept in the freezer. Siberians say that *pelmeni* taste better as a result of such freezing. It is a recognized custom among Siberian housewives to keep several hundred *pelmeni* in their cold cellars, just in case an unexpected crowd of hungry guests drops in. Refrigeration is no problem; those who have no cellars hang pillowcases full of *pelmeni* outside their windows and the temperature does the rest. The filling can be meat, cheese or vegetables.

Serves 4

*1 lb lean ground beef
(or a mixture of beef and
lean pork)
1 onion, finely chopped
salt and pepper
2–3 tablespoons iced
water
noodle paste (p. 32)
1½ quarts beef stock
dill or parsley garnish*

Mix the ground beef with the onion and season to taste. Add the iced water and mix well.

Roll out the noodle paste very thinly, cut out small circles with a cookie cutter about 6 in in diameter and put a little meat filling on each circle of pastry. Crimp up the pastry edges, forming rather a plump semi-circle, and join the tapering ends together, pinching hard to make them stick. Continue until all the *pelmeni* are done, putting them on a lightly floured board, without allowing them to touch.

Drop them a few at a time into boiling stock, allowing boiling to be re-established before adding any more. Simmer gently for 10 minutes or until the *pelmeni* float up to the surface. Serve in the soup, with a sprinkling of chopped dill or parsley. Siberians also like their *pelmeni* served separately with a dressing of 2 teaspoons dry mustard diluted with 3–4 tablespoons of wine vinegar.

Leftover boiled *pelmeni* are delicious well drained and fried in a little butter.

Borshch, with pirozhki *and* vatrushki *– a meal in itself*

VATRUSHKI (RUSSIA AND POLAND)
Cream cheese tartlets

There tartlets, which can have a savory or sweet filling, have always been popular in the Ukraine and Russia. They are so appetizing and easy to eat that, according to Gogol, they 'leap into one's mouth of their own accord'. They can be served with *borshch*, or spinach and sorrel soup, and any left over can be served cold with salad.

Serves 4

*Pastry
2⅓ cups flour
⅓ cup butter or margarine
iced water
salt*

*Filling
1 lb cream cheese
3 tablespoons sour cream
salt
freshly ground pepper
1 teaspoon sugar
2 eggs
a little extra butter*

Sift the flour into a bowl and add a pinch of salt. Cut the butter into small pieces and rub into the flour with fingertips, until the mixture looks like breadcrumbs. Add enough iced water to make a fairly stiff dough. Put it onto a lightly floured board. Knead until smooth, but avoid overworking it.

To make the cream cheese filling, combine the cream cheese and sour cream and season with salt and pepper. Add the sugar and eggs and mix well. Preheat the oven to 375°F. Roll out the pastry and use to line shallow muffin tins. Spoon the filling into the tartlets, dot each with a pat of butter and bake for 20–25 minutes.

PIROZHKI (RUSSIA)
Pies

Pirozhki are a classic accompaniment to many Russian soups and are a must with *borshch*. A good broth and some *pirozhki* can be substantial enough for a main course. They are delicious, especially made with puff pastry.

The fillings can be various: chicken, chicken livers, rice and mushrooms, salmon, veal, chopped hard-cooked eggs, scallions, and many others.

If time is no object – and making *pirozhki* can be a very creative and relaxing pastime – use puff pastry (see page 30). Otherwise make the quick dough given here.

Serves 4

*Beef filling
2 tablespoons butter
1 small onion, finely
chopped
¼ lb lean ground beef
2 tablespoons chopped
mushrooms
1–2 hard-cooked eggs,
chopped
¼ cup stock or water
salt and pepper
½ tablespoon chopped dill
or parsley*

*Quick dough
2⅓ cups self-rising flour,
sifted
¼ teaspoon salt
2 eggs
¼ cup oil
2–3 tablespoons water
1 egg white
1 egg for glazing*

To prepare the filling, melt the butter and fry the onion in it until soft. Add the beef and brown. Add the mushrooms and cook together for 5 minutes, stirring to prevent sticking, adding more fat if necessary.

Add the hard-cooked eggs, stock, seasoning and dill or parsley. Cook, stirring, for 1–2 minutes, remove from the heat and leave to cool completely.

To make the quick dough put the flour into a mixing bowl and sprinkle in the salt. Make a well in the middle, add the eggs, oil and water. Mix well, then knead and roll to a thickness of ¼ in. Cut into circles. Put a spoonful of cold filling on each circle of dough, fold over into semi-circles and pinch the edges together, using egg white to seal them. Beat the egg with salt and brush the *pirozhki* with this to give a beautiful glaze.

Place on a baking sheet and refrigerate for 30 minutes. Preheat the oven to 375–400°F and bake until golden.

SUP IZ VISHNI (UKRAINE)
Cherry soup

The Ukraine, with its hot summers and rich 'black earth', produces an abundance of fruit. So-called 'porch soups', based on all kinds of fruit and berries, are very popular. The soups may be served hot with zwieback or cold topped with sour cream.

Serves 4

*1 lb pitted sweet
  cherries*
2 cups water
¼ stick cinnamon
1 lemon, thinly sliced
¼ cup sugar (or to taste)
¼ cup sweet white wine
1 tablespoon cornstarch
zwieback or sour cream

Put half the cherries in a pan with the water. Bring to a boil and simmer until just tender. Strain into another pan, rubbing the cherry flesh through the strainer, or purée it in a blender.

Return to the heat. Add the cinnamon, lemon and remaining cherries. Simmer for 3–4 minutes. Add the sugar and all but 2 tablespoons of the wine. Simmer, stirring, until the sugar is dissolved.

Dissolve the cornstarch in the remaining wine and stir this into the soup. As soon as the soup thickens, remove from heat and serve with zwieback or sour cream.

UKHA S SYOMGOI I SHAMPANSKIM (RUSSIA)
Salmon and champagne soup

Ukha is a Russian fish soup. This particularly luxurious one is for special festive occasions. *Ukha* served together with fish *coulibiac* makes a splendid main course. Dry white wine may be substituted for champagne.

Serves 4

1 quart good light stock
2 egg whites
*1 tablespoon chopped
  tarragon and chervil*
salt and pepper
4 small salmon steaks
dill or scallions
1 cup champagne
*1 lemon, peeled and thinly
  sliced*

To clarify the stock, which should be a good fish stock strengthened with fumet (p. 240), or a light chicken stock, first warm it gently until lukewarm.

Then put the egg whites in a pan, add the tarragon and chervil and beat to mix. Pour on the stock and bring to a boil, beating all the time. As soon as boiling is established, turn down heat and simmer very gently for 30 minutes. Season to taste. Strain through a dampened napkin. The stock should now be clear.

Twenty minutes before serving, bring the stock to a boil, put in the salmon steaks, lower the heat and poach for 15 minutes. Carefully remove the fish and put in a heated soup tureen. Sprinkle with the dill or scallions and keep warm.

In a separate saucepan, heat the champagne almost to boiling point and add to the soup. Pour the soup over the salmon, put a lemon slice in each bowl and serve at once.

A prosperous peasant home, the source of traditional Polish cuisine

KAVKAZSKIY SUP (CAUCASUS)
Yogurt soup

This is reputed in the Caucasus to be a health-giving summer soup. It is certainly a refreshing one and has the added advantage that it requires no cooking.

Serves 4

3 cups peeled diced
  cucumber
salt
1 clove of garlic
1 tablespoon vinegar
1 pint plain yogurt
1 tablespoon olive oil
1–2 tablespoons chopped
  mint

Put the cucumber in a dish, sprinkle with salt and leave for 30 minutes.

Slice the garlic and with it rub the inside of a bowl large enough to take all the ingredients. Sprinkle in the vinegar and rinse the bowl with it. Spoon the yogurt into this vinegar and garlic-flavored bowl and stir to thin it, adding 2–3 tablespoons of water, if necessary.

Drain the cucumber, add to the yogurt, mix and chill. Stir in the olive oil, a few drops at a time. Chill, sprinkle with the mint and serve.

SUP IZ SHCHAVELIA I SHPINATA (RUSSIA AND POLAND)
Sorrel and spinach soup

This light summer soup is popular in the Baltic countries, in Russia, Poland, the Ukraine and Rumania. Its base can be meat or chicken stock, or a mixture of milk and water.

Serves 4–6

2 tablespoons butter
¼ lb sorrel, chopped
¼ lb spinach, chopped
6 tablespoons chopped
  parsley
1 quart stock or water
1–2 potatoes, peeled and
  diced
salt and pepper
a pinch of sugar
1 cup milk
1–2 egg yolks
1–2 tablespoons lemon
  juice
4 hard-cooked eggs
¼ cup sour cream

Melt the butter in a pan large enough to take all the ingredients. Add the sorrel, spinach and parsley, and cook on low heat, stirring, for 5 minutes. Add the stock or water, then the potatoes and season to taste with salt and pepper. Add the sugar, bring to a boil and cover. Reduce heat and simmer for 25 minutes. Drain, keeping the liquid.

Rub the sorrel, spinach and potatoes through the strainer, or put in a blender, with half the milk, to make a smooth purée. Reheat the stock, add the purée and simmer for a few minutes to heat through.

Dilute the egg yolks with the remaining milk and stir into the soup. Reheat the soup without allowing it to boil; check the seasoning. Remove from the heat, sharpen with lemon juice to taste and serve with a hard-cooked egg in each bowl and a tablespoon of sour cream on top.

Pass *vatrushki* separately.

KRUPNIK (POLAND)
Barley soup

The custom of serving soups is very popular in Poland. This barley soup is so substantial that it is frequently served as a meal in itself.

Serves 6–8

¼ cup pearl barley
1½ quarts stock
2 tablespoons oil
2 onions, sliced
2 carrots, diced
1 parsnip, diced
3 celery stalks, diced
2–3 potatoes, diced
¼ cup sliced fresh
  mushrooms (or 7–8
  dried ones)
1 bay leaf
salt and pepper
chopped dill

Soak the barley in water overnight. Drain and simmer in 1 pint stock for 1½ hours.

In a large pan heat the oil and lightly fry the onions. Add the barley and its liquid, the rest of the stock and the carrots, parsnip, celery, potatoes, mushrooms and bay leaf. Cover and simmer for 30 minutes. Season to taste with salt and pepper. Serve garnished with the dill. If fresh dill is not available, use parsley.

The forestland of Poland, rich in mushrooms and game

ARMIANSKIY SUP IZ MINDALIA (ARMENIA)
Almond soup

Nuts abound in the Caucasus and form a basis for many dishes, such as this smooth, delicate soup. The stock can be made a day in advance and the cooked veal, egg whites and vegetables can be served cold, dressed with mayonnaise.

Serves 6–8

1¼ lb boneless lean veal
1½ quarts cold water
1 medium-sized onion,
  chopped
1–2 celery stalks,
  shredded
1 bay leaf
4–5 white peppercorns
1–1½ teaspoons salt
rind and juice of
  1 lemon
4 hard-cooked eggs
2 cups ground almonds
4–5 bitter almonds,
  blanched and ground
a pinch of verbena salt

Put the veal in a saucepan. Add the water, bring to a boil and skim. Cover and simmer for 1 hour.

Add the onion and celery to the stock, together with the bay leaf, peppercorns and salt. Cook for 1½ hours. Chop the lemon rind finely. Add half of it and all the lemon juice to the stock. Continue to simmer for another hour. Strain the stock, leave until cold, then remove all surface fat.

Halve the hard-cooked eggs and remove the yolks. Keep the whites for another dish, as stuffing or garnish. Combine the yolks, ground almonds, verbena salt and remaining lemon rind and pound to a paste in a mortar or put through a blender. Dilute with 1 cup of stock, adding it a little at a time.

Bring the rest of the stock to a boil. Add the almond mixture, mix thoroughly, simmer for 10 minutes and serve.

Fish

KAVKAZSKAYA OZERNAYA FOREL (CAUCASUS)

Mountain lake trout

Adding prunes to trout the Caucasian way makes an interesting variation. The soaking time for prunes depends entirely on their quality. If the prunes are plump and soft enough to eat uncooked, they will need only twenty to thirty minutes' soaking. If very dry and hard, they may have to be soaked for several hours or even overnight.

Serves 4

- *½ cup prunes*
- *4 trout*
- *salt and pepper*
- *¾ cup oil*
- *¼ cup chopped parsley*
- *1 clove of garlic, crushed*
- *3 tablespoons wine vinegar*
- *4 eggs, beaten*
- *1 tablespoon lemon juice*
- *lemon quarters for garnish*

Cover the prunes with water and soak them until soft and plump. Drain thoroughly; pit and dry them. Wipe the trout and sprinkle with salt. Cut a few slanting incisions in the fleshy part of the fish and put a prune in each slit. Oil an ovenproof dish, sprinkle it with parsley and garlic and lay the fish on top. Add the remaining oil, vinegar and 3 tablespoons of water, and bake in a hot oven (450°F) for 35–40 minutes.

Carefully transfer the trout to a heated serving plate. Heat the pan juices. Season the beaten eggs with salt and freshly ground pepper, and pour the mixture into the pan. Add the lemon juice, scramble briskly and use as a garnish for the trout. Decorate with lemon wedges and serve.

LESHCH PO-KASPIISKI (RUSSIA)

Porgy Caspian style

Great shoals of bream occur in the Caspian, and those of the autumn catch are considered superior in texture and flavor. This popular Caspian recipe calls for bream with horseradish and apple sauce. Porgy is a good substitute for bream.

Serves 6–8

- *2–3 lb porgy*
- *salt*
- *vinegar*
- *1 quart water*
- *bouquet garni*
- *1 onion, sliced*
- *1 leek, sliced*
- *1 celery stalk, chopped*
- *10 peppercorns*
- *2 cooking apples, grated*
- *3 tablespoons freshly grated horseradish*
- *1 tablespoon sugar*

Cut the fish into portions, rub with salt and place in a dish. Bring to a boil enough vinegar to cover the pieces and pour this over them. Allow to stand for 10 minutes.

Make a *court-bouillon* by bringing the water to a boil with the bouquet garni, onion, leek, celery and peppercorns. Season with salt to taste. Remove the fish from its marinade and add the fish with a tablespoon of marinade to the *court-bouillon*. Simmer until done. To test for readiness, press lightly on the thickest part of the fish. If the pressure shows that the flesh comes away from the bones, it is cooked. Remove the fish with a slotted spoon, drain, arrange on a serving plate and keep hot.

Mix the apple with the horseradish, 1 tablespoon vinegar and the sugar. Add strained *court-bouillon* to the desired consistency and serve with the fish.

KARP S KASHEI (UKRAINE)

Carp stuffed with kasha

Carp, originally brought to Russia and other parts of Europe from China, used to be cultivated in the monastery fish ponds. Today they are found in great numbers in the lakes and rivers of Russia and they are also extensively bred on special farms. Ukrainians eat a lot of carp. In this unusual variation a substantial filling is used to stuff this meaty fish.

Serves 4

- *1 carp, weighing 2 lb*
- *salt*
- *¼ cup butter*
- *1 onion, chopped*
- *6 oz cooked kasha (p. 234)*
- *2 hard-cooked eggs, chopped*
- *a pinch of freshly ground pepper*
- *flour*
- *¾ cup sour cream*

Wash and dry the carp thoroughly, then use the end of a cloth to wipe it inside and rub with salt. Melt half the butter and fry the onion lightly. Add the cooked *kasha* and fry together for 2–5 minutes. Remove from the heat, add the eggs and mix well.

Stuff the carp with this mixture and sew up the opening. Sprinkle the fish with pepper, coat lightly with flour and carefully fry it in the rest of the butter to brown both sides. Transfer to a buttered baking dish and put it in the oven preheated to 425°F for 5 minutes. Pour in the sour cream, reduce the heat to 350°F and continue to bake for 30–35 minutes, while basting frequently. Serve in the same dish.

SUDAK PO-MONASTYRSKI (RUSSIA)

Monastery perch

A Russian cook book of 1890 says 'when this dish is served in Orthodox monasteries as Lenten fare, the ham and rum are left out and vegetable oil is used instead of butter.' If perch or pike are not available, substitute a good freshwater fish.

Serves 4

- *2–3 lb perch or pike*
- *1 cup shredded lean cooked ham*
- *¾ cup chopped parsley*
- *salt and pepper*
- *½ cup butter*
- *1 quart fish stock*
- *1–1½ tablespoons vinegar*
- *12 peppercorns*
- *¼ lb mushrooms, sliced*
- *2–3 tablespoons rum*
- *¼ cup olive oil*
- *1 lemon, sliced*

Clean the fish, stuff it with mixed ham and parsley, and season with salt and pepper to taste. Wrap it in a clean napkin, folded in four and generously spread with about ¼–⅓ cup butter; tie with string. Bring the stock to a boil, add the vinegar and peppercorns, put in the wrapped fish and simmer for 15 minutes. Unwrap the fish, place on a serving plate and keep hot.

Lightly fry the mushrooms in a little butter and oil. Pour the rum into a small saucepan, flambé, and add the olive oil, 1 cup of the strained liquid in which the fish was cooked, the mushrooms and the lemon. Season with salt and pepper and thicken by gradually mixing in 2 tablespoons butter in small pieces. Stir briskly, bring to a boil, pour the sauce over the fish and serve.

Russia and Poland

SHCHUKA S GRIBAMI PO-LITOVSKI (LITHUANIA)
Pike with mushrooms

Dill is much loved in Russia, Scandinavia and the Baltic countries. Parsley can often be used as a substitute, but no Lithuanian cook would consider it adequate for this dish.

Serves 4

2 lb pike fillets
salt and pepper
3 tablespoons butter
1 onion, chopped
½ lb mushrooms, sliced
2 tablespoons chopped dill
1 teaspoon grated lemon rind
3 tablespoons dry white wine
1 cup cream
2 egg yolks

Cut the fillets into uniform pieces and season to taste. Melt the butter, soften the onion in it, add the mushrooms and simmer for 10 minutes. Sprinkle with dill and lemon rind and stir. Add the pike fillets, moisten them with the wine, cover and simmer for 10 minutes.

Add all but 2 tablespoons of the cream and stir it in carefully, without breaking up the fish. Simmer for another 10 minutes. Mix the egg yolks with the reserved cream and pour into the pan. Stir together gently and serve.

KAMCHATSKIYE KOTLETY IZ LASOSIA (KAMCHATKA)
Salmon steaks with caviar

The main industry of this huge peninsula of northeast Siberia, like that of Iceland, is fishing and fish processing. Much of the canned crab in Europe comes from Kamchatka. Life is hard there and the climate inhospitable, so people have invented attractive, consoling dishes. These salmon steaks are certainly comforting and are unusual in their garnish of red caviar tartlets. This makes a good buffet dish.

Serves 4

1 quart water
bouquet garni
1 onion, sliced
1 leek, sliced
1 celery stalk, chopped
salt
10 peppercorns
4 salmon steaks, ¾ in thick
aspic jelly (see fish fumet, p. 240)
cucumber, sliced
3 hard-cooked eggs, quartered

Caviar tartlets
1 cup flour
salt
2 tablespoons shortening
2 tablespoons butter
iced water
½ lb red caviar

Make a *court-bouillon* by bringing the water to a boil with the bouquet garni, onion, leek, celery, salt and peppercorns. Poach the salmon in the *court-bouillon* for 10 minutes and allow to cool in the liquid. Drain and skin them, and pat gently with a cloth to dry. Arrange the steaks on a plate and coat them with half-set aspic jelly. Decorate with cucumber and eggs. To make the tartlets, sift the flour with a pinch of salt, cut in the fats with a knife and add enough iced water to bind the pastry, sprinkling it in a tablespoon at a time and mixing it in evenly. Roll it out and line small, if possible boat-shaped, shallow muffin tins. Prick the bottoms and bake in a moderately hot oven (375°F), until lightly browned. This may take 12–13 minutes, but start checking after 10 minutes. Remove and allow the tartlets to cool. Garnish each tartlet with red caviar and place them around the salmon steaks on the serving plate.

KULEBIAKA IZ SYOMGI ILI LOSOSYA (RUSSIA)
Salmon coulibiac

A *coulibiac* is a narrow, tall pie made of one or more kinds of filling arranged in layers. The bottom layer is absorbent to prevent the pastry from becoming soggy and the pie is equally good with rice or *kasha*. You can also use any kind of pastry or dough. For best results use generous amounts of fish filling: salmon, tuna or halibut. *Coulibiac* is delicious hot or cold.

Prepare about 2 hours in advance.

Serves 6

Quick brioche dough
1 package active dry yeast
¾ cup lukewarm water
4 cups flour, sifted
2 eggs
1 teaspoon sugar
pinch salt
¾ cup butter, softened

Creamy sauce
¼ cup butter
¼ cup mushrooms
3–4 sprigs of parsley
10 peppercorns
½ cup flour
1 cup fish stock
½ cup cream

Filling
1 lb salmon, cooked, skinned and boned (or tuna or halibut)
1 onion, finely chopped
½ cup butter, melted
1 cup cooked rice or buckwheat
3–4 hard-cooked eggs, sliced
salt and pepper
2–3 tablespoons chopped parsley, chervil and tarragon
1 egg yolk mixed with 1 teaspoon water

To make the brioche dough, dissolve the yeast in warm water and mix with one-third of the flour. Put the remaining flour in a bowl, make a well in the middle and put in the eggs, sugar, salt and yeast mixture. Mix well and add the butter. Beat the dough until smooth and soft.

Cover and leave to stand in a warm place for about 1–1½ hours.

To make the creamy sauce, melt the butter and fry the mushrooms whole for 5 minutes. Add the parsley and peppercorns and cook for another 3–4 minutes on a low heat. Stir in the flour and cook the roux, without allowing it to color, for several minutes. Stir in the stock, bring to a boil, stirring with a wooden spoon until the first bubble appears, then reduce the heat to simmering point and cook gently for 45–50 minutes, skimming from time to time. Strain the sauce through damp muslin or cheesecloth and continue to stir until quite cold.

Before using, reheat gently and stir in the cream. Remove from heat and check the seasoning. Rinse the mushrooms and use as part of the *coulibiac* filling or as garnish.

To make the filling, flake the salmon or cut it into very thin slices. Lightly fry the onion in 1 tablespoon of the butter and add the mushrooms which were cooked in the sauce (or lightly fry some sliced mushrooms in butter and add these).

Roll the dough into a thin rectangle and cut in two. Place one of the sheets of dough on a lightly buttered baking sheet and moisten the edges. Spread a layer of rice evenly across the dough. Leaving the edges uncovered, spoon over some creamy sauce. Follow with a layer of egg slices, more sauce, then a layer of salmon. Season with salt and pepper. Sprinkle with herbs, onions and mushrooms and spoon over some more creamy sauce. Finish with the remaining rice. Season and sprinkle liberally with butter. Cover with the second sheet of dough and press down the edges to seal.

Brush the top with diluted egg yolk, prick with a fork and bake in a hot oven (425°F) for 30–35 minutes.

Coulibiac can also be made with puff pastry (p. 30). In this case, put the assembled *coulibiac* in the refrigerator for 30 minutes before cooking it, then paint the whole surface with egg and bake for 20 minutes.

left *Three generations of Volga fishermen*

Craftsmanship on the outside . . .

MIDII S SOUSOM IZ KEDROVYKH ORESHKOV (ARMENIA)
Armenian mussels with pine nut sauce

Nuts of various kinds are added to many Armenian dishes. The kernels of pine cones look like enlarged grains of rice and have a very pleasant almond-like flavor. They are used a great deal in cooking and confectionery everywhere, and are commonly known as *pignoli*.

Serves 4

4 dozen mussels	Scrub the mussels thoroughly, and steam to open. After steaming, throw away any mussels which have not opened. Discard the shells and remove the beards from the remaining mussels.
3 eggs	
1 cup milk	
1¼ tablespoons olive oil	
1¼ tablespoons lemon juice	Beat the eggs until thick. Add the milk, olive oil, lemon juice and 2½ cups of flour. Season with ½ teaspoon salt and mix to a smooth batter. Heat the oil.
3 cups flour	
salt and pepper	Dry the mussels on a soft cloth or on paper towels, and coat them with the remaining flour. Dip the mussels in the batter, shaking off any surplus. Deep fry a few at a time for 3–4 minutes, until pale brown. Drain on crumpled paper towels. Put on a heated plate and keep warm.
oil or other fat for deep frying	
3 tablespoons shelled pine nuts	
2 tablespoons currants (optional)	Make a sauce by bringing the pine nuts, currants, wine and stock to a boil in a saucepan. Season with salt and pepper. Simmer for 7–8 minutes.
¼ cup dry white wine	
¼ cup fish stock	Sprinkle the mussels with parsley and serve with the sauce.
parsley, chopped	

RIBNIY BULION (RUSSIA)
Fish fumet

A fish fumet is a concentrated fish stock, used for enriching and giving body to sauces which accompany fish dishes. When cold it jells into an aspic.

1 onion, chopped	Put the onion, mushroom parings, parsley, thyme and bay leaf in a stock pot. Cover with the fish bones and trimmings, add the lemon juice and season with a pinch of salt and pepper. Add the wine and water, and bring to a boil. Simmer gently for 30 minutes, skimming when necessary. Strain through muslin or cheesecloth, and reduce the stock by boiling until it has a fairly thick consistency.
¼ cup mushroom parings (stalks etc)	
2 sprigs of parsley	
1 sprig of thyme	
¼ bay leaf	
2 lb bones, head and trimmings of white fish (whiting, sole, haddock, flounder etc)	
¼ tablespoon lemon juice	
salt and pepper	
1 cup dry white wine	
1 pint water	

M_{eat}

BIGOS MYSLIWSKI (POLAND)
Hunter's bigos

This is a slightly simplified version of the famous Polish mixed-meat casserole. The original recipe uses both sauerkraut and fresh shredded cabbage, a mixture of various

. . . and in the kitchen – Polish hunter's bigos

butcher's meats and a variety of feathered and furred game. Obviously the Polish hunter does not intend to waste away.

Serves 4

1 lb sauerkraut
2 tablespoons butter
¼ cup diced bacon
1 medium onion, chopped
¼ cup ground pork
2 cups diced mixed
  cooked meats (beef,
  veal, lamb, venison)
1–2 cooking apples, diced
¼ lb Polish ham sausage,
  sliced (optional)
salt and pepper
¼ cup stock
¼ cup red wine
½ tablespoon flour

Squeeze out any surplus liquid from the sauerkraut, put the latter in a pan and cover it with cold water. Bring to a boil, simmer for 10 minutes and drain thoroughly. Fry the bacon and onion until the onion becomes soft. Add the pork and brown it lightly. Put in the mixed meats, apples, sauerkraut and sausage. Season to taste, mix well, moisten with stock and wine, and scatter 1 tablespoon butter on top in tiny pieces. Cover and simmer gently for at least 2 hours.

Mix the remaining butter with the flour and pound to a smooth paste. Add this to the meat to thicken the sauce. Simmer for a further 10 minutes and serve piping hot.

BLINCHATY PIROG (RUSSIA)
Crêpe pie

Variations of this de luxe crêpe pie are served all over Russia as an accompaniment to clear soups; but the pie is substantial and interesting enough to be an independent course. Served with a good consommé, it requires only a light dessert or simply fruit to make a complete meal.

The crêpes used are not *blini* but *blinchiki*. These are made of a thin unleavened batter, similar to French crêpes. It is possible to do most of the preparation for the pie well in advance, and bake the pie at the last moment.

Serves 6

BLINCHIKI
1 cup flour, sifted
pinch salt
2 eggs
2 tablespoons water
1 cup milk
2 teaspoons melted butter

To make the batter, beat the flour, salt and eggs together. Gradually beat in the water and milk. Incorporate the melted butter and stir until the batter is smooth and creamy. Chill until needed and stir well before using.

Beef filling
2 tablespoons butter
1 small onion, finely
  chopped
½ lb ground beef
2 tablespoons chopped
  mushrooms
1–2 hard-cooked eggs,
  chopped
¼ cup stock or water
salt and pepper
½ tablespoon chopped dill
  or parsley

To prepare the filling, melt the butter and fry the onion in it until soft. Add the beef and brown. Add the mushrooms and cook together for 5 minutes, stirring to prevent sticking, adding more fat if necessary.

Add the hard-cooked eggs, stock, seasoning and dill or parsley. Cook, stirring, for 1–2 minutes, remove from the heat and leave to cool completely.

Cream cheese filling
1 lb cream cheese
3 tablespoons sour cream
salt
freshly ground pepper
1 teaspoon sugar
2 eggs
a little extra butter

To make the cream cheese filling, combine the cream cheese and sour cream and season with salt and pepper. Add the sugar and eggs and mix well.

BÉCHAMEL SAUCE
2 tablespoons butter
1 tablespoon chopped
  onion
¼ cup flour
1 pint boiling milk
¼ teaspoon salt
3 white peppercorns
1 sprig parsley
pinch grated nutmeg
  (optional)

Melt the butter, add the onion and cook until it is soft and transparent. Stir in the flour and cook gently until it turns a pale gold. Gradually add the milk, beating vigorously. Add the salt, peppercorns, parsley and nutmeg. Simmer gently for 30 minutes, stirring frequently. When it has reduced by one-third, strain the sauce through a fine strainer. This makes about 1 pint of sauce. For the pie you will need only half this amount. The rest can be reserved for later use.

Fry the *blinchiki* on both sides. Butter a deep soufflé dish with the same diameter as the crêpes. Line the bottom with a crêpe. Put a layer of beef filling on top and spread some *béchamel* sauce over it. Cover this with a crêpe and spread it with a layer of the cheese mixture. Continue in this way, until all is used up. Finish with a crêpe. Scatter a few pats of butter on top and bake in a hot oven (450°F), long enough to heat through and brown the top. Unmold onto a heated serving dish and decorate with the parsley.

To serve this pie, cut it in wedges, like a cake.

242

Stuffed cabbage – simple, wholesome country fare from the Ukraine

KHARCHO (CAUCASUS)

This is one of those Highland meal-in-itself dishes: part soup, part casserole. The lamb cooked with plums, the rice and the soup are all served together in deep bowls.

Serves 4

1¼ lb boneless lamb, cut from the leg
1½ quarts beef stock
2 onions, chopped
2–3 cloves garlic, crushed
⅗ cup rice
8 plums
salt and freshly ground pepper
1 tablespoon butter
3 tomatoes, skinned and chopped
1½ tablespoons chopped dill

Cut the meat into pieces, allowing 3 or 4 pieces per portion. Put them in a large saucepan, cover them with stock, bring to boil, skim, cover and simmer for 1½ hours.

Add the onions and garlic. Add the rice to the soup. Bring the soup to a boil, add the plums and season to taste. Simmer for 30 minutes.

Melt butter or use the fat skimmed from the soup, and fry the tomatoes in it until they reduce to a paste. Add this to the soup and cook for 5 minutes. Check the seasoning, sprinkle with dill and serve.

MYASO S AIVOY PO-ARMYANSKI (ARMENIA)
Beef and quince casserole

Armenian cuisine includes many Eastern dishes, though it is uncertain whether or not they originated here; and fruit which is available everywhere is often combined with meat or fish as a main course.

Serves 4

1 lb beef chuck
2 tablespoons drippings
2–3 cups beef stock
1 lb quinces, peeled, cored and sliced
1 onion, sliced
salt and pepper
1 tablespoon chopped dill or parsley

Cut the beef into pieces, allowing 3–4 pieces per person. Melt the drippings in a pan; add the meat and brown it lightly. Cover the meat with stock and simmer very gently for 30 minutes.

Add the quinces to the pan. Fry the onion lightly and add it to the meat. Season with salt and pepper to taste and simmer until the quinces are tender. Pour the stew into a heated serving dish, sprinkle it with the dill and serve.

Russia and Poland

BEEF STROGANOV (RUSSIA)

The Stroganovs were a prosperous family of Russian merchants who went out to develop parts of Siberia in the sixteenth century. Ivan the Terrible had granted them vast lands there, probably for their services in the conquest of Kazan in 1553.

Serves 4

1 lb beef sirloin
1½ tablespoons flour
1 teaspoon salt
¼ teaspoon dry mustard
¼ teaspoon pepper
2 medium-sized onions, sliced
6 tablespoons butter
¼ lb mushrooms, sliced
1 tablespoon brandy
1 tablespoon tomato purée
¾ cup stock
1–2 tablespoons lemon juice
½ cup sour cream
1 tablespoon chopped parsley

Cut the meat into strips about 1 in long and not more than ½ in thick. Mix the flour with the salt, mustard and pepper. Lightly fry the onions in butter. Add the mushrooms and fry them together for 2–3 minutes; remove from heat. Dip the meat strips in the seasoned flour and shake off any surplus. Brown the meat in hot butter and add the onions and mushrooms with their pan juices. Fry together on low heat for 5 minutes, stirring with a wooden spoon.

Sprinkle in the brandy, set it alight, then stir in the tomato purée. Add the stock, bring to a boil, pour in the lemon juice and sour cream, stir, cover with a lid and simmer gently for 15 minutes. Bring back to a boil and transfer to a heated serving dish. Sprinkle with the parsley and serve with new potatoes or rice.

PIROG IZ MYASA PO-GRUZINSKI (GEORGIA)
Beef pie

It is a tradition in Russia to serve a *coulibiac* or some other savory pie at a birthday party, instead of a cake. Guests are not asked in for 'a drink' or a meal; they are simply invited to have some pie. This Georgian beef pie is a great success.

Serves 6

Quick brioche dough (see coulibiac, p. 239)
1½ lb beef sirloin
¼ cup butter
1 bunch scallions, chopped
¼ lb mushrooms, sliced
1 tablespoon chopped chives
2 tablespoons chopped parsley
salt and pepper
2–3 tablespoons stock
2–3 tablespoons fine breadcrumbs

Prepare the dough. Cut the steak into strips about 1 in long and ¼ in thick, and fry it in 3 tablespoons butter. When brown on all sides, add the scallions, mushrooms, chives and parsley. Mix and cook together for 5 minutes. Season with salt and pepper, and moisten with the stock.

Using two-thirds of the dough, roll out the bottom sheet, which must be thicker and slightly larger than the top covering. Put this on a lightly greased baking sheet and spread the filling on it, avoiding the edges. Dot with tiny pieces of butter. Roll out the rest of the dough and carefully cover the filling with it. Moisten the edges slightly with water to make the dough stick together, draw up the edges of the lower sheet of dough to cover the edges of the upper sheet, and seal together. Make a hole in the center for steam to escape, brush the top with melted butter, sprinkle it with breadcrumbs and bake in a moderately hot oven (400°F) for 1 hour. Remove the pie from oven, pour 3–4 tablespoons melted butter into the 'chimney' hole in the center and serve.

GOLUBTSY (UKRAINE)
Stuffed cabbage leaves

Cabbage, like beet, is a staple of the north and is cooked in many ways. As with most Russian cabbage dishes, this reheats well and tastes even better the next day.

Serves 4

12 cabbage leaves
1 small onion, chopped
3 tablespoons oil or butter
1 lb ground beef
4–5 tablespoons cooked rice
salt and pepper
1 cup stock
1 onion, sliced
¼ lb mushrooms, sliced
1 tablespoon flour
2 tablespoons tomato purée
1½ teaspoons sugar
¼ cup raisins (optional)
juice of ½ lemon
1 tablespoon chopped dill or parsley
sour cream

Choose a large white cabbage, remove the largest leaves and cut out the central stems to make the leaves flatter and more pliable. Put the leaves in a bowl, cover with boiling water and let them stand for 3 minutes. This could be enough to soften them. Drain and dry carefully on a soft cloth.

Fry the chopped onion in 1 tablespoon oil until soft. Add the meat and brown lightly. Add the rice, season to taste and stir in 2–3 tablespoons stock. Remove from the heat. Put a generous portion of meat stuffing on each cabbage leaf, fold in the sides, and roll each up into a neat parcel.

Heat the remaining oil and lightly brown the cabbage rolls on all sides, frying them flap-side first so they will not unroll. Put in a baking dish.

In the same oil fry the sliced onion until soft. Add the mushrooms and fry for 2–3 minutes. Sprinkle in the flour and make a roux. Add the tomato purée, then gradually stir in the remaining stock. Bring to a boil and add the sugar, raisins and lemon juice. Season to taste and pour the sauce over the cabbage leaves. Put the rolls in the oven preheated to 350°F and cook uncovered for 25–30 minutes. Sprinkle with the dill and serve in the casserole. Pass the sour cream separately.

For a party or just a picnic – Georgian beef pie

TELYATINA S SOUSOM IZ IKRY (RUSSIA AND POLAND)
Veal with caviar sauce

Veal, being bland, combines well with mild fish flavors. The Italians sometimes serve it with a tuna sauce (*vitello tonnato*), while the Russians enliven it in the following way.

Serves 6

2 lb veal sirloin, in one piece
6 oz bacon slices, sautéed
¼ cup butter
1 onion, thinly sliced
1 parsnip, sliced
1 carrot, sliced
2 celery stalks, chopped
1 bay leaf
10 peppercorns
2 cloves
grated rind of ¼ lemon
¼ cup dry white wine
¼ cup light stock
salt and freshly ground pepper
2–3 tablespoons caviar
1 tablespoon lemon juice

Make incisions in the veal and fill these with a few lardoons of bacon. Put the rest of the bacon in a casserole with half the butter. Add the onion and fry, stirring, until the onion softens. Add the parsnip, carrot, celery and bay leaf. Cook together for 5 minutes. Place the veal on top of the vegetables. Cook, turning the meat until all sides are seared. Add the peppercorns, cloves, lemon rind, wine and half the stock. Cover and simmer gently for at least 1 hour until tender. Season to taste.

Remove the veal; slice it, arrange on a heated plate and keep warm. Strain the pan juices into a small saucepan. Heat the remaining stock. Add the caviar and stock to the pan juices. Simmer on low heat for 2–3 minutes. Sharpen with lemon juice and stir in the remaining butter, adding it in small pieces. Pour the sauce over the veal and serve.

Suzdal, northeast of Moscow, in the heart of old Russia

JEZYK CIELECY (POLAND)
Beef tongue

Either beef or lamb tongue can be used for this dish, since the distinctive Polish touch is the sauce, which combines almonds and raisins. Some Polish cooks say that the flavor of tongue is improved if, after a preliminary soaking in cold water for 3 hours, it is sprinkled with sea salt and left overnight. If you can't spare so much time, you can still do this recipe as follows.

Serves 6

2 lb fresh tongue
salt and pepper
1 onion, roughly sliced
1 carrot, cut in chunks
3–4 celery stalks, chopped
1 tablespoon chopped dill or parsley
6 peppercorns
1 bay leaf
1 cup blanched almonds
¾ cup raisins
1 teaspoon grated lemon rind
1 cup red wine
2 tablespoons sugar
1 tablespoon wine vinegar
2 tablespoons butter
1½ tablespoons flour

Put the tongue in a deep pan, cover it with 3 quarts of cold water and add a tablespoon cooking salt. Bring it to a boil and skim the surface. Add the onion, carrot, celery, dill, peppercorns and bay leaf. Cover and simmer gently for 2½ hours or until the tongue is tender. Remove the tongue; strain and keep the liquid. Dip the tongue in cold water, drain and skin it, and trim away any unsightly tubes.

Cook the almonds, raisins and lemon rind in the wine, over a low heat, for 5 minutes, then remove from the heat.

In a heavy saucepan dissolve the sugar in 2 tablespoons water and the vinegar. Do not allow the sugar to brown. As soon as it melts into a syrup, add the butter and stir in the flour. Dilute with 1 cup of the liquid in which the tongue was cooked. Stir well and season to taste with salt and pepper. Add the wine mixture and let it simmer gently for 5 minutes.

Reheat the tongue in its own broth, then remove it. Slice and arrange it on a heated serving plate. Pour the sauce over and serve.

KABURGA PO-BUKHARSKI (BUKHARA)
Stuffed breast of lamb

In this dry, land-locked area of Uzbekhistan, which until fifty years ago was a secluded emirate, the only meats available were mutton, lamb and horsemeat. As a result much ingenuity has gone into preparing every cut of meat. This dish, served with a salad of thinly sliced onion rings and pitted black olives, dressed with lemon and oil, looks and tastes most appetizing.

Serves 6

1 whole breast of lamb
2 tablespoons butter
¾ cup rice
2 cloves of garlic, 1 sliced, 1 crushed
1 medium-sized onion, chopped
1 green pepper, seeded and chopped
2½ cups chopped parsley
salt
freshly ground black pepper
¼ cup shelled pistachio or pine nuts
⅓ cup water
¼ cup tomato juice

Wash and dry the meat. Slit the skin along one side and pull it away from the flesh to form pockets. With a cleaver crack the bones along the other side (or ask the butcher to do it for you).

Melt the butter and fry the rice lightly with the crushed garlic, onion and pepper. Add the parsley and season to taste with salt and pepper. Add the nuts and the water. Bring to a boil, cover and simmer for 8–9 minutes, by which time the water should be absorbed.

Preheat the oven to 350°F. Stuff the pockets you have made in the breast of lamb with the rice. Secure the openings with toothpicks (in Bukhara, cooks stitch them). Place the stuffed breast of lamb in a roasting pan and rub the outside with the sliced garlic. Season with salt and pepper, add the tomato juice, and cook for 1 hour, basting from time to time. Cover with foil and continue to cook for another 20–30 minutes. To serve, discard the toothpicks and cut the meat into thick slices.

Poultry and game

KOTLETY PO-KIEVSKI (UKRAINE)
Chicken à la Kiev

This famous Ukrainian dish is beautiful to look at, delicious to eat, and a rewarding party dish. It can be prepared a day in advance, covered with a cloth and kept in the refrigerator until needed. It tastes best served as soon as it is cooked.

Serves 4

2 small frying chickens
¾ cup butter
salt and pepper
2 eggs, beaten
fine breadcrumbs
oil for deep frying
lemon wedges and
  watercress for
  garnish

Remove the breasts, each with its wing attached, so that there are 4 identical pieces. Skin and carefully bone them, leaving only the central wing bone attached. Lightly beat the pieces to flatten them, and season.

Cut the butter into 4 'fingers'. Season and roll slightly. Chill thoroughly. Place a piece of frozen butter lengthwise on each breast, fold the flesh over and roll up neatly into a cigar shape with the bone sticking out at one end. It is essential to enclose the butter completely. Dip the pieces in the beaten eggs and roll them in breadcrumbs. Do this twice to make the coating adhere and to seal the butter inside. Refrigerate until ready to fry.

Heat the oil and deep fry the chicken for 4–5 minutes, until uniformly golden. Garnish with lemon wedges and watercress. You can also put a paper frill on each bone.

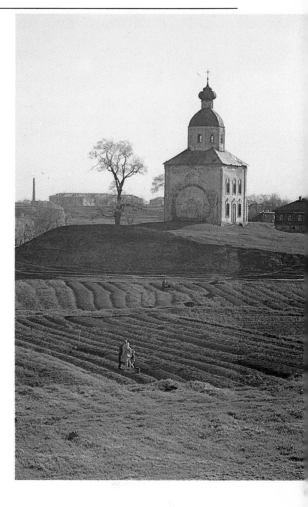

The close-knit pattern of a Russian village

POZHARSKIYE KOTLETY (RUSSIA)
Pozharsky cutlets

This excellent dish is dedicated to the great historical figure, Prince Dimitri Pozharsky. In the early seventeenth century when Russia was threatened with Polish domination, Pozharsky, with Kuzma Minin, headed an army which drove them out. Today a monument to Pozharsky and Minin stands in Red Square, in front of St. Basil's cathedral.

Use only breast of chicken for this recipe. Very nice cutlets can be made using any ground chicken meat, but they won't be Pozharsky cutlets.

Serves 6–8

4 whole chicken breasts
2 cups fresh breadcrumbs
a little cream
1 cup butter
salt and pepper
a pinch of nutmeg
a little flour
lemon wedges and
  watercress for
  garnish

Skin the chicken breasts, remove all sinews and pass the flesh through a fine grinder. Mix the breadcrumbs with enough cream to moisten them, so they are well impregnated, but not so soaked that they require squeezing. Mix the chicken and breadcrumbs, add ½ cup butter and pass the mixture through a grinder.

Season with salt and pepper, and add a mere suspicion of nutmeg. Mix well and reshape into the form of chicken breasts, imprisoning a little piece of butter in each before giving it the final shape.

Lightly coat the cutlets with flour and fry them in sizzling butter for 10–12 minutes, turning to make both sides golden.

Garnish with the lemon wedges and watercress.

KURITSA PO-CHERKESSKI SATZIVI (CAUCASUS)
Circassian chicken

Here is one of the many variations of this most famous of Circassian dishes.

Serves 4

1 chicken
1 medium onion, sliced
a few fresh tarragon
  leaves
a few sprigs of parsley
salt and pepper
2 slices 2-day-old bread,
  cut fairly thick
2 cups shelled, peeled
  walnuts
2 cloves of garlic,
  crushed
1 teaspoon paprika
1–2 tablespoons
  walnut oil

Put the chicken in a pan with enough cold water to cover. Bring it to a boil, simmer for 10 minutes, and skim. Add the onion, tarragon and parsley, and salt and pepper to taste. Simmer until the chicken is tender. Do not overcook.

Allow the chicken to cool. Skin it. Thinly slice the flesh off the bones with a sharp knife and arrange on a serving plate. Skim the surface fat off the cooking liquid and moisten the bread with some stock.

Pass the walnuts through a fine grinder or food mill 3 times, catching any oil which they render. Break up the bread and put it in a pan with the garlic. Stir over a gentle heat and season with salt and freshly ground pepper. Add the walnuts (but not the walnut oil) and, keeping the heat low, gradually stir in enough chicken stock to make a thick smooth sauce. Pour this over the chicken.

Add the paprika to the walnut oil. Mix well and trickle this red oil over the sauce in a zigzag or some other pattern. As a special compliment to your guest of honor, trickle the oil to spell his or her name. Serve cool, but not chilled.

Desserts

VARENIKI (UKRAINE)
Sweet noodle dumplings

This type of dumpling is a Ukrainian specialty that is popular throughout Russia, Czechoslovakia and other Central European countries.

In the Ukraine it is made with a variety of other fillings, including raspberries, cherries, plums and apricots.

Serves 4–6

1 lb cream cheese
2 egg yolks
2 tablespoons sugar
salt
¼ cup sour cream
a pinch of cinnamon
noodle paste (p. 32)
extra sugar for serving

Combine the cream cheese, eggs, sugar, a pinch of salt, ¼ cup sour cream and the cinnamon. Mix well together.

Roll out the noodle paste and cut into small squares. Fill each square with a spoonful of the cream cheese mixture. Join 2 diagonal corners to make a triangle and seal up the edges. Then bring the corners together and pinch them. Alternatively, cut the dough with a round cookie cutter into small circles, fill them with the cheese, and fold and shape them into semi-circles.

Drop a few at a time into boiling salted water, allowing the boiling to be re-established before adding any more. Boil them for 10 minutes, or until they rise to the surface. Remove with a slotted spoon and serve piping hot with sour cream and sugar. *Vareniki* can also be served with melted butter.

MOUSSE CHAINIY (RUSSIA)
Tea ice mousse

The Russians are exceedingly fond of ice cream and of iced desserts of all kinds. It is not unusual to see people of all ages enjoying ices out of doors in the middle of a Russian winter.

Serves 6–8

½ cup boiling water
2 teaspoons China jasmine
*   tea (more if a stronger*
*   flavor is desired)*
2¼ cups scalded milk
4 egg yolks
1 cup sugar
¾ cup whipped cream

Pour the water onto the tea and allow it to infuse. Strain the tea and mix it with the milk. Cream the egg yolks with the sugar. Then slowly add the milk mixture and stir well. Let this cook gently in a double boiler, without boiling, until the mixture thickens. Strain the mousse, cool and freeze it, but do not allow it to become hard. Fold in the whipped cream and freeze the mousse until ready to serve.

Tea ice mousse in the orchard. This dish is served all year round.

Russia and Poland

248

The Ukraine in the nineteenth century: the samovar is still the center of family life today.

KISEL IZ KLYUKVY PO-LATYSHSKI (LATVIA)
Cranberry dessert

The Latvians are fond of berries of all kinds; they play an important part in providing valuable vitamins. Many soups, desserts and preserves are made of bilberries, whortleberries, blueberries, barberries, etc. Some such preserves are served as jams, others as accompaniments to roasts.

Serves 4

¼ lb cranberries
¾ cup sugar
1 stick cinnamon
2 teaspoons cornstarch
whipped cream for
 decoration

Pick over the cranberries, wash them quickly without soaking and put them in a pan with ¼ cup water. Simmer until the skins burst, then rub them through a strainer. Dissolve ⅔ cup sugar with ¼ cup water and add the cranberry pulp and juice with the cinnamon. Simmer for 10 minutes. Remove the cinnamon.

Dissolve the cornstarch in 1 tablespoon of cold water and stir into the cranberries. As soon as the juices thicken, remove the pan from heat and pour the *kisel* into a serving bowl. When the dessert cools, a crust will form on the top. Sprinkle the remaining sugar over this. Chill and serve cold with rosettes of whipped cream.

ZEMLYANIKA PO-ROMANOVSKI (RUSSIA)
Strawberries Romanov

Elena Molokhovetz is the Russian Fannie Farmer. Her enormous cook book, *A Gift to the Young Housewife* which was first published in 1861, was in its twenty-eighth edition by 1914. She calls this a Romanov favorite, without specifying which member of the dynasty was the godfather.

Serves 4

2 lb strawberries
a little fresh orange juice
2–3 tablespoons curaçao
 or other orange liqueur
1½ cups whipping cream,
 chilled
¼ cup sugar
1 teaspoon vanilla sugar

Hull the strawberries, put them into a bowl and pour over just enough orange juice to moisten them. Don't drown them. Sprinkle with curaçao. Make sure the cream is cold and beat it in a bowl until it stands in peaks. Carefully fold in the sugar and vanilla sugar. Serve the cream with the strawberries.

ZEFIR IZ GRETZKIKH OREKHOV PO-ARMYANSKI (ARMENIA)
Walnut drops

The Armenians add nuts to many dishes. These delicious petits fours are served with coffee.

Makes 24

¾ cup butter
¾ cup sugar
¼ teaspoon salt
1½ cups flour, sifted
¼ cup brandy
1 cup finely chopped
 walnuts

Preheat the oven to 350°F. Cream the butter with the sugar, sprinkle in the salt and add the flour. Moisten it with brandy and mix. Add the walnuts and stir well. Drop small spoonfuls of the mixture onto a lightly greased baking sheet and bake for 20–25 minutes.

SLADKOYE IZ GRANATOV PO-SAMARKANDSKI (SAMARKAND)
Pomegranate dessert

Pomegranates appear in the stores each winter and people often wonder what to do with them. Here is a pleasant Uzbek way of serving them, but only really ripe pomegranates are suitable for this treatment.

Serves 4–6

2–3 ripe pomegranates
2–3 tablespoons sugar
1¼ teaspoons lemon juice
*1½–2 teaspoons rose-
    water*

Carefully cut around the base of the pomegranate crowns and lift the tops off. This will enable you to see what happens inside. Carefully cut through the pulp membranes separating each segment. If the pomegranates are ripe, the seeds in the segments should be very red and juicy. Coax the seeds into a serving bowl and bruise them. Add the sugar, lemon juice and rose-water. Stir and chill. Serve this dessert very cold.

KHUSAINE (CRIMEA)
Chilled grape dessert

Grapes of the *vitis vinifera* species are native to the region bordering on the Caspian and the people there claim that theirs are the only 'original' vines in existence. The *Phylloxera* pest, which decimated the European vineyards, did not manage to get across the Caucasus mountains, so they, unlike the rest of Europe, did not have to replant with Californian grapes. Most of the Caucasian grapes are used for wine making. But the Crimea grows one particularly delicious species of seedless dessert grapes, of the long, pale, 'ladies' fingers' variety, which they use for this recipe.

Serves 4

1 lb seedless grapes
1 teaspoon lemon juice
1 tablespoon honey
2 tablespoons brandy
¼ cup sour cream

Wash grapes and remove stems. Combine lemon juice, honey and brandy. Pour over the grapes. Chill for several hours. Decant into dessert glasses. Top with sour cream and serve.

SHARLOTKA IZ VISHNI (UKRAINE)
Cherry charlotte

The Ukrainians make a variety of cherry liqueurs, including a rather treacherous one appropriately called 'the staggerer'. For the charlotte, they use a sweet ratafia. If you aren't in the habit of making your own cherry liqueur, you can use kirsch or cherry brandy.

Serves 4–6

1¼ lb pitted cherries
⅓ cup vanilla sugar
*⅓ cup cherry liqueur or
    kirsch*
*½ lb (about 36)
    ladyfingers,
    preferably homemade*
1 cup whipped cream
*extra whipped cream
    and sugar for serving*

Put 1 lb of the cherries in a bowl with half the sugar and 2 tablespoons cherry liqueur. Liquidize the remaining cherries with a few tablespoons of water. Mix with the rest of the liqueur and use it to moisten the ladyfingers.

Line the bottom and sides of a springform pan with some of the ladyfingers. Fold the remaining sugar into the whipped cream. Put a generous layer of cherries over the ladyfingers on the bottom and cover them with a layer of whipped cream. Cover this with a layer of ladyfingers. Continue in this way, finishing with a layer of ladyfingers. Chill in the refrigerator. Unmold and serve with more sweetened whipped cream.

ZHELE PO-ARMYANSKI (ARMENIA)
Orange blossom gelatin

Armenians, in common with Central Asians and the natives of the Arab countries, Iran and Turkey, are fond of exotic aromatics in their desserts. Rose-water, orange blossom water, etc, are often used to flavor sweets.

Serves 4

*1 envelope unflavored
    gelatin*
juice of 1 lemon
¼ cup sugar
⅓ cup dry white wine
1 cup hot water
*¼ cup double-strength
    orange blossom water*
1 egg white, stiffly beaten
*1 egg shell, washed and
    crushed*

Dissolve the gelatin in the lemon juice. Bring the sugar gently to a boil with the wine and water. Stir until the sugar has dissolved. Add the gelatin and lemon juice and the orange blossom water.

To clarify the gelatin, add the beaten egg white and the egg shell to the pan; beat it over a low heat until boiling. Remove from heat and allow it to settle for a couple of minutes. Boil it up again, beating vigorously; remove from the heat at the first boiling and rest as before. Repeat the beating and boiling up for the third time. Remove from heat, leave to stand for a few minutes and strain it through a jelly bag. Pour the gelatin into a rinsed mold and leave to set.

The wild Caucasus – the home of many exotic dishes

Easter, and the guests were welcomed with the traditional paskha *and* kulich

MAZUREK (POLAND)
Fruit and nut slice

There are many variations of this Polish specialty. This recipe for pastry slices topped with chopped fruit and nuts is a very popular one.

Serves 6

2¼ cups flour, sifted
a small pinch salt
2 cups sugar
1¼ cups butter
3 eggs
⅓ cup sour cream
1 cup raisins, chopped
1 cup dates, chopped
⅓ cup figs, chopped
2 cups chopped walnuts
1¼ tablespoons lemon
 juice

Put the flour, salt and half the sugar into a mixing bowl. Cut in the butter until the mixture looks like crumbs. Beat 1 egg with the sour cream, add this to the flour and mix lightly. Preheat the oven to 350°F. With a fork, press the dough lightly into a greased baking pan 8 in square. Then bake it until set, about 20 minutes.

Mix the raisins, dates, figs and walnuts with the lemon juice. Beat the remaining 2 eggs with the rest of the sugar and add to the fruit and nut mixture. Stir together and spread gently over the dough foundation. Return to the oven and continue to bake for 35–40 minutes. Remove from the oven and, before the *mazurek* cools, cut it into slanting slices about 2 in wide.

PASKHA (RUSSIA)
Easter dessert

Paskha, kulich and colored eggs are the essentials of the Russian Easter table, and special wooden pyramid-shaped molds are used for setting *paskha*.

Serves many

1 lb well drained,
 unsalted cream cheese
⅛ teaspoon salt
⅓ cup seedless raisins
⅓ cup mixed candied fruits
⅓ cup chopped blanched
 almonds
⅓ cup unsalted butter
¾ cup vanilla sugar
3 egg yolks
1 egg, beaten
⅓ cup whipped cream

Rub the cheese through a fine strainer, then add the salt, raisins, candied fruits and almonds. Mix well. Cream together the butter and sugar; add the egg yolks and beat well. Combine this with the cheese mixture, add the beaten egg and stir. Fold in the whipped cream.

Heat the mixture in a double boiler over simmering water, stirring constantly until bubbles emerge around the edge of the pan and the mixture thickens enough to coat a spoon.

If you haven't got the traditional pyramid-shaped mold for *paskha*, use a clean flower pot with a hole in the bottom. Line it with cheesecloth rinsed in water and wrung out. Pour in the mixture, enclose it with the cheesecloth and put a small plate on top with a weight on it. Chill and drain off any surplus moisture. Unmold it, remove the cheesecloth and serve cold.

When your guests depart, return the *paskha* in the cloth to the mold, and keep refrigerated.

Russia and Poland

KULICH (RUSSIA)
Easter cake

This is the traditional Russian Easter cake, always served with *paskha*. The cake must be cylindrical and tall. The diameter may vary, but the proportion of height to circumference must be observed. Russians have special *kulich* pans for the purpose, but tall fruit juice cans, salad oil cans and big coffee cans can be used. It is usual to bake one *kulich* for every member of the family, with small ones for the children. In the Russian home there must be enough *kulich* to offer to the endless stream of friends who drop in over the Easter holiday.

Serves many

1 ounce yeast
¼ cup lukewarm water
1 cup seedless raisins
3–4 saffron threads
2 tablespoons vodka
1 cup lukewarm milk
8 cups flour, sifted
1¼ cups vanilla sugar
a pinch of salt
1¼ cups unsalted butter
4 eggs
½ cup chopped blanched almonds
½ cup chopped candied peel
1 egg yolk mixed with 2 teaspoons water
1 tablespoon fine breadcrumbs

Frosting
½ cup confectioners' sugar
1 tablespoon water
½ teaspoon lemon juice
chocolate vermicelli or confectioner's roses for decoration

Mix the yeast with the lukewarm water. Soak the raisins in water to cover. In a small glass, soak the saffron threads (these are much better than powdered saffron) in vodka leaving them to infuse the liquid. When the infusion is complete, the vodka should have acquired a deep orange color.

In a large bowl combine the milk, one-third of the flour, 1 tablespoon of sugar and the salt. Add the diluted yeast and mix well. Cover and leave to rise, until the dough doubles its bulk.

Soften the butter. Add to this the remaining sugar and the eggs and beat well. Stir this into the yeast mixture.

Drain the raisins and add them to the dough. Strain the saffron infusion into it, discarding the threads, which will have done their work by now. Add the almonds, candied peel and remaining flour. Mix well.

Turn the dough out onto a lightly floured board and knead until it is elastic and silky smooth. This may take 15–20 minutes. Replace in a clean bowl, cover and leave to rise in a warm place until it again doubles in size. Don't be alarmed by the stiffness of the dough; it is slow rising but bakes very well. Grease a baking pan or pans and line the bottom with a circle of buttered brown paper. When the dough has doubled in size, transfer it to the baking pan. Shape into a ball for large pans and into cylindrical rolls for the smaller ones. Do not fill the pans more than half full of dough. Cover with a cloth and leave in a warm place until the dough rises almost to the tops of the pans. When the dough has risen, brush the top with diluted egg yolk. Sprinkle this with breadcrumbs and bake on the bottom shelf of the oven (400°F) for 15 minutes. Reduce the heat to 350°F and bake for a further 35–40 minutes.

In Russian villages a thin smooth wooden spill is inserted into the middle of the unbaked *kulich*. This reaches right down to the bottom and is baked with the *kulich*. To test, the spill is pulled out and if it is clean, without any dough sticking to it, the *kulich* is done. Remove the cake gently on to a cake rack, cover with a clean, dry dish towel and leave to cool.

Mix the confectioners' sugar with the water and lemon juice. Frost the top of the *kulich* and sprinkle the frosting with chocolate vermicelli, or decorate with confectioner's roses. If you have any frosting left over, pipe X B (Russian initials for 'Christ is risen') on the body of the *kulich* near the glazed top.

To serve, first cut off the decorated top, then cut the cake into round slices about 1 in thick. If the slices are large, halve or quarter them. Replace the top as a lid. Serve *paskha* at the same time.

ZAWIJANIEC MAKOWY (POLAND)
Poppy seed roll

In Poland, this is served both as a cake with tea or coffee and as a dessert. It is full of good natural products: milk, butter, honey and poppy seeds.

Prepare 4–5 hours in advance.

1 cake compressed yeast
6 tablespoons sugar
1 cup milk
½ cup butter
4 cups flour
pinch salt
2–3 eggs, depending on size

Filling
2 cups poppy seeds
3 tablespoons honey
2 tablespoons vanilla sugar
1 cup milk
2 tablespoons chopped candied peel
1 teaspoon powdered cinnamon
1 tablespoon melted butter

To make the dough, cream the yeast with ½ tablespoon of the sugar in a bowl or a mixer. Warm the milk gently with the butter until the butter melts. Take care not to overheat the milk; it should be lukewarm. Pour the milk and butter mixture onto the yeast and stir well.

Warm a mixing bowl large enough to take all the dough ingredients and to allow for rising. Sift the flour and salt into it, make a well in the center and pour in the yeast and milk mixture. Work in the flour from the sides and knead until you have a smooth dough. Cover with a lightly floured cloth and leave to rise in a warm place until the dough doubles in size. This may take 1½–2 hours. Sprinkle in the remaining sugar, beat, and work in the eggs. Knead well.

Prepare the filling while the dough is rising, that is before you add the sugar and eggs to it. Rinse the poppy seeds with hot water and drain them well (this is best done in a muslin bag). Then grind them finely. Add the honey and sugar to the milk and bring gently to a boil. Add the ground poppy seeds and cook, stirring frequently, until the mixture thickens. Stir in the candied peel and cinnamon, and remove from the heat. Leave to cool.

On a floured board roll out the dough into a rectangle ¼ in thick. Moisten the edges and spread the filling thickly over the rectangle almost to the edges, then roll it up. Put the roll in a lightly greased baking pan, cover with a cloth and leave again in a warm place to rise for another 1½–2 hours.

Preheat the oven to 375°F. Brush the top of the poppy seed roll with the melted butter and bake for 50–60 minutes.

If desired, mixed chopped dried fruit and/or chopped nuts may be added to the filling.

Part of the secret of success in life is to eat what you like.

Mark Twain (1835–1910)

America's native grain: rich gold piled after the corn harvest

North American cooking isn't hard to define in geographical terms: from the North Atlantic to the Pacific, from the Gulf of Mexico to the Arctic, it is a singular culinary haven. Yet it remains amorphous. It divides easily enough into regions, in which certain influences are noteworthy, yet nowhere is there a cooking style that rules out all others. In the settlement of America, fertile soil in most areas insured family cooks a bounty of agricultural produce, and the dispersal of immigrants made inevitable the mixing of gastronomic modes. Only one factor has remained immutable: North America has been dominated in the kitchen, as elsewhere, by the political realities which resulted in English as a common language.

When that language was established on the Atlantic seaboard, however, it was only one of several, for French pioneers were then settling in Montreal, others were in Savannah and Charleston, and there were the Dutch in New York and the Swedes in New Jersey, while Germans moved into Pennsylvania and a few other places. Before the American Revolutionary War, Spaniards were living among the French in Louisiana and in scattered settlements in Florida, the Southwest and California. In each of these regions ethnic customs have endured, adding multiple accents to the American culinary complexion.

Ethnicity is what America is all about – always remembering that being an American comes first. French-Canadians may try to seem more French every day, but that is politics; their ethnic culture is of the New World rather than Europe, their customs tempered by more than three hundred years of life on the side of the Atlantic away from ancestral shores. So it is with their cultural cousins in Louisiana's bayous. There the Acadians, who were evicted in the eighteenth century from what is now Nova Scotia, have devised a Creole way of life that is more soda pop than vintage wine.

'Pop' may be – it is tempting to say – one of the important New World words. Soda bottles pop open. We venerate pop art, and are lulled timelessly by pop music in elevators and shopping centers, and in buying the billions of recordings by which pop superstars are made. But neither popular music nor popular art need necessarily be vulgar. American musicians gave jazz to the world, and the folk genius that developed the blues has unquestionably enriched the twentieth century.

In this sense, the food of America that is most visible – the meals served by fast-food chains – offers no improvement in quality, as it invades one new country after another. Fast food, instead, exports the pace of life in a computerized environment. It is a little like comparing the comic-strip origins of Andy Warhol's work to the realism of Andrew Wyeth's finest painting. Speed and economy of line characterize the Warhol message, and speed and economy of effort have made fast food a success among those who visualize themselves as constantly 'on the run', no longer devoted to dining rooms or kitchen tables around which families have habitually gathered in the past.

Yet Americans might also be said to be 'on the run' in the sense of foreign travel, and this exercise has awakened men and women alike to the pleasures of dining well, and interestingly. An important result of trips to the world's far places is to be seen in the phenomenon of proliferating cooking schools. Men and women who in the early days of the tourist boom returned from France with yearnings to emulate *haute cuisine* at home have infected others who simply want to learn to cook well. In the 1970s classes for serious students of cooking (male devotees no less than women) are available not just in cosmopolitan centers but in U.S. communities once considered remote from any sophisticated influence. The number of cooking schools multiplies every month, an increase that belies the impression that fast food has overwhelmed America and that the hamburger and fried chicken dominate the nation's eating habits.

Ethnic influence: shallots from a Chinese market and tomatoes, the marvelous red fruit that originated in the New World

left *Vast beef herds reflect the American love of red meat.*

The food that in the beginning made the American eating experience unlike any in the Old World was corn. When the first vessels nudged into landings at Jamestown, Cape Cod and Quebec, or when Conquistadores inched on through the arid Southwest in search of El Dorado, the chief thing of value to be found was Indian maize. For the new settlers, ground corn often took the place of wheat flour and other grains. This was because corn grew more readily and because the first European cooks in America were taught by Indian women how to bake small loaves of bread, called hoe cakes or corn pones, in hot ashes. In Canada and the colonies to the south the Indians grew types of beans unknown in England, and the settlers learned how to combine fresh beans with fresh kernels of corn in the classic dish called *succotash* that is still served, rich with cream, at Yankee Thanksgiving dinners. In the Southwest, Europeans who had come to settle were taught to make pancakes of cornmeal, and as a result stuffed griddle cakes, known as *tacos*, filled with combinations of meat, chilis, vegetables, and cheese or sour cream, have become a favorite 'sandwich' almost everywhere from the Lower Mississippi to southern California.

As corn was used universally by America's Indians, so it is accepted in the twentieth century. There are dozens of delicious ways of making cornbread or Johnny cake as it is called in several regions (see page 26). Crisply fried cornmeal mush, served with maple syrup and country cured ham (like Virginia's famous Smithfield hams which are fed on peanut vines) is a traditional breakfast in the Deep South. And there are even more uses for fresh corn, or corn kernels, canned or frozen. In the heartland, as the Midwest is often called, the corn 'grows as high as an elephant's eye', and it gives succulent character to many dishes, such as corn-stuffed green peppers. But it is corn on the cob – or 'roastin' ears' – that is a national gustatory institution. Slathered with butter, salted and peppered, corn on the cob is eaten much the way a mouth organ is played, a ritual which may tend to cause any eater to feel American.

The world knows the appetite of many Americans for steak, no matter how it is cooked. Aged beef is consumed by some men, especially those who go to restaurants on expense accounts, as often as four times a week. The desire is a part of a deep, lingering lust for red meat in both Canada and the U.S. that goes back to the nineteenth century, when manners were rough and appetites were primitive. It shows itself also in the millions of pounds of chopped or ground beef sold each day to housewives whose families keep crying for more.

The average American family dines from a polyglot menu, not in any pretentious sense, but because the kitchen melting pot is more apt to absorb ingredients and ideas from various lands. Fish and corn chowders (the word derives from the French-Canadian use of *chaudière*, meaning pot) are no more popular in New England, where they gained fame, than is spaghetti with a tomato sauce. Indeed tomatoes, when they are cooked, are as apt as not to make one think of southern Italian cooking styles, in spite of the fact that this marvelous red fruit originated in the New World. Recipes for kabobs, the Middle Eastern way of grilling lamb and ripe tomatoes, are common in standard domestic cook books. So are those for German or Scandinavian pot roasts, which derive from immigrants who settled throughout the Midwest.

254

American contrasts: pop art . . .

fruit pies crossed the Atlantic with the first English settlers, and pie for breakfast was a way of life in early New England. (Apple pandowdy is Yankee argot for a rustic, deep-dish pastry.) Plantation hostesses of the South developed reputations for their unctuous sweet potato puddings and flaming banana confections, but fluffy angel food and devil's food cakes in the American tradition evolved after immigrant cooks from Central Europe began to settle all across the country. Coconut marshmallow cakes may be as indigenous as any, but the real point is that American cooks have been as adventurous in satisfying their families' craving for cakes and other desserts as any cooks anywhere.

Modern developments in cooking utensils have made cooking easier for the American housewife, but shiny and efficient hardware isn't the source of inspiration that results in meals to stir nostalgia or titillate the palate. To find such eating anywhere in North America, simply turn to the food of those who honor traditions. Generations of Portuguese fishing families in Cape Cod, for example, have developed a deep-fried pastry that is stuffed with briskly seasoned corn kernels mixed with fresh sardines. In the Deep South where Soul Food reflects a way of life begun in slave times, corn and green peppers are combined with chicken and shrimp in a glorious one-dish mélange; or the same cooks transform blackeyed peas and ham hocks into the ancient New Year's Day repast called Hoppin' John. In the Texas Hill Country you might try braised beef stuffed with bacon, or in the Northwest the Columbia River salmon that is grilled on planks. All of these dishes are habitually prepared in regional kitchens.

Finding them is worth the search. There is much good food produced by American cooks in every region, and sometimes, as Mark Twain was moved to say of the pompano fish from Gulf of Mexico waters, it is as 'delicious as the less criminal forms of sin'.

. . . to the California dream

Chinese cooks, whose ancestors appeared on the continent with the building of transcontinental railroads, have begun to change cooking habits; in supermarkets throughout Canada, for instance, ample shelving is set aside for Oriental ingredients. More and more it has become apparent that Americans have very catholic taste buds.

Two things make American meals stand out from those of other countries. A serious family dinner, served at the end of the day, is customarily begun with a salad course, and it isn't considered complete without a very serious dessert.

American salads, unlike the simple oil-and-vinegar dressing of greens in France, tend to be what are known as 'composed salads', mixtures of greens and raw vegetables embellished with slightly sweet mayonnaise, or jellied combinations that include fruits with such contrasting ingredients as cheese and nuts. Even plain lettuce is eaten more frequently with a pinkish, sweetened 'French' oil-based mixture. And ubiquitous, sweet coleslaw has increased in popularity since it first appeared in early Pennsylvania homes, while under new chic circumstances avocados are now stuffed with mixtures of crab and shrimp topped with a tart anchovy and tarragon sauce known as Green Goddess dressing. Combinations in this vein – similarly stuffed tomatoes, or a tossing of romaine, croûtons, one-minute eggs and Parmesan cheese, known as Caesar's salad – are often served as a complete luncheon.

Desserts are an American passion. The knack for making

Hors d'oeuvre

OYSTERS ROCKEFELLER (NEW ORLEANS)

The original recipe for oysters Rockefeller, invented in Antoine's restaurant in New Orleans, was named after the founder of the great family fortune because it was so exotic. Antoine's has never disclosed its recipe; but every good restaurant in New Orleans' *Vieux Carré* has its own version of the dish, and thousands of family cooks serve it as a festive appetizer, using recipes similar to this one.

Serves 4

1 lb spinach
8 scallions
3 tablespoons finely chopped celery
¼ cup coarsely chopped parsley
1 cup butter, melted
¼ cup finely chopped chives
½ teaspoon crushed fennel seeds
1¼ cups fresh breadcrumbs
salt and freshly ground pepper
3 tablespoons Pernod or Ricard
48 fresh oysters on the half shell
rock salt

Rinse the spinach thoroughly and drain. Put it in a large saucepan with no water added, and cook gently until tender. Drain well. Chop the scallions, including the green stems, and combine with the spinach, celery and parsley. Put half or less of the mixture in an electric blender and blend with about half of the melted butter. When all the mixture is well blended, transfer to a mixing bowl and stir in the chives, fennel seeds, breadcrumbs, salt, pepper and Pernod or Ricard.

Loosen the oysters in their shells and arrange them on beds of rock salt in 4 pie pans or ovenproof serving plates. Spoon a generous amount of the spinach mixture over each oyster, pat it down and bake in a hot oven (450°F) for 5–8 minutes, or until the sauce bubbles and the oysters are heated through.

CRAB AND PROSCIUTTO ROLLS (NEW YORK)

Crabmeat from Maryland's eastern shore is combined with thin slices of ham (produced by Italo-Americans in the traditional way) to make this splendid appetizer.

Serves 4

16 thin slices of prosciutto
½ lb fresh lump crabmeat
9 tablespoons butter
¾ teaspoon Worcestershire sauce
Tabasco sauce
juice of 1 small lemon
1½ tablespoons finely chopped parsley
freshly ground pepper

Arrange 4 slices of prosciutto on a flat surface, each slice overlapping another. In the center place a heaped tablespoon of crabmeat. Now roll the ham slices over the filling, cigar style. Make 3 more rolls in the same way.

Melt the butter in a large skillet. When it foams add the rolls. (The ham will cling to the crabmeat when heated.) Cook, turning the rolls once, until the ham starts to frizzle and the crab is heated through. Transfer to a hot plate. Add the Worcestershire sauce, a liberal shaking of Tabasco and the lemon juice to the juices in the pan. Heat for about 30 seconds, then pour over the rolls. Sprinkle each with parsley and freshly ground pepper.

Crab and prosciutto rolls: one of many appetizers inspired by a passion for cocktails

SHRIMP COCKTAIL (MIDWEST)

Although the recipe given below comes from Kansas City, the so-called shrimp cocktail is to be found everywhere in America; indeed it is the country's most popular appetizer. The tiny shrimp that are used come from the waters off Alaska, Maine or the Pacific Coast.

Prepare several hours in advance.
Serves 4

4 cups cooked shelled shrimp
juice of 1 lemon
1 teaspoon paprika
salt and freshly ground pepper
¼ cup vinegar
1 tablespoon tomato juice
1 teaspoon finely chopped onion or ¼ clove of garlic, crushed
1 teaspoon finely chopped celery
1 teaspoon prepared mustard
1 pint olive oil
1 head of lettuce

Season the shrimp with the lemon juice, paprika, salt and pepper and chill thoroughly. Mix together the vinegar, tomato juice, onion or garlic, celery and mustard. Add the oil a little at a time. Shake well in a tightly covered jar and let the sauce mature for several hours in the refrigerator.

When ready to serve line 4 cocktail dishes with lettuce leaves, divide the shrimp between them and moisten well with the sauce.

CHILI-CHEESE-TOMATO DIP (SOUTHWEST)

Cocktail parties are endemic in all the states, as is the notion of filling the stomach to minimize the effects of drinking. The mixtures known as dips, designed to be scooped up with a cracker of some sort, are legion and give free rein to inventive cooks.

Serves 4

2–3 tablespoons butter
2 large onions, finely chopped
2 cloves of garlic, crushed
3 tablespoons finely chopped canned green chili peppers, or
1 tablespoon chili powder
1 tablespoon Worcestershire sauce
1 cup grated Mozzarella cheese
2½ cups canned tomatoes, drained and finely chopped
1 tablespoon cornstarch

Melt the butter in a saucepan and sauté the onions, garlic and chili peppers for about 4 minutes. Stir in the Worcestershire sauce.

In a double boiler melt the cheese. Stir in the tomatoes and cooked onion-chili mixture. When it begins to bubble, add the cornstarch and stir until thick. Serve hot in a chafing dish with corn chips.

GUACAMOLE (SOUTHWEST)

The name *guacamole* is derived from an Aztec word meaning 'concoction', and was brought north with Spanish and Indian migrations. The mixture is very adaptable: some cooks stir in crushed garlic and finely chopped tomato. This recipe is common in Arizona and New Mexico.

Serves 4

2 ripe avocados
1 small onion, grated
a 4-oz can green chili peppers, minced
1 freshly hard-cooked egg
3 tablespoons butter
2 tablespoons mayonnaise
2–3 tablespoons lemon juice
dash of Tabasco sauce
salt

Peel the avocados, reserving the pits. Mash the flesh and stir in the onion and chili peppers. Grate the warm hard-cooked egg over the butter and work in the mayonnaise with a whisk. When the mixture is smooth, stir in the seasoned avocado, a little at a time; add lemon juice and Tabasco. Taste and add salt as needed. Bury the pits in the *guacamole* to prevent it discoloring and chill in the refrigerator.

Eating 'alfresco' Nebraska 1886 – a tradition that continues today

Soups

CANADIAN HABITANT DRIED PEA SOUP (QUEBEC, GASPE)

The early settlers in French Canada, in Quebec and the Gaspé Peninsula, may have been no more dependent on dried legumes and other easily stored foods than any other pioneers, but the soup made by the first *habitants* – a delicious *potage* to which various vegetables and seasonings are added at the cook's whim – has become a tradition.

Prepare the beans 24 hours in advance.
Serves 4

¼ lb salt pork, diced
1 small onion, finely chopped
2 cloves of garlic, crushed (optional)
1 lb dried yellow split peas, soaked overnight
2 quarts tongue or ham stock, or water
4 celery stalks, chopped
1 ham bone or small smoked hock
2 teaspoons salt
freshly ground pepper
1 bay leaf
¼ teaspoon dried summer savory

Sauté the salt pork in a large saucepan, removing when crisp and brown. To the fat in the pan add the onion and garlic, if used, and cook, stirring, until the onion is transparent. Stir in the drained peas, the stock or water, celery and the ham bone. Add seasonings and simmer, skimming when necessary, until the peas are very tender, about 2 hours.

BLACK BEAN SOUP (FLORIDA)

Once a Spanish settlement and now a haven for Caribbeans of Spanish blood, Florida has had a distinct culinary style from its earliest days. It is not the only region to have a version of black bean soup, but Floridian cooks add their own flavors and serve this soup with pride.

Prepare the beans 24 hours in advance.
Serves 4

½ lb black beans, soaked overnight
¼ lb boneless veal, cubed
1 small veal knuckle bone
2 small onions, chopped
½ lemon, halved
2 whole cloves
ground allspice
1½ tablespoons salt
freshly ground pepper
sherry to taste
1 hard-cooked egg, finely chopped
slices of fresh lime or lemon

Put the drained beans in a large saucepan with about 1½ quarts of water, the veal, knuckle bone, onions, lemon pieces, cloves, allspice, salt and several turns of the pepper grinder. Bring to a boil and simmer for about 5 hours, or until the beans are very soft.

Take out the meat and bone and set aside. Discard the lemon and cloves. Purée the soup in a blender. Return to the saucepan and shred the veal into the soup. Add sherry to taste and simmer for 5 minutes. Serve with chopped egg and lime slices in each dish.

PEANUT AND OYSTER SOUP (DEEP SOUTH)

The highly praised Southern style of American cooking began in the days of slavery when black cooks made the most of the bounty available in plantation kitchens, often serving innovative combinations of ingredients.

Serves 4

1 quart oysters
1 tablespoon butter
4–5 scallions, finely chopped
¼ cup peanut butter
3 tablespoons flour
1 pint chicken stock
¼ cup heavy cream
salt and cayenne pepper
chopped fresh summer savory
2–3 tablespoons sherry
finely chopped parsley

Shuck the oysters, reserving the liquid in the shells. Melt the butter in a large saucepan and sauté the scallions for 2–3 minutes over a moderate heat. Stir in the peanut butter and flour and mix well. Remove from the heat and stir in the stock to make a smooth mixture. Return to the heat and cook slowly until the soup thickens. Stir in the cream and oyster liquid. Season to taste with salt, cayenne and summer savory, then add the oysters and sherry and heat through gently. Sprinkle each serving with parsley.

A solitary harvester cuts through the rich Louisiana wheatlands. At the turn of the century everyone joined in the harvest

CLAM CHOWDER (NEW ENGLAND)

The word chowder is derived from the French *chaudière*, and it is possible that this 'meal in a dish', which is so popular in Canada and the United States today, was originally invented by the early Breton fishermen. A more modern version, Manhattan chowder, is distinguished by the addition of tomatoes.

Serves 4

1 pint shelled clams and their liquid, or
2 10-oz cans minced clams
¼ lb salt pork or bacon, diced
1 medium onion, chopped
3 medium potatoes, diced
¼ teaspoon salt
freshly ground pepper
1 pint milk
paprika
butter

Drain the clams, measure the liquid and add enough water to make 1 pint. In a large saucepan brown the salt pork or bacon, then stir in the chopped onion and cook over a very low heat for about 5 minutes. Add the potatoes, clam liquid and seasoning and simmer for about 15 minutes or until the potatoes are tender.

Chop the clams, if whole, and add to the pan with the milk. Bring the chowder slowly back to boiling point. Top each serving with a sprinkling of paprika and a pat of butter.

CORN CHOWDER (NEW ENGLAND)

The New England states are famous for dishes that have stick-to-the-ribs propensities – the homey corn chowder is one of them.

Serves 4

¼ cup diced salt pork
1 medium onion, chopped
1 pint boiling water
2 medium potatoes, sliced
2 cups fresh, canned or frozen corn kernels
1½ cups hot milk
salt and freshly ground pepper
4 cream crackers, split (optional)

In a saucepan cook the salt pork until it is crisp and brown. Add the onion and cook until transparent, stirring occasionally. Remove the salt pork and stir in the boiling water and potatoes. Simmer for about 15 minutes. Add the corn, hot milk and seasoning to taste – do not let the mixture boil. If you wish, add the crackers just before serving.

PUMPKIN SOUP (NEW ENGLAND)

American cooks have always been inventive in the culinary use of pumpkin and other squashes and often, as in this recipe, one vegetable may be exchanged for the other.

Serves 4

2 tablespoons butter
3 tablespoons finely chopped onion
1 pint chicken stock
2 cups cooked pumpkin, fresh or canned
1 pint milk
¼ teaspoon each of ground cloves, ground ginger and ground allspice
¼ teaspoon salt
¼ cup heavy cream
¼ cup dry sherry

In a large heavy saucepan melt the butter, add the chopped onion and cook until transparent. Stir in the chicken stock, well drained pumpkin, milk, spices and salt. Bring to a boil, then reduce the heat and simmer for 15–20 minutes, stirring frequently.

Rub the soup through a fine strainer, then return it to the saucepan. Stir in the cream and sherry, and heat but do not boil.

Cornmeal, rice and vegetables

SPOON BREAD (DEEP SOUTH)

Southern spoon bread derives from the 'Indian pudding' that was a mainstay in colonial times. It is served today with meat or poultry as a substitute for potatoes or rice.

Serves 4

1 cup white cornmeal
1 teaspoon baking powder
¼ teaspoon baking soda
½ teaspoon salt
3 medium eggs, beaten
2 tablespoons butter
1 pint buttermilk

Sift the cornmeal, baking powder, baking soda and salt together into a mixing bowl. Make a well in the center and pour in the beaten eggs. Put either an 8 × 8 × 2 in baking pan or a 1½ quart soufflé dish in a moderately hot oven (400°F) to warm, adding 2 tablespoons butter to melt. Mix the eggs into the cornmeal, then gradually beat in the buttermilk. Remove the pan or dish from the oven and tip it to coat all inside surfaces with melted butter. Pour the excess butter into the batter and stir quickly to mix. Pour the batter into the pan or dish. Bake for 35 minutes and serve immediately with lots of butter.

Anglers' pride c. 1890

WILD RICE AND MUSHROOM CASSEROLE (MIDWEST AND UPPER CANADA)

In Minnesota and Wisconsin, and in Manitoba and Ontario, the Chippewas and the other American Indians have for generations been harvesting the grain of the aquatic grass called wild rice. In modern kitchens, the unique texture and flavor of wild rice make it a favorite accompaniment for all kinds of game, and it is also very good when used to stuff domestic duck or turkey.

Serves 4

1 cup wild rice
¼ teaspoon dried thyme
¼ teaspoon dried basil
salt and pepper
1½ pints beef stock
¼ cup butter
1 medium onion, finely chopped
¾ lb mushrooms, sliced

Wash the wild rice under running water. Put it in a heavy saucepan and stir in the herbs, salt and stock. Cover tightly and bring to a boil, then simmer over low heat for about 45 minutes or cook until tender.
  Lightly butter a 1½ quart casserole. Melt the remaining butter and cook the onion for 2–3 minutes. Stir in the sliced mushrooms and cook until they change color. Combine the mushrooms, onion, and rice (which should have absorbed most of the stock) in the casserole and season with salt and pepper to taste. Bake in a moderate oven (350°F) for 15–20 minutes.

PENNSYLVANIA DUTCH FRIED CUCUMBERS

Since long before the American Revolutionary War the Pennsylvania Dutch (who came from Germany, not Holland, and whose name is derived from the word *Deutsch*) have been setting standards for good food. The farms of southeastern Pennsylvania are among the finest in the world, and farming families deliver their own produce and tend market stalls in agricultural centers such as Lancaster, which is a few miles west of Philadelphia.

Serves 4

2 cucumbers,
  7–8 in long
salt and freshly ground pepper
1 egg, beaten
1 cup fresh breadcrumbs
¼ teaspoon dried savory
¼ teaspoon dried thyme
6 tablespoons corn oil
juice of ¼ lemon

Peel the cucumbers and cut into ¼ in slices. Let them steep with a sprinkling of salt for about 20 minutes, then drain and pat dry. Dip the cucumber slices in beaten egg, then in the breadcrumbs well mixed with the herbs, salt and pepper. Fry the slices in oil for about 15 minutes, turning once to give them an even color. Sprinkle with lemon juice and serve with flank steak.

North America

BAKED WALLEYE PIKE (MIDWEST)

Pike is popular among American sportsmen. Throughout the Great Lakes country, the Midwest, western Canada and Alaska it is known by various local names and cooked in many different ways. It is particularly delicious served with a simple, tasty stuffing.

Serves 4

1 pike weighing 3 lb, scaled
½ teaspoon salt
1 cup cracker crumbs
1 celery stalk, chopped
½ small onion, peeled and chopped
½ small green pepper, chopped
¼ cup chopped cooked ham
1 egg
cayenne
½ teaspoon mustard
a few slices of bacon

Wipe the fish with a damp cloth and salt the cavity. Combine the cracker crumbs, celery, onion, green pepper and ham. Break in the egg and mix well, adding a dash of cayenne and the mustard. Stuff the fish and sew or close tightly with skewers. Put in an oiled baking pan and top with bacon slices. Bake in a moderate oven (350°F) for 1 hour, or until fish flakes easily when tested with a fork.

BAKED SHAD WITH CORNBREAD STUFFING (ATLANTIC STATES)

Shad has always been considered a delicacy, particularly now that polluted rivers have made it difficult to come by. In the Carolinas, where this recipe comes from, the season begins in February; in New York and New England it is slightly later.

Serves 4

2 shad fillets (about 1 lb)
6 tablespoons butter
2 tablespoons finely chopped scallion
2 tablespoons chopped green pepper
¼ lb mushrooms, finely chopped
⅔ cup crumbled cornbread
⅔ cup crumbled water biscuits
salt and freshly ground pepper
2 teaspoons chopped fresh dill
lemon wedges

Wipe the fillets with a damp cloth and lay them in a lightly greased shallow baking dish.
Melt ¼ cup of the butter in a skillet and sauté the scallion, green pepper and mushrooms for about 5 minutes. Stir in the crumbled cornbread and biscuits, sprinkling generously with salt and some pepper, then add the herbs and mix well.
Spread this stuffing on the fillets, then fold them lengthwise and tie in 3 places. Dot with the remaining butter and season with salt and pepper. Pour at least ½ cup water into the baking dish and cover loosely with foil. Bake in a moderately hot oven (375°F) for 30 minutes. Remove the strings, cut the fillets in half and garnish with lemon wedges.

McLeod lake, British Columbia: fishing today on one of North America's many beautiful lakes

F*ish*

COLD POACHED SALMON (NORTHWEST)

Most of the salmon available in the United States comes from the Columbia River, Puget Sound and Alaska while in Canada that from the Frazer and Campbell rivers is thought by some to be the best. The Maritime Provinces supply the Eastern seaboard with salmon, especially smoked Nova Scotia – a popular delicacy that is known in New York as 'Novy'.

Serves 4

4 salmon steaks
1½ cups chicken stock
¼ cup white wine
3–4 tablespoons finely chopped fresh dill
salt
½ lemon, to garnish

Put the salmon steaks in a deep, oiled baking dish large enough to accommodate them. Barely cover with all the combined remaining ingredients, except the lemon. Poach in a hot oven (425°F) for 20 minutes. Allow to cool, then chill the salmon, in the baking dish. Carefully transfer to a cold serving platter and garnish with lemon slices. Tartare sauce makes a good complement.

A banquet of fish and seafood: chicken and oysters over cornbread, shrimp cocktail, crab Louis, Cajun gumbo, sablefish Alaska and fish stuffed avocados

LOBSTER NEWBERG (NEW YORK)

Throughout the nineteenth century, Delmonico's restaurant in Manhattan set standards for all good American cooks. Its most famous dish was originally named after a patron, Ben Wenberg, but the first three letters of Ben's surname were reversed after he quarreled with the restaurateur. The following way of preparing Lobster Newberg has since become a classic.

Serves 4

*2 live lobsters, each
    weighing about 2 lb
6 tablespoons butter,
    clarified
⅛ teaspoon salt
1 cup heavy cream
2 tablespoons Madeira
3 egg yolks, well beaten
cayenne pepper*

Boil the lobster until the shells are barely red. When cool, remove the lobster meat from the shells and cut it into small pieces. Put in a saucepan with about ¼ cup of the butter and the salt and sauté lightly, turning the lobster pieces to cook without browning. Remove lobster. Pour the cream into the pan and bring to a boil. Reduce the liquid by half. Stir in the Madeira and bring back to boiling point, then remove from the heat.

Stir some of the liquid into the beaten egg yolks, and add this mixture to the pan, stirring to make a slightly thick sauce. Return lobster. Stir in the remaining butter and a little cayenne and reheat without boiling. Arrange the lobster in a heated serving dish and top with the sauce.

CRAB LOUIS (WEST COAST)

From Seattle and Portland to San Francisco and Los Angeles, crabmeat dressed with a mayonnaise mixture – a dish devised by a chef whose last name is forgotten – has become an American classic. Crab Louis is either served as a bountiful salad for lunch or sometimes, as in this recipe, as an appetizer.

Serves 4

*1 cup mayonnaise
¼ cup heavy cream
¼ cup chili sauce
¼ cup chopped
    green pepper
2 tablespoons finely
    chopped chives or
    scallion
2 tablespoons chopped
    pitted green olives
salt
lemon juice
3 cups flaked cooked
    crab
1 large head of lettuce,
    shredded and chilled*

Mix together the mayonnaise, cream, chili sauce, green pepper, chives or scallions and olives. Add salt and lemon juice to taste. Chill the crabmeat on beds of shredded lettuce and top with the Louis dressing.

FISH-STUFFED AVOCADO (FLORIDA)

Avocados are cultivated in both southern California and southern Florida for consumption throughout the United States. More often than not they are served uncooked in salads, but the ways to use avocados are limited only by the cook's imagination. This recipe originated in Key West.

Serves 4

2 tablespoons butter
2 tablespoons flour
1 cup cream
salt and pepper
2 cups flaked cooked fish
(turkey or chicken may
be substituted)
2 tablespoons finely
chopped red pepper
2 tablespoons finely
chopped green pepper
2 medium avocados, at
room temperature
2 tablespoons fine crumbs

Melt the butter in a saucepan. Stir in the flour, then gradually stir in the cream and salt to taste. Stir constantly until the sauce thickens. Add the flaked fish and peppers and adjust the seasoning.

Cut the avocados in half lengthwise and remove the pits. Put the avocados in a greased shallow pan, cut sides up, if necessary cutting thin slices from the rounded surfaces of each half so the avocados do not tip over. Fill the cavities with the creamed fish and sprinkle with crumbs (preferably from water biscuits). Place 4 in from broiler heat, just long enough to heat the flesh of the avocados and brown their tops.

SAUTÉED POMPANO (GULF STATES)

Pompano, which is related to the mackerel, is considered one of the very best fish found in American waters.

Serves 4

2 pompano weighing
1¼ lb each, split and
boned
⅓ cup butter
coarse salt
freshly ground pepper
6 tablespoons dry
vermouth
3 tablespoons finely
chopped fresh chervil

Wipe the fish with a damp cloth. Melt about ⅓ cup of the butter in a skillet large enough to hold the fish pieces in one layer. When the butter foams, turn the heat to moderately high and sauté the fish, flesh side down, for about 3 minutes. Turn, sprinkle with a little salt and pepper and sauté for 5 minutes, spooning over the melted butter. Transfer the fish to a warm serving plate.

Stir the vermouth into the pan and boil to reduce to about half. Sprinkle in the chervil and stir in the remaining butter. Pour this sauce over the fish.

CODFISH CAKES (MARITIME PROVINCES)

Along the seaboards of New England and Canada fried cakes made of a mixture of fish and mashed potatoes are as traditional as they are delicious.

Soak the cod 24 hours in advance.
Serves 4

1 lb boneless salt cod,
soaked in cold water
overnight
2 cups mashed potatoes
1 small onion, finely
chopped or minced
2 tablespoons butter,
melted
1 egg, beaten
2–3 tablespoons finely
chopped parsley
salt and pepper
flour (optional)
⅓ cup dry breadcrumbs
oil for frying

Drain the cod then cover it with fresh water in a saucepan and heat slowly until almost, but not quite, boiling. Drain and flake. Place in a mixing bowl and stir in the mashed potatoes, onion, butter, beaten egg, parsley, and salt and pepper to taste. Shape the mixture into 8 cakes, using a little flour only if necessary to help hold them together. Coat in breadcrumbs and fry in hot fat or oil, turning to brown both sides.

SABLEFISH ALASKA (PACIFIC COAST)

The rich, succulent sablefish, at least as well known to Oregonians and Californians as black Alaska cod, is served both fresh and smoked and is frequently barbecued over charcoal. Alaskans sometimes make a sablefish pie with cheese and peppers, or cook the fish in this straightforward Anglo-Saxon way and serve it with curried tomato sauce.

Serves 4

4 sablefish fillets
flour
salt and pepper
2 eggs, beaten
1 cup dry breadcrumbs
¼ cup butter

Curried tomato sauce
¼ cup butter
3 tablespoons flour
½ cup fish stock
1 cup milk
salt and pepper
freshly grated nutmeg
3 tablespoons tomato
purée
1 tablespoon curry powder

Dip the fillets into flour mixed with salt and pepper and then into beaten egg. Coat generously with breadcrumbs. Cook in butter over medium heat until the fillets are golden on both sides and the fish is tender.

To make the sauce, melt the butter and stir in the flour to make a smooth paste. Cook until slightly colored. Carefully stir in the fish stock to avoid making lumps, then gradually add the milk and continue cooking, stirring all the time, until thickened. Season to taste with salt, pepper and a little nutmeg, then mix in the tomato purée and curry powder. Serve hot with the fish.

CAJUN GUMBO (LOUISIANA)

Louisiana's Cajun people trace their ancestry back to Acadia, as Nova Scotia was known before the Treaty of Utrecht in 1713 when the British took it from the French. After their removal to the *bayou* marshlands of Louisiana they brought the French touch to many local dishes with origins in the West Indies and Africa. *Gumbo* is derived from a dialect word for okra and means a much embellished okra soup flavored with various seafoods or meat. Filé powder is made from the young tender leaves of the sassafras tree. American Indians used it to bind and thicken sauces.

Serves 6–8

½ lb cooked ham
1 clove of garlic, crushed
4 onions, chopped
¾ lb okra, sliced
1½ lb raw shelled shrimp
1½ lb tomatoes, skinned
and chopped
a 6-oz can tomato purée
1½ pints chicken stock
Tabasco sauce
1 green pepper, chopped
1 lb crabmeat
grated rind of 1 lemon
1 tablespoon filé powder
(optional)
18 mussels

Trim excess fat from the ham and cut the meat into cubes. Render enough of the fat to make about 2 tablespoons in the bottom of a heavy skillet. Reserve the remainder. Sauté the garlic, onions and okra in the melted fat for about 10 minutes, then add the shrimp and cook, stirring occasionally, for 5 minutes. Remove the shrimp and okra and allow to cool. Keep in the refrigerator if needed.

Stir the tomatoes into the pan, add the tomato purée, stock and several dashes of Tabasco and simmer for about 2 hours. Half an hour before serving add the ham cubes and okra. Heat some of the reserved fat and sauté the green pepper and crabmeat for about 10 minutes. Add to the tomato mixture with the lemon rind, filé powder, if used, crabmeat and shrimp, then top with the mussels. Cover tightly and steam until the mussels open. (Discard any that remain closed.) Fluffy rice should accompany this dish.

North America

Meat

CHILI CON CARNE (SOUTHWEST)

The *New York Times* once said that if anything is more typically American than apple pie, it is chili con carne. As the name implies, this dish of Texan origin is composed of chili pepper with meat although beans or rice are popular accompaniments.

Serves 8

4–5 onions, finely chopped
4 cloves garlic, crushed
2 tablespoons corn oil
3 lb lean beef, cut into ½ in cubes
5–8 tablespoons fresh chili powder
1 teaspoon dried oregano
2 teaspoons ground cumin
2 dashes Tabasco sauce
3 tablespoons tomato purée
1½ cups beer

Sauté the onions and garlic in the oil. Stir in the beef cubes and brown quickly. Add the chili powder, oregano, cumin, Tabasco, tomato purée and beer. Cover and simmer for about 45 minutes, adding more liquid if necessary. Uncover, taste for seasoning, then simmer for about 15 minutes more. Serve with hot rice and red kidney beans.

SWEDISH MEATBALLS (MIDWEST)

Scandinavians influenced eating habits wherever they settled, and the *smörgåsbord* – cold table – is a commonly accepted meal in the Midwest and all along the Pacific coast. No such array of food is considered complete without meatballs, which may be either bite-size to pop into your mouth at a cocktail party or served in a sauce for dinner.

Serves 4

½ lb lean beef
½ lb lean pork
½ cup soft fresh breadcrumbs
1 cup milk
1 egg, slightly beaten
1 teaspoon salt
freshly ground pepper
½ teaspoon ground allspice
1 medium onion, finely chopped
2 tablespoons bacon fat
6 tablespoons butter
1 teaspoon beef extract
1½ tablespoons flour
1 cup cream
1 tablespoon finely chopped parsley

Grind the beef and pork together 4 times. Soak the breadcrumbs in half the milk. When soft, add it to the meat and mix thoroughly. Stir in the egg and seasonings and gradually add the remaining milk.

Cook the onion in the bacon fat for 4–5 minutes, then drain on paper towels and stir it into the meat mixture. Shape the mixture into small balls. Melt 2 tablespoons butter in a skillet and fry the meatballs a few at a time, shaking the pan so that they roll and brown evenly.

Meanwhile, dissolve the beef extract in 1½ cups boiling water, and pour half of this into a baking dish. As the first meatballs brown, put them in this dish in the oven to keep warm. Repeat the process – using a further 2 tablespoons butter for frying – until all the meatballs are cooked. Pour the remaining beef extract mixture into the skillet, stir well to scrape up the pan juices and pour this over the meatballs.

Melt the remaining 2 tablespoons butter in the skillet. Stir in the flour and cook for 2–3 minutes. Stir in all the liquid from the meatballs. When the sauce thickens, stir in the cream and again pour over the hot meatballs. Sprinkle with parsley and serve immediately. Fluffy mashed potatoes are a good accompaniment.

MEAT LOAF (MIDWEST)

Eaten hot or cold, doused with tomato catsup or chili sauce, stuffed with walnuts as in North Carolina or with sausages as in Quebec, meat loaves are universally popular in Canada and the United States. This one from Minnesota makes a meal for four, with plenty left over for sandwiches another day.

Serves 4

1½ lb ground round (silverside)
¾ lb ground lean veal
¾ lb ground pork
4 slices of white bread
1⅓ cups milk
3 whole eggs
3 tablespoons finely chopped celery
2 medium onions, finely chopped
2 tablespoons finely chopped parsley
¼ teaspoon dried thyme
¼ teaspoon dried marjoram
¼ teaspoon dried basil
freshly ground salt and pepper
3 bacon slices
dry vermouth

Put all the meat in a large bowl. Tear the bread into small pieces and soak in the milk. Break the eggs on top of the meat and add the celery, onions, parsley, herbs, salt, pepper, bread and milk. Mix lightly but thoroughly to distribute the bread and seasonings throughout the meat.

Shape the mixture into a firm loaf and place it in a buttered loaf pan. Lay the bacon slices on top. Bake in a moderately hot oven (375°F) for 45 minutes or until the surface begins to brown. Pour ½ cup boiling water over the meat loaf and continue baking for about 45 minutes, basting once or twice with a little dry vermouth and any juices that rise. When cooked, run a knife around the edges and turn the loaf on to a hot platter. Serve with buttered noodles.

TOURTIÈRE (FRENCH CANADA)

Pork pies have been made in Canada for *Reveillon* – a midnight feast served after Mass on Christmas Eve – since the first French settlements in the seventeenth century. Modern versions of the *tourtières* are sometimes made with chicken or veal.

Prepare the dough several hours in advance.
Serves 4

Dough
3–3½ cups flour
2 teaspoons baking powder
1 teaspoon salt
1 cup lard
½ cup hot water
2 teaspoons lemon juice or vinegar
1 egg, well beaten

Filling
1 lb ground lean pork
1 medium onion, finely chopped
1 tablespoon finely chopped celery leaves
½ teaspoon salt
freshly ground pepper
pinch of ground cloves
½ teaspoon dried savory
1 small bay leaf
½ cup boiling water
2–3 tablespoons dry breadcrumbs

First make the dough. Sift the flour, baking powder and salt into a mixing bowl. Add ½ cup of the lard and cut in with 2 knives until the mixture becomes mealy. Melt the remaining lard in the hot water and add the lemon juice or vinegar and half of the beaten egg. Mix into the flour mixture and knead until the dough leaves the sides of the bowl. Turn out onto a lightly floured board and knead for about 1 minute or until well mixed. Wrap in wax paper and chill for several hours.

To make the filling, mix the pork, onion, celery leaves, seasonings and water together in a saucepan and simmer for about 10 minutes or until the meat loses its color, stirring occasionally. Cover and continue cooking over the lowest possible heat for about 30 minutes. Remove the bay leaf, drain and set the filling aside to cool.

Line an 8 in pie plate with half the dough and sprinkle the breadcrumbs on the flat surface (to absorb the meat fat). Fill with the meat mixture. Cover with the remaining dough, seal the edges and slash the top to let steam escape. Brush with beaten egg remaining from dough mixture. Bake in a hot oven (425°F) for 10 minutes, then reduce the heat to moderate (350°F) and continue baking for about 30 minutes.

Chili con carne: lean beef spiced with hot chilis – a Texan specialty

Butterflied leg of lamb and baked spareribs: barbecues prove that food cooked outdoors always tastes better . . .

LES COTES DE PORC QUÉBECOISE (QUEBEC, GASPÉ)

Pork recipes are very popular among French-Canadian cooks: dishes like this one, combining pork with apples, cider and maple syrup, are often served in the orchard country of Charlevoix County, Quebec.

Serves 4

1 tablespoon butter
4 pork chops, about 1¼ in thick
salt and freshly ground pepper
1½ tablespoons flour
1½ tablespoons maple syrup
1 cup cider or apple juice
2 tart apples, cored but not peeled

Melt the butter in a heavy skillet, just large enough to hold the chops snugly in one layer. Brown the meat on both sides and sprinkle with salt and pepper. When both sides are brown, sprinkle with the flour and divide the maple syrup evenly between the chops, rubbing into the meat with the back of a spoon. Pour in the cider or apple juice, cover the pan and simmer for 20 minutes over a low heat.

Cut the cored apples in half horizontally and place a half on each chop. Cover the pan again and continue to cook for about 30 minutes or until the apples are soft and form a thick sauce.

CASSEROLE OF HAM AND SWEET POTATOES (DEEP SOUTH)

Surprisingly enough, country-cured hams are still available in some parts of the United States, including the South, New England and the Midwest. Sweet potatoes, or yams, make perfect foils to the strong-flavored ham when combined in what are known throughout the country as 'one-dish meals'. There are numerous variations of this South Carolina recipe.

Serves 4

1½ lb slice uncooked ham
3 medium sweet potatoes or yams, peeled and quartered
salt
⅓ cup brown sugar
2 tablespoons butter
1 orange, peeled and sliced
1 teaspoon lemon juice

Put the ham in a shallow casserole and pour on about ¾ cup hot water, not quite enough to cover. Arrange the sweet potato quarters in the casserole. Sprinkle with salt and sugar and dot with butter. Separate the sweet potato pieces with orange slices, and add the lemon juice. Bake in a low oven (300°F) for 1 hour or until the sweet potatoes are tender and candied. Baste with the juices 2 or 3 times. Serve in the same dish.

FRANKFURTERS FLAMBÉ (NEW YORK)

American hot dogs make one think of baseball games and county fairs; but they are also affectionately treated in American kitchens. The recipe below is sometimes prepared and served in a chafing dish.

Serves 4

1 lb frankfurters
6 tablespoons butter
⅓ lb mushrooms, quartered
1 clove of garlic, crushed
⅓ teaspoon salt
freshly ground pepper
1 tablespoon finely chopped parsley
¼ cup applejack or brandy

Cut the frankfurters in quarters lengthwise, then in ½ in pieces, and in a large skillet heat for 5 minutes in foaming butter. Add the mushrooms, garlic, salt and pepper. Stir to coat the mushrooms with butter, then cover and cook for 5 more minutes. Sprinkle with parsley, and just before serving pour on heated applejack or brandy and set it aflame.

JAMBALAYA (LOUISIANA)

Although recipes vary greatly, Jambalaya is one of the most instantly recognizable Creole dishes.

Serves 4

1 tablespoon bacon fat
2 small onions, chopped
4 highly seasoned pork sausages
1 tablespoon flour
⅓ lb cooked smoked ham, diced
2 medium tomatoes, skinned, seeded and chopped
¾ cup rice
1 clove of garlic, crushed
1½ cups chicken stock
creole or cayenne pepper to taste
⅓ teaspoon dried thyme
salt
1 small green pepper, diced
3 tablespoons chopped parsley
1 lb raw shelled shrimp
1 pint fresh oysters, shucked

Melt the bacon fat in a heavy saucepan with a tightly fitting lid and fry the onions and sausages. Stir in the flour and let it brown slightly. Add the ham and tomatoes, cover tightly and simmer for about 30 minutes. Add the rice, garlic, stock, creole or cayenne pepper, thyme, salt to taste, green pepper and parsley. Cover and continue simmering until the rice is cooked but not mushy. Do not stir. Add the shrimp and cook for 2 minutes. Add the oysters and cook for 3 minutes more.

BUTTERFLIED LEG OF LAMB (ROCKY MOUNTAIN WEST)

For a nation in which hundreds of thousands of families engage in 'cook-outs' and backyard barbecues, this is a recipe that makes barbecued lamb a new experience – and it can be accomplished indoors with equal success. Some British Columbians use a honey-and-mustard basting sauce for barbecued lamb, while in the High Sierras a simple mixture of garlic and oil may be brushed on the meat with a bunch of fresh herbs and parsley.

Prepare the meat several hours in advance.
Serves 4

1 leg of lamb, about 4 lb, with excess fat removed
2 cloves of garlic, crushed
1 teaspoon salt
freshly ground pepper
1 teaspoon dried oregano
juice of 1 lemon
2 tablespoons olive oil
4 scallions, finely chopped
1 tablespoon butter
1 cup soft fresh breadcrumbs
1 tablespoon finely chopped parsley
¼ cup freshly grated Parmesan

Ask your butcher to remove the bone from the lamb by making a long cut on the under side (not the fat side). Spread the meat out flat so that it looks like an irregularly-shaped butterfly. Mix the garlic, salt, pepper, oregano and juice of lemon into a grainy paste. Rub this onto the meat on both sides. Leave to stand at room temperature for several hours.

If cooking outdoors, arrange a grill 3 in above the charcoal to give a medium heat. Indoors, the broiler should be preheated and the rack placed about 4 in below the heat. Boned lamb is of varying thickness so you will have some meat cooked on the rare side, some faintly pink, and the rest well done. On a barbecue, put the meat fat side down; if it is very lean brush with 1 tablespoon oil. Leave to cook undisturbed for 30 minutes, then turn it over, permitting the fat side to baste the meat, and cook for 15 minutes more. For kitchen cooking, do the same but watch the meat carefully – if there are signs of burning reduce the heat.

Meanwhile, sauté the scallions in the butter and 1 tablespoon of the oil. Stir in the breadcrumbs, parsley and cheese. Spread this mixture over the meat just before removing it from the heat. Let the lamb rest for a few minutes before carving perpendicularly as you would a large steak.

BAKED SPARERIBS (MIDWEST)

When Americans speak of spareribs they mean pork: the traditional butchers' cut containing the breastbone, the rib bones, and rib cartilages; or the rib bones from the back, known as 'back ribs' among Southerners, or sometimes 'country spareribs'. In Canada it is traditional to serve sauerkraut with ribs, and the Pennsylvania Dutch often make a 'rib sandwich', putting a layer of apple stuffing in the center. Chinese workers who helped to build the transcontinental railroads established the custom of 'sweet and sour' barbecuing, but a more common way of barbecuing – in the kitchen or outdoors – is represented by this recipe from Missouri.

... and the New World provides beautiful settings for them.

Serves 4

1 onion, chopped
2 tablespoons bacon fat
2 tablespoons vinegar
2 tablespoons sugar
¼ cup lemon juice
1 cup tomato catsup
3 tablespoons Worcestershire sauce
2 teaspoons sharp mustard
¼ cup water
chopped parsley
1 teaspoon dried basil
1 tablespoon chili powder (optional)
4 lb pork spareribs
salt and pepper

Cook the chopped onion in bacon fat for about 5 minutes, then add the vinegar, sugar, lemon juice, catsup, Worcestershire sauce, mustard, water, parsley, basil and chili powder, if used. Simmer for 30 minutes. Wipe the ribs and sprinkle with salt and pepper before putting on a rack in a shallow roasting pan. Bake in a hot oven (450°F) for 30 minutes. Take out of the oven and drain the fat from the pan. Remove the rack and replace the ribs, brushing them with the cooked sauce. Reduce the heat to cool (300°F), and bake for at least 1½ hours, brushing the ribs frequently with the sauce until tender.

BAKED LIVER HILO STYLE (HAWAII)

The culinary influences of the East and West meet in Hawaii and this recipe, using both Oriental and Occidental ingredients, shows how successfully they can be combined.

Prepare 2 hours in advance.
Serves 4

1 lb beef liver, in 4 slices
a 6-oz can water
* chestnuts, sliced*
4 bacon slices, cut in
* squares*
¼ cup butter
½ cup fresh
* breadcrumbs*
2 bananas, sliced

Marinade
¼ cup soy sauce
¼ cup peanut oil
¼ cup brandy
2 tablespoons sugar
1 teaspoon finely chopped
* lemon rind*
¼ teaspoon ground ginger

Wipe the liver with a damp cloth. Mix together the marinade ingredients, add the liver and marinate with the water chestnuts for 2 hours.

About 30 minutes before serving, sauté the bacon pieces and drain on paper towels. Melt most of the butter in a small saucepan and stir in the breadcrumbs. Butter a shallow baking dish with the remaining butter. Drain the liver and water chestnuts thoroughly and put them in the baking dish. Arrange the bananas on top and spread with the buttered crumbs. Bake in a moderate oven (350°F) for 20 minutes.

BRUNSWICK STEW (DEEP SOUTH)

The fabled and traditional Brunswick stew of the South used to be based on squirrel meat and was a feature of backwoods political rallies in the days when candidates fed hordes of voters outdoors. Today it is more often made with chicken and it is markedly American in style.

Serves 6

3 bacon slices, cut
* in small squares*
½ lb chuck steak, cubed
½ lb lean veal, cubed
1 chicken, weighing
* 2½–3 lb, in small pieces*
salt and freshly ground
* pepper*
4 tomatoes, skinned and
* quartered*
3 medium onions, chopped
1½ pints boiling water
2 cups fresh lima beans
½ lb potatoes, diced
2 cups sliced fresh okra
Tabasco sauce
2 cups fresh or canned
* corn kernels*
¼ cup breadcrumbs
2 tablespoons butter
* (optional)*

Fry the bacon squares in a heavy saucepan. Add the beef and veal cubes and brown all over. Remove the meat and brown the chicken pieces. Pour off all the fat, return the meat and chicken to the pan and season well with salt and pepper. Add the tomatoes, onions and water, then simmer for about 45 minutes.

Remove the chicken pieces, let them cool, then pull the meat from the bones and cut into small chunks. Return these to the pan with the beans, potatoes, okra and several dashes of Tabasco. Simmer for about 1 hour, skimming fat at intervals.

Add the corn and cook for about 10 minutes, then stir in the breadcrumbs and butter. When done the stew should almost be the consistency of oatmeal and have a pronounced peppery taste. Freshly baked corn sticks are the traditional accompaniment.

Baked liver Hilo style: East and West meet in this Hawaiian dish.

BROILED FLANK STEAK (CALIFORNIA)

A popular item in New York restaurants for many years, the so-called 'London broil' was simply a well broiled flank steak, cut diagonally in thin slices. When marinated in this Chinese-American sauce it makes the flavor of other American steaks almost tasteless in comparison.

Prepare at least 1 hour in advance.
Serves 4

1 flank steak
  (about 3 lb)

Marinade
1¼ cups soy sauce
¼ cup dry sherry
¾ cup sugar
1 clove of garlic, crushed
¼ teaspoon grated ginger
  root

Put the steak in a shallow container just large enough to allow it to lie flat. Mix the marinade ingredients and pour over the meat. Marinate for at least 1 hour, turning several times and spooning the marinade over the surface. Broil about 3 in from a high heat, so that the sugar in the marinade chars slightly. Save the marinade for another time.

WISCONSIN POT ROAST (MIDWEST)

This Wisconsin pot roast was developed by the American actor, Alfred Lunt. It is based on the classic Swedish *slottstek* with its characteristic taste of anchovies – enhanced by Wisconsin maple syrup instead of molasses.

Serves 4

3½ lb rolled rump of beef
  without fat
2 tablespoons beef suet
¼ cup cider vinegar
2 tablespoons maple syrup
2 medium onions, chopped
16 peppercorns
12 allspice berries
2 bay leaves
3 anchovy fillets
1 pint beef stock
1 teaspoon arrowroot

Brown all surfaces of the meat in the melted suet. Add the vinegar, maple syrup, onions, peppercorns, allspice, bay leaves and anchovies. Pour in the stock and bring to a boil. Simmer gently for 2½–3 hours, or until the meat is tender. Thicken the sauce with the arrowroot mixed in a little water, and spoon the sauce over the meat before serving.

Poultry and game

ROAST TURKEY WITH ORANGE-FLAVORED STUFFING (WEST COAST)

Turkeys are an important part of traditional Thanksgiving Day celebrations in Canada and the United States, especially in New England where the custom of serving cranberry sauce as an accompaniment began. American cooks, however, are irrepressibly inventive, and the following recipe profits from the use of California oranges.

Serves 4

1 lb sausage meat
8 cups stale white bread
  cubes
8 celery stalks, diced
1 onion, finely chopped
2 teaspoons grated
  orange rind
¼ teaspoon grated lemon
  rind
salt and freshly ground
  pepper
1 teaspoon dried thyme
¼ teaspoon dried marjoram
¼ teaspoon dried sage
¼ cup finely chopped
  parsley
¼ cup orange juice
a 12–14 lb turkey
¼ cup butter, melted

Preheat the oven to 325°F. Break the sausage meat into pieces and cook it slowly in a saucepan, stirring to keep the particles separate. Drain off the fat and reserve. Combine the sausage meat with the bread cubes and celery.
  Sauté the onion in 2 tablespoons of the sausage fat and add to the bread mixture with the orange and lemon rind, salt and pepper to taste, thyme, marjoram, sage, parsley and orange juice. Stir in ¼ cup of the sausage fat, then stuff the mixture into the turkey cavity.
  Truss the turkey, rub it with the butter and put it on a rack, breast side down, in a shallow roasting pan. Roast for 2½ hours, basting frequently with the remaining melted butter. Turn breast side up and continue roasting, basting with the pan drippings, for a further 1½–2 hours.

CRUSTY BAKED DUCK (NEW YORK)

Long Island duckling is a standard commercial description in most of the United States, and the best Canadian ducks are said to come from Brome Lake in the eastern townships of Quebec. In both cases the birds are plump and fat, and so the method given here eliminates the excess fat and results in an unusual and tasty dish.

Serves 4

a 5 lb duck
2 teaspoons salt
freshly ground pepper
1 egg
2 tablespoons milk
¼ teaspoon dried savory
2 cups fresh breadcrumbs
2 tablespoons flour

Preheat the oven to 350°F. Peel all the skin from the duck except the wings, tearing away as much fat as possible to reserve. With a sharp knife, cut out the backbone and neck and put in a saucepan with the giblets, 1 teaspoon or less of salt, a little pepper and enough water to cover. Simmer for about 2 hours.
  Divide the duck legs into drumsticks and thighs, remove the wings and divide the breast into 4 pieces, easing the flesh away from the ribs. Add the bones to the simmering stock. Cut the skin and fat into small pieces and render over a low heat.
  Beat the egg with the milk, 1 teaspoon salt, a little pepper and the savory. Dip the duck pieces in the egg mixture, then roll in the breadcrumbs. Brown in 2–3 tablespoons of the rendered fat. Transfer to a shallow casserole large enough to hold all the pieces in one layer. Cover the casserole and bake in the oven for about 50 minutes.
  Meanwhile stir the flour into 2 tablespoons of the rendered duck fat and mix in enough of the duck stock to make a thinnish gravy. Season to taste and serve with the crisp pieces of duck.

ROAST WILD GOOSE (ROCKY MOUNTAIN WEST)

Great flocks of Canada geese traverse the Mississippi flyway north from Louisiana and are often hunted in the Rocky Mountain region. This recipe is a variation of one from Alberta.

Prepare the goose 24 hours in advance.
Serves 4

1 wild Canada goose
coarse and fine salt
freshly ground pepper
1 onion, chopped
2 celery stalks, chopped
5 tart apples
1 tablespoon flour
1 teaspoon dried sage
1 teaspoon paprika
1 cup apple juice
1 cup orange juice
½ cup prune juice
¼ cup butter
2–3 tablespoons brown sugar
3 tablespoons currants soaked in Cognac

Clean the goose and remove pinfeathers. Rinse the cavity, dry it with paper towels and rub in coarse salt and fresh pepper. Stuff with the onion, celery and one of the apples, chopped. Put the goose in a covered roasting pan and leave to stand overnight in a cool place.

Next day mix together the flour, 1 teaspoon salt, ½ teaspoon pepper, sage and paprika, and rub well into the skin of the goose. Mix the 3 juices. Roast the goose, uncovered, in a moderately hot oven (400°F) until light brown. Pour off excess fat, and reduce the heat to warm (325°F). Baste every 15 minutes with the mixed juices. Allow 20 minutes per 1 lb cooking time.

About 20 minutes before the goose is ready, core and peel the remaining apples and slice them thickly. Fry them in foaming butter, turning after 5 minutes and adding the brown sugar. Continue to fry until golden, then add the currants. Place the apples around the goose on a hot platter.

California market, Dawson, 1901

CHICKEN TETRAZZINI (NEW YORK)

Hundreds of recipes evolve as tributes to distinguished people. Luisa Tetrazzini, a spellbinding *coloratura* whose career reached its peak just before World War I, had such a passion for pasta that she inspired a Delmonico's chef to name in her honor his dish of chicken, spaghetti, bubbling cream sauce and melted Parmesan. It is one of many American recipes deriving from Italy's cuisine.

Years later another New York restaurant kitchen produced a more calorie-conscious adaptation, substituting broccoli for pasta; and the result, chicken divan parisienne, is now a popular buffet party dish among Americans everywhere.

Serves 4

5 tablespoons butter
2 tablespoons flour
1 pint chicken stock
salt and freshly ground pepper
grated nutmeg
1 cup heavy cream
3 tablespoons medium dry sherry or white wine
½ lb mushrooms, sliced
6 oz thin spaghetti
3 cups shredded cooked chicken
½ cup freshly grated Parmesan

Melt 3 tablespoons of the butter and stir in the flour. Cook for 3 minutes before gradually stirring in the stock. Stir until the sauce thickens, and season with salt, pepper and a little nutmeg. Stir in the cream and sherry or wine.

Sauté the mushrooms in the remaining 2 tablespoons of butter. Cook the spaghetti, drain well and mix with the mushrooms, then put in a shallow buttered flameproof dish. Stir the shredded chicken into the hot sauce and pour over the spaghetti and mushrooms. Sprinkle with cheese and broil long enough to brown the top. Serve bubbling hot.

CHICKEN ILE D'ORLÉANS (QUEBEC)

As in Normandy and Brittany, there are many fruit orchards in Quebec and Ontario, and so it is not surprising to find certain similarities in the cuisine of the two regions. Apples grow abundantly on the Ile d'Orléans, near Quebec City.

Serves 4

1 chicken (about 3 lb)
applejack or Cognac
salt
paprika
1 cup diced toasted bread
1 celery stalk, sliced
1 small apple, peeled, cored and chopped
2–3 tablespoons raisins
1½ tablespoons butter, melted
a pinch of dried thyme
a pinch of finely chopped parsley
bacon fat
3 apples, cored and thickly sliced
bacon slices
½ cup heavy cream

Rub the inside of the chicken with some applejack or Cognac and sprinkle inside and out with salt and paprika. Mix the toast with the celery, chopped apple, raisins, butter, thyme and parsley. Stuff the chicken with this mixture and truss.

Brown the chicken in bacon fat and remove. Lightly brown the apple slices. Cover the bottom of a casserole with the apple slices, then put in the chicken and top with the bacon slices cut in half. Cover the casserole and bake in a moderate oven (350°F) for about 1¾ hours. Just before serving baste with cream and 2 or more tablespoons of applejack or Cognac, then transfer the chicken and cooked apples to a hot platter.

SOUTHERN FRIED CHICKEN (DEEP SOUTH)

Although purveyors of fast food may have tarnished the image of Southern fried chicken, it is an American specialty that deserves to be made in the home with love and care.

Serves 4

1 frying chicken,
  weighing 2–2½ lb
bacon fat
1 cup flour
1 tablespoon coarse salt
1 teaspoon freshly ground
  pepper
the chicken's liver and
  heart

Gravy
1¼ tablespoons flour
1¼ cups milk
1 tablespoon finely
  chopped parsley
salt and pepper

Divide the chicken into pieces, separating thighs from legs, removing backbone, dividing breast into 2 pieces, and detaching the wings. Melt a 1 in layer of bacon fat over a moderate heat in a skillet just large enough to hold the pieces in one layer.

Meanwhile put the flour, salt and pepper in a plastic bag. Drop in the chicken pieces 1 or 2 at a time, and shake well to cover each piece thoroughly with the flour mixture.

When the bacon fat is sizzling but not quite smoking, add the chicken pieces 3 or 4 at a time and brown quickly on all sides. Repeat until all the pieces are crisply golden. Now lower the heat and arrange all the pieces snugly in the pan. Cook for about 45 minutes, turning frequently. About 10 minutes before cooking is finished, add the chicken heart; and 5 minutes later add the liver.

Put the chicken pieces in the oven to keep warm. Chop the cooked heart and liver and reserve. Pour off all but about 1½ tablespoons of fat from the pan and stir in the flour. Scrape the bottom of the pan and let the flour brown slightly as it melds with the fat. Heat the milk and stir into the pan. Cook until the gravy thickens, then add the chopped heart and liver, parsley and salt and pepper to taste. Serve the chicken on a hot platter, and the gravy separately.

CHICKEN AND OYSTERS OVER CORNBREAD (VIRGINIA)

Combining chicken and oysters has been popular among American cooks since the earliest colonial days, and was especially popular as a supper dish in the nineteenth century. The recipe given below dates back to the days when Virginia was known as the Old Dominion.

Serves 4

2 cups diced cooked
  chicken
1¼ pints fresh shucked
  oysters
¼ cup butter
5 tablespoons flour
1¾ cups chicken stock
¼ cup heavy cream
¼ teaspoon salt
4–5 drops Tabasco sauce
1 teaspoon lemon juice
2 tablespoons finely
  chopped parsley

Cornbread
1 cup flour
1 tablespoon sugar
¾ teaspoon salt
5 teaspoons baking
  powder
1 cup yellow cornmeal
3 tablespoons butter,
  melted and cooled
  slightly
1 cup milk
1 egg, lightly beaten

To make the cornbread sift together the flour, sugar, salt and baking powder. Sift again, then stir in the cornmeal. Mix together the melted butter, milk and egg, and combine with the dry ingredients. Beat for about 1 minute. Pour into a buttered 8 in square baking pan and bake in a hot oven (425°F) for 25 minutes. Cool on a cake rack.

Have the chicken and oysters at room temperature. In a saucepan melt the butter and stir in the flour until smooth. Gradually stir in the chicken stock and simmer over very low heat, stirring constantly, for about 5 minutes or until thickened. Stir in the cream, salt, Tabasco and lemon juice.

Poach the oysters in their own liquid (from the shells) for 5 minutes or until their edges have just become plump. Drain and fold the oysters into the sauce. Add the diced chicken.

To serve, cut squares of cornbread, then split them, putting the bottom halves on a platter. Cover them with half of the chicken and oyster mixture, top with the remaining cornbread squares and cover with the rest of the sauce. Sprinkle with parsley.

Southern fried chicken with traditional accompaniments

Pecan pie satisfies the North American craving for cakes and desserts.

PECAN PIE (DEEP SOUTH)

Americans say that their pecan pie is an improvement upon British treacle tart because the nuts counteract the sweetness of the filling. In this recipe, adding Kentucky's bourbon whiskey is a further adaptation.

Serves 4

¼ cup butter
½ cup brown sugar
3 eggs
¼ teaspoon salt
1 cup dark corn syrup
1 tablespoon bourbon whiskey
1 cup chopped pecans
1 tablespoon flour
flaky pastry (p. 30)
9–10 whole pecans for decorating top
¼ cup whipping cream, whipped with 2 tablespoons sugar and 2–3 tablespoons bourbon whiskey (optional)

Cream the butter and add the brown sugar slowly, beating until the mixture is light and fluffy. Add the eggs one by one, beating continuously, then add the salt, corn syrup and bourbon. Toss the chopped pecans in the flour and fold into the syrup mixture.

Line a 9 in pie pan with flaky pastry and cover with foil. Fill this shell with dried beans and bake in a hot oven (450°F) for 10 minutes. Remove the foil and beans. Pour in the filling. Lower the heat to moderate (350°F) and bake for 35 minutes, or until the pie is firm. Decorate the top with a border of whole pecans and bake for 5 minutes more. Cream whipped with sugar and bourbon may be used as a garnish.

Desserts

BAKED ALASKA (NEW YORK)

This showy dessert, said to be the invention of Charles Ranhofer, one-time chef of Delmonico's restaurant in New York City, celebrated the American purchase of Alaska in 1867. It can be made in individual meringue-covered portions, or as a single crisp and creamy mountain to be cut into at the table.

Serves 8

4 egg whites
¾ cup confectioners' sugar
a 1 quart brick of vanilla ice cream
2 1-in thick slices of sponge or pound cake

Beat the egg whites until they form stiff peaks, then fold in the sugar. Arrange the ice cream on 1 slice of cake and top with the other. Arrange on a wooden board and cover completely with the meringue mixture. Bake in a very hot oven (475°F) for about 1–2 minutes, or until delicately brown. Serve immediately.

MAPLE WALNUT ICE CREAM (NEW ENGLAND)

When the first English settlers arrived in America they discovered that the natives sweetened their food with tree sap. Maple syrup and maple sugar still come from the woods of Vermont, New Hampshire, Maine, Quebec, as well as northern Minnesota, Wisconsin and Michigan. Although maple products are expensive, many families serve the syrup as a breakfast treat on pancakes, or use it as a flavoring in many kinds of food.

Prepare at least 5 hours in advance.
Serves 4

1 cup maple syrup
3 egg yolks, lightly beaten
¼ teaspoon salt
1 teaspoon vanilla extract
3 egg whites, stiffly beaten
1 cup heavy cream, whipped until thick
½ cup chopped walnuts

Put the maple syrup in the upper part of a double boiler and heat carefully; do not let it boil. Stir 2 tablespoons of the warm syrup, a spoonful at a time, into the beaten egg yolks, then stir this mixture into the remaining syrup. Cook slowly, stirring all the time, until the mixture thickens. Stir in the salt and vanilla and chill for about 1 hour. When cold, fold in the stiffly beaten egg whites and cream alternately.

Remove the dividers from an ice cube tray and fill it with the ice cream mixture. Freeze for about 1 hour, or until the mixture has frozen around the edges. Put the partially frozen mixture in a bowl and beat well. Add the chopped nuts. Return to the tray and freeze for 3 hours.

SHOOFLY PIE (PENNSYLVANIA)

The housewives of the Amish settlements of southeastern Pennsylvania became very adept at creating dishes with limited ingredients and their innovative recipes have now become traditional. The sweetness of shoofly pies, when brought to the outdoor markets, attracted more than eager buyers and therefore suggested the name.

Serves 4

1½ cups flour
1 cup brown sugar
¼ teaspoon salt
⅓ cup butter
¼ teaspoon baking soda
⅔ cup hot water
⅔ cup dark molasses
2 eggs
an unbaked 8 or 9 in pie shell (p. 30)

Sift the flour, sugar and salt into a mixing bowl. Rub in the butter until the mixture forms crumbs. Dissolve the soda in the hot water and mix with the molasses and the two beaten eggs. Pour into the pie shell and sprinkle with the crumb mixture. Bake in a moderate oven (350°F) for 30–40 minutes, or until the filling sets.

OZARK PUDDING (MIDWEST)

This simple apple and nut pudding from the Ozark mountains in Missouri and Arkansas is a typical 'down home' American dish. When the Truman family was in the White House, from 1945 to 1952, it was frequently served to visitors – including Winston Churchill after he gave his famous 'Iron Curtain' speech in Fulton, Missouri.

Serves 4

1 egg
¾ cup sugar
⅓ cup flour
1¼ teaspoons baking powder
⅛ teaspoon salt
½ cup chopped apples
½ cup chopped walnuts
1 teaspoon vanilla extract
1 cup heavy cream, whipped with 3–4 tablespoons rum

Beat the egg and sugar together until the mixture is light and creamy. Sift the flour, baking powder and salt into the egg mixture and mix well. Fold in the apples and nuts, and add the vanilla. Pour into a greased and floured 1 quart baking dish. Bake in a warm oven (325°F) for about 30 minutes. Cool slightly, then serve with cream whipped with rum.

Morrison County c. 1900

BLUEBERRY BREAD PUDDING (VERMONT)

Newcomers from various parts of Europe brought with them frugal recipes similar to this one, but the most popular ways of making bread puddings, or summer puddings as they are called in Britain, seem to date back to early British settlers. Recipes calling for blueberries are common throughout Canada and the United States where both wild and domestic blueberries thrive.

Prepare at least 6 hours in advance.
Serves 4

2 cups blueberries
about ⅓ cup sugar
  depending on tartness of
  berries
4 slices of homemade
  bread, 1 or 2 days old
butter

Pick over the berries and put them in a heavy saucepan with 2 tablespoons water and the sugar. Bring slowly to a boil, then simmer for 5–10 minutes, depending on the ripeness of the fruit; the berries should be soft but still holding their shape.

Meanwhile, remove the crusts from the slices of bread and butter lightly on one side. Line a small bowl with them, buttered side down, trimming other pieces to fit snugly into the spaces so that the bowl is completely lined. Spoon the blueberry mixture into the bowl, reserving some of the juice. Fold the tops of the bread slices over the filling and add a slice to cover the top completely. Spoon some of the reserved juice over the top so that all the bread is saturated. Put a saucer on top and press down. Chill in the refrigerator for at least 6 hours. Turn out on a dish. If any bread has remained white, color it with the rest of the reserved juice. Serve with cream.

GREENGAGE PLUM ICE CREAM (VIRGINIA)

This ancient dessert is served at the restored King's Arms in the reconstructed colonial town of Williamsburg, Virginia.

Serves 4

¾ cup greengage preserves
juice of 1 small lemon
⅓ cup sugar
salt
1½ cups heavy cream
1½ cups milk

Mix all the ingredients thoroughly. Remove the dividers from 2 ice cube trays and fill with the mixture. Freeze for 2 hours, remove and beat. Freeze again until firm, about 3 hours.

below *Picking berries, 1916;* **right** Still life *by Isaac W. Nuttmann, c. 1870*

Al dente
Italian term, meaning firm to the bite. Used of pasta when just cooked.
All-i-oli
A garlic and oil sauce from Spain.
Anis
French for aniseed.
Anise
Aniseed liqueur.
Akvavit
A spirit distilled from grain or potatoes and flavoured with caraway.
Armagnac
A brandy distilled from wines of the Gers *département* in France.
Aspic
A savoury jelly used as a garnish or a mould for vegetables, fish, meat, poultry and game.
Bain-marie
A shallow vessel half filled with very hot water, containing a smaller pan in which custards, and egg- or cream-based sauces may be cooked or kept hot without spoiling.
Bake blind
To bake flan crusts and tarts without a filling. The pastry shell is lined with greaseproof paper, filled with dried beans or rice, and baked. The paper and beans are removed about five minutes before it is ready to allow the surface to cook.
Béarnaise sauce
A French sauce made with shallots, chervil or tarragon, cooked in white wine or vinegar, and thickened with butter and egg yolks. It is served with grilled meat.
Béchamel sauce
A basic French white sauce made by melting butter with flour to form a roux, then gradually stirring in warmed milk which has been infused with flavourings such as parsley, nutmeg and white peppercorns.
Beignet
French name for fruit, vegetable or cheese dipped in batter and deep fried.
Beurre blanc
A sauce made with shallots, butter and Muscadet wine vinegar. The vinegar is reduced with the chopped shallots and the butter is whisked in.
Beurre manié
A paste of flour and butter used to thicken sauces and soups.
Black pudding
A sausage made of pigs' blood and suet.
Blanch
To plunge food into boiling water. Some vegetables, and nuts such as almonds, are blanched to make them easier to peel. Some meats are blanched to clean them, or to harden their skins and draw out surplus fat.
Bouquet garni
Parsley, thyme and a bay leaf, and sometimes other herbs, tied together and used to flavour stews.

Bourguignonne, à la
Any dish simmered in red Burgundy with salt pork, mushrooms and small onions.
Brioche dough
Dough made with flour, butter, eggs, yeast and sugar.
Calvados
An apple brandy named after a town in Normandy, France.
Cannelloni
The largest type of Italian pasta, in the form of a tube, which is stuffed and baked with a sauce.
Caramel
Sugar melted to a rich brown colour, used as a flavouring and colouring and to coat moulds for desserts.
Cardoon
A plant of the artichoke family with a flavour between those of artichoke and celery.
Catalane sauce
A French sauce for pork or partridge, made with tomatoes, oranges, garlic and olive oil.
Caul
A fatty membrane from sheep's or pigs' innards, used for wrapping minced meats, or covering roasts.
Celeriac
The root of a true celery plant, rare in England but used extensively in France, Italy and Germany. It is served both raw and cooked.
Cervelas
A French cooked pork sausage seasoned with garlic.
Chafing dish
A metal container used to cook dishes at the table, usually heated by a spirit stove.
Charcuterie
French term for pork butchery. A pork butcher prepares and sells various meats, particularly pork, cooked or cured in many ways.
Chaudron
French cast-iron cooking pot.
Chianti
One of the best known Italian wines, produced in Tuscany and often bottled in characteristic straw flasks.
Cèpe
French name for an edible mushroom, usually a particular variety, *Boletus edulis*. It is often available dried.
Chorizo
A Spanish pork sausage, flavoured with garlic and paprika.
Choucroute
The French term for pickled cabbage or sauerkraut.
Chouriço
A spiced Portuguese pork sausage.
Clarified butter
Butter that has been heated gently and strained through muslin to remove salt and impurities. It is used for cooking, to seal potted shrimps and meat, to coat moulds, to moisten meats and fish for grilling.

Clarified stock
Stock that has been brought to the boil with an egg white added, and beaten with a whisk, then strained through a cloth. The impurities in the stock adhere to the egg white.
Coeur à la crème
Fresh curd cream cheese made in heart-shaped moulds, served as a dessert in France.
Confit d'oie
Preserved goose.
Cornbread
Bread made from ground maize.
Court-bouillon
A stock in which fish or vegetables are cooked, prepared with vinegar or wine, carrots and shallots.
Crème fraîche
A thick cream with a distinctive flavour made by adding lactic acid to fresh double cream. If *crème fraîche* is not available, a substitute may be made by mixing together equal quantities of fresh double cream and sour cream and leaving it in the refrigerator for a day.
Crêpe
French term for pancake.
Croûtons
Cubes of stale bread, fried in butter or baked in the oven.
Crudités
Raw vegetables served as a first course in France.
Curaçao
A liqueur of Dutch origin made from brandy or gin and flavoured with orange rind.
Cutlet bat
A metal bat used to flatten and tenderize cutlets, steaks or escalopes.
Daube (en daube)
Meat dish cooked by braising gently in liquid, often made with red wine in which the meat has marinated.
Diable sauce
A sauce made by cooking shallots in white wine and vinegar, with pepper, meat stock and tomato purée.
Eau-de-vie
French name given to liqueurs, especially brandies. Marc, often called eau-de-vie, is a spirit distilled from grape skins left after wine making.
Flambé
To flavour a dish by pouring warmed spirit over it and setting it alight.
Filé powder
Made from the young shoots of the Sassafras tree and used by American Indians to thicken sauces.
Fish fumet
A concentrated fish stock which, when cold, gels into an aspic.
Flat parsley
A parsley with plain leaves and a more distinctive flavour than the curly-leaved variety.
Fondue
A Swiss national dish, usually of melted cheese, served communally

from a dish which is kept warm over a spirit stove. Cubes of bread are dipped into the cheese with a fork.
Forcemeat
A mixture of ingredients, minced and spiced, used to stuff meat, fish, poultry, game, eggs and vegetables.
Fritter
Fruit, vegetable or cheese dipped in batter and deep fried.
Glaze
To coat food with condensed meat or fish stock, egg, or fruit jelly, giving it a glossy, smooth surface.
Gratin, au
A dish with a thin crust achieved by topping with breadcrumbs or cheese, and browning under the grill or in the oven.
Griddle
A round sheet of iron with a handle on which flat cakes are cooked.
Hamburg parsley
A root vegetable with a flavour between those of celeriac and parsley. It is served raw or cooked.
Haricots verts
Commonly known as French beans.
Heidelberg vinegar
A sweet Danish vinegar.
Infuse
To steep herbs or other flavourings in boiling liquid.
Jugged hare or goose
Hare or goose cooked in an earthenware pot or 'jug'.
Juliennes
Meat or vegetables cut into matchsticks, or finely shredded, and used as a garnish, or added to soup.
Kirsch
A spirit distilled from wild cherries, usually made in Germany or eastern France.
Kügelhopf
A fluted mould, used in the Alsace region of France, which gives its name to the raisin-studded yeast cake cooked in it.
Kümmel
A colourless spirit flavoured with cumin and caraway seeds.
Lardons
French term for lardoons – strips of pork fat inserted into meat, poultry and game to add fat and flavour.
Lye solution
Alkaline solution for preserving fish, commonly used in Scandinavia.
Madeira
A fortified wine, ranging from dry to sweet, made in the Portuguese island after which it is named.
Mâitre d'hôtel butter
Butter flavoured with parsley and lemon juice, and served with grilled meat and fish.
Maraschino
A liqueur made from morello cherries.
Marinate
To soak in a marinade – a liquid which often includes wine, olive oil,

spices and herbs. This is done to impart or release flavour, and to tenderize certain meats.

Marrow (bone)
A fatty substance with a very delicate flavour found in the centre of bones, and often added to stock. The shank bone of an ox is very rich in marrow.

Marsala
A sweet fortified wine made in Sicily.

Molasses
A thick brown liquid, the residue left after refining sugar, known in England as black treacle.

Mortadella
A Bolognese pork sausage flavoured with coriander and white wine.

Mortar
A bowl, traditionally of stone, in which foods are pounded and crushed with a pestle.

Mouli-légumes
A utensil for making fruit or vegetable purée.

Ouzo
A Greek spirit distilled from grapes and flavoured with aniseed.

Okra
The fruit pods of the okra plant, a native of the West Indies, served as a vegetable. They are known in England as 'ladies' fingers'.

Paëllera
A shallow two-handled iron pan from Spain, used for cooking paella.

Paprika
Dried and ground sweet peppers, available in several varieties and strengths. Paprika is chiefly made and used in Hungary.

Parboil
To boil food until it is partly cooked, prior to cooking in another way.

Pastis
French generic term for an aniseed-flavoured spirit.

Pernod
An aniseed spirit, made in France.

Pesto
A basil and garlic paste from Genoa, Italy, used as a sauce on pasta.

Petits pois
Fresh garden peas picked before they reach maturity.

Pilau
Rice cooked in stock, to which vegetables, meat, fish, poultry or game are then added.

Pine nuts
The kernels of pine cones. They look like large grains of rice and have a nutty flavour. They are used especially in confectionery, and in Mediterranean cooking.

Potato flour
Dried and ground potatoes, used to thicken soups and sauces.

Poussin
The French name for a very young chicken.

Pot herbs
Finely chopped leeks, onions, carrots,

celery hearts and parsley, used to flavour soups and stews, also known as soup greens.

Presunto
Smoked ham from Portugal.

Prosciutto
Raw, smoked ham from Italy.

Provençale, à la
Any dish flavoured with garlic, olive oil, tomatoes and fresh herbs.

Pumpernickel
A firm, dark brown bread made from coarsely ground rye flour, originally from Westphalia in Germany.

Purée
A soft pulp made by mashing and sieving cooked or raw foods. A mouli-légumes or an electric blender may also be used to make a purée.

Ricard
A French aniseed-flavoured spirit.

Quenelle
A savoury dumpling of minced fish or meat.

Quiche
A savoury flan.

Ragôut
French term for stew.

Ratafia
A liqueur made by infusing fruit juice, syrup and spices in alcohol.

Reduce
To boil liquid rapidly, causing it to evaporate and reduce in volume. This thickens and concentrates the flavour.

Rémoulade sauce
Mayonnaise flavoured with gherkins, capers, parsley, spring onions, chervil, tarragon and anchovy essence.

Render
To melt down fat.

Rice flour
Rice milled to a fine powder and used to thicken cakes and puddings.

Ricer
An implement for giving mashed potato a rice-like appearance.

Romesco
A hot pepper sauce from Spain.

Roux
A mixture of flour and butter cooked gently together, and used as a basis for sauces and to thicken soups.

Saddle of hare
The main part of the hare's body without fore or hind legs.

Saltpetre
Potassium nitrate, used in preserving meat and other foods.

San Daniele ham
A type of prosciutto.

Sauté
To cook in oil or fat, shaking the pan so that the contents 'jump' and do not stick.

Scald
To cover with boiling water. Some vegetables are scalded to make them easier to peel.

Schnaps
A popular term for grain spirits.

Schnitzel
A thin slice of veal, associated particularly with the cooking of Germany and Austria. In Vienna it is dipped in egg and breadcrumbs, quickly fried in butter, and known as a *Wiener Schnitzel*.

Sippets
Small pieces of bread, toasted or fried, used to soak up liquid.

Skim
To take fat or impurities from the surface of a liquid.

Slivovitz
Rumanian plum brandy.

Smørrebrød
Danish open sandwich.

Speck
A thick white pork or bacon fat, the traditional Central European cooking medium.

Strong flour
Flour made from hard wheat which has a high gluten content. It is used in bread making and produces light, protein-rich bread.

Suppevisk
The outer leaves of leeks, parsley (including the stalks) and celery, tied together and used for flavouring in Scandinavian cookery.

Sweat
To release the juices from food by heating very gently in butter or fat.

Tartare sauce
Mayonnaise flavoured with mustard, parsley, tarragon, shallots and gherkins.

Terrine
A French earthenware dish. The name also refers to the meat, game or fish pâté cooked in it.

Tocino
Salted pork fat, used in Spanish cookery. Fat bacon may be used instead.

Trito
A mixture of chopped vegetables cooked in oil or lard and used as a basis for sauces.

Truss
To secure the legs and wings of poultry and game with string.

Unleavened
Used to describe batter or bread made without a raising agent.

Vanilla sugar
Sugar flavoured by leaving a vanilla pod in a sealed container of sugar for several weeks. One vanilla pod to 450g sugar is usually sufficient.

Vermicelli
Very fine spaghetti.

Vinaigrette
A cold dressing for salads or vegetables, made with three parts oil to one part vinegar and flavoured with various seasonings.

Whipping cream
Cream sold ready to whip, or made by whipping together equal quantities of single and double cream.

Acknowledgements

Special thanks are due to the following people, all of whom helped to make this book possible:

Hilary Adamson, Anglodal Ltd, Chesterfield House, 15–19 Bloomsbury Way, London, WC1, P. S. Birrel Props Hire, 5 Chepstow Villas, London W11, John V. Brindle, Art Curator, Hunt Institute for Botanical Documentation, Diana Buirski, Michel Bourdin, Connaught Hotel, John Carrod, Cucina Pot Shop, 8 Englands Lane, London NW3, Danish Centre, 2 Conduit Street, London W1, Danish House, 16 Sloane Street, London SW1, Danish Royal Copenhagen Porcelain, 5 Old Bond Street, London W1, Patrick Ensor and Judith Thomas, Mimi Errington, Finnish Embassy, Emma Fisher, Goethe Institute, Great Britain–USSR Society, Gow's Restaurant, Old Broad Street, London EC2, Graham and Green, 7 Elgin Crescent, London W11, Susan Harle, Biddy Hobbs, Pineapple Pottery, 104 Leith Mansions, Grantully Road, London W9, Hungarian Embassy, Georg Jensen Silversmiths, 15b New Bond Street, London W1, Anne Johnson, Justin de Blank Provisions, 42 Elizabeth Street, London SW1, Jenny Kane, Catherine Shakespeare Lane, Sally Lawford's Country Kitchen Antiques, Royal College Street, London NW1, Pietro Larenzelli, Maison Sagne, 105 Marylebone High Street, London W1, Martinez Restaurant, Swallow Street, London W1, David Mellor, 4 Sloane Square, London SW1, Rob van Mesdag, Netherlands National Tourist Office, C. J. Newnes, 11 Billingsgate Market, London EC3, Norway Food Centre, 166 Brompton Road, London SW3, Polonez, 129 Shepherds Bush Centre, London W12, Quality Chop House, 94 Farringdon Road, London EC1, Selfridges, Oxford Street, London W1, F. Slaby Ltd, Importers, 176 Upper Richmond Road, London SW15, Sol e Mar Restaurant, 77 Dean Street, London W1, Jana Sommerlad, Lucretia Stewart, Marie Stone, Bella Thompson, Treasure Island, 81 Pimlico Road, London SW1, John and Dianne Turner, The Surprise, Christchurch Terrace, London SW3, William E. Wiltshire III, Zenka Woodward, and all the people in Kent, Wiltshire and Richmond, Surrey, whose farms provided superb photographic locations.

Photographers, illustrators and picture sources

1 Kenneth Griffiths
2-3 Collection Sirot-Angel
4-6 Vana Haggerty
10-11 Anna Pugh
12 Batsford Books
14-15 Tessa Traeger
15 Jane Walton
16 Tessa Traeger
17 Jane Walton
18-19 Tessa Traeger
22 Terence LeGoubin/Colorific!
22-24 Tessa Traeger
26 Jane Walton
27-28 Tessa Traeger
29 Jane Walton
31 Claus and Liselotte Hansmann
32 Jane Walton
33 Tessa Traeger
35-36 Kenneth Griffiths
36 (t) Marc Riboud/Magnum/from John Hillelson Agency
  (b) John Bulmer
37 (t) J-N Reichel/Top, from Colorific!
  (b) Collection Sirot-Angel
38 Tessa Traeger
39 Snark International
40 Tessa Traeger
41 (t) Vana Haggerty
  (b) Tessa Traeger
42 (t) Popperfoto
  (b) Frank Horvat/John Hillelson Agency
43-44 Popperfoto
45 Tessa Traeger
47 Roger-Viollet
48 Radio Times Hulton Picture Library
49 (t) Vana Haggerty
  (b) Tessa Traeger
50 (t) Bruno Barbey/Magnum/from John Hillelson Agency
  (b) Vana Haggerty
51 Tessa Traeger
52 (t) Popperfoto
  (b) Bruno Barbey/Magnum/from John Hillelson Agency
53 Tessa Traeger
54 (t) Victor Englebert/Susan Griggs Agency
  (m) Vana Haggerty
  (b) Tessa Traeger
55 Popperfoto
56 John Bulmer
57 Tessa Traeger
58 François Hers/Viva/from John Hillelson Agency
59 (t) IBA, Zurich
  (b) Tessa Traeger
60 Jean-Loup Charmet
60-61 Scala
62-63 Tessa Traeger
63 Vana Haggerty
64-65 Erich Lessing/Magnum/from John Hillelson Agency
66 IBA, Zurich
66-67 Ernst Haas/Magnum/from John Hillelson Agency
67 (t) Swiss National Library
  (b) Horst Munzig/Susan Griggs Agency
68 Henri Cartier-Bresson/Magnum/from John Hillelson Agency
69 Heini Schneebeli
71 Collection Fontanet, Geneva
72 Popperfoto
73 Heini Schneebeli
74 (t) IBA, Zurich
  (b) Vana Haggerty
75 Claus and Liselotte Hansmann
76 Heini Schneebeli
77 Thomas Hopker/Magnum/from John Hillelson Agency
78 Claus and Liselotte Hansmann
79 Georg Gerster/John Hillelson Agency
80 (t) Heini Schneebeli
  (b) John Garrett/Susan Griggs Agency
82 Popperfoto
83 Heini Schneebeli
84 (t) Georg Gerster/John Hillelson Agency
  (m) B. Benjamin/ZEFA
  (b) John Moss/Colorific!
85 Popperfoto
86 Adam Woolfitt/Susan Griggs Agency
87 Popperfoto
88 (t) Alan Randall
  (m) Vana Haggerty
  (b) Popperfoto
89 Alan Randall
90 (t) Alan Randall
  (b) Popperfoto
91 (t) Vana Haggerty
  (b) Rijksmuseum/Cooper Bridgeman Library
92-93 Alan Randall
93 Kunsthistorisches Museum, Vienna/Cooper Bridgeman Library
94-95 Adam Woolfitt/Susan Griggs Agency
96 (t) Adam Woolfitt/Susan Griggs Agency
  (b) Rijksmuseum, Amsterdam/Cooper Bridgeman Library
97 Popperfoto
98 Alan Randall
99 Popperfoto
100-101 Alan Randall
102 Roger Perry
103 Tate Gallery
104 Steve Herr
105 (t) Tessa Traeger
  (b) Vana Haggerty
106 (t) Popperfoto
  (b) Frank Meadow Sutcliffe/Sutcliffe Gallery
107-109 Tessa Traeger
110 Vana Haggerty
111 John Bulmer
112 Tessa Traeger
113 Royal Photographic Society
114-116 Tessa Traeger
117 Robert French/Lawrence Collection/National Library of Ireland
119 Tessa Traeger
120 Vana Haggerty
123 (t) Ted Spiegel/John Hillelson Agency
  (b) Georg Gerster/John Hillelson Agency
124-125 Anna Pugh
125 Jane Walton
127 Alexander Law/John Hillelson Agency
128 Horst Munzig/Susan Griggs Agency
129 Keith Collie
130-131 Keith Collie
131 Norsk Folkemuseum
132 Keith Collie
133 Adam Woolfitt/Susan Griggs Agency
134-137 Keith Collie
138 Popperfoto
139 Norsk Folkemuseum
141 Ted Spiegel/John Hillelson Agency
143 Keith Collie
144 Brian Seed/John Hillelson Agency
145 Tessa Traeger
146 (l) Robert Golden
  (m) Robert Golden
  (r) Bruno Barbey/Magnum/from John Hillelson Agency
147 F. de Zurbaràn/Coll. Privata, Bergamo, Italy
149 (t) Robert Golden
  (b) Tessa Traeger
150 (t) Popperfoto
  (b) Vana Haggerty

Italic page numbers denote illustrated dishes.

Changing to metric

The metric system of measurement is simpler than our present one, because all relationships between the various units work in powers of ten, as do those in our monetary system. The basic metric units are liters (for volume), grams (for weight) and meters (for length). By adding a prefix, the quantity of the basic unit is designated – milli: one-thousandth of the basic unit; centi: one-hundredth of the basic unit; deci: one-tenth of the basic unit; kilo: one thousand times the basic unit.

The metric terms which will be used in recipes are millimeters (mm) and centimeters (cm) for length, milliliters (ml) and liters (l) for volume, and grams (g) and kilograms (kg) for weight. Oven temperatures will be measured in degrees Celcius instead of degrees Fahrenheit. Foods sold by weight, such as meat and vegetables, will be measured in grams and kilograms. Cookware volumes will be marked in liters, and bakeware dimensions in centimeters.

New metric measuring utensils are being developed which will be similar in appearance and use to present utensils, but based on metric units. Liquid measuring cups will be available in a 250 ml size (slightly larger than the 8 fluid ounce cup), graduated in 25 ml, a 500 ml cup and a 1000 ml or 1 liter cup. Dry measures will include a 250 ml cup (slightly larger than the 1 cup measure now), a 125 ml cup and a 50 ml cup. Spoon measures will be marked as 1 ml, 2 ml, 5 ml (1 teaspoon), 15 ml (1 tablespoon) and 25 ml. From this you can see that the *method* of measuring will be the same, but different utensils will be used.

Because exact conversion from the inch/pound system of measurement to metric produces unworkable amounts, approximate measures will be used. The following tables illustrate this.

Volume

Present measure	Precise metric equivalent	Approximate metric equivalent
1 cup (8 fluid ounces)	0.236 liter (or $\frac{1}{4}$ liter less $\frac{3}{4}$ tablespoon)	$\frac{1}{4}$ liter or 250 ml
2 cups (1 pint)	0.475 liter (or $\frac{1}{2}$ liter less $1\frac{1}{2}$ tablespoon)	$\frac{1}{2}$ liter or 500 ml
4 cups (1 quart)	0.95 liter	1 liter

Weight

Present measure	Precise metric equivalent	Approximate metric equivalent
1 ounce	28.35 grams	30 grams
4 ounces ($\frac{1}{4}$ pound)	113.4 grams	115 grams
8 ounces ($\frac{1}{2}$ pound)	226.8 grams	225 grams
16 ounces (1 pound)	453.6 grams	450 grams

Metric tables

Length

One inch is exactly 2.54 centimeters, and there are 39.37 inches in a meter. As these are inconvenient working quantities, the equivalent measures for common pan sizes will be rounded off.

Present measure	Metric equivalent
9 × 9 × 2 inches	22 × 22 × 5 centimeters
8 × 8 × 2 inches	20 × 20 × 5 centimeters
9 × 5 × 3 inches	22 × 20 × 7.5 centimeters
8 inch round	20 centimeter round
9 inch round	23 centimeter round
10 inch round	25 centimeter round

Oven temperatures

Temperature guide	° Fahrenheit	° Celcius
Very slow	225	110
	250	120
Slow	275	140
	300	150
Moderate	325	160
	350	180
Moderately hot	375	190
	400	200
Hot	425	220
Very hot	450	230